Preface

Educate Your Nose and Abide by It
Angelo M. Pellegrini

In late September 1949, my wife and I were walking along the ancient Appian Way, a few miles from the Coliseum in Rome, enjoying the *campagna*, loitering in the shade of the pines, observing the ruins of tombs and monuments that reflected the historic antiquity of the landscape. It was a fair day, with not even the whisper of a breeze as the sun began its decline on the western horizon.

The long walk had given edge to our appetites; and as we paced ourselves along the lengthening shadows of the pines, we compared our preferences for the dinner we would have at the Trattoria di Righetto: Stracciatella? Saltimbocca? Osso Buco? Scaloppine? Salivating with anticipation, and as we moved along briskly, my nose, trained from infancy to sniff, told me, in so many sniffs, so to speak, that we were approaching the source of a strangely seductive culinary smell. Illusory? Successive sniffs confirmed its reality. And yet, where was its source?

Off to our right, several hundred yards away, was what appeared to be a monastery. Surely the fragrance of food in preparation for the table could not reach us from that distance. However, it had lodged in our nostrils from somewhere; and its authenticity was unmistakable. The source could not be far away. Immediately ahead of us, on our left and adjacent to the road, was a tomb in partial ruin, a structure of thick walls, about four yards square. At the top the walls were truncated, as if by an explosion. Since there was no other building in sight, that ruin must be a residence and its occupant must be preparing dinner. My wife agreed, and we trotted toward it.

The ruin was what we expected and its address was 249 Via Appia Antica. It had an opening as for a door and another as for a window. I peeked in and saw a lady stirring a skillet. As if I had been expected, she invited me in and told me her name, Signora Coscia. There were seven children; her husband was in a sanatorium. Victims of the war, they were waiting for the government to provide them living quarters.

My habitual sniffing is about to reveal to you a perfect example of natural simplicity in cookery, the essential doctrine of this book by Paul Bertolli, as opposed to refinement, sophistication, and rigid formulas. But first, a word about odor, the sense of smell, and of taste, its corollary.

The eminent medical scientist and brilliant essayist, Lewis Thomas, has noted that "we might fairly gauge the future of biological science by estimating the time it will take to reach a complete, comprehensive understanding of odor." No doubt it will. Meanwhile, let us educate the nose by constant practice. In the kitchen, it is an indispensable aid in testing the olfactory correctness of, let us say, a broth, a sauce; while an appropriate sniff at the table will add to the pleasure which the palate will derive from what is ingested. Furthermore, and more to the point, the pleasure of reading the vivid, appetizing descriptions of food in preparation given in this book will be enhanced by engaging the nose in the learning process, precisely what I have done.

The sensitivity of one's nose and palate can be easily improved by repeated smelling and tasting; but it may be more difficult for some people to develop a taste and olfactory memory, to remember the smell and taste of, let us say, a glass of wine drunk months ago, or recall a smell in its absence. Since my father began training me to sniff when I was a child, a training I have passed on to my children, I can recall at will, for example, the smell of frogs cooked in a tomato sauce flavored with *puleggio*, wild mint, last eaten when I was a boy in Italy. I tested my memory of this in our kitchen when I had found *puleggio*, and repeated the recipe substituting catfish for frogs. Perhaps you have had a similar experience. At any rate, it is worth the effort to cultivate these faculties since their use is so important in the kitchen, at the table, and in sniffing, shall we say, the landscape along the Via Appia Antica.

As soon as I had smelled what Signora Coscia was stirring in her skillet, my nose told me what she herself confirmed: wild mushrooms. She and her children had gathered them early that morning. They were now being sautéed in olive oil, garlic, parsley, and *nepitella*, colloquially called *erba da funghi*, mushroom grass, the appropriate herb for mushrooms. I knew immediately what was in the skillet for I had cooked wild mushrooms precisely the same way hundreds of times in our kitchen in Seattle. *Nepitella* grows wild in certain regions in Italy; and when one buys mushrooms there, a few sprigs of the herb are included in the purchase.

Could there be a more perfect example of natural simplicity in cookery than wild mushrooms, freshly gathered and immediately cooked as described above, using the indispensable herb, also freshly taken from the soil? Prime raw materials with the appropriate condiment, such is the basic premise of this book. Elsewhere I have written that herbs are the soul of cookery—fresh herbs. And the wise restaurateur, intent on excellence, will know where to find them. In a small restaurant in London, I was so elated when I was served oven-roasted potatoes aromatized with fresh rosemary that I consulted the manager. He took me to the storage room and showed me chests of the indispensable ones. Fresh rosemary and other herbs in an unpretentious restaurant in London! And, of course, at Chez Panisse in Berkeley.

The best book on the cuisine of Italy, *L'Arte di mangiar bene*, the art of eating well, was written about a half century ago by an amateur, Pellegrino Artusi. "Select prime raw materials from the two kingdoms of nature and respect their integrity in the kitchen." Such is his basic culinary principle. This book, for which I am delighted to write the preface, is Artusi brought up to date gastronomically. I have given you an example of natural simplicity in cookery; here is another from my own kitchen. Leeks organically grown and using only the bleached white portion are split lengthwise, braised in butter, and given a sacramental drop or two of balsamic vinegar.

The recipes in this book offer an invitation to engage the senses while cooking. It is not a rigid culinary rule book; rather it gives helpful suggestions culled from the experience of a professional cook whose instructions are animated by an interest in the details that distinguish food that is full of savor from that which is plain. Inevitably, this means becoming involved in the whole process, to use the hands rather than fancy gadgets or machinery. When an Italian cook in London was asked why his pasta was the best, he spread his capable hands and said, "Ah! Ci vol quella man." It requires that hand. And when an aging baker was asked why he did not use a mechanical mixer, his reply was that when he could no longer mix with his hands he would quit baking.

The section on risotto is introduced by an essay on that justly favored northern Italian dish, which can be prepared in a number of different ways. The most typical of these is saffron risotto; all others are variations on that theme. With taste memory as guide and inspiration, and his innate culinary talent, Paul not only re-creates, but enlarges on what he remembers. Hence the classic variations on the basic theme. Each variation is composed of several ingredients, which combine to produce what the author describes as a harmonious whole. This is precisely the result sought in the preparation of all composite dishes. Artusi calls it an amalgam of flavors.

And what does this mean in terms of the nose and kitchen procedure? Give the nose a peach and it smells the odor that emanates from it; add to it a strawberry and a liqueur and it records a bouquet. When I recall the frog dish, I do not smell frog, *puleggio*, or the several other ingredients; I smell the harmonious whole.

The kitchen procedure that produces it is roughly scientific. There is the hunch in the mind of the cook, the intuitive guess that if A is done, B will follow. Hence the hypothesis. Then the experimental verification. In other words, the creative cook, drawing from knowledge of the raw materials of the two kingdoms of nature, imagines the harmonious whole that will result when certain elements are combined in the preparation of a dish. Sound procedure. As an example, note how Bertolli created what he calls a "rabbit salad."

Such is the metaphysic of the culinary art: reasoning in the kitchen from what is known about prime raw materials to that which one intends to extract from them, a harmonious whole, a cuisine of natural simplicity purged of refinement and rigid formulas. Doctrinally inspired, well written, this book is an encompassing variety of culinary preparations designed to satisfy man's innate desire for that which is pleasant, and for an explanation. Accordingly, Paul provides enlightening reasons for the ingredients and the procedure he has chosen in preparing a composite dish. And it is, of course, an important feature of this inspired book on the culinary art; for the amateur must be taught not only *how* to prepare a given dish but also *why* it must be done in a certain way. That is sound pedagogy in the kitchen as well as in the classroom.

And now that I have given you a hint of what this remarkable book contains, if you are of the breed who mind their stomach very carefully and very studiously, you will want to read it with utmost care. Do so and engage your nose in the learning process; for as you sniff your way from one appetizing recipe to another, the book will be your Via Appia Antica, with Paul Bertolli stirring the skillet instead of Signora Coscia. Read and enjoy what I am pleased to recommend. Pleased and privileged.

Foreword

Not long ago my mother gave me a patined copy of an Italian cookbook and kitchen manual, *La scienza in cucina e l'arte di mangiar bene* by Pellegrino Artusi, which had belonged to my grandmother. It was clear from the condition of the book, with its mangled binding and tattered pages, that my grandmother had indeed consulted this book; but what was more interesting were scraps of paper on which her own recipes (if they could be called that) were scrawled in her patient, florid script. Ingredients were listed, but with only vague indications of proportions—one spoon of this, a little of that—or simply the ingredient itself without measure. Recipes such as these were a source of amused frustration for my mother. Excited at the prospect of re-creating for our family the dishes she ate as a child, the translucent hand-rolled pasta, fanciful frittate, golden mounds of polenta, breaded sole, and braised beef with rosemary, to name only a few, my mother was not encouraged by my grandmother's loosely approximated estimations. But evidently it has rubbed off some: my mother's recent instructions to me for potato gnocchi, a dish I have always loved, were a familiar echo, rivaling if not outdoing my grandmother's indefinite style.

As I understand it now, a recipe is at the very least a method of accounting for a cooking process. At best, it captures a memory or inspired moment in cooking. But it can never quite tell enough nor can it thoroughly describe the ecstatic moments when the intuition, skill, and accumulated experience of the cook merge with the taste and composition of the food. In this sense, cooking is not about following recipes. Quarter cups and tablespoons are ridiculously inadequate measures for a process that defies this kind of dry formulization. My grandmother knew this and her cursory reminders to herself, serving only to jog her memory, exhibited a refreshing impatience with formula. She was a cook and required no magical instructions. Yet recipes are enormously valuable for all kinds of cooks—for those who are interested beginners, they introduce an approach and technique and provide structure. For more seasoned cooks, recipes offer a different vision and style and stimulate fresh ideas. The danger in any cookbook is that it be slavishly followed at the expense of the enjoyment that comes in becoming engaged in the process of cooking.

Good cooking is inextricably linked to a desire to eat (this is easily demonstrated: try cooking on a full stomach!). It is perhaps a failing of our times that we have forgotten that we are hungry, or better stated, what we are hungry for. We are distracted. Our desire to eat well has been eroded and compromised by tasteless diets and the empty enticement of pop food designed to appeal to our eyes rather than our stomachs. Never has food looked better and tasted worse. The appeal is more insidious than we think; subtle advertisements summon our groaning instincts—indeed we are hungry, but what we are offered is too often disappointing. Modern food technology has triumphed in addressing our hunger with fast food, frozen food, chemically treated food, and out-of-season food, making of our supermarkets a fairyland in which tomatoes are always ripe and watermelons appear in the dead of winter. Amid the threatening pile-up of packages and cans we have forgotten that food comes from the earth. More specifically, we have forgotten what food should taste like and thus our ability to compare and evaluate is diminished. The sweet crunch of just-picked corn, a glistening chunk of fresh local salmon, vine-ripened tomatoes sliced while still hot from the sun, and figs that are left on the tree until they grow heavy with sweetness remind us of the most basic pleasures, and create a perspective for our eating. Most important, they make us truly hungry and satisfy us fully.

Good cooking begins with good ingredients—fresh, ripe, seasonal, unadulterated raw materials. The challenge in creating a nightly changing menu at Chez Panisse lies less in dreaming up abstract and novel combinations than in keeping apace with the season and welcoming its produce. Responding in this manner lends concreteness, continuity, and ease to the cooking. There is both an anticipatory delight and security in knowing that in November we will have Dungeness crab and the first wild mushrooms, that our local salmon will be running back to the river mouths in June, that Frank and Enid from Amador will be calling in late March ready to send their spring lambs, and our friends at the Chino Ranch are harvesting their ambrosial strawberries. Choosing seasonal foods is not only a privilege of a restaurant, but an available option for anyone who wants to cook well. Educate yourself about the seasons and what they bring; find out about your own locality. What you select, if it is seasonal, fresh, and ripe, will give your cooking integrity, will taste more lively, and will appropriately reflect the mood of the time of year.

There is no better classroom for a cook than the garden, no matter how modest. There the most direct appreciation can be developed for the seasons, for the vibrant quality of fresh fruits, vegetables, and herbs (a quality you will discover is fully present in your finished dishes), and where the senses can be awakened to nuances of taste, texture, and color. It is in the garden that you will discover variety and the great generosity of the soil. Pleasure comes in waiting for the right moment to pick from the garden, in knowing the destiny of certain crops in dishes you plan, and in improvising with what you have planted as it ripens. Planting your own garden is one of the best ways to become engaged in the kitchen. Of course not all of us have the luxury of a garden. It then becomes important to learn to evaluate what one encounters in the market. Is it fresh? in season? what does it smell like? where does it come from? how has it been grown or raised? does it excite me in any way to think of cooking it? does it make me hungry?

Developing skills and technique in the kitchen has much to do with practice, like any physical activity requiring coordination. Yet it seems more to the point to address the question of how one develops a feel for cooking or how to arrive at the point when the recipe can be put aside and instinct and confident intuition take over. Good cooking is in the very best sense a craft, involving the heart, head, and hands simultaneously. It is important to know what you are doing and why you are doing it, to keep your knives sharp and to teach your hands, above all, to remember that you are preparing food, not culinary artwork, that is to be savored and shared with others at your table. Cooking is a commonsense practice, not alchemy. Listening and watching closely while you cook will reveal a richly shaded language understood by all the senses—the degrees of a simmer, the aroma of a roast telling you it is done, the stages of elasticity of kneaded dough, the earthy scent of a vegetable just pulled from the ground—it is everything to mind these details. This is cooking. Following a recipe rigidly is a dry, mechanical exercise unless you re-create it yourself by asking questions along the way, remaining alert and responsive, and making judgments of your own.

It is my wish that someday this book will appear on your shelf as well-worn as my grandmother's gift to me, and that it may likewise include a few of your own jottings, memorializing a dish or happy moment in the kitchen when you discovered you were a cook.

Acknowledgments

I owe a great deal to the staff of Chez Panisse; many have contributed to the sum of the parts that is Chez Panisse cooking and upon publication of this book we will all share that credit. Warm thanks to Peggy Smith, Jeff Stoffer, Gordon Heider, and Catherine Brandel; and to Lindsey Shere and the pastry department; Tom Guernsey, Bill Staggs, and Janet Hankinson-Lee, skillful attendants, whose goading and firm administrations in the dining room often made my dishes more palatable. I thank them too for their critical admonishments, memories of which continue to keep my cooking in line.

My gratitude to Steve Sullivan for generously contributing his bread recipe; Jeff Hvid, mushroom sleuth; Paul Johnson of Monterey Fish; Heidi Crawford, who tends the salad gardens and supplied information on the varieties we grow; Bob Cannard, for his model organic farm and delicious fruits and vegetables; Bill Fujimoto of Monterey Market; and the Chinos whose weekly deliveries of produce, fit for the heavenly banquet, are a continual source of surprise and inspiration.

Gail Skoff's eloquent painted photography punctuates this text; evermore I admire her high craft. I am privileged to have had the benefit of Pat Curtan's counsel at various times and her clean design, which graces these pages. Elaine Ginger edited the manuscript with unusual acuity and put me to task; I am indebted to her for timely encouragement in my moments of dispirit and for helping me believe that I could write.

I am proud of the dessert recipes that Dianne Wegner and Mary Jo Thoresen developed and tested, often on the basis of sketchy notions. My appreciation to Jerry Rosenfield who researched numerous topics in this book with honorable thoroughness, and who wrote the essay "On Nitrites in the Curing of Meats"; he, along with Abigail Shaw, organized research and wrote lucidly in the section Fresh and Pure Ingredients.

Many thanks to Angelo Pellegrini, and to our friends Jean Flaum and Brad Golinsky for the faithful company they keep at our kitchen table.

Furthermore I am obliged to Bob and Susan Lescher for their good faith and to Jason Epstein at Random House for his generous allowances.

When my pen would stall, my wife, Donnis, listened and questioned while I attempted to rattle loose some thought. She also transcribed my illegible scratchings and shared my labor pains in many dreary hours before the word processor. I am thankful to Craig and Jennifer, who endured their mother's and my preoccupations with patience and good spirit, and who gave me their unabashed opinions on trial recipes at the dinner table.

It is Alice's remarkable gift to see the larger picture and it was she who proposed this book. Smiling off my reluctance, she believed in me sooner than I did. Well aware of the daunting scope of the project and my shortcomings, she pushed me beyond my limits.

Contents

Fish and Shellfish

Fish Soup

Fish and Bread Soup

Fish Soup with Onions Stewed in Saffron

Grilled Fish Wrapped in Fig Leaves with Red Wine Sauce

Clam and Sorrel Soup with Cream and Mirepoix

Poached Cod with Pickled Vegetable Relish

Salt Cod

Creamed Salt Cod

Salt Cod Hash

Soft-Shell Blue Crabs

Pan-Fried Soft-Shell Crabs with Yellow Pepper Sauce

Crab Cakes

Soufflés

Dungeness Crab Soufflés with Chervil and Green Onions

Double Consommé of Crab

Fried Flounder and Poached Flounder with Tomato Sauce and Basil

Lobster Salad with Garden Lettuces, Beans, Tomatoes, Basil, and
   Edible Blossoms

Lobster and White Corn Chowder

Winter Lobster Salad

Mussel Soup with Saffron, Fennel, Cream, and Spinach

Mussels Steamed with New Zinfandel

Oyster Soup

Fish and Shellfish Soup

Salmon

Salmon Carpaccio

Salmon in Court Bouillon with Herb Butter

Grilled Salmon with Tomatoes and Basil Vinaigrette

Spring Salmon Salad

Buckwheat Crêpes with Smoked Salmon, Crème Fraîche, and Capers

Grilled Sea Bass with Sliced Artichokes Stewed in Olive Oil

Fried Shellfish with Herb Mayonnaise

Shrimp Bisque

Squid with Cherry Tomatoes, Olive Oil, Parsley, and Garlic Toast

Garlic-Baked Squid

Squid Stuffed with Shrimp

Squid, Romano Bean, and Tomato Salad with Garlic Mayonnaise

Grilled Tuna, Green Onions, and Radicchio with Cannellini Beans

Grilled Tuna and Red Onion Salad

Fish Soup

The most memorable fish soups I have eaten have always been an expression of a locality and season—the ebullient and colorful stews of the Mediterranean, bouillabaisse and *cacciucco*; the austere *cotriade* from Brittany, Alsatian *matelote* made of local fresh water river fish and Riesling; and the forthright simplicity of fall San Francisco crab *cioppino*.

I am most compelled to make and eat fish soup in the month of November. It is then that the ingredients most clearly associated with fish soup converge. Pale green Florence fennel is piled high in the market and wild fennel stands tall on roadsides. Spiny lobster, crab, and shellfish of all kinds from various sites along our coast are in prime season.

Making fish soup is engaging and gratifying. It is also one of the most authentic dishes, as the ocean is still a wild place and fish are, by and large, immune from the technology of improvement that has bred the flavor and soul out of certain vegetables, livestock, and poultry. If you fish yourself or know a reliable fishmonger, you can bring to your table the ancient and mysterious flavor of the sea.

Fish soup mirrors the ocean. Just as there are kelp beds and reefs populated by a diversity of colorful rockfish and crustaceans and quieter, clearer tide pools, so there are soups that vary in their complexity of flavor and variety of elements. Fish soups modeled after bouillabaisse, which contain many types of fish and shellfish, make an arresting presentation and form the focus of an informal meal. Clams, mussels, crab, and lobster are added in the shell and the soup is eaten with the hands as well as with a spoon.

Other more manageable soups are made from one or an assortment of fileted fish cut into pieces and poached in a broth made from the bones and heads. The broth can be left alone, or perfumed with wine or herbs, or embellished with seasonal vegetables such as leeks and young garlic stewed with saffron in spring; ripe tomatoes, roasted peppers, and basil in summer; or fennel, potatoes, yellow onions, and bay leaves in the fall. When one or a variety of smaller rockfish is available, the broth and fish can be sieved and made into an aromatic soup that is slightly thickened by the small bits of fish that fall through the sieve. This soup is delicious with thin noodles, egg pastina, or can be used as a broth for a crusty panade (a sort of rustic bread and broth soup) made with garlic bread and Parmesan cheese. Provençal sauces redolent of garlic, such as *aioli* or *rouille*, unify and enliven fish soups remarkably and have become an almost indispensable accompaniment to various kinds of fish soups here in the restaurant.

Fish broth itself can be emphasized by making a double consommé—a clear broth simmered with the shells of crustaceans such as lobster, crab, or shrimp. The meat of the shellfish is reserved and added as garnish to the strained soup. A consommé of crab scented with lemon peel and scattered with sliced green onions and the leaves of chervil or coriander is a particularly fine example.

Shellfish can be the basis for a number of preparations. We rarely combine clams and mussels in one soup because of the special qualities of their flavor and the liquid they release. The simplest soup of mussels is made by tossing them in a pot on a bed of sliced onion or shallots with bay leaves and dry white wine, covering the pot, and putting it to cook until the mussels open. They are then transferred to a bowl and a little extra virgin olive oil, garlic, and chopped parsley are stirred into the hot liquid. This fragrant broth is served alongside the mussels with grilled bread rubbed with garlic and seasoned with black pepper. Clams can be cooked in just the same way.

Mussels, clams, and oysters have a particular affinity for soups enriched and smoothed with cream, and the liquid they release while cooking provides a foundation of flavor for the soup. We remove the meat from the shell and either chop it or leave it whole. The fresh briny flavor of oysters and clams is more widely dispersed through the soup if they are chopped and added in the last minutes to the cream-bound liquid. Shucked mussels have a powerful richness and are better left whole in the soup.

Cream-enriched soups invite countless possibilities for other additions. A small amount of finely diced mirepoix is present in virtually all these shellfish soups and adds an aromatic sweetness to the broth. The chopped leaves of spinach or sorrel, wilted into the cream and shellfish liquid before the addition of the shellfish meat, adds color and interest, particularly to oyster soup. Herbs such as thyme, parsley, lovage, and bay add a distinct character and are perhaps best used singly so that their perfumes do not conflict. Chowders can be fashioned of any of these shellfish soups by adding small diced parboiled potatoes, bits of smoked bacon, and diced onion that has been reserved from the initial steaming of the shellfish. I have never found it necessary to thicken cream soups with flour or other binders as this adds weight where it isn't needed.

Soups made from clams, mussels, and oysters are at their best in the cold months (October through March). Because these bivalves spawn in the late spring or summer months they are not then in prime condition. In general, oysters are more fatty-tasting in the spawning season and have a milky appearance. Mussels, and to a lesser extent clams, are leaner and more watery than oysters. Wild bivalves are quarantined at various times during the year (May 1 through October in California) because of red tide, a toxic plankton bloom that bivalves feed on. Commercial shellfish beds are monitored for these toxins and harvesting is brought to a halt if the risk is significant.

Crustaceans such as lobster, shrimp, crab, and crayfish surrender the essence of their flavor in bisques that are highly spiced, puréed soups where the shells are used to give the soup its unique flavor and smoky overtones. The process is the same as that for double consommé, with the exception that bisques are not clear and they are slightly thickened. Fish broth or water is poured over aromatic vegetables and the meat and shells of the crustaceans are pounded and cracked and allowed to simmer together. The mixture is then strained and the shells are passed through a sturdy sieve, or food mill, and pressed against the sieve to extract as much flavor and bits of meat as possible. A much quicker and less laborious method, provided you are working with shells that are fairly soft, is to put small amounts of broth and shells in a food processor or blender before sieving and pulse it on and off until the shells are cracked, but never puréed— the presence of ground shells in the soup gives it an unpleasant, chalky texture. After sieving, a thin but flavorful liquid remains.

Bisques can be thickened with flour, rice, or a combination of starchy vegetables such as potatoes, carrots, and fennel. Bisques thickened with flour have a creamy quality, a textural refinement that to my taste is out of keeping with the highly spiced, slightly rough qualities of these soups. Rice is another option, but can give the soup a glutinous texture. The combination of puréed starchy vegetables produces a heavier consistency and the texture, without a lot of sieving, can be a bit grainy. The classic method of thickening bisques with soft white bread crumbs, in the proportion of one cup crumbs to one quart sieved broth, is probably the best. The crumbs are cooked briefly in the liquid and then both are passed for a second time through a finer sieve, resulting in an almost weightless suspension of bits of shellfish and clean, strong flavors.

Fish soup, depending on the type and degree of complexity, can be the focus of a menu with other simple courses to frame it or it can play a more understated role. Soups modeled after bouillabaisse are festive and have a fullness and complexity that puts them in the main course category. Simple chowders, consommés, and bisques provide contrast and relief in the midst of a progression of dishes. Perhaps the best way to decide what soup you will make is in the market. Fish and shellfish have their definite seasons but their availability is subject to the whims of weather. It is important that you go to the market with a flexible attitude, to be informed and inspired by the choices and even prepared to postpone your plans for fish altogether. Buy what is in season, and if you live near the ocean, what is local. Aquaculture and foreign importation has blurred the seasonality and locality of fish and shellfish. Such fish appears as a distracting and an often expensive temptation. I remember an instance when I had my sights set on a glistening chunk of Hawaiian bluefin tuna, but instead bought several pounds of hours-old, local-run herring at a fraction of the cost, which we then grilled over rosemary branches.

For anyone who has fished for supper in the ocean, the experience of buying fish in the market could never compare except under the best of circumstances. Very fresh fish has vigor—flesh that is firm to the point of rigor mortis, skin and scales that are brilliantly colored and tightly attached, and a briny fragrance of seaweed and tide pools. Fileted and skinned fish reveals a bloom, a first freshness, a glow. This is what to look for in the market. The popular notion that the eyes of fish tell all and the degree of clarity in the eyes is a sign of freshness is often contradicted. The eyes of certain fish that have been subjected to the ruinous practice of freezing are hardly affected. Rockfish that is brought up from deep water often reflects the change in pressure in eyes that are swollen and anything but clear, although the fish itself is only hours old. Obviously, this one criterion is not enough. Gills are another means of judging the freshness of fish. Here again, depending on the method of capture, the conditions of the gills at first glance can be misleading. This is particularly true of bottom fish such as halibut. If dragged through the mud, the gills will appear dirty-brown to black. The gills of all fish should be rinsed to reveal their condition, which should be in lively shades of dark red to pink.

Plan to cook fish the day you buy it. Microorganisms and enzymes spoil fish quickly even under refrigeration. Fish is cold-blooded and enzymes in the flesh work at much lower temperatures than animal meat. If you buy whole fish, remove the gills and viscera immediately. Never freeze fish or buy it frozen. As the fish freezes, ice crystals puncture the cell membranes in the flesh. The result is fish with tissue that has been damaged, has lost moisture, and becomes dry, mushy, or stringy when cooked.

Perhaps the most important aspect of shopping for fish is to find a merchant you can trust, one who can give you reliable information about the origin, method of capture, and handling, as well as the freshest and most interesting seasonal choices available. Not only will you discover more about fish, but your cooking will be all the more animated.

Fish and Bread Soup

For 8

Bread soup appears often on the winter menus at Chez Panisse. The soup has its roots in the most frugal peasant dishes that utilize leftover crusts of bread mixed with water, or broth, and little else. Forms of this soup still exist as a sort of tired tribute to forgotten ancestry. French onion soup is the obvious example, and no authentic Florentine trattoria would fail to include on its menu *ribollita* (a minestrone thickened with bread) or *pappa col pomodoro* (bread and tomato soup). Bread soups are a reminder of times past, of conditions of scarcity, when bread was the main source of nourishment. It is ironic that these soups live on in times of affluence, in the midst of a varied five-course dinner at the restaurant; but somehow it strikes the same chord, and is no less nourishing or soul warming.

Bread will carry the flavor of any broth. One of the more unusual and interesting bread soups is one made with fish. The broth is made in the manner of a bisque—whole pieces of fish are used and it is pushed through a sieve to extract small bits, which then slightly thicken the broth. The broth is poured over layers of toasted or grilled garlic bread and leeks that have been stewed in olive oil with saffron. Sprinkled with Parmesan cheese and put into the oven, the soup forms a dark brown crust on top, while the bread beneath absorbs most of the broth. A spoonful of this layered mixture with its crusty top and moist triflelike strata below is placed in each bowl, and more of the broth, into which rouille—a spicy red pepper-garlic sauce—has been stirred, is poured around it.

Leftover fish soup, which can taste a little indifferent the second time around, is put to ideal use in this recipe, and as is the case with many spontaneous dishes derived from leftovers, is both extended and redeemed.

4 slices of sourdough levain bread (8 ounces), cut ½ inch thick (see page 218 for a description of levain bread)
4 tablespoons olive oil
2 large leeks (8 ounces), quartered lengthwise and sliced thinly
Pinch saffron (about 20 threads)
¼ teaspoon dry thyme
¼ teaspoon salt
⅛ teaspoon ground pepper
Pinch ground cayenne

2 quarts leftover fish and shellfish soup
   or,
2 quarts fish broth (see page 428), substituting an equivalent amount of whole small
   rockfish or larger rockfish that has been gutted, gilled, and cut into pieces, for the
   fish carcasses. In addition to the other ingredients, include ½ pound shrimp.
½ recipe Rouille (see page 9)
Raw garlic, peeled
2 heaping tablespoons freshly grated Parmesan cheese
2 tablespoons chopped fresh Italian parsley

Preheat oven to 350°F.

Brush the bread slices with 2 tablespoons of the olive oil, set on a baking sheet, and bake for about 25 minutes, or until the bread is completely dried out, brown, and crisp.

Warm the remaining 2 tablespoons olive oil in a heavy, 3-quart saucepan. Add the leeks, saffron, thyme, salt, pepper, and cayenne and cook the mixture slowly, stirring often, for about 12 minutes, or until the leeks are soft. Remove from the heat and set aside.

Remove the mussels, or other hard-shell fish, from the fish broth and strain the broth in batches through the medium-size holes of a food mill, extracting all the liquid and pushing as much of the fish and shrimp through the sieve as possible. Be patient with this step. The soup will be all the richer for your efforts. Next, prepare the rouille.

Assembling the soup: Rub the bread with the raw garlic, break it up into coarse pieces, and lay half of it in a square baking dish (8 by 8 by 2 inches). Cover the bread in an even layer with the leeks. Form an even top layer with the remaining bread. Pour 1 quart of the sieved fish broth over the bread and leeks, sprinkle with the Parmesan, and bake in the oven for 50 minutes, or until the top is nicely browned and almost all of the broth has been absorbed.

Bring the remaining fish broth to a boil. Stir in the rouille and parsley. With a knife, divide the bread and leeks into six portions. Keeping the browned side up, scoop out portions of the bread and place them in warmed bowls. Ladle some of the fish broth around each and serve.

Rouille (Red Pepper Sauce)

1 cup, for 8 servings

There are few more natural matches in cooking than fish soup and rouille, the Provençal red pepper sauce. A spoonful of the sauce is stirred into the soup at the last moment; the fresh flavor of garlic, grilled peppers, hot chiles, and olive oil invigorate both the broth and the fish and give a depth and unity of flavor to the soup. Like pesto, rouille is a coarse sauce made in a mortar with a pestle. A Japanese mortar with its gritty inner surface is particularly helpful in reducing the slippery pepper flesh to a paste. Choose thick-fleshed red bell peppers and char them well so that the flesh softens thoroughly. This can be done on a charcoal grill or on the stove over an open flame. Grilling the peppers adds a smoky dimension and gives the sauce a more authentic quality.

There are a number of piquant chiles to choose from. I have had most consistent results with the Serrano chile—a small, smooth, green variety with a rounded, sometimes slightly pointed end. While the degree of piquancy can vary with jalapeño or Fresno chiles, the fresh Serrano is always fiery and has a potent, fresh flavor. Make this sauce just before you serve it so that the flavors remain lively.

½ cup soft white bread crumbs
¼ cup fish broth (see page 428)
1 fresh Serrano chile (1½ inches long), stem removed, sliced
2 cloves garlic
Pinch saffron (about 20 threads)
1 large red bell pepper (8 ounces), charred, peeled, seeded, juice reserved
Freshly ground pepper
⅜ teaspoon salt
¾ teaspoon red wine vinegar
¼ cup extra virgin olive oil

Put the bread crumbs in a bowl. Add the fish broth and any juices from the peppers and mix well. Put the Serrano chile, garlic, and saffron in a mortar and pound and grind them to a paste. Add the red pepper and work it to a similar consistency. Add the moistened bread crumbs. Stir and grind until the mixture resembles a fine porridge. Grind a little black pepper into the sauce, add the salt and vinegar, and stir in the olive oil. Use at once.

Fish Soup with Onions Stewed in Saffron

This soup is modeled after the Brittany-style fish soup called *cotriade*, but is more associative in its use of ingredients than true to the original process and presentation. Fish broth is simmered briefly. Onions are stewed in olive oil with bay leaves and thyme and a pinch of saffron, which gives the soup a golden cast and a pleasing perfume. Small, peeled red potatoes are cooked until tender in a separate pot of salted water so as not to compete with the fish for salt in the broth. The potatoes are then added to the broth with fileted fish that has been cut into chunks. Finally, just before serving, parsley and garlic are pounded into a paste in a mortar with a little olive oil and is stirred into the soup to enliven it.

Rather than serving the soup as soon as the fish is cooked, I let it stand a little longer on the stove so that the fish will absorb some of the salt and the flavors of the broth. Nothing is lost if you choose a fish that won't break apart or turn to mush. Avoid small flat fish such as sole, which tend to be too delicate. Thick, meaty-fleshed rockfish such as Golden Eye, Yellowtail, or sea bass are ideal.

By itself, this soup is satisfying with the final addition of parsley and garlic. A pot of Garlic Mayonnaise is also welcome. Or, in keeping with the soup's original roots, put on the table a bowl of vinegar mixed with crushed black pepper. Good bread, grilled or toasted and rubbed with garlic, is essential. When making this soup at home, for the sake of simplicity, I buy only one fine rockfish of about 4 pounds. The broth is made from the fish carcass and a pound or so of mussels. The filets, cut into pieces, are returned to the pot as described above. Made in this manner, the soup is both simple and economical.

For the broth:
1 rockfish (about 4 pounds), fileted
1 pound, 4 ounces mussels
1 tablespoon pure olive oil
⅓ cup dry white wine
1 medium carrot (3 ounces), peeled, finely diced
½ large stalk of celery (2 ounces), finely diced
½ yellow onion (5 ounces), finely diced
3 sprigs parsley
3 sprigs fresh thyme
2 bay leaves
6 cups cold water
¾ teaspoon salt

Prepare the broth: Remove the gills, eviscerate the fish, and cut the carcass into three or four large pieces. Rinse the head, carcass, and filets under cold running water. Make cuts on either side of the pin bones running vertically down the filet and remove this strip of fish containing the bones. Reserve these scraps for the broth. Cut the filets into 1-inch pieces on the bias and set aside on a plate. Scrub the mussels thoroughly. It is not necessary to de-beard them.

Warm the olive oil in a 6-quart stainless-steel pot. Add the pieces of fish carcass and cook them, turning them over to expose all surfaces to the heat, until their color changes to white and the fragrance of the fish is released. Add the wine and scrape up any bits of fish adhering to the bottom of the pot. Add the vegetables, mussels, herbs, bay leaves, water, and salt. Make certain all pieces of the fish are submerged in the water. Bring to a simmer, skim any white froth that comes to the surface, and cook slowly for 30 minutes. In the meantime, prepare the onions and potatoes.

3 tablespoons pure olive oil
2 yellow onions (14 ounces), thinly sliced
3 bay leaves
¼ teaspoon dry thyme
Pinch saffron (about 20 threads)
¼ teaspoon salt
⅛ teaspoon freshly ground pepper
1½ quarts water
1 teaspoon salt
4 to 5 small red potatoes (12 ounces), peeled, cut into eighths

Warm the olive oil in a heavy, 3-quart saucepan. Add the onions, bay leaves, thyme, saffron, salt, and pepper. Combine well and cook the onions over low heat, without letting them brown, for 25 minutes, or until they are very soft. Stir the onions often to prevent them from sticking.

In a pot, bring the water to a boil, add the salt and the potatoes, and cook for 5 to 6 minutes, or until just tender throughout. Drain. Prepare the garlic and parsley mixture.

3 cloves garlic
¾ cup finely chopped fresh Italian parsley
1 tablespoon extra virgin olive oil

Pound the garlic to a paste in a mortar, add the parsley, and pound it to a similar consistency. Stir in the olive oil.

To finish the soup, pour the fish broth over the onions and simmer for 5 minutes. Add the potatoes and fileted fish and cook at a bare simmer for 10 minutes. Let stand for 5 to 8 minutes, then stir in the parsley and garlic mixture. Serve the soup in warm bowls.

Grilled Fish Wrapped in Fig Leaves with Red Wine Sauce

For 4

Every autumn while I was growing up my father would organize the family workforce to collect the fallen leaves and prunings from our backyard plum, apricot, peach, walnut, apple, and fig trees. We would make enormous piles and throw ourselves on them for fun; then we'd set them on fire. Throughout the day the backyard was afog with smoke—at first, dense, billowy, and bluish; toward evening, it would trail off in a wispy vapor. The fires were set near their respective trees in the orchard, each contributing its own particular scent to the overall perfume. Yet the smoke of the fig was preeminent, more aromatic and penetrating, defying combination.

In the middle of the day we would break for lunch. The smoky leaves (primarily fig) heavy on our clothes mingled with the aromas of the food on the table—cold cuts, the previous night's rewarmed spaghetti Bolognese, vinegar, onions, my father's bitter chicory salad.

I am certain that my nostalgia for this scent accounts for fig leaves finding their way into this recipe. For those to whom it is served, it may provoke curiosity that I hope this story satisfies. It is more than delicious; it is for me a fond reminder of past autumn days.

For the red wine sauce:
2 cups red wine
½ cup finely diced onion (2 ounces)
3 tablespoons finely diced celery (1 ounce)
3 tablespoons finely diced carrot (1 ounce)

1 tablespoon sirop de cassis
8 tablespoons cold unsalted butter, cut into ½-inch chunks
Salt and pepper

4 fig leaves (about 6 inches long)
3 tablespoons pure olive oil
Four 4-ounce filets of sea bass, salmon, or halibut, cut into even 1-inch-thick pieces
Salt and pepper

Prepare a medium-hot grill.

Prepare the red wine sauce: Combine the red wine, vegetables, and cassis in a 1½-quart stainless-steel saucepan. Bring to a boil and reduce until the wine just covers the bottom of the pan and a scant ¼ cup remains. Working over low heat and whisking constantly, add the butter, 3 pieces at a time. Just as the butter has melted, add the next 3 chunks. Never let the mixture reach a boil. Adjust the heat or move the pan off the flame if you notice the surface bubbling. When all the butter has been incorporated, pour the sauce through a fine sieve into a warm (not hot) bowl or double boiler and press gently on the vegetables to extract as much sauce as possible. Salt and pepper the sauce to taste. For added flavor, stir in chopped herbs such as parsley (add 2 teaspoons) or dill (add 1 teaspoon) a few moments before you serve the sauce.

Rinse the fig leaves in water and allow them to remain wet. This will create a little steam inside the package, helping to cook the fish and assure that the leaf does not char before the fish is done. Stem and brush the pale side of the leaves with about half the olive oil.

Oil each filet on both sides, salt and pepper it, and center it on the oiled fig leaves. Fold the leaf around the fish to enclose it and set the fish aside on a plate, folded edges down, until you are ready to grill it.

Place the fish on the grill folded side down (the leaf will adhere to itself once heated) and grill it for about 4 to 5 minutes per side, until the leaf is lightly charred and the fish is just firm.

To serve: Set the package on a warm plate folded edges up. Carefully pull back the leaf so that it frames the fish and spoon a little red wine sauce over each filet. The fig leaf is not particularly good to eat—it is only meant to perfume and garnish the fish.

Clam and Sorrel Soup with Cream and Mirepoix

This soup can be made with either hard- or soft-shell clams. Soft-shell clams and razor clams have an exceptional flavor, but they ingest large amounts of sand; the liquid released in steaming them must be put through a very fine sieve and the shucked meat must be rinsed well or the soup will have an awful grittiness.

Two processes are involved in making this soup. First, the clams are steamed opened on a bed of vegetables—the mirepoix—with wine and bay leaves added. The clams are then removed and shucked; cream is added to the vegetables and liquid. The clams are then returned with cream and sorrel to heat.

If you make this soup with soft-shell clams, steam them open with 4 ounces diced onions, several bay leaves, and the same amount of wine listed below. Pass the liquid through a very fine sieve and discard the contents of the sieve. Soften the mirepoix in a separate pot and assemble the soup as described above.

Hard-shell clams become tougher as they increase in size. Those larger than a quarter should be chopped. Not only does this minimize any toughness, but it makes for better flavor. Sorrel offsets the sweetness of this soup; you may also add diced potatoes and bits of smoked ham or bacon, which will thicken the combination to a chowder.

Good crusty bread in the form of buttered croutons or a freshly baked or warmed loaf to pull apart at the table are indispensable to this soup. Finally, portions are intended to be small. The soup is plenty rich and flavorful.

3 ounces mirepoix in all (3 tablespoons each of diced carrot and diced celery and 4 tablespoons diced onion)
2 small bay leaves
½ cup dry white wine (such as Muscadet or Sauvignon Blanc)
2 pounds small, hard-shell clams
1 cup heavy cream
1 cup loosely packed, chopped sorrel
Freshly ground pepper

Put the mirepoix, bay leaves, and wine in a 3-quart stainless-steel pot. Rinse the clams of any sand and add them to the pot. Bring to a simmer, cover the pot, raise the heat, and steam the clams for 4 to 5 minutes, or until they are open. Turn off the heat and transfer the clams with tongs or a slotted spoon to a bowl to cool, leaving the juice, mirepoix, and bay leaves in the pot. Be sure to taste

14   FISH AND SHELLFISH

the liquid the clams release. If it is very salty, pour off some of it and dilute the base with the same amount of fish broth or water.

Shuck the clams when cool enough to handle and add any juices and mirepoix that have drained from them back to the pot. Chop the clams coarse into ¼-inch bits. Add the cream and sorrel to the pot. Bring to the simmer, add the clams, and heat for 2 minutes. Grind pepper on top and serve.

Poached Cod with Pickled Vegetable Relish

For 6 as a first course

Poaching has a softening effect on the flavors of fish. Consequently, poached fish invariably needs a sauce—one that either complements the mildness of the fish with equal delicacy or one that provides a contrast with forward flavors. Pickled Vegetable Relish is a tart and colorful condiment of finely diced vegetables, chopped cornichons, onions, capers, and anchovies. It is used like salsa atop this chilled fish and is similarly a lively accompaniment to boiled beef tongue or veal shoulder.

For the poaching liquid:
2 quarts water
3 tablespoons thinly sliced carrots (1 ounce)
4 tablespoons thinly sliced onion (1 ounce)
3 tablespoons thinly sliced celery (1 ounce)
3 sprigs parsley
3 sprigs thyme
1 clove garlic, sliced
1 teaspoon salt
Six 1-inch-thick fish filets (2 pounds, 4 ounces), rockfish, such as Golden Eye cod, halibut, or sea bass

Combine the water, vegetables, herbs, garlic, and salt in a pot large enough to contain the filets. Bring the mixture to a boil, reduce the heat, and let simmer for 10 minutes to allow the vegetables to release their flavor. Add the fish and poach until it is just firm in the center of the filet. Remove the filets with a slotted spoon or strainer and let cool. Discard the poaching liquid, vegetables, and herbs.

For the pickled vegetable relish: makes 1½ cups
3 tablespoons finely diced carrot (1 ounce)
3 tablespoons finely diced red pepper (1 ounce)
4 tablespoons finely diced red onion (1 ounce)
1 clove garlic, finely chopped
3 tablespoons finely diced cornichon pickles
4 tablespoons pitted chopped green olives
1 tablespoon capers, rinsed in several changes of water and drained
2 salt-packed anchovies, fileted, soaked in several changes of cold water for 15 minutes, chopped
1 tablespoon red wine vinegar
¼ cup plus 2 tablespoons extra virgin olive oil
2 tablespoons chopped fresh parsley

In a ceramic bowl, combine the vegetables, garlic, pickles, olives, capers, and anchovies. Stir in the vinegar, olive oil, and parsley. Correct to taste with more vinegar. Cover and let stand in the refrigerator for 1 hour.

Assembling the dish: Break the fish up into chunks or large flakes. Place the fish on individual plates or a platter. Scatter the relish liberally over the top and serve.

Salt Cod

Dried and salted cod is most commonly associated in cooking with the countries of the Mediterranean, Italy, Spain, and Portugal, and the South of France. The flavor and texture of fresh cod, a lean fish with delicate, flaky white flesh, is radically transformed in the process of salting—it becomes firm, slightly yellow in color, and pungent in aroma. Salt cod varies greatly in its salt content according to its origin and the type of cure. Salt cod that is cured in the damp sunless regions of the Arctic, where conditions of temperature and humidity are variable, require more salt as compared with the milder, more even climates of the Mediterranean.

The salting of cod is carried out in one of two ways. Method one: The fish is deheaded, split open, backbone removed, and stacked between alternating layers of salt. The brine that forms is allowed to run off. The other method is a pickling process in which the cod is dry-salted along the thick portion of the filet where the backbone was removed and set in barrels. The brine is contained in this process and penetrates the thinner sections of the fish. Both methods can produce a heavier or lighter cure depending upon the amount of salt applied and the length of exposure.

There are several different salt cods available, and they differ in size, moisture content, and the manner in which they were processed for curing (whether bones and skin were left on). We have had best results with salt cod sold in boneless strips from Canada. This cod has a high moisture content and relatively low salt content. It rehydrates quite quickly (2 to 3 days depending upon the thickness) and the filets are generally taken from large fish resulting in thick, finely flaked chunks. When purchasing salt cod, buy the thickest fish with the lightest color. Examine the salt cod and pass over those filets that are discolored. Avoid salt cod that is thin and stiff as a board; this is an indication that the fish underwent a heavy cure, which is more often than not damaging to the texture of the fish.

Salt cod must be soaked in fresh water to remove excess salt and rehydrate the fish. Soaking time depends upon the thickness of the filet and the type of cure. Generally speaking, a filet that is 1 inch thick at the head end will require about three days with changes of fresh water each half day. When the cod is soaked enough, it will have swelled considerably, will appear evenly white, and lose its firmness in the center.

Salt cod will never rival the refinement of a fresh filet and should not be used as a substitute for fresh fish. But the flavor of salt cod is unique for certain preparations where its distinctive, assertive character is essential.

Creamed Salt Cod

2 cups, for 6 servings

Creamed salt cod, or *brandade de morue*, is poached salt cod worked to a fluffy texture with boiled potatoes, olive oil, garlic, lemon juice, and cream. It is suitable for stuffing raviolis or baked tomatoes, or can be rolled in egg and bread crumbs and fried as croquettes. In making this dish it is important that you think ahead. You will need two to three days to soak the fish. Both the quality of the olive oil and garlic you use is critical: creamed salt cod is a particularly transparent medium for these flavors.

The classic presentation of this dish is in a mound surrounded by fried or toasted bread (fried polenta, cut into triangles, is another option). Creamed salt cod is ideal as a warm appetizer and surprisingly harmonious with both white and black truffles, the aroma of which will fill the room if the truffles are shaved directly over the warm mixture just before it is served.

³⁄₄ pound Canadian salt cod (boneless strip), about 1 inch thick at the head end of the filet
³⁄₄ cup yellow onion (3 ounces), sliced
2 bay leaves
2¹⁄₂ quarts water
³⁄₈ cup extra virgin olive oil
1 red potato (3 ounces), peeled, boiled in water until soft, mashed
¹⁄₂ cup heavy cream
2 to 3 cloves garlic, pounded to a paste in a mortar
1¹⁄₂ teaspoons lemon juice
Freshly ground pepper

Rinse the surface salt from the cod and soak the cod 2 to 3 days in 1 gallon water, changing the water twice daily.

Put the onion and bay leaves in a 3-quart pot, add 1¹⁄₂ quarts of the water, and bring to the boil. Add the salt cod, reduce the heat to a bare simmer, and poach it for 10 to 12 minutes. Remove the cod and cool it. Taste a piece from the thicker portion of the fish. If it is strongly salty, break up the chunks into flakes and return the cod to the hot water to release more salt. Pour the cod and water into a colander over the sink and let it cool. Pick out the onions and bay leaves and discard them.

Pour the olive oil into a heavy, 3-quart saucepot and warm it gently. Add the cod and stir it vigorously with a wooden spoon over low heat about ¹⁄₂ minute, breaking the cod up until it is reduced to a matted, fibrous texture. Stir in the mashed potato. Pour the cream over the garlic in the mortar, mix well, and add to the cod. Season with the lemon juice, a little freshly ground pepper, and salt, if necessary. Work the mixture with the spoon to a fluffy consistency and serve while still warm.

Creamed salt cod will keep well for 2 to 3 days. If you think this recipe yields more than you need, set the excess aside before you add the garlic-cream (the flavor of garlic quickly goes stale). Accordingly, adjust the amount of cream and garlic. Leftover creamed salt cod should be rewarmed in a *bain-marie*.

Salt Cod Hash

This recipe came about as a way to use leftover poached salt cod. It is a colorful scramble of browned potatoes, hard-cooked eggs, bits of bacon, small crisp croutons, parsley, and the cod, whose pungent, slightly salty quality stands out amid the other ingredients. First the potatoes are well-browned in a cast-iron pan, then the bacon and salt cod are mixed in, warmed together, seasoned, and sharpened with vinegar. The eggs, croutons, and parsley are tossed in at the last.

The hash ends up with a fairly dry consistency. Garlic Mayonnaise is a requisite sauce, which blends perfectly with the various flavors of the dish. Serve the hash for lunch with plenty of cold rosé wine followed by a simple salad of mixed greens.

3 quarts water
2 bay leaves
4 ounces salt cod, previously soaked (see page 19)
1 cup ½-inch-square sourdough croutons
4 tablespoons pure olive oil
Salt and pepper
2 ounces smoked bacon, sliced ¼ inch thick, diced
1 pound red potatoes, peeled, cut into small odd-sized chunks
2 large eggs
⅛ teaspoon ground cayenne
1 teaspoon red wine vinegar
1½ tablespoons chopped fresh parsley
½ recipe Garlic Mayonnaise (see page 115)

Preheat the oven to 375°F.

Bring 1 quart of the water and the bay leaves to a boil. Reduce to a simmer and in it poach the salt cod for 10 to 12 minutes. Pull apart the thickest portion of the fish; if it is still strongly salty in the center, return the fish to the water and let it simmer a few minutes more. Remove the salt cod from the water, drain in a colander, and set aside on a plate.

Toss the croutons in 1 tablespoon of the olive oil and bake in the oven for about 15 minutes, or until very crisp.

Bring the remaining 2 quarts water to a boil. Parboil the bacon in it for 45 seconds and remove it from the pot with a strainer. Lightly salt the same water, add to it the potatoes and cook them for about 8 minutes, or until tender but not mushy, and drain in the colander. Let them cool and dry out without running water over them.

Cover the eggs with cold water, bring to a boil, turn off the heat, and let them stand for 8 minutes. Cool the eggs under running water and peel them. Chop the eggs coarse.

Pull the salt cod apart in flakes. Put the remaining 3 tablespoons olive oil in a seasoned 12-inch cast-iron or steel sauté pan. Heat the oil and add the potatoes. Salt and pepper the potatoes and cook them over medium-high heat for 10 to 12 minutes, turning them over and over until they are crusty brown. Reduce the heat and stir in the bacon, salt cod, cayenne, and vinegar. Warm the mixture for about 3 minutes. Just before serving, toss in the eggs, croutons, and parsley. Correct to taste with a little more vinegar, if necessary, and grind pepper over the top. Serve and pass the garlic mayonnaise at the table.

Soft-Shell Blue Crabs

The blue crab is a soft-shell crab only at a particular phase of its life—after it has shed the old shell and a new shell has not begun to harden, a process called molting. Throughout maturation the molting process periodically reappears, some twenty times in the three-year life span of a healthy crab, and is an accommodation to its increased size. Unlike mammals, the external skeleton cannot grow as the crab expands.

Blue crabs are in season from late spring to early fall and are found along the western Atlantic shoreline from Cape Cod to Brazil and from the Gulf Coast of Louisiana and Texas to the shores of the Mediterranean. Blue crabs are particularly abundant in the estuaries of the Gulf of Mexico and the marshy grasses of the shoreline of Chesapeake Bay, where the industry is centered. The optimal period for shipping soft-shell crabs is critical as the newly formed exoskeleton begins hardening within 2 hours of molting. Soon the "paper shell" stage is reached, identifiable as a wrinkled texture on the crab's back, and it is no longer in prime commercial condition. Crab fishermen are by necessity close observers of the molting cycle. They are able to identify, through observance of the thin border of a new shell within the margin of the old shell, how soon a "peeler" (soon-to-molt crab) will shed its hard outer covering. Crabs are taken from the marshes before they molt and held in floats where the process can be clearly observed. Once the old shell has been shed, the crabs are removed and shipped live.

Make sure that the crabs you buy are alive and that you cook them the day you buy them. Soft-shell crabs deteriorate very quickly and are not suitable for cooking if they develop any strong odors. The crabs can be eaten whole, but must be cleaned and drained first.

To clean live soft-shell crabs: Turn the crab on its back and with your fingers pry up the apron (appearing as a triangular or T-shaped flap) on the underside of the crab. The apron is attached to the crab just below the back legs. Pull it away and discard it. Turn the crab right side up, lift the soft flaps on either side above the legs, and remove the gill tissues. Rinse the crab thoroughly.

To aid in sloughing off the old shell, the crab takes on water in its final preparation to molt, which causes swelling and rupture along the shell lines. Crabs are often quite bloated, and should be properly drained before being cooked. Make small punctures on the underside of the crab and let the water drain out. When drained, pat the crabs dry.

The crabs are perhaps most appetizing when pan fried in brown butter and served with a spicy mayonnaise.

Pan-Fried Soft-Shell Crabs with Yellow Pepper Sauce

For 6 to 8

About 3/4 cup all-purpose flour
12 small soft-shell crabs, cleaned, drained, patted dry (see above)
6 tablespoons brown clarified butter

Put the flour in a bowl. One by one, coat the crabs with flour on both sides. Remove from the bowl, shake off any excess flour, and transfer to a plate.

Preheat a 12-inch cast-iron pan over low heat. Add 3 tablespoons of the butter and heat it until a speck of flour sizzles when added to the pan. Raise the heat a little and fry the crabs, 6 at a time (or as many as will fit in a single layer without crowding), for about 5 minutes per side, or until they are a deep brick red on the shell side and orange-brown underneath. Keep the first batch of cooked crabs warm in a low oven. Meanwhile, discard the butter in the pan and wipe out the browned bits. Add the remaining 3 tablespoons butter and fry the remaining crabs similarly. Serve with lemon wedges or Yellow Pepper Sauce.

Yellow Pepper Sauce

Makes about 1½ cups

This sauce was developed to accompany pan-fried or grilled soft-shell crabs. The color of the sauce is pleasing and the flavor of yellow peppers, slightly milder than red, goes well with crab. It is also good with shrimps cooked in a spicy court bouillon, boiled lobster, or fried fish cakes. Charring the skins of the peppers over a charcoal fire lends an interesting smokiness to the sauce. The skins can also be blistered over the open flame of a stove.

2 yellow peppers (13 ounces)
2 egg yolks
¾ cup refined peanut oil or vegetable oil
1 large clove garlic, mashed in a mortar
¼ teaspoon salt
1/16 teaspoon black pepper
⅛ teaspoon ground cayenne
1 teaspoon lemon juice

Thoroughly char the skins of the peppers over a charcoal fire or the open flame of a stove, allowing the flesh to soften. Place the peppers in a plastic bag and close it tightly. Let the peppers sweat for 15 minutes—this will loosen the skin.

In the meantime, make a stiff mayonnaise with the egg yolks and peanut oil (refer to process on page 115). Remove the peppers from the bag, peel them, cut them in half, and discard the seeds and the stems. Purée the peppers in a food processor or blender. Slowly whisk the pepper purée into the mayonnaise. Season the sauce with garlic, salt, pepper, cayenne, and lemon juice.

Crab Cakes

12 small crab cakes

This recipe is an extraordinarily delicious way of serving freshly picked crab meat. I remember one particular night when an old friend of the restaurant dispensed with the rest of the menu and repeated this course four times and then again for dessert(!).

Trimmings or leftover odd-sized scraps of fish are put to good use when made into fish cakes; the fish is chopped, seasoned with shallots or onions and fresh herbs, bound with mayonnaise, formed into a small patty, rolled in bread crumbs, and fried. Crab cakes, unlike fish cakes that utilize leftover trimmings, are an extravagance requiring time (if you should decide to cook the crabs and pick the meat yourself) or the considerable expense of purchasing picked crab meat. If you use only crab meat, you will never be happier; however, the recipe includes a certain amount of chopped cod (any firm fleshed white fish will do) to extend the mixture if time or your budget does not permit.

Serve the cakes as an appetizer (in which case one 3-ounce cake is adequate) with just lemon wedges, Red or Yellow Pepper Sauce, Garlic Mayonnaise, or with a salad of lettuces vinaigrette, sliced fennel, and radishes.

8 ounces fresh filet of cod
2 cooked Dungeness crabs (3 1/4 pounds), picked clean to yield 1 pound crab meat, or an
equivalent quantity of blue crabs

Mayonnaise:
1 egg yolk
1/4 cup plus 2 tablespoons vegetable oil

1/2 cup loosely packed green onion, dark green part included, sliced very thin
1 tablespoon lemon juice
Zest of 1/2 lemon
1/2 teaspoon salt
1/4 teaspoon ground cayenne
1 1/4 cups fresh sourdough bread crumbs
4 tablespoons clarified butter

Make a cut on either side of the pin bones in the cod filet. Remove and discard this thin scrap of fish and bones. Cut the cod into thin strips, dice it, and then chop it into small bits. Combine the chopped fish with the crab meat in a bowl.

Make the mayonnaise: In a separate small bowl, whisk the egg yolk while adding the oil in droplets, until the mixture begins to thicken. As the mixture thickens add the oil faster in a thin stream until all of it has been incorporated.

Add the mayonnaise and green onion to the fish and crab, season the mixture with the lemon juice, zest, salt, and cayenne, and combine well. Divide the mixture into 12 portions, about 2 ounces each. Pour the crumbs into a small baking dish. Flatten each portion into a small patty about 2 1/2 inches in diameter and ¾ inch thick. Lay each crab cake in the crumbs, pat it gently to coat with crumbs on all sides, and transfer to a baking pan. Cover and refrigerate the cakes if you don't plan to fry them right away. The cakes can be made up several hours ahead.

Fry the cakes in two batches of six in a 12-inch cast-iron skillet. Heat 2 tablespoons of the clarified butter until it sizzles when a crumb is dropped in. Fry the cakes over medium-high heat for about 2½ minutes per side, or until the surfaces are well browned. Transfer the cakes to a platter lined with a paper napkin or absorbent towel. Keep the first six cakes warm in a low oven while you fry the second batch. Serve while still hot.

Soufflés

With the exception of some dessert soufflés, which rely only on beaten egg whites for their structure and rise, soufflés begin as a béchamel sauce bound with egg yolks. Beaten egg whites are folded in just before cooking and account for the expanded form and barely substantial consistency. Essentially, the structural components of a soufflé are bland. The challenge in creating savory soufflés (as opposed to sweet soufflés, which begin with pastry cream) lies more in introducing and balancing flavor; whereas the marvel of its puffy top and airy consistency is the function of a simple and reliable formula. To make solid additions (bits of meat, vegetables, shellfish) to the béchamel is not enough. The béchamel itself must be infused with flavor or the soufflé will taste dull.

An ideal way to introduce flavor to the béchamel is to purée aromatic vegetables or, if appropriate, a proportion of the main ingredient of the soufflé with the milk that is to be added to flour to make the béchamel. In the case of a leek or garlic soufflé, for instance, the milk is poured over the stewed vegetables, the mixture is puréed and then stirred into the flour. Cheese is added for additional flavor. A soufflé of crab utilizes the near-liquid mass of edible organs, called the "crab butter," found inside the top shell and body cavity to flavor the béchamel. Some soufflés, such as lobster, are flavored by adding a cream-bound reduction of the shells to the béchamel or by simmering the béchamel with meats, poultry, or fish previously pounded in a mortar. Cheese soufflés are generally made with an unseasoned béchamel since the cheese melts in and flavors the béchamel sufficiently. Cheeses with a firm texture that are not too moist and with full flavor are excellent for soufflés. Gruyère, Cantal, Swiss Emmenthaler, Comte, Appenzeller, and Parmesan are fine choices.

The guideline for all savory soufflés is the same: The béchamel must be well seasoned and taste clearly of the main ingredient. As a general rule, I follow the proportion of 1¼ cups béchamel sauce made with 5 tablespoons butter, 3 tablespoons flour, and 1 cup milk to 4 eggs. This produces a light soufflé texture with a creamy interior. I am indebted to Richard Olney for the idea of a soufflé pudding, which is really a sunken soufflé, unmolded and gratinéed in a bath of cream in the oven. We make soufflé puddings of all kinds in the restaurant, with Parmesan cheese, wild mushrooms, white and black truffles, oysters, and crab. The base mixture contains extra egg yolks and is stiffer than that of a regular soufflé so that it can stand up to being unmolded and cooked twice.

The way the ingredients are assembled is very important. The beaten egg whites are the very last addition. Any solid garnishes are added before the addition of the egg whites. For light soufflés with a creamy center, the egg whites are beaten to firm, but not stiff, peaks. Stiff egg whites would not blend well with the batter. In general, the degree of stiffness of the egg whites is adjusted to the consistency of the batter—the stiffer the batter, the stiffer the egg whites should be.

Egg whites should be beaten in a very clean copper, stainless-steel, glass, or ceramic bowl. Egg whites are particularly sensitive to the presence of fat; a speck of egg yolk, for instance, will drastically reduce the volume when beaten. Never use plastic bowls to beat egg whites, as even washed-out plastic retains traces of fats.

Always use the freshest eggs available when making soufflés. The whites of fresh eggs achieve good volume when beaten and are less likely to collapse when folded in. Although acid (in the form of cream of tartar) or the use of a copper bowl have no effect on volume, they do chemically stabilize beaten egg whites. Distilled white vinegar appears to do the same: Before beating the whites I add about ½ teaspoon to the bowl and wipe down the entire inner surface with a clean towel until it is dry. The whites are less inclined to leak, form lumps, or break.

Egg whites should be incorporated immediately after being beaten. Work quickly when folding the whites into the batter. First, fold in half of the whites with a large spatula or spoon working from the bottom center, turning up and out. Turn the bowl and continue folding until the mixture is blended. Add the remaining whites similarly. Keep the mixture light and voluminous. Do not overfold the whites or the mixture will deflate. Transfer the mixture directly to buttered soufflé dishes and place them on the middle rack of a preheated oven. The soufflés are placed on the middle rack so that they benefit from the top heat of the oven, which helps the caps to brown evenly. I prefer to cook soufflés at a fairly high temperature, 400°F to 425°F. This temperature has proven ideal for cooking the interior edges and browning the top, but leaving the center with a creamy, saucelike consistency. Cooking soufflés at temperatures below 375°F gives a more uniformly solid texture.

There are several options for soufflé dishes. A large, low-sided, oval gratin can be used to serve a family-style soufflé. Cooking time will be shorter, however, because of the shallower dimensions of the dish. Individual soufflés are made in deeper ceramic dishes, ramekins, or charlotte molds.

A soufflé can serve as an intermediary course, an entrée, or dessert. Our experience in the restaurant has taught us that soufflés are not best served as first courses; they dull rather than awaken the appetite. Furthermore, we have found that in a succession of courses, it is wise to serve a small soufflé (4-ounce ramekins). Despite their lightness, soufflés are deceptively filling.

Dungeness Crab Soufflés
with Chervil and Green Onions

Eight 4-ounce soufflés

For this recipe buy a whole, preferably live, crab. You will use both the meat of the crab and the edible organs (crab butter) inside the carapace. The crab butter flavors the béchamel base of the soufflé, and the meat of the crab is shredded and added for texture. It is important that the crab meat be as dry as possible so as not to introduce too much moisture in the soufflé mixture—it may be necessary to squeeze out the crab meat in a towel or cheesecloth before adding it. A 1½- to 2-pound crab will yield up to 1½ cups meat but only ¾ cup is necessary for this recipe. If made in small (4-ounce) ramekins, this soufflé makes a light second course or a delicious entrée with a lemony chervil butter and a sauté of tender spring vegetables, such as carrots, leeks, asparagus, artichokes, and peas.

1 gallon water

1 tablespoon salt

1 live Dungeness crab

¼ cup finely diced leek (2 ounces), white part only

3 tablespoons celery from the tender inner stalk (1 ounce), thinly sliced

¾ cup water

½ teaspoon white wine vinegar

½ teaspoon salt

Freshly ground pepper

1 cup milk

5 tablespoons unsalted butter

3 tablespoons all-purpose flour

¼ teaspoon lemon zest

2 pinches ground cayenne

1 tablespoon chopped fresh chervil

1 tablespoon very finely chopped green onion or chives

5 large eggs

Bring the water to the boil in a pot large enough to contain the crab. Add the salt and then the crab. Cook the crab for 12 minutes from the time the water returns to the boil. In the meantime, put the leeks and celery in a 3-quart saucepan. Add the ¾ cup water, the vinegar, salt, and a little freshly ground pepper. Bring to a simmer, cover the pot, and cook the vegetables for 10 minutes. Remove the cover, raise the heat, and allow all of the water around the vegetables to evaporate. Remove the crab from the pot and set it aside to cool. Add the milk to the vegetables and bring it to just below the simmer. Purée the vegetables with the milk in a blender for 1 minute.

Clean out the saucepan and melt the butter in it. Stir in the flour until the mixture is smooth and well combined. Over low heat, add the puréed vegetables and milk and stir for about 2 minutes, until the mixture thickens. Transfer this béchamel immediately to a 2-quart bowl.

Pull the top shell away from the body and legs of the crab. Set a fine sieve over a bowl. Using a spoon, remove the crab butter (the white-orange-colored internal organs from the top shell and body cavity of the crab), letting it fall into the sieve. Discard the watery liquid that falls through the sieve. With the back of the spoon, push the crab butter through the sieve. Stir ¼ cup of sieved crab butter into the béchamel.

Preheat the oven to 425°F. Butter eight 4-ounce ramekins.

Crack the shells of the crab and pick the meat out. Measure ¾ cup crab meat and squeeze it out in a towel or piece of cheesecloth until dry. Add it to the béchamel with the lemon zest, cayenne, chervil, and green onions.

Separate the eggs. Stir the yolks into the béchamel and combine the ingredients. Correct, if necessary, with salt to taste. Beat the egg whites to firm but not stiff peaks. Fold in half of the whites first, then the other half. Work quickly, keeping the mixture light and voluminous. Ladle the mixture into buttered ramekins, filling them very nearly to the top. Run your thumb around the inside rim to form a cap. Bake the soufflés for 10 to 12 minutes on the middle rack of the oven, until they are brown and puffy and just set everywhere except the center. Serve immediately.

Double Consommé of Crab

For 6

If you want to eat something clean and warm but not rich, this consommé is an agreeable choice. The soup is made by simmering the crab shells in fish broth. Extracting flavor first from the fish, then from the crab, results in a clear broth and the name double consommé. You'll need two crabs, one for flavoring the broth, the other to pick clean and add as garnish to the soup. We use Dungeness crabs or Rock crabs—both local varieties—which we must fish for ourselves. Atlantic hard-shell blue crabs will work as well, as will lobster. Make this soup if you already have fish broth on hand, or this recipe can be time-consuming.

4 quarts water
1 tablespoon salt
2 live Dungeness crabs (3 pounds)

Put the water and salt in a pot large enough to contain one of the crabs and bring it to the boil. Plunge in the crab and cook it for 12 minutes. Remove from the pot and let cool.

Dress the other crab live. Use a towel or wear oven mitts. Approach the crab from behind and grasp the two legs furthest to the back. Hold the crab steady and twist off the pincers. With the crab resting right side up and holding the underbody down at the point where the legs protrude, pull away the top shell. Discard the top shell and the internal organs, some of which will remain in the crab cavity. Remove the ivory-colored, tapered gills attached to either side of the body and discard them. Turn the crab over and lift off the apron, or breast-plate, the hinged piece of shell on the midsection of the crab. Remove the legs and rinse all parts of the crab under cold running water. Crack the shells of the crab under a towel with a rolling pin or mallet or pound them, piecemeal, in a mortar. The crab need not be pulverized, just broken into small pieces.

1 tablespoon olive oil
3 ounces mirepoix (3 tablespoons each of finely diced carrot, and celery and 4 table-
spoons finely diced leek, white part only)
½ small red bell pepper (2 ounces), finely diced
¼ cup fennel (1 ounce), finely diced
1 bay leaf
1 sprig thyme
5 cups fish broth (see page 428)
2 small pieces (about 1 inch) lemon peel, yellow part only
3 tablespoons sliced green onion
Optional: ¹/₁₆ teaspoon ground cayenne

Warm the olive oil in a 6-quart stainless-steel pot. Add the vegetables, bay leaf, and thyme and cook over medium heat for 8 minutes, until the vegetables release their aroma and soften slightly. Raise the heat, add the crab shells, and stir them constantly until they turn orange colored all over. Bits of crab will adhere to the bottom of the pan. Scrape them up and continue turning the shells for about 5 minutes. Add the fish broth, bring to a simmer, and skim the white froth that rises to the surface. Cover the pot and cook gently for 20 minutes.

In the meantime, use a nut cracker, kitchen shears, or meat mallet to crack or cut the shells of the boiled crab and pick the meat from the shells. (A 1½-pound Dungeness crab, picked clean, will yield a heaping cup or roughly one-third of its weight of meat.) Strain the crab broth and discard the vegetables and shells.

Assembling the soup: Add the lemon peel to the crab broth and warm it gently. Stir in the crab meat and the cayenne, if desired. When the soup is hot, pour it into warm bowls, scatter the green onion over the top and serve. The leaves of fresh coriander or chervil are also refreshing additions to this soup.

Fried Flounder and Poached Flounder
with Tomato Sauce and Basil

This recipe is an opportunity to present small flat fish cooked two different ways. The difference is textural—one crunchy, the other soft and delicate. The cook must work rapidly and know the steps involved, as both fish cook at once and very quickly.

Four 3-ounce filets, flounder or sole
3 tablespoons clarified butter (see page 414)

For breading for fish:
1 egg
⅛ teaspoon salt
Freshly ground pepper
1 cup fresh sourdough bread crumbs

Mix together the egg, salt, and pepper in a shallow bowl. Spread the bread crumbs on a plate. Coat two of the four filets only in the egg mixture, coating them on both sides. Remove and place them on the bread crumbs. Press the surrounding crumbs on the top and sides of each filet. Set aside.

Simply salt and pepper the remaining two filets lightly and set aside.

For the tomato sauce:
2 tablespoons unsalted butter
1 large, very ripe tomato (9 ounces), peeled, seeded, diced, juice strained and poured back over the tomato
⅛ teaspoon salt
Freshly ground pepper
½ teaspoon balsamic vinegar
Fresh basil

Melt the butter in a saucepan. Add the tomato, the salt, some pepper, the balsamic vinegar and stir well. Cook over medium heat, reducing the liquid in the pan and allowing it to thicken slightly, approximately 4 minutes. Turn off the heat.

Proceed directly to cooking the fish: Use two separate 10-inch sauté pans, placing them side by side on the stove. In one pan put ¼ cup water; in the other, put 3 tablespoons clarified butter, and turn the heat on under both. Drop a crumb in the pan with butter. When it sizzles, the pan is ready. Bring the water in the other pan to a simmer. First place the breaded fish in the butter, then the unbreaded fish in the simmering water. With a spatula, gently turn the fish to the other side. Cook all the filets roughly 1 minute on each side.

Transfer the poached fish to two warm plates. The fried fish should first be placed on a paper towel to drain, then be transferred to the plates.

Chop enough basil to measure 1 tablespoon. Add it to the sauce and stir well. Using half the sauce for each plate, spoon it over the unbreaded filets and around the breaded ones. Serve immediately.

Lobster Salad with Garden Lettuces, Beans, Tomatoes, Basil, and Edible Blossoms

For 2

This refreshing, colorful salad makes an extravagant presentation for festive occasions. There are a number of lobster salads that we make throughout the year at Chez Panisse. This is a summer one and is the most colorful because of the tomatoes, peppers, beans, garden lettuces, and edible blossoms then available.

Although there are many ingredients in this salad, it is the flavor of lobster that is central; the vegetables that have been chosen balance and complement it. The whole lobster is used, not just the parts with meat. A rich reduction derived from the head section is used as a sauce rather than as the basic seasoning for the salad. The vegetables and lettuces, dressed separately with vinaigrette, provide a tart base in contrast to the richness of the lobster and its sauce.

For composed salads, the raw torso of the lobster is used to make a sauce. It is necessary, clearly, to deal with a live creature. Unless you trap your own, their pincers will probably be held with thick rubber bands, so there is no reason to fear their claws. First, twist off the claws using a towel or oven mitt to protect your bare hands from sharp points on the shell. Grasp the tail at the point at which it enters the torso and twist it away. Position the lobster on its back and cut directly through the middle of the torso. Remove the sand sac behind the eyes, reserve the tomalley (liver), the greenish matter inside the shell, the roe, which is pink to orange, and any liquid. Wash out the two halves of the shells under cold running water.

This salad is best served chilled. The preparation should be completed, therefore, at least an hour ahead of serving.

For the lobster sauce:
1 tablespoon unsalted butter
4½ tablespoons carrot (1½ ounces), finely diced
3 tablespoons celery (1 ounce), finely diced
6 tablespoons onion (1½ ounces), finely diced
1½ tablespoons red bell pepper (½ ounce), finely diced
½ tomato (2 ounces), diced
One 1½-pound live Maine lobster, killed, claws and tails removed, head section split and rinsed (see above)
1 sprig thyme
1 sprig parsley
2 cups water
⅛ cup heavy cream

Prepare the lobster sauce: Melt the butter in a 1-quart saucepot. Raise the heat and brown the butter. Add the vegetables, reduce the heat, and stew them for 10 minutes, stirring often. Cut up the lobster head section, crack the small legs, and add to the pot with the vegetables. Raise the heat, add the thyme and parsley, and sauté the shells, turning them over and over until they turn red all over. Add 2 cups cold water, bring to the boil, and skim off any foam that rises to the surface. Reduce the heat and simmer the *fumet* for 20 minutes.

Bring a pot of 2 quarts water plus 2 tablespoons salt to a boil. When the water has come to a hard boil, plunge in the lobster tail and large claws and cook for 5 minutes. Remove the lobster pieces and let them cool on a plate. When they are cool, crack the shells, extract the meat, and after de-veining the tail, slice the meat into thin medallions. Slice the claws lengthwise down the middle and remove the claw membrane, if any, inside. Cover and refrigerate the lobster meat.

When the *fumet* is done, strain the shells and vegetables through a sieve into a sauté pan. Over high heat reduce the *fumet* until it barely covers the bottom of the pan and has thickened slightly. There should be a scant ¼ cup. Whisk in the heavy cream, bring the mixture back to the boil, then remove it from the heat immediately and transfer to a small bowl. Cool and refrigerate the sauce.

Vegetable garnishes:
1 small handful (1 ounce) green beans
1 small handful (1 ounce) yellow wax beans
6 red cherry tomatoes, halved
6 yellow cherry tomatoes, halved
1½ tablespoons red bell pepper (½ ounce), cut in thin julienne strips
2 tablespoons finely diced seeded cucumber
1 tablespoon finely diced shallot (½ ounce)
1 tablespoon light red wine vinegar
2 tablespoons extra virgin olive oil
Salt and pepper
4 basil leaves (lemon basil if possible)
2 handfuls small garden lettuces (mâche, young rocket, red leaf, bronze leaf, Boston,
* bibb, romaine, chervil, blanched curly endive), washed*
Edible blossoms (borage, rocket, rose petals, calendula petals, nasturtiums)

In separate batches parboil the beans in 1 quart water plus 1 teaspoon salt. Remove them from the water while they still have a slight crunch. Let the beans cool, combine them with the tomatoes and peppers, and refrigerate.

Combine the cucumber, shallot, and vinegar in a bowl and add the olive oil. Season the vinaigrette with salt and pepper and refrigerate it.

Assembling the salad: Chop the basil leaves coarse and add them to the vinaigrette. When all the salad ingredients are well chilled, dress the greens with half the vinaigrette and correct with salt to taste. Dress the vegetables with the other half of the vinaigrette. Divide the greens between large white plates. Distribute the lobster meat equally between them and arrange the vegetables around the plate. Pour any remaining vinaigrette over each salad. Drizzle the lobster sauce over all the salad ingredients. Coarsely mince the edible blossoms with a very sharp knife and sprinkle the flower confetti over the top.

Lobster and White Corn Chowder

This soup matches two sweet flavors, corn and lobster, which share an unusual affinity. There are again two procedures involved in making this soup. The first is to prepare a lobster *fumet*, which is then added to stewed onions and corn. The mixture is puréed, seasoned, and then garnished with lobster meat, whole corn kernels, and tomatoes. The success of this soup depends on the quality of the corn—it should be as fresh as possible.

For the lobster fumet:
Two 1½-pound live Maine lobsters
2 tablespoons unsalted butter
1 small yellow onion (4 ounces), diced
1 small carrot (2 ounces), diced
¼ large stalk of celery (1 ounce), diced
½ red bell pepper (2 ounces), diced
2 sprigs thyme
1 sprig parsley
2 bay leaves
6 cups water

Prepare the lobster *fumet*: Kill the lobsters and remove the tails and claws (see page 33). Split the head section in two and discard the green tomalley, the gill tissues, and the digestive tract. Rinse the head sections and cut them into small pieces. Put a gallon of water on to boil with 2 tablespoons of salt for cooking the tails and claws.

Melt the butter in a 6-quart pot and add the onion, carrot, celery, and pepper. Stew the vegetables over low heat for 15 minutes, stirring occasionally. Raise the heat, add the thyme, parsley, bay leaves, and lobster head pieces. Sauté them, turning them often until their shells redden all over. Pour the 6 cups water over the shells and vegetables, bring it to a boil, reduce the heat, and simmer for 30 minutes.

In the meantime, plunge the lobster tails and claws into the salted boiling water for 5 minutes. Remove and let cool on a plate. Remove the meat from the shells and de-vein the tails.

Strain and reserve the lobster *fumet*, discarding the shells, vegetables, and herbs.

For the corn soup:
2 tablespoons unsalted butter
1 yellow onion (6 ounces), finely diced
¼ cup water
7 ears white corn, shucked, kernels cut free from the cob
2 ripe red tomatoes (8 ounces), peeled, seeded, diced
⅛ teaspoon salt
⅛ teaspoon freshly ground pepper
1/16 teaspoon ground cayenne
3 tablespoons chopped fresh chervil

Prepare the corn soup: Melt the butter in a 6-quart stainless-steel pot. Add the onion and water, cover the pot, and sweat the onion for 10 minutes over low heat. Set aside 1 cup of corn kernels, then add the rest to the pot. Add the lobster *fumet*, bring it to a simmer, and cook for 5 minutes. Purée the corn and lobster *fumet* in batches in the blender for a full 3 minutes, then pass the liquid through a medium-fine sieve into another pot. Season the soup with salt, pepper, and cayenne.

Five minutes before serving, dice the meat from the lobster tails and claws. Add it with the tomatoes and the reserved corn to the soup and warm gently. When hot, serve the soup in warm bowls and garnish with the chervil leaves and freshly ground pepper.

Winter Lobster Salad

For 4

The method of preparing this salad is identical to that of summer lobster salad. It is the seasonal vegetables that are used as garnish that create the different effect.

Like the summer version, the head section of the lobster is used to make a sauce, which gives a single focus of flavor. We often make this salad with Pacific spiny lobster rather than Maine lobster. The tail of the spiny lobster is very fat and full and the meat is relatively firm-textured. It has a lean, briny flavor and has no claws.

Use this recipe as a model and improvise with other winter vegetables: leeks or tender scallions, carrots, hearts of celery, red and golden beets, oyster mushrooms, artichokes. Winter salad greens might include the blanched centers of curly endive and Belgian endive, young tender spinach and sorrel leaves, watercress, mâche, and the deep-colored red lettuces. Black truffle will lend its distinctive aroma to the salad if pounded and added to the vinaigrette.

Preparing this salad involves a number of steps: boiling and extracting the meat of the lobster, making the lobster sauce and vinaigrette, and washing, cutting, and precooking the vegetables. If you wish to pace the preparation of this dish, both the lobster and sauce can be made a day ahead.

For the lobster sauce:
2 tablespoons pure olive oil
4½ tablespoons finely diced carrots (1½ ounces)
3 tablespoons finely diced celery (1 ounce)
1 shallot (1 ounce), finely diced
Two 1½-pound live lobsters, killed, claws and tails removed, head section split (tomalley reserved), and rinsed (see recipe page 33)
1 sprig parsley
1 sprig thyme
1 small bay leaf
¼ cup heavy cream
Pinch ground cayenne
Water

Prepare the lobster sauce: Warm the olive oil in a 6-quart non-corroding pot. Add the vegetables and soften them over medium heat for 8 minutes. Cut up the lobster head, crack the small legs, and add to the pot with the vegetables. Raise the heat, add the parsley, thyme, bay leaf, and sauté the shells, turning them over and over until they turn red all over. Add water to just cover the shells (about 4 cups). Bring to the boil, skim off any foam that rises to the surface, reduce the heat, and simmer the *fumet* for 20 minutes.

Put on a pot of 2 quarts water plus 2 tablespoons salt in which to cook the lobster claws and tails. Plunge in the lobster and cook it for 5 minutes from the time the water returns to the boil. Remove the lobster from the water and let it cool on a plate. Crack the shells, extract the meat, and after de-veining the tail, slice the meat into thin pieces. Slice the claws lengthwise down the middle and remove the claw membrane, if any, inside. Cover and refrigerate the lobster meat.

When the lobster *fumet* is done, strain through a sieve into a sauté pan. Over high heat reduce the *fumet* to about ⅓ cup (it will have thickened slightly). Add the heavy cream and cayenne, bring the mixture to the boil, add the reserved tomalley and whisk it constantly for 15 seconds. Strain the sauce immediately through a medium-fine sieve pushing the tomalley through. Cover the sauce and refrigerate it until you are ready to dress the salad.

Vegetable garnishes:
2 large handfuls mixed winter lettuces (tender blanched curly endive or Belgian endive, watercress, mâche, bronze leaf or ruby red, watercress, young spinach, or a few leaves of sorrel, burnet, and chervil)
2 globe artichokes (1 pound, 8 ounces), pared down to bottoms
8 small leeks (2½ ounces), or green onions, peeled down to tender shoots
8 baby carrots (2 ounces)

Wash and dry the lettuces. Cook the artichoke bottoms in 1 quart lightly salted water with 1 tablespoon vinegar for 15 minutes. Parboil the leeks and carrots separately in lightly salted water until tender. Let all the vegetables cool on a plate.

For the vinaigrette:
1 large shallot (1½ ounces), finely diced
1 tablespoon Champagne vinegar
Optional: ½ ounce black truffle, pounded in a mortar
Salt and pepper
4 tablespoons extra virgin olive oil

Prepare the vinaigrette: Combine the shallot and vinegar and black truffle, if used. Dissolve a little salt in the mixture, add pepper, and stir in the olive oil.

Assembling the salad: Slice the artichokes thin. Toss the lettuces with about half the vinaigrette and use the other half to dress the artichokes, carrots, and leeks. Distribute the lettuces and vegetables on large white plates. Place pieces of the lobster tail and claws on each. Stir the sauce well, drizzle it over the lobster and vegetables, and serve.

Mussel Soup with Saffron, Fennel, Cream, and Spinach

The most common mussel available in the United States is the blue mussel (*Mytilus edulis*), which is cultivated in New England, Nova Scotia, and along the northern points of the Pacific Coast. Cultivated mussels hang on ropes or stakes between the surface and the ocean bottom where there is little variation in tide. These mussels are remarkably refined, both in appearance and flavor, and require little scrubbing or cleaning. Wild mussels are available only to those who gather them. Although much less uniform in size, a little tougher, and more trouble to clean, they have a truer flavor.

Mussels will gape if exposed to the air or to changes in temperature, such as removing them from the refrigerator to room temperature before cooking. Press any opened shells back together with your thumb and forefinger. The shells should close tightly. If they do not, the mussel is dead and should be discarded. Storing mussels in sea water is ideal. However, they will keep for a day in a dry container, refrigerated, and covered with a damp towel.

To clean mussels, remove the "beard," the tangled tuft protruding from mid-shell, which the mussel uses to attach itself to the rope, rock, or seawall (the beard of wild mussels can be particularly tenacious). Pull off any grasses clinging to the shell and scrub the mussel under running water with a small vegetable brush to remove any mud or silt.

No fish broth is required for this recipe. The liquid that the mussels release when steamed open is sufficient to provide a base for the soup. This recipe yields small portions—about 4 ounces each—a just amount considering the richness and persistent flavors of mussels, not to mention the other ingredients in the soup.

1½ pounds live mussels
1 large shallot (1½ ounces), finely diced
½ cup dry white wine (such as Muscadet or Sauvignon Blanc)
3 bay leaves
2 sprigs thyme
1 tablespoon unsalted butter
Pinch saffron (about 20 threads)
½ cup finely diced fennel (4 ounces)
⅛ teaspoon salt
¼ cup water

1 cup chopped fresh spinach
²/₃ cup heavy cream
Freshly ground pepper

Clean the mussels thoroughly. Put the shallot, wine, bay leaves, and thyme in a 3-quart stainless-steel saucepan and bring to a bare simmer. Add the mussels, raise the heat to high, cover the pot, and cook for 3 to 4 minutes, shaking the pot occasionally until all the mussels have opened. Pour the mussels into a colander over a bowl to catch the liquid from the pan. Let the mussels cool and shuck them, checking inside each and pulling away the base of the beard, if any remains.

Wash the saucepan. Over low heat, melt the butter, add the saffron, fennel, and salt, and stew for 8 minutes, until it is softened. Add the strained mussel liquid, the water, spinach, and cream. Bring the mixture to just under the boil and simmer for 2 minutes. Add the mussels and simmer 2 minutes more. Generously pepper the soup and serve.

Mussels Steamed with New Zinfandel

For 2

We served these mussels during New Zinfandel Week, when we celebrated the bottling of newly fermented wine from our friends at Phelps Vineyard several years ago. We decided to use this youthful, somewhat raw wine to steam open the mussels and as a foil for their richness.

This dish is very simple to prepare. Once the mussels have been cleaned and the parsley and garlic are chopped, it is on the table in minutes.

1 large shallot (1½ ounces), diced
3 bay leaves
2 sprigs thyme
½ cup young red wine (young Zinfandel or Beaujolais Nouveau)
1½ pounds live mussels, de-bearded and cleaned
1 tablespoon extra virgin olive oil
1 small clove garlic, finely chopped
1 tablespoon chopped fresh Italian parsley

Put the shallot, bay leaves, thyme, and wine in a 3-quart stainless-steel pot and bring to a simmer. Add the mussels, cover the pot, raise the heat to high, and cook for about 3 minutes, or until all the mussels have opened. Transfer the mussels to a large bowl with a slotted spoon. Stir the olive oil, garlic, and parsley into the broth (about 1 cup) in the pot. Serve the broth in small bowls with toasted sourdough bread brushed with olive oil and rubbed with raw garlic. Use the broth as a bath, to pour over both the mussels and bread.

Oyster Soup

For 4

Reminiscent of oyster chowder, this soup is much lighter and fresher and retains the briny flavor of the sea. Although the combination is not too rich, a small portion of it is sufficient. A favorite way we present it in the restaurant is in a 3-ounce serving, with a crouton topped with caviar floating in the center.

1 dozen live oysters
2½ tablespoons unsalted butter
1 cup baguette croutons, cut into ½-inch squares
¼ cup water
2 sprigs fresh thyme
2¾ ounces fine mirepoix (1 tablespoon each of ⅛-inch diced carrot, celery, and onion)
2 small red potatoes (4 ounces), cut into ¼-inch dice, parboiled in lightly salted water
    for 3 minutes
1 cup milk
½ cup heavy cream
Large pinch lemon zest
1 tablespoon chopped fresh chervil
Salt and pepper

Preheat the oven to 375°F.

Shuck the oysters, drain them, and reserve their liquor. Chop the oysters coarse. (This should yield about ⅓ cup.) Melt 1½ tablespoons of the butter, pour it over the croutons, and mix well. Spread the croutons on a small baking sheet and bake in the oven for 15 minutes, or until they are crisp and toasted brown.

Melt the remaining 1 tablespoon butter in a saucepot, add the water, thyme, and mirepoix, and cook about 3 minutes, until the vegetables soften and release their flavors. Add the potatoes, the reserved oyster liquor, the milk, cream, and lemon zest. Bring to a simmer and add the chopped oysters and chervil. Continue to simmer for 3 minutes. Correct the soup for salt and pepper. Serve in warm bowls with a small handful of warm croutons added to each.

Fish and Shellfish Soup

For 8

The late fall is a good time to make fish soup in the style of a bouillabaisse. A plentiful supply of various rockfish are available and shellfish of all kinds are in prime season. Avoid strong-flavored, oily fish, such as herring, sardines, or mackerel, and salmon and sole, the fine flavor of which would only be lost. Select fish for a variety of texture and flavor. Grouper, tautog, red snapper, hake, haddock, skate, black drum, sea bass, halibut, monkfish, shark, and Pacific rockfish are all good candidates. There is no need to go overboard—three different kinds in combination with shellfish such as clams, mussels, crab, shrimp, or lobster make a colorful and varied soup.

The broth is derived from the carcasses of fish; when this is done the filets of fish are cut into pieces and poached in the broth along with the shellfish. Well-made, richly flavored fish soup is moistened with fish broth rather than water. Unfortunately, the small varieties of "soup fish," which are ideal for broth making, are not common to our markets. Nevertheless, Chinese markets are a good, inexpensive source for the stranger and smaller varieties, and using them will enrich the broth considerably.

A soup of this kind makes a whole meal. In the restaurant the dishes we send to the table before and after are simple and insubstantial—a plate of olives, a bowl of mixed lettuces, an uncomplicated dessert. However, presenting a soup with as many components as this poses some problems. Following the model of bouillabaisse or *pot au feu*, the most graceful way is to disassemble the soup and serve it in separate dishes, rather than all together. Each person is given a bowl containing some of the broth and a toasted slice of bread. The fish and shellfish, transferred to separate bowls and kept warm in some of the broth, are passed around. Fish and shellfish soup, as served at Chez Panisse, would not be the same if not accompanied by the wines (both red and rosé) of the Domaine Tempier, the generosity and good nature of which complete this soup.

3 quarts fresh fish broth (see page 428, omit the mussels and tomatoes)
1 recipe Garlic Mayonnaise (see page 115)
2½ pounds mixed fileted, skinned fish: rockfish, monkfish, sturgeon or bass, halibut
3 tablespoons olive oil
3½ cups thinly sliced yellow onions (14 ounces)
Pinch saffron (about 20 threads)
3 bay leaves
¼ teaspoon thyme
¼ teaspoon salt
⅛ teaspoon freshly ground pepper
6 tomatoes (2 pounds), peeled, seeded, diced, juice reserved and strained
1½ teaspoons salt
Pinch ground cayenne
1 pound small clams, rinsed
1 pound small mussels, scrubbed and rinsed
¾ pound thin-fleshed squid, cleaned, cut into ringlets
4 tablespoons chopped fresh Italian parsley
8 slices sourdough levain bread, toasted and rubbed with garlic (see page 218 for a
    description of levain bread)

Have ready the fish broth and garlic mayonnaise.

Locate the bones running vertically down the rockfish and make a cut on either side of the bones. Remove these bony strips and add them to the broth. Cut all the fish filets into pieces about ½ inch thick and 2 to 3 inches long and set aside, keeping the types of fish separate.

Warm the olive oil in a heavy, 3-quart saucepan, add the onions, saffron, bay leaves, thyme, salt, and pepper. Stir the mixture well and cook the onions slowly for about 20 minutes, or until soft. Strain the fish broth and discard the carcasses and vegetables. Transfer the onions to a large pot (8-quart capacity), add the tomatoes, the strained tomato juice, and pour the fish broth over these ingredients. (For a wonderful smoky flavor, try using grilled tomatoes.) Add the salt and cayenne and bring to a low simmer.

Warm eight bowls in a low oven or on top of the stove.

Add the firmest fish first, in this case the monkfish and sturgeon. Cook for 2 minutes, maintaining a simmer. Raise the heat if necessary. Next, add the clams and mussels, then the rockfish, allowing each to cook for 2 minutes. Lastly, add the squid, cook 3 minutes more, and stir in the parsley. Transfer the fish and shellfish to deep serving dishes or a platter and pour a few ladlefuls of the broth over each. Put the remaining broth into a soup tureen. At the table, put a slice of toasted bread in each bowl and pour a ladleful of broth over the bread. Pass the fish, shellfish, and garlic mayonnaise around the table.

Salmon

Living on the Coast, we are privileged with an abundance of wild Pacific salmon. Although there are a number of distinct species, the salmon most highly regarded, and commonly available, is the Chinook, also known as the King salmon. It is impossible to characterize salmon consistently. The flavor, color, size, and oil content are variable from one run to the next and depend on the season or point of origin of the fish. Generally speaking, the leanest and most delicately flavored salmon appears in the late spring. The summer months bring fish that are progressively fatter with a more pronounced oil content and flavor.

Salmon is an ancient species and has developed a remarkable adaptability to both fresh and salt water. Born in fresh water, salmon travel thousands of miles to ocean feeding grounds only to return to spawn and die. Salmon are caught in the ocean just prior to their migration upstream. It is at this point that the fish are in prime condition, having fed for years on rich marine sources. Their silvery bodies are plump and firm, the flesh is brightly colored. Mature salmon do not feed while in fresh water, but store fat and protein in preparation for an often perilous return to the spawning grounds. The oil content and color of the flesh of salmon clearly reflect the diet of the fish. The brilliant orange-to-red colors are derived from carotenoid pigments found in crustaceans, such as the tiny shrimp or krill, on which the salmon feed. There is one type of Alaska salmon called Ivory, which suggests an altogether different food source.

Some of the choicest fish of the year come from the Columbia River and are called Winter King salmon. This is a distinct population of late-run fish returning to the river in mid-February. They are characterized by prodigious size and fat content and the most brilliant red color, which indicates a long period of ocean life. The flavor and texture of this fish is the finest I know.

Aquacultured salmon has caught on as a major source for salmon year round. These salmon are hatchery bred and transferred after six months to square net pens just off the shore. The fish are fed a controlled diet of ground fish and shrimp and are harvested after two years in the pens. Because of their restricted movement, and diet, which is high in fatty fish, aquacultured salmon tend to be rich in fat, paler in color, and have a pronounced oily flavor compared to wild salmon.

Salmon is probably the most versatile fish in the kitchen. It is delicious grilled, poached, steamed, baked in parchment, pan-fried, served cold or warm, used in salad and soups, or made into mousses and rillettes. The bones and head of the fish can be used to make *fumets*, if care is taken not to include any of the skin of the fish—the skin contains oils that give the *fumet* a disagreeable flavor. Use the skin to season the charcoal grill. Lay the skin on the hot grill and let its oils transfer to the metal grates. Remove the skin, clean the grates with a wire brush, and grill the salmon immediately. This will prevent the fish from sticking and leave attractive grill marks.

When choosing salmon, look for fish with a bright red color. A diet of shrimp-like animals makes a fine-flavored salmon. If you are buying a whole fish check to see that it is firm and has bright silver skin with smooth, unruffled scales, which means that the fish has been caught by hook and line rather than in a gill net which can bruise the fish.

When buying fileted salmon, know from what part of the fish the piece has been cut. The various sections of the fish—head, tail, belly, and midsection—all have specific uses in the kitchen. The salmon uses its tail primarily to move through the water. Consequently, this section, extending from the tapered end one third of the way up the filet, is the most exercised, tightly bundled, and leanest portion of the fish. The tail will be less tender and juicy, and firmer in texture than other parts of the fish. Its flavor can be excellent, however. The tail section is best cooked in a moist medium, such as baked with tomatoes and bacon, or steamed in parchment where none of its juices are lost. If you choose to grill or poach the tail, serve it with a sauce. The mid-section of the fish is ideal for wide-cut escalopes, an attractive way of presenting grilled salmon. Hold your knife at a 25-degree angle and cut even ½-inch-thick slices. Cut in this manner, salmon cooks very quickly on the grill, which sears the surface and seals in the juices. The head section of salmon, resting just below the nape of the fish on either side, is the thickest and choicest section of the filet. The flesh is large flaked and ideal for grilling or poaching when cut in block portions, also called *tranche*.

Thick cuts of salmon from large fish, sealed on the surface of a hot grill and left slightly less cooked in the center, can have an incomparable buttery texture. Poaching exposes the bare flavor characteristics of the fish. To my taste it is preferable to choose head or midsections from smaller, delicately flavored fish for this purpose. The flavor of larger, oil-rich fish is tempered by the smoke of a wood or charcoal fire.

Unfortunately, most fishmongers either discard, or sell as scrap, the belly flaps of salmon. Resting under the stomach, it is the fattest section of the fish. Salmon bellies are generally paler in color, with a wide, flaked grain. The belly is normally trimmed after the fish is fileted, resulting in a long strip an inch or two wide. First skinned, poached or sautéed, and broken up and combined with finely minced shallots, a little sweet butter, and herbs, this makes a refined spread for croutons. The belly is also suited to mousses and *quenelles*.

Salmon Carpaccio

This dish has always been a popular appetizer at the restaurant because it looks so good. The raw salmon, the colors of the pepper mélange, and the edible blossoms make it wildly colorful. Its appearance belies its delicate flavor, however. By itself it is insubstantial; but like oysters or caviar, it is satisfying in its elegance and very well matched with Champagne.

Choose very fresh fish that is a brilliant red color. Pacific Chinook salmon is the best. And buy the choice center or head of the filet. Don't use the tougher tail section.

Two 1-ounce escalopes of salmon, cut 1/3 inch thick
Four 6- by 8-inch pieces of baking parchment, oiled lightly on one side

For the garnish:
2 tablespoons mixed peppers (red, yellow, green), cut into 1/8-inch dice
1 small shallot (1/2 ounce), minced
Juice of 1 small lemon (Meyer, if possible)
1/2 teaspoon balsamic vinegar
1/4 cup extra virgin olive oil
Salt and pepper
Chervil leaves
Edible blossoms (borage, rocket, wild radish, rose petals, johnny jump-ups, calendula petals)

Have ready two chilled plates, about 8 or 9 inches in diameter.

With a pair of flat tweezers or needle-nose pliers, remove any small white pinbones in the fish. Place each salmon escalope between two pieces of the parchment paper, oiled side up. With a flat meat mallet, or better, a lightweight cleaver turned on its side, gently flatten the escalope, holding the paper secure so that it does not slip. Alternate direct downward movements with those that draw the escalope out to a dimension that conforms to the serving plate. Flatten until the salmon appears evenly translucent when held up against the light. Carefully peel the top sheet of parchment away from the fish and invert the carpaccio onto a cold dry plate. Peel off the other piece of paper.

Mix the diced peppers, shallot, lemon juice, balsamic vinegar, and olive oil together. Season to taste with salt and pepper. Spoon the mixture liberally over the fish and garnish with the fresh chervil leaves and the edible blossoms. Serve immediately, or the salmon will begin to "cook" in the lemon juice and vinegar.

Salmon in Court Bouillon with Herb Butter

Salmon for poaching is best cut from the section of the fish closest to the head. This part is moist, meaty, and finely flaked. The tail section of the fish is much leaner and tends to stiffen and go dry in a poaching liquid.

Court bouillon is an aromatic bath of herbs and vegetables. Its flavors combine with the salmon to make a delicate soup. The herb butter, which acts as a kind of condiment, can be altered in any number of ways to suit your taste. The shallots cooked in red wine and wine vinegar add bits of burgundy color and a tart emphasis. The addition of chopped parsley, capers, and anchovies creates a more forceful taste. Herbs with a minty character—tarragon or basil—stand out clearly and enhance the flavor of the salmon greatly.

Cut the salmon perpendicular to the filet in block portions as opposed to escalopes. Exposing less of the surface area of the fish to the hot liquid will keep it moist inside.

For the court bouillon:
4½ tablespoons very thinly sliced carrot rounds (1½ ounces)
3 tablespoons very thinly sliced celery from the heart (1 ounce)
½ cup very thinly sliced rounds yellow onion (2 ounces)
3 sprigs fresh lemon thyme
1 large sprig Italian parsley
3 cups water
½ cup Sauvignon Blanc
1½ teaspoons salt

For the herb butter:
4 tablespoons unsalted butter at room temperature
1 small shallot (½ ounce), finely diced
1½ heaping tablespoons chopped fresh chervil
½ tablespoon thinly sliced chives
Zest of ¼ lemon
Pinch of salt and pepper

Four 4-ounce pieces of salmon, cut 1 inch thick

Prepare the court bouillon: Combine all the ingredients for the court bouillon in a noncorrosive pot large enough to hold the salmon pieces side by side with room to spare. Bring to a simmer, cover, and cook for 20 minutes.

In the meantime, prepare the herb butter: Mix the butter together with the herbs, lemon, salt, and pepper. Set the butter aside in a small bowl and keep it at room temperature.

Taste the court bouillon and correct it to your taste for salt. Bring the court bouillon to a bare simmer and add the salmon. If you are using a small pot, the salmon will be submerged and will require about 3 to 4 minutes cooking time. (It should be removed when slightly undercooked in the center. With a small knife, part the filet to check.) Otherwise, gently poach the salmon slices, cut side down, in the hot liquid for about 2½ minutes on each side. Do not raise the heat during this time. Transfer the salmon to warm soup bowls and put a dollop of herb butter on each slice. Pour hot court bouillon over the butter and salmon, add some of the vegetables from the pot to each bowl, and serve.

Grilled Salmon with Tomatoes and Basil Vinaigrette

For 6

This is an excellent way of serving salmon, particularly the larger late-season fish, which are rich in oil. The tomatoes vinaigrette has a tart, clean flavor that relieves the richness of the fish. Although salmon of this kind is very well suited to the charcoal grill, it can also be cooked in a hot, well-seasoned cast-iron pan. Get the pan very hot before adding the fish. It is not necessary to add oil to the pan—there is enough in the flesh of the fish to seal the surfaces.

Another simple treatment for this fish is to serve it with a vinaigrette made with Champagne vinegar, extra virgin olive oil, and finely diced shallots. Scatter a mixture of herb blossoms like thyme, marjoram, sage, rosemary, basil, chervil, or coriander and other edible blossoms over the top. Be careful, the herbs' flowers are powerful.

2 shallots (2 ounces), finely diced
1½ tablespoons red wine vinegar
2 tablespoons extra virgin olive oil
2 ripe tomatoes (1 pound), peeled, seeded, diced
2 tablespoons coarsely chopped fresh basil
Salt and pepper
1½ pounds salmon filet

Prepare a charcoal fire.

Combine the shallots, vinegar, and olive oil in a small bowl. Add the tomatoes and basil. Spoon the vinaigrette over the tomatoes and mix well. Salt and pepper the tomatoes to taste and correct them for vinegar if necessary.

Holding a sharp knife at about a 25-degree angle to the fish, cut 6 slices of salmon to an even thickness of ⅜ inch. Lightly oil and salt and pepper both sides of the salmon. While the fire is hot grill the salmon. Salmon cut this way cooks very quickly, 1 to 2 minutes per side, and it is advisable to remove it from the grill while it is still pink in the center. Feel the salmon after you have flipped it to the second side. It should be a little firm (never hard) and the color will have changed from red-orange to a paler pink.

Put the salmon on warm plates, spoon the tomatoes vinaigrette over the filets, and serve.

Spring Salmon Salad

For 4

We make this salad in the restaurant when the first spring salmon appear. The fish has a refined and delicate flavor and is characteristically lean and not at all oily. The salad keenly represents spring with its pastel colors, tender growths from the garden, and soft flavors. Substitutions or other additions to the salad might include small sorrel leaves, young leeks parboiled until tender, spring artichokes, and blanched endive.

Salmon poaching liquid (court bouillon):
4½ tablespoons very thinly sliced carrot rounds (1½ ounces)
3 tablespoons very thinly sliced celery from the heart (1 ounce)
½ cup thinly sliced yellow onion (2 ounces)
3 sprigs lemon thyme
1 large sprig parsley
½ teaspoon salt
3 cups water
½ cup Sauvignon Blanc

Combine all the ingredients for the court bouillon in a 3-quart noncorrosive pot. Bring to a simmer and cook for 20 minutes, covered. In the meantime, prepare the vinaigrette and the other elements of the salad.

For the vinaigrette:
⅜ cup English cucumber, cut into ¼-inch dice
1 shallot (1 ounce), finely diced
1 tablespoon Champagne vinegar
Salt and pepper
2 tablespoons extra virgin olive oil

Combine the cucumber and shallot in a small bowl. Add the vinegar and a pinch of salt and pepper. Let the salt dissolve in the vinegar and stir in the oil. Set aside.

2 handfuls young ruby red or bronze leaf lettuce
2 bunches (16) scallions
½ cup shelled peas
2 to 3 stalks asparagus, sliced on the diagonal to measure ½ cup
8 nasturtium blossoms
A 12-ounce piece of salmon

Wash the lettuce. Trim the scallions so that they are about 4 inches long and remove several layers of the outer skin to reveal the tender pale green shoots. Parboil the scallions in lightly salted water for 1½ minutes. Parboil the peas and asparagus in separate pans until each is just tender.

Poach the salmon in one piece in the hot court bouillon. The time this takes will vary according to the thickness of the fish. A 1-inch-thick piece of fish will take about 3 minutes if it is submerged. The fish should be cooked all the way through but be a bit darker colored in the center. If you are in doubt about the degree of doneness, lift the fish out of the court bouillon. It should feel slightly firm all over. Make a small incision in the center and check to see if it is cooked inside. When the salmon is cooked, transfer it to a plate to cool.

Assembling the salad: Have four chilled plates ready. Dress the lettuces with about half the vinaigrette. Correct the salad for vinegar and salt if necessary. Lay the lettuces loosely on the plates. Break the salmon up by hand into large flakes and divide it among the plates. Dress the scallions, peas, and asparagus with the remaining vinaigrette and scatter them over the salmon and lettuces. Chop the nasturtium blossoms and sprinkle them over the salads as garnish.

Buckwheat Crêpes with Smoked Salmon, Crème Fraîche, and Capers

This is perhaps the lightest possible version of a pizza and a genuine appetizer—the slightly salty, tart, and smoky flavors are stimulating to the appetite. And the combination is nearly weightless.

Precooked crêpes are crisped in the oven and topped while still warm with thin slices of smoked salmon, green onions, capers, and crème fraîche. The crêpes themselves can be made and fried several days in advance. Although crème fraîche is available commercially, it is very simple to make and at much less expense (see page 417). If you want to render this dish even more attractive, sprinkle each crêpe with chopped edible blossoms, such as borage or nasturtium. In addition to their pleasing colors, edible blossoms contribute nuances of flavor that only add to this dish.

4 buckwheat crêpes
8 slices smoked salmon (6 ounces), very thinly sliced
1 tablespoon brined capers, soaked in several changes of cold water and drained
4 teaspoons crème fraîche
2 tablespoons green onion, quartered lengthwise and sliced very thinly
Ground pepper

Preheat the oven to 375°F.

Have four plates warming. Place the crêpes on a sheet pan and put them in the oven for 4 to 5 minutes, until they feel somewhat dry but not brittle and are crisp at the edges. Transfer the crêpes to the warm plates. Drape several slices of smoked salmon over each crêpe so that its surface is nearly covered. Sprinkle one-fourth of the capers on each crêpe. Stir the crème fraîche and thin it with a little water if it is very thick; it should be slightly thicker than heavy cream. Drizzle 1 teaspoon of crème fraîche over the salmon, sprinkle each crêpe with green onions, grind pepper lightly over the top, and serve.

For the buckwheat crêpes: makes twelve 7-inch crêpes
2 tablespoons unsalted butter
1 cup milk
⅛ teaspoon salt
¼ teaspoon sugar

½ cup all-purpose flour
2½ tablespoons buckwheat flour
1½ teaspoons vegetable oil
2 small eggs
¼ cup beer

Make the buckwheat crêpes: Melt the butter in a small saucepan. Add the milk, salt, and sugar, stir well, and turn off the heat. Put both flours in a mixing bowl, make a well in the center, and pour in the vegetable oil and eggs. Mix the eggs and oil with a whisk, gradually bringing in flour from the sides until it begins to thicken. Add the milk mixture little by little until all of it has been incorporated and the batter is smooth. Whisk in the beer. Pour the batter through a medium strainer into a bowl and refrigerate it for at least 2 hours before using. (This resting time will allow the batter to relax and the flour to absorb the liquids fully.) Crêpe batter can be made a day ahead and kept refrigerated.

Cooking the crêpes: Preheat a seasoned 9½-inch steel crêpe pan over medium-low heat until it sizzles when you pour a drop of water onto its surface. Stir the crêpe batter well. Bring the pan from the stove to the mixture. Using a small ladle, pour about 1 heaping fluid ounce of batter in one spot at the edge of the pan. Immediately tilt and swirl the pan, moving the batter around the periphery and down over the center, until the cooking surface is covered. Dribble batter over any bare spots. This takes a little practice and works if the pan is not too hot. If it is, the batter will set before it can be spread. On the other hand, if the pan is too cool, the crêpe will not brown well, nor will it be lacy in appearance. The pan is hot enough if the batter sizzles upon contact and the batter immediately becomes riddled with small holes. Your first several crêpes may not take. Don't be deterred. Adjust the heat and try again. Establish an even rhythm so that the pan is always filled. (When you perfect this technique, you may wish to try cooking crêpes in staggered intervals in several pans at once. This will cut your time at the stove in half and is particularly recommended if you are cooking a large batch.) Use only as much batter as will cover the bottom of the pan in a thin layer.

Cook the crêpes for about 1 minute per side. The first side is ready to be turned when you see the edges browning. Loosen and quickly flip it over with your other hand. Side two will never brown as attractively as side one because as it rests more lightly in the pan, it does not make as thorough contact with the hot surface. Remove the cooked crêpes with a fork and your fingers and stack on a cool plate. Fill the pan with batter immediately. Continue making crêpes until all the batter is used. If you do not intend to serve the crêpes right away, cover them with plastic wrap and store in the refrigerator.

Grilled Sea Bass
with Sliced Artichokes Stewed in Olive Oil

For 6

The tender leaves and hearts of small artichokes (the size of golf balls) are treated here as a condiment for grilled fish. The artichokes are first stewed in olive oil with plenty of lemon juice, slivered garlic, and thyme until very tender. What sounds at first like a strong and aggressive mixture is actually a soft blend of flavors that harmonize well with the fish. Artichokes cooked this way suit rock cod, halibut, or salmon as well.

24 small artichokes (4 pounds)
½ cup extra virgin olive oil
10 cloves garlic (⅓ cup), slivered
1 teaspoon salt
⅛ teaspoon freshly ground black pepper
1 tablespoon fresh thyme leaves
Juice of 1 lemon (2½ tablespoons)
Six 4-ounce sea bass filets
Salt and pepper

Prepare a wood or charcoal fire.

Pull away the tough outer leaves of each artichoke until the yellow-green heart is revealed. Slice off the pointed top at about halfway between the point and the base of the artichoke. Cut off the stem and pare off what is left of the dark green outer leaves surrounding the bottom. Submerge the prepared hearts in water to prevent them from turning brown. When all the chokes have been pared to the heart, turn them choke side down, and slice them about ⅛ inch thick.

Warm the olive oil in a stainless-steel pot and add the sliced artichokes, garlic, salt, pepper, thyme, and lemon juice. Cover, and cook the artichokes slowly, stirring often, for 20 minutes, or until tender.

Just before the artichokes are done, brush the sea bass filets with olive oil and salt and pepper both sides lightly. Quickly grill them over a hot fire until they are just done, transfer them to warm plates, and pile stewed artichokes over each filet.

Fried Shellfish with Herb Mayonnaise

For 6

Delicate shellfish, such as oysters, scallops, mussels, and shrimp, are better suited to shallow pan-frying than deep-frying. Pan-frying is a much gentler process and, since the pieces cook separately, both the texture and flavor of the individual shellfish is more sharply defined. Deep-frying, although an ideal way to seal flavor in foods, imparts a certain uniformity of flavor to the breading on shellfish. Generally one pot of oil is used and the shellfish are added successively, according to the cooking times; the oil is very quickly spent. At home, without the use of a deep fryer designed to maintain the necessary high temperature, frying more than a small batch of shellfish can be a frustrating process. Home stoves, in general, do not have the heat output to return the oil to a high enough temperature once the shellfish have been added, resulting in breading that takes longer than it should to brown and crisp, and shellfish that have absorbed too much oil.

Cast-iron pans are excellent for pan-frying as they retain heat well, and, if seasoned, will prevent any sticking. The choice of oil or fat is a matter of personal preference. In the restaurant we most often use clarified butter. Occasionally we use pure olive oil. Fried shellfish need little more than a wedge of lemon or a small bowl of vinegar, shallots, and chopped parsley for dipping. A tart herb mayonnaise is delicious, particularly with oysters, but adds considerable richness to the dish. A salad of lettuces vinaigrette, thinly sliced fennel, or in the summer, tomatoes and cucumbers, is a good accompaniment.

The recipe that follows calls for an array of the most common shellfish. Squid, though delicious cooked this way, can be dangerous to work with—its high moisture content, which flows when heated, causes the hot oil to spatter. Squid are better floured and deep fried. Here too, precautions must be taken when adding squid to hot oil. If you wish to simplify this recipe, serve only one shellfish.

Although the amount of bread crumbs and egg will vary according to the kind and quantity of shellfish selected, the amount of clarified butter in which you will fry shellfish in a 12-inch cast-iron pan will remain at 3 tablespoons per batch. Don't crowd the shellfish in the pan; leave space between the pieces for turning. A pair of V-shaped stainless-steel tongs is very useful. If you decide to serve a number of different shellfish, fry them separately, in batches. Work quickly, as it is best to serve the shellfish immediately, although they won't suffer if held for 5 minutes in a warm oven while you prepare the next batch. Another option is to use two pans at the same time and stagger your additions so that not all of the pieces need to be turned at the same moment.

12 live, plump oysters in the shell
½ pound shrimp
½ pound sea scallops
1 shallot (1 ounce), sliced
¼ cup dry white wine
2 bay leaves
18 mussels (10 ounces), scrubbed
About 2 cups fresh sourdough bread crumbs
2 eggs, beaten
9 tablespoons clarified butter

For the herb mayonnaise:
1 egg yolk
½ cup neutral-flavored oil
1 teaspoon water
⅛ teaspoon salt
Freshly ground pepper
2 teaspoons lemon juice
1½ teaspoons brined capers, soaked for 10 minutes in water, squeezed out, and minced
1 tablespoon finely diced cucumber
1½ teaspoons sliced chives
1 tablespoon chopped watercress
½ teaspoon chopped fresh thyme
1½ teaspoons chopped fresh parsley

If you plan to serve the fried shellfish with herb mayonnaise, make the mayonnaise first and let it stand for 30 minutes before you serve it.

Shuck the oysters and set them aside in a small bowl. Peel and de-vein the shrimp. If the shrimp are large (2½ to 3 inches long), make a lengthwise cut down the back, but not all the way through, and splay them open. If the scallops are large, cut them in half horizontally to render slices about ½ inch thick.

Combine the shallot, wine, and bay leaves in a 3-quart saucepan, bring to the boil, and add the mussels. Cover and steam the mussels over high heat for 2½ minutes, shaking the pot vigorously during this period. Pour the mussels into a bowl and let cool. When the mussels have cooled, remove them from their shells and debeard them, if necessary.

Divide the bread crumbs in half. Dip the shellfish by type one by one into the egg, letting some of it drip off so that the piece is just coated, then into the bread crumbs. Transfer the pieces to a platter. Keep the crumbs as dry as possible.

If you are using one 12-inch pan, it will be necessary to fry this amount of shellfish in three batches. Just before you are ready to serve, heat 3 tablespoons of the clarified butter in a 12-inch cast-iron pan until it sizzles when you drop in a bread crumb. Have ready a large platter lined with an absorbent towel or napkin warming in a preheated slow oven. Working quickly, transfer the shellfish to the pan and fry them for about 1 minute per side, or until the crumbs are brown and crisp. Turn them carefully with the tongs. Transfer the shellfish to the platter and return the platter to the warm oven. Discard the butter in the pan. Heat 3 more tablespoons of butter and pan-fry the remaining shellfish in the same manner.

Prepare the herb mayonnaise: Place the egg yolk in a small, deep bowl (1-quart capacity). Secure the bowl by wrapping a damp towel around the base of it. Drop by drop add the oil, whisking all the time. When the mixture begins to thicken, add the oil a little faster in a thin stream until about half of it is incorporated. Whisk in ½ teaspoon of the water. Then add the rest of the oil in a thin stream. Whisk in the remaining ½ teaspoon water to thin the consistency. Add the salt, a little pepper, the lemon juice, capers, cucumber, and herbs, and mix well. Let stand for 30 minutes before serving.

Shrimp Bisque

4 large servings

A bisque is a puréed soup that is highly seasoned and slightly thick. In general, bisques are the focus of one particular flavor. Although the process of making a bisque can apply to fowl or fish, I primarily associate it with shellfish, particularly crustaceans. A good deal of flavor is contained in the shells of shrimp, and it is the carotenoid pigments in the shell, combined with browned vegetables, that gives this soup its characteristic burnt-umber color. The technique for making shrimp bisque is like that for double consommé. Fish broth is added to vegetables and the sautéed shrimp and the two are simmered together. Make certain you sauté the shrimp until their shells are well caramelized—this is essential to the deep flavors of the soup. If you have no fish broth on hand, water or light chicken broth can be substituted, although water will result in a soup with less body.

The bisque is then sieved with as much of the shrimp and vegetables pushed through. Screen sieves are not strong enough for this process. In the restaurant we use a heavy metal conical sieve (a *chinoise*) and a tapered wooden pestle to actually pound the meat through. Shrimp pose fewer problems in sieving than do crab or lobster, which have harder shells. Alternatively, if the whole shrimp are ground to a coarse paste in a food processor before they are combined with the broth, the job of sieving can be handled in a food mill without too much effort.

There are two types of shrimp that produce excellent bisques—white Louisiana Gulf shrimp and Pacific Ridgeback shrimp. The Louisiana shrimp is a larger variety and has a deep, lingering flavor. The Ridgeback is quite small and is incomparably sweet and fine flavored. When buying fresh shrimp choose those that are firm and fresh smelling with shells that adhere tightly. Use your nose. Shrimp that is old has an offensive ammonia-like odor and a mat gray color.

Shrimp bisque is rich. A simple red wine makes a fine match.

2 tablespoons unsalted butter
1½ ounces each: 4½ tablespoons each of diced carrot and celery, 5 tablespoons diced fennel, and 6 tablespoons diced onion (1½ ounces each)
6 tablespoons diced red bell pepper (2 ounces)
1 large clove garlic, sliced
1 bay leaf
½ ripe tomato (3 ounces), diced
12 ounces Gulf or Ridgeback shrimp
½ cup water
4 cups fish broth (see page 428)
1 cup soft white bread crumbs
⅛ teaspoon salt
⅛ teaspoon ground cayenne

In a 3-quart saucepan brown 1 tablespoon of the butter over medium heat. Add the carrot, celery, onion, fennel, red pepper, garlic, and bay leaf and cook, stirring occasionally, for 10 minutes, until lightly browned. Add the tomato and reduce the heat to very low.

In a sauté pan brown the remaining 1 tablespoon butter. Add the shrimp and sauté them over high heat, turning often, for 4 to 5 minutes, or until the shells are browned all over and encrusted with bits of butter. Transfer the shrimp to the bowl of a food processor. Deglaze the sauté pan with the water and add it to the vegetables. Process the shrimp to a coarse paste and add the paste to the vegetables. Add the fish broth, bring to a simmer, and cook for 10 minutes.

Pass the mixture through the medium blade of a food mill into another pan, sieving through as much of the shrimp and vegetables as possible. Take as much time as you need with this step—it is critical to the final texture and flavor of the soup. Clean off the underside of the food mill with a rubber spatula and add the extra to the sieved broth. Return the broth to the stove. Over very low heat, stir in the bread crumbs and let them sit in the warm soup for 10 minutes. Wash out the food mill and fit it again with the medium blade. Pass the bisque again through the food mill. Season the bisque with the salt and cayenne. Correct with more salt if necessary, warm the bisque gently, and serve.

Squid with Cherry Tomatoes, Olive Oil, Parsley, and Garlic Toast

For 4

This is a quick and very simple sauté. Served with a glass of Beaujolais, followed by cheese and a salad of mixed lettuces, it makes a very satisfying light lunch.

Squid is best either cooked briefly or braised for a long time. Otherwise its texture can be tough and chewy. Early summer, thin-fleshed squid are preferable for this recipe as they are more tender than thicker-bodied squid. If only larger squid are available, cut them into ringlets about ⅛ inch thick. Also, squid readily absorbs water, which reduces its flavor; after cleaning, therefore, it should only be rinsed—never soaked—and immediately patted dry.

1 pound squid
3 tablespoons extra virgin olive oil
2 cloves garlic, minced
Salt and pepper
8 ounces small cherry tomatoes, red and yellow, if possible
3 tablespoons chopped fresh Italian parsley

Separate the head and tentacles from the body of the squid. Cut the head free from the tentacles and discard the head. Clean and rinse the squid, then cut the tentacles in half and the body into ringlets. In a saucepan, gently warm the olive oil and add the garlic. When the garlic begins to sizzle softly, add the squid, lightly salt and pepper them, and stir well. Raise the heat a little and cook the squid until it turns from opaque to white. When it has turned white, add the tomatoes and cook gently, warming the ingredients in the olive oil. Taste one of the tomatoes. When it is warmed through, turn off the heat. Stir in the parsley. Serve in wide bowls with a few spoonfuls of the juice over the top. Accompany with toasted sourdough bread that has been drizzled with olive oil and rubbed with raw cut garlic.

Garlic-Baked Squid

For 2

This recipe is best made with tender, thin-fleshed squid. Thicker-skinned varieties will not take much longer to cook; however, their texture is just not as pleasing.

8 whole fresh squid, each approximately 5 inches long
4 cloves garlic, thinly sliced
1 tablespoon extra virgin olive oil
1 tablespoon dry red wine
Salt and pepper
1 tablespoon chopped fresh parsley
½ recipe Garlic Mayonnaise (see page 115)

Preheat the oven to 500°F.

Separate the head and tentacle section of the squid from its body. Cut the head free from the tentacles and discard it. Clean and rinse the squid. Put the squid, including tentacles, in a bowl. Toss it with the garlic, olive oil, and red wine. Arrange the squid on a baking pan and pour any wine, garlic, and olive oil left in the bowl over it. Salt and pepper both sides lightly.

Bake the squid for 5 minutes. When done, transfer the squid to a warm plate. Collect the juice in the pan and add the chopped parsley to it. Arrange the squid on two plates, pour half the juice over each, and serve with the garlic mayonnaise and warm bread.

Squid Stuffed with Shrimp

For 8

Choose squid with flesh that is less than ⅛ inch thick. Larger squid are unsuitable for this recipe as they can be tough and would take longer to cook than the shrimp stuffing. Stuffed squid are delicious with garlic mayonnaise and/or ripe tomatoes vinaigrette, which complement the richness of the shrimp and make the dish more lively, colorful, and fresh-tasting.

8 squid (1 pound), approximately 4 inches long
1½ tablespoons unsalted butter, melted
1 cup coarse sourdough bread crumbs
10 ounces small sweet shrimp (Ridgeback or Louisiana)
1 tablespoon chopped fresh Italian parsley
1 small clove garlic
Juice of ⅛ lemon (1 teaspoon)
1 tablespoon extra virgin olive oil
Salt and pepper

Preheat the oven to 450°F.

Separate the head and tentacles from the squid body. Cut the head free from the tentacles. Discard the head. Clean and rinse the bodies. Melt the butter in a sauté pan. Add the bread crumbs and fry them until crisp and golden brown. Peel the shrimp and chop them coarse. Transfer the shrimp to a bowl. Add the parsley, garlic, lemon juice, and olive oil, and salt and pepper the mixture lightly. Add the bread crumbs and stir well.

Pack the squid bodies with the shrimp mixture—not too tightly—to within 1 inch of the opening. Make a stitch with a toothpick to close the squid. Arrange the stuffed squid and the tentacles on a baking sheet. Brush the bodies and tentacles with olive oil and salt and pepper them lightly. Bake for 15 minutes. When they are done, transfer them to plates and drizzle any juices from the pan over each portion.

Squid, Romano Bean, and Tomato Salad with Garlic Mayonnaise

For 8 as a first course

¾ pound Romano beans, cut diagonally in 1-inch pieces
1½ pounds fresh small squid (ideally no longer than 5 inches)
4 tablespoons extra virgin olive oil
2 cloves garlic, minced
Salt and pepper
5 ripe tomatoes, red and yellow, if possible
2 shallots (2 ounces), finely minced
1 tablespoon red wine vinegar
2 tablespoons chopped fresh basil
Garlic Mayonnaise (see page 115)

In 2 quarts rapidly boiling water seasoned with 2 teaspoons salt, cook the Romano beans until tender but slightly firm. If the beans are very fresh, they will take approximately 2 minutes. Transfer to a colander immediately and cool the beans under running water. Do not soak them as they will absorb water and lose flavor.

Separate the head and tentacles from the squid body. Cut the head away from the tentacles and discard the head. Keep the tentacles separate. Cut the bodies crosswise into ⅛-inch-thick ringlets.

Put a pot of water on to boil for blanching the tomatoes. In the meantime, in a large (10-inch) sauté pan or cast-iron pan, place 2 tablespoons of the olive oil and heat it until sizzling hot. Add the squid tentacles to the pan first and sauté for 1 minute, turning them to expose all sides to the heat. Add the ringlets and the garlic and salt and pepper the mixture. Continue to cook the squid over the highest heat for 2 minutes. The squid will change from grayish to white, will release a pink liquid, and be slightly firm but yielding when bitten into. Pour the squid into a colander with a bowl beneath it to capture the juice. Transfer the drained squid to a bowl.

Blanch the tomatoes in boiling water for 15 seconds. Remove the core. Peel, seed, and dice them into 1-inch pieces. Strain the tomato juice through a sieve and add it to the squid juice. Mix the shallots and vinegar with the remaining 2 tablespoons olive oil and stir in the basil leaves. To this vinaigrette add the squid juice and strained tomato juice. Correct for salt and pepper.

Combine the beans and tomatoes in a bowl and season them with ¼ teaspoon salt and ⅛ teaspoon freshly ground pepper. Add half the vinaigrette to the tomatoes-beans combination and half to the cooked squid. Mix each well. On a large cold platter spread the tomatoes and beans. Distribute the squid over the top and pour any vinaigrette juices from the bowls over all.

Serve the garlic mayonnaise in a separate bowl and accompany the squid with plenty of warm sourdough bread.

Grilled Tuna, Green Onions, and Radicchio with Cannellini Beans

For 4

The combination of tuna and beans is a typical Italian antipasto. The most notable variations include one served in vinaigrette with chopped tomatoes and fresh basil; and one made as a salad bound with mayonnaise (chick peas are often substituted for the more familiar white beans). Perhaps the most basic version is made in Tuscany with chopped red onion, ground pepper, and new green olive oil. It is not only the flavors of tuna and beans that so agree, but their soft textures—the creaminess of the beans and the tenderness of the tuna—make the two very appealing.

In Italy, tuna that has been preserved in oil is generally used. Fresh albacore, big eye, or bluefin tuna is a definite refinement; the delicate flavor and meatlike texture is lost in the preserved versions. Since it cooks very rapidly, it is wise to buy tuna that has been cut into thick slices (1 inch). Overdone tuna loses its moisture and becomes awfully dry. Thick slices can be grilled with more control, and should remain pink in the center.

Beans and tuna come alive when sharply accented with a tart dressing, salty bits of chopped anchovies, or a pungent garlic mayonnaise. In this recipe, chopped anchovies are stirred into a lemon and olive oil dressing, which is used to season the grilled fish and the accompanying salad of grilled radicchio and green onions. Garlic mayonnaise is passed around the table.

This dish makes a fine lunch. Don't worry about delivering everything to the table hot. It is good served slightly warm or at room temperature with plenty of bread and cold rosé or a simple white wine.

1 cup dry cannellini beans
5 cloves garlic, peeled
One 3-inch sprig fresh rosemary
3½ cups water
Salt and pepper
4 tuna steaks (1 pound, 8 ounces) cut about 1 inch thick
16 green onions, trimmed to 6 inches, roots cut off (4 ounces)
2 firm heads radicchio (7 ounces)
½ recipe Garlic Mayonnaise (see page 115)

Wash the beans in a colander and pick through and discard those that are discolored or broken. Check also for small pebbles, which sometimes find their way into the beans. Soak the beans in cold water to cover in the refrigerator for 12 hours or overnight. Beans that have been presoaked cook more quickly and evenly and tend not to burst.

Drain the beans and put them in a 2-quart noncorroding pot, add the garlic cloves, rosemary, water, and ¾ teaspoon salt. Bring the beans to a simmer, cover, and cook them gently for 1 hour (unsoaked beans will take about 1½ hours), or until they are tender. Turn the heat off and allow the beans to stand in the cooking liquid.

Prepare a charcoal fire. While it is burning down, prepare the tuna, green onions, and radicchio for grilling. Cut the radicchio heads in half, leaving the root end attached, and lay them out on a large tray with the onions and tuna. Brush the vegetables and tuna with vegetable oil and lightly salt and pepper them on both sides. Have ready the garlic mayonnaise.

4 salt-packed anchovies (8 filets)
2 shallots (2 ounces), finely diced
2 tablespoons lemon juice (Meyer lemon, if possible)
Salt and pepper
3 tablespoons extra virgin olive oil

Make the lemon-anchovy dressing: Debone the anchovies and soak them in a bowl of cold water for 15 minutes. Squeeze them out and chop them coarse. Combine the anchovies and shallots with the lemon juice. Grind a little pepper over the top and stir in the olive oil. Taste the dressing and correct it to your taste with more lemon juice, olive oil, or a pinch of salt.

Grill the vegetables and tuna over a medium-hot fire: the onions will take about 6 minutes and should be turned every 2 minutes, until they soften and become lightly charred. Place the radicchio on the grill cut side down and turn them every 2 to 3 minutes so that the leaves do not burn. Remove them from the grill after about 8 minutes, when their red color has faded to brown, the leaves appear wilted, and the heads are tender in the center.

Grill the tuna for about 2½ to 3 minutes per side on the hottest part of the grill. After 1 minute, rotate the tuna 90 degrees with a spatula so that the fish cooks evenly and picks up the attractive pattern of the grill. Repeat after turning the fish to the second side. Take care not to overcook the fish. It should be slightly pink in the center and moist throughout.

Assembling: Cut out the root end of the radicchio to free the leaves. Pull the leaves apart and combine them with the green onions in a bowl. Toss with about 2 tablespoons of the lemon-anchovy dressing. Transfer the grilled tuna to a platter or individual plates and spoon the remaining dressing over each piece. Serve with a spoonful of the beans warm from the pot (you may wish to drizzle them with olive oil), garlic mayonnaise, the grilled onions, and radicchio, and a simple, crisp white wine.

Grilled Tuna and Red Onion Salad

For 4

One of the most lively and immediately recognizable themes of Italian life is food. Wonderful food is displayed everywhere in Italy, in the marketplace, on street corners, behind the enormous plate-glass windows of bakeries, butcher shops, and delicatessens. Upon entering many Italian restaurants or *trattorie*, you first encounter a wide table laden with food; the experience of eating there begins with this enticement rather than the first bite. There is a quality of openness, informality, and generosity about displaying food in this manner and it is this spirit we have tried to capture in the restaurant, particularly on special occasions. I think of this salad as one of the components of a large table of varied and colorful appetizers.

Preparing a table of appetizers as part of a dinner, outdoor lunch, or picnic presents the challenge of bringing foods together that complement one another. On a table with grilled tuna and red onions, for example, could be roasted, marinated peppers; grilled eggplants or a ratatouille; a large platter of shell beans dressed with olive oil, garlic, rosemary, hard-cooked eggs, and garlic mayonnaise; salt-packed anchovies; bowls of spicy arugula and radicchio from the garden; chilled rice salad with capers; a variety of olives; sliced tomatoes with basil; colorful jars of pickled vegetables; and plenty of cold white wine.

The possibilities are endless. Let the season and your imagination be the guides. This salad is delicious by itself or in combination with any of the dishes mentioned above.

1 large red onion (10 ounces)
1½ quarts water
2 tablespoons balsamic vinegar
4 tablespoons extra virgin olive oil
2 teaspoons salt
¼ teaspoon freshly ground black pepper
12 ounces fresh tuna, cut into 1-inch-thick slices
Juice of 1 small lemon
2 tablespoons chopped fresh Italian parsley

Prepare a small charcoal fire. While it is burning, prepare the onion. Peel it and cut it in half lengthwise (from root to stem). Cut each half into eight segments. Separate the layers of each segment. Bring the water to a boil with 1½ teaspoons salt, add the onions, and parboil them for 2 minutes. Drain in a colander. Transfer the onions to a bowl. While still hot, dress them with the vinegar, 2 tablespoons of the olive oil, ¼ teaspoon of salt, and the pepper.

Lightly oil and salt and pepper the tuna on both sides and grill it to medium-rare, about 2 minutes on each side. Let it cool and break it up into chunks by hand. Season the tuna with ¼ teaspoon salt, the lemon juice, and the remaining 2 tablespoons olive oil. Combine the tuna and onion, sprinkle them with the parsley, and let them marinate together for 1 hour.

Serve at room temperature.

Vegetables

Grilled Asparagus with Olive Oil and Parmesan

Artichokes

Baked Stuffed Artichokes

Soup of Cannellini Beans with Pasta and Rosemary

Minestrone of Shell Beans, String Beans, Tomatoes, and Pesto

Salad of String Beans, Shell Beans, and Tomatoes

Fava Beans with Olive Oil, Garlic, and Rosemary

Romano Beans Sautéed with Oregano

Beets with Vinegar and Tarragon

Long-Cooked Broccoli

Brussels Sprouts Leaves Cooked with Bacon and Mirepoix

Cabbage Braised with Riesling and Bacon

Wilted Flat Black Cabbage

Double Soups

Carrot and Red Pepper Soup

White Corn Cakes with Caviar

Corn Puddings with Blue Crab Sauce

Corn Soup with Garlic Butter

Baked Eggplants and Tomatoes with Bread Crumbs and Basil

Eggplant Croutons

Grilled Eggplants with Shallots and Parsley

Grilled Eggplant Tart

Gratin of Belgian Endive

Fennel, Mushroom, Parmesan Cheese, and White Truffle Salad

Gratin of Florence Fennel and New Potatoes

Green Garlic

Green Garlic and Cheese Soufflés

Green Garlic Soup

Garlic Butter

Garlic Mayonnaise

Leeks Vinaigrette with Anchovies and Eggs

Wild Mushrooms

Cèpes Baked in Parchment

Chanterelle Custard

Morels Baked with Bread Crumbs, Garlic, and Parsley

Bread and Onion Soup with Red Wine

Sugar Snap Peas with Brown Butter and Sage

Pimiento Soup with Fried Polenta

Potato and Black Truffle Croquettes

Purée of New Potatoes and Green Garlic

Potatoes and Onions Roasted with Vinegar and Thyme

Potatoes Cooked in the Coals

Straw Potato Cake

Spinach Soup

Grilled Tomato Croutons with Red Onion Vinaigrette, Anchovies, and Fresh Basil

Tomato, Green Garlic, and Herb Soup

Ratatouille

Grilled Late-Season Tomato Soup with Bacon, Garlic, and Croutons

Chilled Red and Yellow Tomato Soups with Peppers, Cucumbers, Onions, and Basil

Black Truffle Puddings

Black Truffle Soup

Garden Salad

Apples Baked with Orange and Riesling

Citrus Fruit Salad

Fall Fruit Salad with Warm Goat Cheese and Herb Toast

Spiced Quince

Grilled Asparagus with Olive Oil and Parmesan

For 2

Cooking asparagus on the charcoal grill is unusual but a good alternative to boiling it in water. Grilling imparts a soft smokiness and chars the surface slightly. The flavor is more vivid.

8 fat asparagus spears
1 tablespoon pure olive oil
Salt and pepper
2 tablespoons extra virgin olive oil
½ lemon
6 thin slices pancetta
1 large egg, hard-cooked and chopped
Fresh Parmesan cheese

Prepare a charcoal fire.

Toss the asparagus in the pure olive oil and salt and pepper them lightly. Grill the asparagus over a medium-hot fire for about 5 minutes, turning the spears until the skin is shriveled and slightly charred all over. Test the asparagus for doneness at its thickest point with the tip of a knife. The asparagus should feel soft in the center. Transfer the asparagus to warm plates. Drizzle extra virgin olive oil and squeeze lemon juice over the asparagus.

Grill the pancetta for several minutes until it renders some of its fat and just begins to crisp. Chop the pancetta coarse and strew it over the asparagus while still warm; sprinkle with the chopped egg. Using a cheese slicer—the hand-held kind that you pull toward you—cut thin shards of Parmesan and place them over the top. Serve right away.

Artichokes

Artichokes can be cooked in various ways depending on the season, their size, and at what stage they are picked. In the market artichokes are graded according to size, and their appearance varies by season. The largest winter artichokes, named "green globe," have a compact, full form and rounded leaves. Summer artichokes are more conical, open, and have pointed leaves. The smallest artichokes, which appear to be immature, are in fact fully grown buds. The thickness of the stem determines the size of the bud and these small artichokes are taken from the thinner stems of the plant.

The normal flowering of the plant occurs from fall to early spring. However, it is possible to induce the artichoke to produce at other times by pruning out stems that have borne harvestable buds. The plants then put out new stems that bloom again, hence the summer crop. The summer artichokes are usable but are never as tender as those picked in the spring. The smallest spring artichokes have virtually no fuzz inside and are delicious sautéed whole in olive oil, skewered and grilled, or even sliced very thin and eaten raw, with olive oil and salt, pepper, and shavings of Parmesan cheese. The largest buds have a meaty base section that encases the chokes. This is referred to as the bottom and is delicious stuffed, and in salads with shellfish. Together with celeriac it makes a very fine soup.

Don't discard the mountain of leaves removed from large artichokes. These leaves can be boiled until tender, then scraped at the end that attaches to the choke. This coarse purée can be mixed with shallots, lemon, and olive oil and spread on toast, or can be used as the base of a risotto. The medium-size artichokes are best stuffed, either hollowed out whole, or sliced in half lengthwise. If the leaves are very tender, you can also deep-fry artichokes whole.

Whatever size is available, look for artichokes that have tightly closed leaves. Those that have opened-out leaves have remained on the plant too long and will be tough.

Baked Stuffed Artichokes

This recipe very clearly represents the abiding kinship that exists between the cooking at Chez Panisse and the cuisines of Northern Italy and the South of France. Ingredients typical of those regions and common to our own are brought together in this dish. Artichokes, pared down to their bottoms and scooped free of the chokes, are stuffed with a mixture of toasted bread crumbs, chopped anchovies, garlic, and parsley, and are then set on a bed of onions and peppers, stewed in olive oil, and put in the oven to bake slowly. When tender, the artichokes, onions, and peppers are allowed to cool a bit and are served with garlic mayonnaise, briny Niçoise olives, anchovy filets, and chopped parsley.

The artichokes you choose should be medium size, weighing about eight ounces each. The large chokes with thicker leaves tend to be too tough and fibrous unless they are pared down considerably, in which case they are not that much bigger than the medium-size ones.

Baked stuffed artichokes make a colorful first course and can be prepared ahead of time. The lively flavors of this dish are most evident if the artichokes are served slightly warm or at room temperature, but not cold. Wine with artichokes is problematic. The strong astringency present in mature, raw artichokes fades almost entirely when cooked, but nevertheless affects the taste of wine consumed afterward. Choose a simple, thirst-quenching low-alcohol white or rosé wine. A finer or more complex bottle would certainly be wasted on an artichoke.

This recipe takes some time to prepare, but the finished result, a perfect union of down-to-earth flavors, will fully satisfy those who love to eat.

8 medium artichokes, about 4 pounds
3 cups fresh sourdough bread crumbs
½ cup plus 3 tablespoons virgin olive oil
8 cloves garlic, 2 reserved whole and 6 sliced
14 salt-packed anchovy filets, soaked for 15 minutes in several changes of cold water,
    drained, patted dry
4 tablespoons chopped fresh Italian parsley
3 large onions (2 pounds), thinly sliced
4 mixed colored bell peppers (1 pound, 4 ounces), seeded, cut into thin strips
Small bunch of thyme
3 bay leaves
¾ teaspoon salt

¼ teaspoon ground pepper
3 tablespoons red wine vinegar
½ cup water
1 recipe Garlic Mayonnaise (see page 115)
⅓ cup brined Niçoise olives

Preheat the oven to 350°F.

Choose artichokes that have about an inch of the stem attached. With a serrated knife, cut through the leaves of the artichokes crosswise (perpendicular to the stem) removing about half of the bodies of the plants just above the chokes. Using a small sharp knife, trim the stems down to their tender cores (visible if you look at the cut portion of the stems) and pare away the tough leaves around the bottoms of the artichokes. Scoop and scrape out the hairy chokes and set the hearts in a bowl of water.

Toss the bread crumbs in 3 tablespoons of the olive oil and toast them for 15 minutes, or until golden brown and crisp. Pound the 2 reserved garlic cloves and 6 of the anchovies to a paste in a mortar and combine them with the bread crumbs and 2 tablespoons of the parsley.

Warm the ½ cup olive oil in a large sauté pan. Add the onions and peppers, thyme, bay leaves, sliced garlic, salt, pepper, and vinegar. Stew the mixture for about 15 minutes, stirring often, until the vegetables have softened. Turn the onions and peppers out into a large crockery or enameled baking pan. Pack the bread crumb mixture into the artichoke bottoms and invert them stem up onto the bed of vegetables. Salt and pepper the inverted artichokes and pour the water around them. Cover with baking parchment, then tightly with foil— artichokes blacken when in direct contact with aluminum foil. Bake in the oven for 1 hour and 15 minutes, or until the artichokes yield easily to the tip of a knife. While the artichokes are cooking, make the garlic mayonnaise.

Allow the artichokes to cool until just warm. Serve the artichokes directly from the baking pan or on individual plates, each with some of the onions and peppers. Sprinkle with the remaining 2 tablespoons parsley and drape with the remaining anchovies, cut lengthwise into thin strips. If the artichokes appear dry on the outside, drizzle them with a little olive oil. Strew the olives around the plates and pass the garlic mayonnaise separately.

Soup of Cannellini Beans with Pasta and Rosemary

For 10

This is a substantial bean soup. Presoaked beans are cooked in broth with diced vegetables, garlic cloves, and rosemary until tender. A portion of the beans and broth is then puréed to thicken the soup. Tomatoes, shell pasta, and chard are added and the whole is brought together with Parmesan and extra virgin olive oil (preferably a fresh, green Tuscan oil) at the table. Pork goes well with beans; a piece of prosciutto, bone and rind included, adds enormously to the flavor of the soup. If prosciutto bones or trimmings are not available to you, substitute a fresh rind of pork boiled until tender and chopped, or pancetta cut into wide dice, or fresh Italian sausage.

It is important that the beans cook in the pot with some salt; otherwise they taste bland. Correcting with salt after the beans have cooked is impossible unless the pot is allowed to stand overnight; salting affects the cooking broth but does not penetrate the beans and the seasoning tastes curiously out of balance. If you use a prosciutto bone, do not add salt to the pot until the soup has simmered for 30 minutes or so. Prosciutto is a salt-cured ham and will release salt into the pot as it cooks. More salt may not be necessary.

Numerous variations of this soup are possible using other types of greens such as kale, mustard greens, or cabbage and by adding small diced vegetables like squash, peppers, and artichoke hearts. Pesto is a delicious last addition in summer when basil is in season. Substitute any good dry pasta you have on hand. Choose shapes and sizes that are easy to pick up with a spoon.

The soup will cook in much less time if you soak the beans in cold water and store them in the refrigerator for about twelve hours or overnight. At higher temperatures they may ferment.

2 tablespoons pure olive oil
½ medium yellow onion (4 ounces), finely diced
1 medium carrot (3 ounces), finely diced
½ stalk of celery (2 ounces), finely diced
5 cloves garlic, sliced
Two 3-inch sprigs rosemary
12 ounces dried cannellini beans, covered with cold water and soaked for 12 hours
2 cups chard leaves (6 ounces), ribs cut out, sliced
1 piece of prosciutto bone and rind (about 6 ounces), split
8 cups chicken broth (see page 426)
1 cup peeled seeded tomatoes

1¼ cups small shell pasta (conchigliette)*, boiled in lightly salted water for 7 to 8*
  minutes, rinsed
Salt and pepper
Freshly grated Parmesan cheese
Extra virgin olive oil

Warm the olive oil in a large saucepot, add the onion, carrot, celery, garlic, and
rosemary and soften over low heat, without browning, for 8 to 10 minutes.
Drain the beans, add them and the chard and prosciutto bone, pour in the
broth, bring to a simmer, and cover the pot. Taste the liquid after 30 minutes. It
should be slightly salty from the prosciutto. If not, add a little salt to the pot.
Cook slowly for about 1 hour and 10 minutes more, or until the beans have
softened throughout.

When the beans are cooked, transfer 2 cups of the broth and beans to a blender
and purée them thoroughly. Return the purée to the pot. Stir in the tomatoes
and pasta; correct the soup to your taste with salt and pepper. Remove the
rosemary sprigs, heat the soup thoroughly, and dish it up into warm bowls.
Sprinkle the Parmesan and about a teaspoon of extra virgin oil over each portion
at the table.

Minestrone of Shell Beans, String Beans, Tomatoes, and Pesto

For 8

In Italy minestrone, despite its numerous regional guises, is essentially vegetable soup, which is often extended with a starch—small macaroni, rice, or beans.
More than a conglomeration of its many elements, a good minestrone unifies
diverse flavors through slow simmering into a single statement, without sacri-
ficing textural integrity. The following minestrone celebrates beans and fresh
shell beans. The shell beans are cooked first with other aromatic vegetables and
a piece of prosciutto bone, a common indispensability, to form a flavorful base.
Later, tomatoes, string beans, and spinach are added, and the soup is left on the
flame to harmonize for twenty minutes longer. Pesto is served as a condiment to
the soup, which, by the way, may be served hot or cold.

1 small yellow onion (5 ounces), diced
2 small leeks (2 ounces), sliced into thin rounds
½ large stalk of celery (2 ounces), diced
1 large carrot (4 ounces), diced
1½ cups red cabbage (4 ounces), sliced
1½ cups Napa cabbage (4 ounces), sliced
2½ cups fresh mixed shell beans (cranberry, flageolet, fava, black-eyed peas, lima), shelled
1 piece of prosciutto bone with rind (4 ounces)
1 cup water
6 tomatoes (1 pound, 4 ounces)
6 cups chicken broth (see page 426)
2 ounces yellow wax beans, ends trimmed, cut into 1-inch pieces
2 ounces fresh Romano beans, ends trimmed, cut into 1-inch pieces
2 ounces green beans, ends trimmed, cut into 1-inch pieces
Handful of fresh spinach leaves, de-stemmed
Pesto (see page 419), approximately ½ cup

Put on a pot of water to blanch the tomatoes. Put the onion, leeks, celery, carrot, cabbages, shell beans, and prosciutto bone into a 6-quart stainless-steel soup pot. Add the water, bring to the boil, reduce to a simmer, and cover the pot. Sweat the vegetables over low heat for 30 minutes.

In the meantime, parboil the tomatoes for 15 seconds. Remove them and discard the water. Peel, seed, and dice the tomatoes and strain and reserve their juice. When the vegetables have cooked for 30 minutes, add the tomato juice with the chicken broth and simmer the soup for 25 minutes. Add the tomatoes, wax, Romano, and green beans, and spinach. Cover the pot and simmer for 20 minutes more. Remove the prosciutto bone and discard it. Season the soup with salt and pepper and serve. Garnish each bowl with a spoonful of the pesto.

Salad of String Beans, Shell Beans, and Tomatoes

For 6 as an appetizer

Our efforts to find and support small farmers in California have been rewarding for the much greater variety of produce now available. Fresh shell beans of many colors, sizes, and flavors are an example of this and the inspiration for this salad. Cranberry beans, with their pink speckled pods, have appeared in midsummer produce markets for as long as I can remember; however, the recent arrival of fresh flageolets, the French shell bean used in dried form in cassoulet and preferred for its resistance to disintegration under prolonged cooking, opened up new possibilities in the kitchen. This year, farmers have supplied us with fresh French horticultural beans, favas, black-eyed peas, purple-hulled crowders, limas, borlotti, and brown Portuguese beans. Usually three to five varieties are available at one time and of course the more that can be found to make this salad the more interesting it will be.

There is a vast difference between fresh and dried beans. Fresh beans are distinctly sweeter and are not at all starchy. Choose shell beans with pods that are tight and vividly colored: This is the best way of telling that they have been recently picked. The beans inside should reflect the color condition of the pod. Although it is much easier to remove the beans from dried pods, they will be much less sweet in this state.

Serve this salad as an appetizer with slices of prosciutto and/or dry-cured Italian sausages.

For the vinaigrette:
1 small red onion (4 ounces), finely diced
3 tablespoons red wine vinegar
¼ teaspoon salt
⅛ teaspoon freshly ground black pepper
1 small clove garlic
4 salt-packed anchovy filets, soaked and squeezed dry
⅓ cup extra virgin olive oil

Prepare the vinaigrette: Mix the onion with the vinegar in a bowl. Add the salt and dissolve it in the vinegar. Add the pepper. Pound the garlic and anchovies to a paste in a mortar and add them to the bowl. Stir in the olive oil.

3 cups fresh shell beans (1 cup flageolets, 1 cup black-eyed peas or purple-hulled crow-
  ders, 1 cup cranberry beans, or any combination available)
4 ounces mixed string beans (yellow wax, haricots verts, Romanos)
2 small red tomatoes (6 ounces), peeled, diced
1 large yellow tomato (8 ounces), peeled, diced
3 tablespoons chopped fresh Italian parsley
8 salt-packed anchovy filets, soaked, squeezed dry, cut in half lengthwise, tossed in 2
  teaspoons olive oil

Cook each type of shell bean in a separate small pot in 1 quart water with 1 teaspoon salt. Depending upon the variety, each will take from 20 to 25 minutes. Sample the beans. When they are tender, take them off the heat. Combine all the shell beans in one container and remove all but enough of their cooking liquid to just cover them. Let the shell beans cool in the cooking liquid in the refrigerator.

Parboil each type of string bean in a separate pot in 1 quart water with 1 teaspoon salt. Remove from the water with a sieve or slotted spoon when they have softened but are still slightly crunchy. Spread the string beans out on a plate to cool. Cooked string beans absorb water quickly when cooked. Do not soak them in cold water to cool them. Combine the string beans in one container and put in the refrigerator.

Assembling the salad: When the dried and fresh beans are cool, drain off the water in the bowls and combine all of the beans. Season the tomatoes with 2 tablespoons of the vinaigrette and 1 tablespoon of the parsley. Taste the tomatoes and correct them to your taste with salt, pepper, and vinegar. (I like to be able to taste the vinegar. While the beans are not quite bland or starchy, they can stand up to a sharp vinaigrette.) Pour the rest of the vinaigrette over the beans and shell beans, add the rest of the parsley, and mix well.

On a large plate, place the beans down first and arrange the tomatoes over the top. Add all vinaigrette and juices to the plate and garnish the top with the anchovy strips.

Fava Beans with Olive Oil, Garlic, and Rosemary

For 4

Fava beans, also called broad beans, are a fast and easy crop to grow if you have your own garden. They also can be found in some produce markets in the spring (Italian green grocers or markets offer a wide range of vegetables), although they are not as common as some of the other shell beans. Mature fava beans—one stage at which they may be eaten—have long, glossy green pods, six to eight inches long. In addition to having to strip them from the pod, you must also remove the tender beans from the pale green, bitter skin enclosing them. To do so, strip the beans from the pod. Plunge them into boiling water for 1 minute, drain, and let cool. Pierce the smooth top of the shell with your thumbnail and squeeze out the bean inside.

The distinctive flavor and somewhat creamy texture of favas is delicious with roast lamb or chicken. The simplest way to prepare them is to briefly stew them in olive oil with rosemary leaves and chopped garlic; their subtle flavor harmonizes perfectly with these ingredients. Otherwise, butter can be substituted for the olive oil and the favas can be stewed with diced pancetta or parboiled smoked bacon, thyme sprigs, a little lemon juice, and be enriched toward the end of the cooking with cream.

Dried fava beans, available in Middle Eastern and Indian markets, have a yellow to pale orange color and make an ideal purée. They need only be simmered in salted water with garlic cloves, an herb such as thyme, rosemary, or savory, and bacon rind. Purée them in a food mill and enrich with butter or perfume with extra virgin olive oil.

5 pounds fava beans
3 tablespoons extra virgin olive oil
A loose tablespoon of fresh rosemary leaves
¼ cup water
3 large cloves garlic (about 1 tablespoon), coarsely chopped
½ teaspoon salt
Freshly ground pepper

Remove the beans from the pods, parboil for 1 minute, and drain in a colander. Run cold water over the beans to cool them. Using your fingernail, break the outer skin of the beans and squeeze the beans out between your forefinger and thumb.

Warm the olive oil with the rosemary in a 9-inch sauté pan. Add the beans, water, garlic, salt, and a little ground pepper. Bring the mixture to a low simmer, cover the pot, and allow to stew for about 5 minutes, or until the water has evaporated and the beans are slightly softened. Continue to cook the beans for about 20 minutes more so that the flavors combine and penetrate. Stir the beans often to prevent them from sticking. Grind a little more pepper over the beans just before serving.

Romano Beans Sautéed with Oregano

For 4

The usual methods of cooking beans is (1) to plunge them into boiling water until they just surrender their resonant crunch, or (2) to steam them to a similar degree for a truer flavor. Well . . . , there may still be a better way to preserve their squeaky crispiness. Namely, to sauté them raw in olive oil laced with herbs. Try this with any fresh beans, string or wax. Romano beans, the flat, stout Italian variety, both yellow and green, are my favorite.

3 tablespoons pure olive oil
1 pound Romano beans, stems and tips removed
Scant 1/4 cup very loosely packed fresh oregano leaves
Salt and pepper
2 cloves garlic, chopped

Heat the olive oil in a 10-inch sauté pan. Add the beans and oregano, salt and pepper them lightly, and cook them over medium heat, stirring often, for about 10 minutes, until they lose their hard crunch. For the last 2 minutes of cooking time, mix in the garlic. Serve immediately.

Beets with Vinegar and Tarragon

For 6

Beets have a sweet, rooty flavor. Their striking colors, both golden and deep burgundy, are a delight. I prefer them as a garnish or accompaniment to salads of pigeon or lobster or as one of the components of a varied plate of fall vegetables that might include julienned celeriac, sliced fennel, tender boiled leeks, and soft-cooked eggs. Cooked in the following manner they can also be puréed, and a small spoonful can be swirled into carrot, spinach, or fennel soups.

The beets are baked in their skins in the oven and retain their full flavors and strong staining pigments. It is wise to peel them over the sink and to slice them directly on a ceramic plate rather than on a bare wood chopping block—the stains are tenacious. The time required to cook the beets depends on their size. Small beets, 1 to 1½ inches in diameter, require about 1 hour. Larger beets will need 15 to 20 minutes more in the oven.

8 beets (1 pound, 10 ounces), topped
1 cup water
Salt and pepper
1 tablespoon white wine vinegar
1 tablespoon olive oil
1 tablespoon chopped fresh tarragon leaves

Preheat the oven to 375°F.

Place the beets in a 10- by 8-inch baking dish, add the water, and cover the dish tightly with aluminum foil. Bake the beets for 1 hour to 1 hour and 15 minutes, until they are tender throughout (poke the beets with a knife or toothpick to test them). Remove the foil, allow the beets to cool, and peel them over the sink. Their skins will rub off very easily. Slice the beets thin and season them with salt and freshly ground pepper. Toss the beets with the vinegar, olive oil, and tarragon and chill until ready to serve.

Long-Cooked Broccoli

For 4

Broccoli (and artichokes), because of its toughness and fiber content, is well suited to lengthy cooking which enhances its cabbagelike flavor. Choose broccoli that is mature, with large florets and a thick stem. Young broccoli does not have the flavor or enough developed vegetable fiber to hold up under long cooking.

This dish is quite strong in taste and should be thought of more as a condiment than as a vegetable accompaniment. It is delicious as an appetizer, served on grilled bread with strips of anchovies and pitted Niçoise olives. Or use it as a topping for pizza that has been sprinkled with grated Parmesan or Caciocavallo cheese. It is very good, too, with grilled steak or sautéed squid.

½ cup extra virgin olive oil
1 pound, 8 ounces broccoli, stem included, cut into small pieces
10 cloves garlic (scant ¼ cup), sliced
Juice of 1½ lemons (3¾ tablespoons)
1 teaspoon salt
¼ teaspoon freshly ground black pepper
¼ teaspoon dry cayenne flakes
2⅔ cups water

Warm the olive oil in a 10-inch stainless-steel casserole or saucepot. Add the broccoli, garlic, lemon juice, salt, pepper, and cayenne. Stir the mixture to combine. Add the water and bring to a boil. Immediately reduce the heat to a low simmer, cover tightly, and cook for 1 hour. Check the broccoli every once in a while to make sure that it stays at a gentle simmer. Adjust the heat if necessary.

After 1 hour remove the lid, raise the heat a little, and cook the broccoli another 15 minutes, or until any water in the pan evaporates. During this time stir often, breaking up the broccoli with a spoon to a coarse texture. Let cool slightly before serving.

Brussels Sprouts Leaves Cooked with Bacon and Mirepoix

4 large portions

The leaves of Brussels sprouts are very tightly bound to their core, but they can be pulled away and cooked like shredded cabbage or other greens. Separating and cooking the leaves is a pleasant change from boiling, braising, or steaming the whole buds. Sweating the leaves is also quicker to do and preserves the fresh flavor of this miniature cabbage, allowing for more subtle combinations with other foods. Brussels sprouts leaves are an ideal accompaniment to roast or braised pork and poultry, and to Guinea hen, in particular.

Despite their size, the small leaves of Brussels sprouts are tough and require 15 to 20 minutes cooking in a covered pan to tenderize them. As an alternative to butter or olive oil, duck fat adds considerably to the finished flavors. Finally, if you are going to serve the leaves with a roast, stir in some of the juices from the roasting pan just before serving.

1 pound Brussels sprouts
2 tablespoons olive oil or rendered duck fat
Mirepoix: 1 small carrot (2 ounces), diced
  ½ large stalk of celery (2 ounces), diced
  ½ yellow onion (3 ounces), diced
2 ounces pancetta, thinly sliced, diced
⅓ cup water
½ teaspoon salt
Freshly ground pepper
White wine vinegar

Working with one sprout at a time, remove as many of the outer leaves as you can until you reach those firmly attached to the core. Trim the stem end freeing more leaves and repeat until you reach the dense center. Slice the center thin.

Warm the olive oil or duck fat in a 6-quart noncorroding saucepan. Add the mirepoix and pancetta and cook over medium heat for 5 to 8 minutes, without browning the vegetables, until they have softened. Add the water and the Brussels sprouts leaves, sprinkle with the salt, and stir well to combine. Cover the pan and cook for 15 to 20 minutes, stirring every so often until the leaves are tender. Season the leaves with a little freshly ground pepper, correct for salt, and add a dash of vinegar. Serve while the color is still vivid.

Cabbage Braised with Riesling and Bacon

For 4

Cabbage is a good vegetable to braise. Slow cooking tones down its pungent, peppery qualities and its tough leaves are softened. Cabbage readily takes on the aromas of the elements with which it is cooked—in this case, aromatic vegetables, Riesling, and smoked bacon. Cabbage also carries the flavors of meat juices and the smooth richness of certain animal fats, giving this dish a wintry feel.

If you have rendered duck or goose fat, substitute it for the olive oil in this recipe, or if you serve this cabbage with roast fowl, lamb, or pork (for which it has a great affinity), season the cabbage with some of the juices released from the meats after they have rested.

This dish can be made with either red or Dutch winter white cabbage or Savoy cabbage, the lighter, loose-growing head with crinkled leaves.

1 cabbage (1 pound)
2 tablespoons pure olive oil
1 small carrot (3 ounces), peeled, cut into ¼-inch dice
½ large stalk of celery (2 ounces), cut into ¼-inch dice
1 small yellow onion (5 ounces), peeled, cut into ¼-inch dice
4 ounces smoked bacon, sliced ¼ inch thick, cut crosswise into 1-inch pieces
1 teaspoon fresh thyme leaves
¾ cup slightly sweet Riesling or Gewürztraminer
2 teaspoons salt
Freshly ground pepper
1 tablespoon white wine vinegar or cider vinegar

Slice the cabbage in half, remove the core, and cut the cabbage into rough chunks about 1 inch wide. Warm the olive oil in a 6-quart noncorroding casserole. Add the vegetables, bacon, thyme, and wine and bring to a simmer. Put half the cabbage in the pot and sprinkle 1 teaspoon of the salt and a little freshly ground pepper over the layer. Repeat with the remaining cabbage.

Cover the pot tightly and braise the cabbage slowly over low heat. After 20 minutes, stir the cabbage gently so that the leaves on top move to the bottom and the vegetables and bacon are mixed throughout. Replace the cover and cook another 15 to 20 minutes, or until the cabbage is tender. Taste the cabbage and correct for salt and pepper if necessary. Add the vinegar and toss well.

The cabbage can be made several hours in advance, or while a roast is cooking, and warmed just before serving it.

Wilted Flat Black Cabbage

For 4 as an accompaniment

Tat Tsoi, which our friends at Chino ranch call flat black cabbage, is an unusual Oriental brassica that grows low to the ground and sends out a spray of glossy, dark green leaves, unlike heading cabbage. Although this vegetable is not common in markets, I include this recipe because we use this cabbage frequently in the restaurant. You may wish to buy seeds and grow the plant in your own garden.

There is no need to cook flat black cabbage as long as you would other cooking greens. In fact, its greatest virtue, besides its spicy, mustardlike flavor, is its refreshing crisp texture, which brightens the softness and richness of braised duck legs, pork, or grilled pigeon. Flat black cabbage is also good chilled and served with boiled lobster, shrimp, or grilled sausages. Mature heads of flat black cabbage are roughly ten inches across. To prepare, make a cut just above the base of the plant to separate the leaves. Wash and dry the leaves as you would salad greens.

2 shallots (2 ounces), finely diced
1 tablespoon lemon juice
1 tablespoon red wine vinegar
¼ teaspoon salt
3 tablespoons olive oil
3 large heads flat black cabbage (8 ounces), topped to include 2 inches of the stem
Freshly ground pepper

Combine the shallots, lemon juice, and vinegar. Add the salt and let it dissolve. Stir in the olive oil. Warm the vinaigrette in a large sauté pan. Add the cabbage leaves, raise the heat, and wilt the leaves for about 3½ minutes, until the leaves are soft but the stems are still crunchy. Grind a little pepper over the cabbage and serve at once, while still warm.

Double Soups

Well-made puréed soups capture the essence of their primary ingredients. In the restaurant we have made puréed soups out of almost every vegetable. Carrying the process further, we began experimenting with the combination of two soups made separately, then served together in the same bowl. Many of the combinations we initially tried failed, either because of a bad match or for one of the technical reasons mentioned below. The visual presentation—two solid colors meeting midway in the bowl—only abetted the problem by turning the course into a cute contrivance. Despite these flops, though, we had our fun and discovered several things in the process.

The first discovery was that the most successful soups don't conflict with each other; neither soup should be stronger in flavor, more viscous, texturally opposed, or significantly more or less rich than the other. This balance is achieved by adjustments the cook makes along the way. For instance, combining the peppery flavor and leaner consistency of watercress with the suavity of fennel may require the addition of a little cream to the watercress soup. An alternative would be to pour less of the watercress directly into the fennel, to mitigate the watercress. The second lesson we learned is that the flavors should be kept direct. Together they should illustrate a simple interaction, not a complex argument. This insight influenced the manner in which we made the soups, as well as the decisions regarding the use of herbs and spices, aromatic vegetables in the base, and the choice of liquid.

In order that both soups be poured together but meet in the middle of the bowl, it is not only necessary that they be similar in consistency. A thin soup poured with one that is thicker will be invaded. We also learned that no two vegetables are alike when puréed. Some have more starch or fiber than others and consequently produce a thicker (or thinner) consistency. The visual effect of these soups suggests sleight of hand or rare expertise in the kitchen; it is accomplished by nothing more than thinning the thicker of the two soups with broth until both soups are uniform and then pouring them simultaneously into a bowl with two separate ladles.

Experiment with different combinations, but strive to balance the flavors by using your sense of how two vegetables will taste together. I find it helpful to think of the relative strength of the featured flavor of both soups. Once you have experimented with double soups you will want to do it again. A common pitfall, even among professionals, is to begin thinking in terms of colors, food painting rather than flavors. The real intent of the process and presentation of double soups is the interplay of tastes. A recipe follows to illustrate the principle of double soups. You may wish to consider the following combinations as well:

Spinach with carrot, green garlic, new potato or leek (spinach and carrot in equal portion with a slash of red beet is a feast of color).

Carrot and spring pea—two orders of sweetness.

Celeriac and butternut squash—two voluptuously smooth-textured vegetables when puréed.

Artichoke and green garlic.

Yellow crookneck squash and cucumber—both soups must be thinned with water for a poised delicacy.

Roasted eggplant and tomato—summer vegetables that if first grilled will convey smoky flavors.

Asparagus and a lemon soup that is thickened with egg and rice.

Carrot and Red Pepper Soup

For 8

Our first double soup: The carrot soup acts as a backdrop for the more pungent red pepper flavor. Pour the carrot soup first into the bowl, then add a smaller proportion of the red pepper soup; the red pepper taste will remain distinct and provide a spicy accent to the deeper carrot flavor.

For the carrot soup:
4 tablespoons unsalted butter
6 cups water
6 large carrots (1 pound, 4 ounces), cut into ½-inch dice
½ yellow onion (4 ounces), cut into ¼-inch dice
1 teaspoon salt
⅛ teaspoon freshly ground black pepper
1½ teaspoons lemon juice

Prepare the carrot soup: Melt the butter in a 6-quart stainless-steel soup pot. Add 1 cup of the water, the carrots, and onion. Bring to a low simmer, cover, and stew for 30 minutes.

Remove the cover from the pot. The vegetables should be very soft and the water almost entirely evaporated. If not, continue cooking the vegetables until they are. Add the remaining 5 cups water and bring to a boil. In the blender, purée the soup in batches, for 3 minutes each, and season it with salt, pepper, and the lemon juice. The soup should have a velvety consistency and be slightly thicker than heavy cream.

For the red pepper soup:
2 tablespoons unsalted butter
3 medium red bell peppers (14 ounces), halved, seeded, and diced
⅔ cup water
¼ teaspoon salt
⅛ teaspoon freshly ground pepper

Prepare the red pepper soup: Melt the butter in a 3-quart saucepan. Add the peppers and the water, bring to a simmer, and cook, uncovered, for 20 minutes, or until the peppers are very soft. Most of the water will have evaporated during this time.

In the blender, purée the peppers with ½ cup of the water and pass the purée through a medium-fine sieve to catch any bits of skin. If the pepper soup lacks depth, correct it with a few drops of red wine vinegar. If necessary, thin the red pepper soup with a little of the remaining water so that its consistency is similar to that of the carrot soup.

Serve the soups in warm bowls, pouring 6 ounces of the carrot into each. Stir 2 tablespoons of the red pepper soup into the center. Optional additions are chopped chervil leaves and crème fraîche thinned with a little warm water to approximate heavy cream. Draw the cream over the surface with the tines of a fork.

White Corn Cakes with Caviar

Eighteen 2-inch cakes, for 6

This dish was created to celebrate Chez Panisse's fifteenth birthday and is a spin-off of the more familiar blini with caviar. These corn cakes, unlike blini that are made with yeast, are leavened with baking powder and can be made and cooked immediately. The addition of beaten egg white just before cooking lightens the batter and allows for a suspension of whole kernels of corn throughout the mixture, giving the cakes a pleasantly crunchy texture.

Corn flour (not to be confused with corn meal) is distinctly gritty and has a slightly sweet flavor. It comes in yellow or white and is finely milled, although not as fine as wheat flour. Either color of corn flour will do for this recipe. Corn flour can be found in some health food stores, from the source listed on page 211 and in stores specializing in Indian groceries. Smell the corn flour before you buy it; it readily absorbs surrounding aromas such as the strong Indian spices it may be stored next to. It should smell faintly of corn. The recipe also calls for whole kernels of corn. Use the freshest you can find with kernels that are sweet and not at all starchy.

The cakes behave similarly on a griddle as those made with wheat or buckwheat flour except that they brown very rapidly. When they are done they will feel firm on the surface, particularly the middle, but do not let them cook any longer than that. Serve them immediately, as they have a tendency to go slightly dry inside.

2 to 3 ears of corn, cut from the cobs to yield 1½ cups kernels
1 cup milk
1½ cups corn flour (see above; corn meal is not a substitute)
1½ teaspoons baking powder
½ teaspoon salt
1 tablespoon honey
2 eggs, separated
¼ cup vegetable oil

12 tablespoons unsalted butter
4 ounces sturgeon caviar

Put 1 cup of the corn kernels and the milk in a blender and purée for 3 minutes. Pass the purée through a sieve into a bowl and press out as much liquid as possible. This should result in 1¼ cups liquid, the maximum amount to be used in this recipe. Sift the corn flour together with the baking powder and salt into a bowl. Add the honey, egg yolks, and vegetable oil and whisk the corn-milk in little by little until the mixture is smooth. Stir in the remaining ½ cup raw corn.

Melt the butter in a double boiler. Heat a seasoned griddle or cast-iron pan. Beat the egg whites to firm but not stiff peaks and fold half into the batter to lighten it. Fold in the other half, quickly working the spatula from the center of the bowl, out and around. The batter should be light and almost frothy.

Pour out about 3 tablespoons of batter, cook over medium-low heat for about 1 minute, or until the bottom of the cake is set. Flip them over and cook for about 1 minute more. Transfer to warm plates. Generously spoon melted butter over the cakes and garnish with a dollop of caviar. Serve immediately.

Corn Puddings with Blue Crab Sauce

For 8

Blue crabs from the Chesapeake Bay are available in late summer and through the fall and are normally caught before they grow large. Because of their scanty amount of meat, they are most practically used in *fumets*, bisques, and sauces. The blue crab is delicate but carries flavors with spicy, peppery overtones, which combine well in this instance with the sweet, grassy flavor of corn.

The puddings puff up like a soufflé and are later taken out of their ramekins and returned to the oven to brown 15 minutes before serving. The puddings can be made several hours or even a day ahead, but should be unmolded while still warm and covered, as they absorb other aromas.

For the crab fumet *for the sauce:*
4 live blue crabs
1 tablespoon unsalted butter
1 small carrot (2 ounces), diced
¼ large stalk of celery (1 ounce), diced
½ yellow onion (3 ounces), diced
½ tomato (2 ounces), diced
¼ red bell pepper (2 ounces), diced
2 sprigs parsley
1 bay leaf
5 cups water

To kill blue crabs: Set the crab right side up in front of you. Press down on the back of the shell to constrict the movements of the crab and quickly twist off the claws and legs using a towel or oven mitt to protect your hands. Turn the crab on its back and separate the body of the crab from its carapace by applying force in opposite directions (one hand holding the top shell down, the other prying the body free) at either of the top corners of the crab where the shell flares out in a point. Remove the sac behind the head, reserve the roe, if any, and tomalley inside (the soft, orange-colored and pale green, nearly liquid mass in the cavity). Rinse all parts of the crab under cold water.

Melt the butter in a large saucepot and in it stew the vegetables over low heat for 10 minutes, stirring occasionally. Meanwhile, with a heavy knife, crack the claws and cut the bodies of the crabs into small pieces. Raise the heat, add the crabs, parsley, and bay leaf, and sauté for 5 minutes, turning the shells over often. Add the water and let the *fumet* bubble gently for 30 minutes, skimming any foam that rises to the surface. While the *fumet* is cooking, prepare the puddings.

For the pudding mixture:
1 cup milk
2 ears of corn, cut from the cob to yield 1½ cups kernels
2 tablespoons unsalted butter
¼ teaspoon salt
⅛ teaspoon freshly ground black pepper
¼ cup all-purpose flour
3 whole eggs
1 cup heavy cream

Preheat the oven to 375°F.

Put the milk and 1 cup of the corn kernels in the blender and purée for 3 minutes. Pour the purée through a medium-fine sieve into a bowl and, using a spatula, push through as much of the milk as possible. Discard the corn skins left in the sieve. Put the purée into a pot on low heat. When it is warmed add the butter, salt, and pepper. After the butter is melted whisk in the flour little by little. Cook the mixture for 2 minutes, whisking constantly, until it thickens. Transfer to a bowl and let cool.

Butter eight ½-cup ramekins. Separate the eggs. When the pudding mixture is cool, stir in the yolks and the remaining ½ cup corn. Beat the whites to firm but not stiff peaks. Fold in half of the whites to lighten the mixture, then fold in the other half, working quickly. Fill the ramekins three-quarters full and place them in a *bain-marie*—a shallow dish large enough to hold all the ramekins. Fill the bain-marie with hot water to reach half way up the ramekins. Bake the puddings in the bain-marie for approximately 40 minutes, or until they are puffed and set and evenly browned on top.

While the puddings are baking, remove the *fumet* from the heat, strain the liquid into a wide saucepan, and discard the shells and vegetables. When the puddings are done remove them from the bain-marie and let them cool for 15 minutes. Run a knife around the inside edge of each ramekin, invert onto one hand, and carefully remove the puddings. Set the puddings, browned side up, in a baking dish just large enough to accommodate them, but do not let them touch. Pour ½ cup of the heavy cream over and around the puddings just to cover the bottom of the dish. Put the dish in the oven for 20 minutes, or until the puddings are browned on top, puffed, and the cream bubbles lightly.

While the puddings are heating, over high heat reduce the *fumet* to ½ cup. Add the remaining ½ cup heavy cream and reduce slightly. The sauce will appear a dark orange-brown and should not be reduced beyond the consistency of heavy cream. When the puddings are finished, transfer them immediately to small warm plates and spoon the crab sauce around them.

Corn Soup with Garlic Butter

For 6

Second best to eating just-picked corn on the cob is this soup, which is made of nothing more than corn, a little onion, water, salt, and pepper. Picking farm-fresh corn and then transferring it immediately to a pot of boiling water is not a matter of false urgency or sentimentality. Unrefrigerated, corn (like peas) can lose a large percentage of its sugar within hours of being picked. Just-picked corn will favor you with a surprisingly rich, sweet soup.

2 tablespoons unsalted butter
1 medium onion (6 ounces), diced
4¼ cups water
5 ears of corn (1½ pounds), the kernels cut from the cob
Salt and pepper
1 recipe Garlic Butter (see page 114)

Melt the butter in a soup pot and add the onion and ¼ cup of the water. Cover and simmer for 10 minutes. Add the remaining water and bring to the boil. Add the corn kernels and simmer for 5 minutes.

Purée the soup in batches in a blender, allowing the blender to run a full 3 minutes for each batch. Press the purée through a coarse sieve, one that will catch the fibers and skins but will permit the starchy juice to pass through into another pot. Season with ½ teaspoon salt and ⅛ teaspoon black pepper or to taste. Gently reheat the soup, divide it among heated bowls, and garnish each serving with a dollop of garlic butter.

VEGETABLES   99

Baked Eggplants and Tomatoes with Bread Crumbs and Basil

For 8

At the restaurant, where large numbers of people are served at definite times, the success of any dinner, from the standpoint of the kitchen, depends upon how well prepared we are. Timing is critical, and accordingly, many dishes that would be impossible to assemble and cook to order are designed so that they can easily be finished and served. This logic and organization is valuable at home as well and can often help to simplify the work of the cook, particularly just before mealtime, when many tasks need to be attended to simultaneously. This eggplant dish may be prepared well in advance of being served.

I have never liked to cook eggplant in oil as it acts like a sponge and becomes heavy and indigestible. So before even assembling the ingredients for this dish, the eggplant is salted and peppered and baked in a little water. Precooking the eggplant also releases its brown, sometimes bitter juice and insures that the raw tomatoes, which will later be layered with the cooked eggplant, will finish cooking at the same time. The bread crumbs are also precooked for proper texture. An important part of this recipe is the reduction that occurs in the final moments. As the vegetables cook they release their juices, which mingle with the vinaigrette, basil, and garlic. Serve this dish with grilled meats, lamb, in particular. It is also excellent with grilled chicken, salmon, sea bass, or cod.

3 globe eggplants (2 pounds)
Salt and pepper
3 large beefsteak tomatoes (2 pounds)
12 ounces sourdough bread, to yield 2½ cups bread crumbs
4 tablespoons unsalted butter
2 tablespoons freshly grated Parmesan cheese

For the vinaigrette:
2 large cloves garlic, minced
1 tablespoon plus ½ teaspoon red wine vinegar
⅛ teaspoon salt
⅛ teaspoon fresh ground pepper
¼ cup extra virgin olive oil
4 tablespoons chopped fresh basil

Preheat the oven to 400°F. Put a pot of water large enough to hold the tomatoes on to boil.

Peel the eggplants with a sharp knife. Slice the eggplant into ½-inch rounds, discarding the hard end piece near the stem. Lay the eggplant out on a cutting board and salt and pepper one side. Then turn them over and arrange them, slightly overlapping, in a noncorroding baking dish approximately 16 by 10 inches. Pour over enough water (about ⅛ inch) to come barely up the sides of the eggplant. Lightly salt and pepper the other side of the eggplant. Cover the dish and bake about 1 hour, or until the eggplant is soft but not mushy.

Core the tomatoes and drop them into the pot of boiling water for 15 seconds. Remove from the water. When cool, remove the skins and cut the tomatoes into ½-inch slices.

Cut the crust off of the bread, break the bread up into small chunks, and grind into coarse crumbs in a food processor. (If you have no processor, pull the bread apart and break it up by hand.)

Melt the butter, add to the bread crumbs, and mix well so that all pieces are coated. Spread the crumbs on a baking sheet. Put into the oven with the eggplant and bake for about 15 minutes, or until golden brown. Turn the bread crumbs over with a spatula every so often, so they will brown evenly.

Prepare the vinaigrette: Whisk the garlic, vinegar, salt, and pepper together until the salt is well dissolved. Add the olive oil and 2 tablespoons of the basil and whisk until blended.

When the eggplants are ready, remove from the oven, transfer to a plate to cool, and discard any juices remaining in the pan.

Cut the eggplant and tomato slices in half, making half-moon shapes. Layer them, by alternating and overlapping them in the same pan used for baking the eggplant. Fit any extra pieces into the cracks. Stir the vinaigrette again and spoon it over the slices, distributing the basil and garlic evenly. Lightly salt and pepper. At this point, the vegetables can be covered and held for 3 hours before being baked.

To finish: Scatter the Parmesan evenly over the top. Put the dish in the oven, reduce to 350°F, and bake for 30 minutes. Sprinkle the bread crumbs over the top and bake 15 minutes more. Let cool slightly, garnish with the remaining 2 tablespoons basil, and serve.

Eggplant Croutons

These croutons are perfect pass-around appetizers. The eggplant itself is delicious as an accompaniment to cold sliced leg of lamb. Or it can be used as a filling for stuffed baked tomatoes.

Salt and pepper
1 large globe eggplant (12 ounces), peeled, cut in 1-inch dice
2 tablespoons olive oil
⅔ cup water
1 large shallot (1½ ounces), minced
1 clove garlic, pounded to a paste in a mortar
1 tablespoon red wine vinegar
1 baguette
1 tablespoon chopped fresh Italian parsley

Preheat the oven to 400°F.

In a bowl, lightly salt and pepper the eggplant and mix it with 1 tablespoon of the olive oil. Arrange the eggplant on a shallow baking dish just large enough to contain it. Add the water and cover tightly. Bake for 45 minutes. The eggplant will turn from white to olive green in color and become very soft. Drain the eggplant in a colander and let cool.

When cool, put the eggplant in a bowl and add the shallot, garlic, vinegar, and the remaining 1 tablespoon olive oil. Mix well so that the eggplant has the texture of a coarse purée. Correct for salt and pepper. Chill the eggplant for 3 hours, or until it is very cold.

Preheat the oven to 350°F. Cut rounds ⅓ inch thick from the baguette and brush them lightly on one side with olive oil. Toast until golden brown. Just before serving, mix the parsley into the eggplant and serve with the warm croutons.

Grilled Eggplants with Shallots and Parsley

For 4

Because of its blandness, eggplant is commonly treated as a vehicle for other flavors. As is, eggplants benefit greatly from the charcoal fire. When picked ripe and grilled soon after, they need very little in the way of seasoning to be satisfying. Eggplants contain a lot of water and it is best to cut them into thick slices because they shrink considerably while grilling or baking. Choose eggplants that are firm (not hard) with shiny unwrinkled skin and a deep color.

In addition to the garnish of shallots and parsley suggested below, grilled eggplants are delicious with pesto, or garlic mayonnaise, or marinated in an anchovy vinaigrette seasoned with orange zest and chopped Niçoise olives.

This dish can stand alone as a first course but also works well as an accompaniment to grilled butterflied leg of lamb, beef steak, or chicken.

12 medium-size Japanese eggplants (2 pounds)
3 tablespoons extra virgin olive oil
¼ of a large lemon
2 shallots (2 ounces), finely diced
2 tablespoons chopped fresh Italian parsley

Prepare a charcoal fire. While it is burning down, remove the stem cover of the eggplants. Trim the eggplants. Cut lengthwise into slices that are an even ⅝ inch thick with two flat, exposed surfaces (save the trimmings for eggplant soup). Arrange the eggplant on a baking sheet. Using 2 tablespoons of the olive oil, brush the eggplant slices with oil and add salt and pepper lightly. Turn the slices and repeat.

Grill the slices over a hot fire, using a pair of tongs to turn them and periodically to check their progress. Once eggplant begins to brown it finishes quickly, so be careful not to blacken the flesh. Four to five minutes on each side should be enough. Work quickly and turn the slices when they are a deep brown.

Transfer the slices to a warm platter and squeeze the lemon juice over each. Mix the shallots and parsley together and sprinkle them over the top. Drizzle the remaining 1 tablespoon olive oil over all the slices. (The simplest way to do this is to cover the top of the olive oil bottle with your thumb, and let a thin stream fall through.) Serve while still warm.

Grilled Eggplant Tart

This tart captures the smokiness of the charcoal grill and the happy union of Provençal flavors—eggplant, peppers, garlic, anchovies, and basil. Its tart and salty accents pique the appetite and it makes a provocative first course. The tart resembles a pizza, but is much lighter and crisper because of the puff pastry crust. The pastry is treated like a large cracker with the toppings added after the shell is baked and cooled. Assembled, it is dressed at the last moment with sharp vinaigrette.

The shell itself is versatile and can support a number of different toppings, for instance, a warm stew of caramelized onions cooked with fresh thyme, vinegar, chopped parsley, olives, and eggs. Or leftover ratatouille, provided it is not too juicy, makes a colorful topping and is well matched with the basil, chopped egg, and anchovy garnishes.

Make the puff pastry ahead of time and refrigerate or freeze the shell. Bake it while you prepare the other ingredients. Be sure to let the shell cool well before you assemble the tart.

8 Japanese eggplants (1 pound, 4 ounces)
4 tablespoons pure olive oil
Salt and pepper
1 sweet red bell pepper (8 ounces)
4 salt-packed anchovies
1 large egg
2 shallots (2 ounces), finely diced
1 small clove garlic, very finely chopped
1½ tablespoons red wine vinegar
1½ tablespoons extra virgin olive oil
2 tablespoons chopped fresh basil for garnish
One 10-inch puff pastry tart shell (see page 322), prebaked

Prepare a charcoal fire.

Cut the eggplants lengthwise into ¼-inch slices. Lay the slices on a baking sheet, brush them with olive oil, and lightly salt and pepper them on both sides. While the fire is still quite hot, grill the pepper until its skin is well blistered and blackened all over, turning it often to expose all sides to the heat. When the pepper is well charred, remove it from the grill and place it in a sealed container to steam. This will help to loosen the skin from the flesh. When the fire has burned down a bit, grill the eggplants, being careful not to blacken the flesh. This should take about 2 minutes per side.

Remove the bones from the anchovies and soak the filets in a small bowl in several changes of cold water for 15 minutes. Put the egg in a small saucepot, cover with cold water, bring to the boil, then immediately turn the heat off. Let the egg stand in the hot water for 8 minutes. Remove, cool the egg in cold water, and peel it.

Combine the shallots, garlic, and vinegar in a small bowl. Add a pinch of salt and pepper and mix well to dissolve the salt. Add the extra virgin olive oil, stirring constantly.

Remove the pepper from the bag and peel off the blackened skin. Cut the pepper in half over a small bowl, saving any juices. Strain the juices into the vinaigrette through a sieve, to capture the seeds. Cut away the stem and seeds and cut the pepper into ¼-inch strips. Toss the peppers with a little of the vinaigrette and set aside. Drain and squeeze the anchovies and cut them lengthwise into ⅛-inch strips. Chop the egg coarse.

Assembling the tart: Just before you intend to serve the tart, lay the sliced eggplant, slightly overlapping, on the puff pastry tart. Next, distribute the anchovies and peppers evenly. Using your hands, sprinkle the vinaigrette and shallots over the vegetables. Garnish with the chopped egg and basil. Serve immediately with a bowl of olives and chilled Bandol rosé.

Gratin of Belgian Endive

The white tender shoots of Belgian endive are the result of a gardening process called blanching, a method of tempering and refining the disagreeable qualities in certain lettuces, such as the bitter or prickly chicories (e.g., the Italian radicchios, curly leaved endive). When the plant develops a thick, sturdy root, the foliage is cut just above the neck and the roots are transplanted in a moist bed of rich soil and placed in total darkness in a cool environment. My grandfather stored his endive in sawdust-filled bushel baskets in the cellar.

Blanched leaves of Belgian endive are ivory white with yellow tinges at the leaf tips, crisp and sweet, and they retain only traces of the harsh bitterness of the unblanched plants. Blanching also causes the leaves to thicken and gather very tightly together. Because of this it is possible to cook Belgian endive without its going limp. It makes an unusual and delicious accompaniment to roast fowl. The endives are first parboiled, then wrapped in thin slices of prosciutto and set in a baking dish. Fresh thyme and a little cream are added, finely grated Gruyère and buttered bread crumbs sprinkled on top, and the dish is set in the oven.

2 quarts water
1 teaspoon salt
Juice of 1 lemon
8 firm Belgian endives (1½ pounds)
16 very thin slices of prosciutto
¼ cup plus 2 tablespoons heavy cream
1½ tablespoons unsalted butter
1 cup fresh coarse bread crumbs
⅓ cup finely grated Gruyère cheese

Preheat the oven to 350°F.

Bring the water to a boil in a 4-quart noncorroding pot. Add the salt and lemon juice. Cut the endives in half vertically and plunge them into the boiling water for 5 minutes, adjusting the heat so that the water simmers gently. Remove the endives and set them on a plate to cool. Making a V-shaped cut, remove the root at the base of each endive, and wrap each in a slice of prosciutto. Pour 2 tablespoons of cream into the bottom of an 8½- by 10½-inch baking dish and set the endives in snugly next to one another. Pour the remaining cream over the endives. Melt the butter and mix it with the crumbs. Sprinkle the cheese over the top, then scatter the crumbs over the endives in an even layer. Place the dish in the oven and bake for 35 minutes, or until the cream appears bubbly at the edges and the crumbs are nicely browned.

Fennel, Mushroom, Parmesan Cheese, and White Truffle Salad

For 2 as a first course salad

This is a delicate, pastel-colored salad to make in late autumn when fresh Italian white truffles are available. It is one of the most striking combinations of flavors and textures I know of. The success of this dish depends upon all the ingredients being very fresh and shaved thinly and for this, a mandoline is a very useful tool. If the outer skin of the truffle appears at all tough or dry, peel it. The most flavorful mushroom to use is the fresh bolete, which is deliciously nutty even when raw. Unless the bolete is in absolutely firm, fresh condition, substitute the white-capped button mushroom commonly available throughout the year. It too should be firm and moist with gill covers that have not yet opened. Dress this salad with fine golden extra virgin olive oil that has a buttery smooth character. Avoid green oils, which can be piquant in the finish.

Salads like this one have prompted other combinations of seasonal vegetables—spring fava beans in their raw form, if absolutely fresh from the garden, picked before they come to full size (about the size of a dime), and peeled of their outer skins, with shaved radishes, fennel, or the pale hearts of celery; thinly sliced Belgian endive, dressed as above with lemon juice and extra virgin olive oil, are a virginal delicacy.

If you grow artichokes yourself or have access to the smallest, most tender buds in very firm, fresh condition, you may wish to serve them raw as well. Pare the leaves down to the pale yellow-to-green hearts, then trim the base and tapered top to the point at which there is no resistance to your knife. Slice as thin as possible (here again the mandoline is useful) and dress immediately (to prevent them from turning brown) with lemon juice, extra virgin olive oil, salt, and pepper. Thin shavings of Parmesan cheese are delicious here as well. I first encountered artichokes prepared in this manner in Florence, where they were dressed and served on top of thinly sliced *bresaola*, cured air-dried beef. In fact, raw artichokes are a wonderful complement to raw meat dishes and we have served them frequently in the restaurant on top of carpaccio (a slip of lean beef pounded to translucent thinness) and veal tartare.

1 teaspoon lemon juice
1½ tablespoons extra virgin olive oil
Salt and pepper
1 very fresh bulb Florence fennel (see page 109)
1 Boletus edulis mushroom (about 3 ounces), brushed clean
Reggiano Parmigiano cheese
1 white truffle (about 1 ounce), brushed clean

Combine the lemon juice and olive oil in a small bowl and season it to taste with salt and pepper.

Have two large, flat white plates ready. Remove any tough outer leaves of the fennel. On the mandoline or with a sharp, thin-bladed knife, slice as thinly as possible enough of the heart to loosely cover the bottom of the plates. Transfer the fennel to a bowl and dress with a little of the olive oil and lemon mixture. Taste and correct for salt and pepper. Scatter the fennel loosely over the plates.

Shave the mushrooms on the mandoline or slice with a knife, producing thin, almost transparent cross sections. Strew the mushrooms over the fennel, covering it with an airy layer. With a hand-held cheese slicer or knife blade make shavings of Parmesan and put them on the two other layers in a similar fashion.

Drizzle the remaining lemon oil over and around everything on the plates. With a truffle cutter (a small hand tool with a flat surface and adjustable protruding blade) run the truffle across the surface and through the blade to produce very thin slices. Or, with a vegetable peeler, shave truffle slices all over the top. Grind a little black pepper over each plate and serve.

Gratin of Florence Fennel and New Potatoes

Florence fennel (*Foeniculum azoricum*) is different from wild fennel (*F. vulgare*), common garden fennel (*F. officinale*), and sweet fennel (*F. dulce*): it is a small annual, thick set, and has a much more swollen base than the other varieties. Although Florence fennel derives from Italy, it is the variety most commonly found in our markets.

Fresh Florence fennel exhibits a very pale green to white smooth bulb. It is delicious as a raw vegetable sliced and served with olive oil, lemon juice, and coarse salt; or with anchovy filets and garlic slivers gently warmed in olive oil until they form a paste. The following recipe is a dish of baked fennel and new potatoes, which rest in tender layers beneath a crisp, golden topping of bread crumbs. It is well matched with grilled veal chops.

3/4 pound Florence fennel, bulbs only, feathery leaves reserved for garnish
1 pound new red potatoes
6 cups water
1 1/4 teaspoons salt
4 large cloves garlic (1 ounce), peeled
Juice of 1/4 lemon (2 teaspoons)
1 cup heavy cream
1/4 cup grated Reggiano Parmigiano cheese
Freshly ground pepper
3/4 cup fresh sourdough bread crumbs
1 tablespoon unsalted butter

Trim the root of the fennel so it is flat at the base of the bulb, remove any tough, stringy, or discolored outer leaves, and slice the whole bulb lengthwise into 1/8-inch-thick pieces. Peel the potatoes and slice them similarly, into 1/8-inch-thick rounds. Place the fennel slices in a 2-quart saucepot. Add 3 cups of water, 1/4 teaspoon salt, the garlic, and the lemon juice. Bring to the boil, reduce to a simmer, and cook gently for 15 minutes.

In the meantime, put the potatoes with the remaining 3 cups water and the remaining teaspoon of salt into another pot. Bring to a boil, reduce the heat, and cook for 5 to 8 minutes, or until the potatoes just lose their crunch. Do not allow them to soften beyond this point. Drain the potatoes in a colander, discard the water, and let them cool.

Remove the fennel from the water with a pair of tongs (leave the garlic in the pot) and transfer the slices to a plate to cool. Raise the heat and reduce the liquid until it is nearly all evaporated and a scant ¼ cup remains. Add the heavy cream and whisk well. Turn off the heat and force the cream mixture through a medium sieve into a bowl, using a spatula to push as much of the softened garlic through as possible.

Assembling the gratin: Preheat the oven to 350°F.

Pour several spoonfuls of the garlic cream (just enough to cover the bottom) into a small 8-inch-square baking dish or oval gratin. Alternate slices of fennel and potato, using up all of the fennel in this first layer. Spoon a little more of the garlic cream over the layer, lightly sprinkle it with one-third of the Parmesan cheese, and a little freshly ground pepper.

Use the remaining slices of potato to form the top layer, arranging them in an overlapping scalloped pattern. Lightly press the gratin with the palm of your hand so that it is evenly flat. Pour over the remaining cream, making sure to moisten all of the potatoes, grind pepper over the top, and sprinkle over the remaining Parmesan. Bake in the oven for 1 hour and 15 minutes.

While the gratin is baking, sauté the bread crumbs in the butter to a golden brown and transfer them to a bowl. Five minutes before the gratin is to come out of the oven, distribute the crumbs over the top with about 1 tablespoon chopped fennel leaves. Let the gratin cool slightly before serving.

Green Garlic

Garlic is commonly used as a mature plant when the bulb containing many cloves has formed. Green garlic is the same plant pulled from the ground at a much earlier stage, before the bulb forms and when the plant resembles a leek, with a stalk about ½ inch in diameter. Until recently, green garlic never appeared in the market and was largely unrecognized by cooks. The quality of green garlic is unique and of great use in the kitchen. When cooked, it has none of the hot, pungent qualities of fresh garlic cloves. Its flavor, although unmistakably associated with the mature form, is much milder.

Green garlic is a year-round staple of my garden. I stagger the plantings to insure a constant supply, leaving some in the ground to form mature bulbs. The rich, earthy aroma of green garlic has inspired numerous dishes at the restaurant. Garlic broth, made by pouring water or, better, poultry stock, over a good amount of stewed, green garlic, simmered and seasoned with salt, vinegar, chopped parsley, and plenty of freshly ground pepper, is a comforting restorative. Although it cannot be claimed as a remedy, garlic broth is particularly soothing to those with a winter cold or touch of the flu. Similar soups, slightly altered or embellished, are made in the restaurant. Garlic consommé is a stew of green garlic, leeks, and ripe tomatoes to which we add a rich poultry or lamb broth. The soup is simmered gently until the elements soften and the flavors combine. The same ingredients, moistened with water or fish broth, make a flavorful poaching medium for fine-textured fish such as halibut, salmon, and sole. Soups of this kind are light and are good between richer or heavier courses.

The flavor of green garlic is most clearly captured in a puréed soup made with new potatoes and finished with cream. Without the potatoes, the puréed and creamed garlic, seasoned with vinegar and salt and pepper, can serve as a sauce, or sauce element, and is good with grilled pigeon, roast chicken, and veal. Stewed green garlic is delicious in soufflés and braised preparations or substituted for onions or leeks in the aromatic bases of soups such as corn, pepper, or eggplant.

Green Garlic and Cheese Soufflés

5 tablespoons unsalted butter

*6 young garlic plants, white to pale green part only (4 ounces), washed, halved
  lengthwise, and sliced thin to yield 1¼ cups*

¼ teaspoon salt

Freshly ground pepper

¾ cup water

½ teaspoon white wine vinegar

1 cup milk

3 tablespoons all-purpose flour

¼ teaspoon chopped fresh thyme

¾ cup finely grated Gruyère cheese

5 tablespoons freshly grated Parmesan cheese

Butter for ramekins

4 large eggs, separated

Melt 1 tablespoon of the butter in a 3-quart noncorroding saucepan. Add the
garlic, salt, a little pepper, water, and vinegar. Bring to a simmer, cover, and
cook for 10 minutes. Remove the cover, raise the heat, and cook another 4 to 5
minutes, until all the water has evaporated. Add the milk and heat it to just
below the simmer. Transfer the mixture to a blender and purée it for 1 minute.

Preheat the oven to 425°F.

Melt the remaining 4 tablespoons butter in a small saucepan. Add the flour
and thyme and stir until all lumps disappear and the mixture is evenly combined. Over low heat, stir in the garlic purée little by little until the mixture is
smooth and thick. Make sure to stir the flour along the bottom edge of the pan.
Transfer the mixture to a larger (2-quart) bowl. Add the Gruyère and 2 tablespoons of the Parmesan and mix well. Let the béchamel cool.

In the meantime, lightly butter six small (4-ounce) ramekins. Then dust them
with Parmesan, using about 2 tablespoons. Stir the egg yolks into the cool
béchamel.

In a very clean bowl, beat the egg whites to firm but not stiff peaks. Fold half
the egg whites into the béchamel first, then the other half. (The mixture need
not be uniformly combined.) Work quickly and keep the mixture light and
fluffy.

Ladle the soufflé base into each ramekin, filling it to just below the top rim.
Run your thumb around the inside rims of the ramekins so that the soufflés form

a cap. Sprinkle the tops with the remaining Parmesan. Set the ramekins on the middle rack of the oven and bake for 10 to 12 minutes, or until the soufflés are brown on top and just set everywhere except the center. Make sure your guests are seated before the soufflés are finished cooking. Transfer the ramekins to plates and rush them to the table.

Green Garlic Soup

Ten 6-ounce portions

5 tablespoons unsalted butter
24 young garlic plants, ½ inch in diameter at the root end, white part only (8 ounces), halved lengthwise
¾ cup water
1 pound, 6 ounces small red potatoes, peeled and quartered
1½ quarts light-bodied chicken broth
½ cup heavy cream
1½ teaspoons salt
2 to 2½ teaspoons white wine vinegar
Freshly ground black pepper
Sourdough bread

Melt the butter in a 6-quart noncorroding pot. Add the garlic and ¼ cup of the water. Bring to a simmer, cover tightly, and cook for 15 minutes. Add the potatoes and remaining ½ cup water and cook at a simmer for 20 minutes. Add the chicken broth, cover the pot, and allow to bubble gently for 20 minutes.

Purée the soup in batches in a blender for 2 minutes. Pass the purée through a medium-fine sieve into a bowl. Stir in the cream and salt. Add the vinegar, 1 teaspoon at a time, tasting the soup after each addition before you add the next. (Some vinegars are more acidic and strongly flavored than others.)

Reheat the soup gently and serve it in warm bowls. Grind black pepper generously over each portion and serve with grilled slices of sourdough bread that have been brushed with melted butter and sprinkled with chopped fresh thyme or small croutons tossed in butter and baked until very crisp.

Garlic Butter

About 6 tablespoons

As a garnish, this butter is very versatile. At the restaurant we use it primarily to enrich and flavor water-based vegetable soups, such as spinach or white corn. Or the butter is used as the final addition in a sauce. The combination is also tasty when tossed with noodles and a little Parmesan, as an accompaniment to roast chicken or spread on warm grilled bread with thin slices of smoked ham.

The flavor of garlic cooked this way has an entirely different character from raw or sautéed garlic. Its strong, hot quality is softened and its flavor, although distinct, resembles stewed onions in sweetness and intensity. It is best to use garlic butter soon after it has been made. Exposed to the air, or even when it is wrapped and refrigerated for as few as eight hours, it loses its fresh, sweet quality and develops an aggressive flavor.

An alternative to cooking the garlic cloves in water is to gently simmer them until they are very soft in goose or duck fat. The cloves are then smashed to a paste and used—without the addition of butter—to enliven sauces, or spread on grilled toasts to accompany salads. As with garlic butter, this paste should be used soon after it is made; and, if you are stirring it into a sauce, it should be the last step, as prolonged cooking will also cause the garlic to lose its mild fresh quality.

12 cloves garlic (approximately ⅓ cup), peeled
Water
Salt
5 tablespoons unsalted butter, softened
¼ teaspoon Champagne vinegar
1/16 teaspoon ground cayenne
Pepper

In a small saucepan, parboil the garlic for 1 minute. Discard the water. Return the garlic to the pan. Add 2 cups water, ¼ teaspoon salt, and bring to the boil. Reduce the heat and simmer for 20 minutes, or until the water has almost entirely evaporated and the garlic cloves are very soft.

Transfer the cloves to a bowl and smash them to a paste with a spatula or spoon. Add the butter, Champagne vinegar, cayenne, and season with ⅛ teaspoon salt and 1/16 teaspoon freshly ground pepper. Mix well, transfer to a small bowl, and cover tightly. Store in a cool place until ready to use, but for no longer than 8 hours.

Garlic Mayonnaise

This garlic mayonnaise was developed with the thought of a lighter, more digestible everyday sauce to complement so many of the dishes in the restaurant that cry for garlic—fish soups, mixed grills of fish and shellfish, salt cod and potatoes, spit-roasted lamb, baked squid, and summer vegetables such as eggplants, tomatoes, peppers, and Romano beans, to name only a few. The cooking at Chez Panisse would be very different if we didn't make this sauce as frequently as we do. Based on *aioli*, the celebrated garlic mayonnaise of Provence made with fresh garlic, egg yolks, and good olive oil in a mortar and pestle, this mayonnaise is much lighter because it is whisked instead of churned in a mortar. The palatability of authentic *aioli* relies, more than any other ingredient, on the quality of the oil. Those oils typical of the French Riviera are buttery soft and intensely fruity. It is difficult to find an imported oil with these qualities any more. Green oils that are often piquant, heavy bodied, or strong flavored are unsuitable for classic *aioli*.

Most of the oil used to make this mayonnaise is flavorless and light bodied. We use a refined peanut oil or vegetable oil and then correct it by seasoning the mayonnaise with extra virgin olive oil. Mixing oils in this manner captures the best of both in a mayonnaise that is light, yet carries the fruity perfume of the olive.

2 large egg yolks
1 cup neutral-flavored oil (peanut or vegetable oil)
3 tablespoons extra virgin olive oil
4 cloves garlic, smashed to a paste in a mortar
1½ tablespoons warm water
1 teaspoon white wine vinegar
¼ teaspoon salt
⅛ teaspoon ground pepper

Place the egg yolks in a bowl with about a 1-quart capacity. Wrap a damp towel around the base of the bowl to steady it. Whisk the egg yolks together and begin adding the peanut or vegetable oil very slowly in droplets, whisking all the time, until the mixture begins to thicken. Add the oil in a thin, continuous stream until all of it has been incorporated, including the olive oil. The mayonnaise should be fairly stiff at this point. Whisk in the garlic paste. Add the water to the mortar, scrape any remaining bits of garlic together, and add them and the water in a thin stream to the mayonnaise, whisking all the time. (The water will thin the consistency of the mayonnaise considerably.) Whisk in the vinegar, salt, and pepper and serve. Garlic mayonnaise should be used the day it is made or the flavor of the garlic turns stale.

Leeks Vinaigrette with Anchovies and Eggs

For 6

If you grow them yourself, or can find them in the market, young leeks with shoots about ½ inch in diameter are perfect for this recipe. Young leeks have a fresh grassy flavor and are much more tender and less stringy than the larger, more mature ones. Leeks vinaigrette make an appetizing first course, providing contrast in a menu that includes a rich braised dish or roast; they also work well as a light lunch, by themselves, with sliced sausage or ham, or with grilled fish.

30 young leeks (13 ounces)
1 gallon water
1½ tablespoons salt
3 large eggs
6 salt-packed anchovies

For the vinaigrette:
1 large shallot (1 ounce), finely diced
2 tablespoons plus 1 teaspoon white wine vinegar
Salt and pepper
4 tablespoons extra virgin olive oil
1 tablespoon chopped fresh Italian parsley

Trim the root end of the leeks and make a cut just above the white part where the green leaves open out. Discard the leaves. The leeks should be about 5 inches long. Make 2-inch slits on either side of the top end of each leek so that any sand or dirt can escape when you wash them. Remove any tough outer skin and plunge the leeks into a large bowl of water. Check the cut tops and shake any sand out under water.

Bring the water and salt to a boil in a large pot and add the leeks. Adjust the

heat so that the water gently bubbles and cook the leeks for 15 to 18 minutes, or until tender throughout.

Meanwhile, filet the anchovies and soak them in several changes of cold water for 15 minutes.

Prepare the eggs and the vinaigrette: Cover the eggs with cold water, bring to a boil, turn off the heat, and let the eggs stand for 8 minutes. Cool the eggs under cold water. Combine the shallot and vinegar in a bowl and add a little salt and pepper. Stir in the olive oil.

Carefully remove the leeks from the pot and put them on a plate to cool. Squeeze them gently to remove excess water and chill them in the refrigerator for 30 minutes.

Assembling and dressing the leeks: Peel the eggs and chop them very coarse. Drain and squeeze the anchovies so that they are quite dry and slice them into small bits. Stir the anchovies into the vinaigrette. Pour the vinaigrette over the leeks and toss gently so that the leeks don't fall apart. Arrange the leeks on individual plates or a large platter in a single layer, adding all of the vinaigrette. Scatter the eggs and parsley over the top and serve.

Wild Mushrooms

Nearly ten years ago, while spending some time in the Veneto region of northern Italy, I ate a plate of porcini mushrooms that I will never forget. It wasn't my first encounter with these mushrooms—both my mother and grandmother kept their precious stashes of the dried form to add conservatively to pasta sauce and risotto. As a child I wondered how anything that looked and smelled that bad could be so special. When I first began working in restaurants, in the early days of local commercial mushroom collecting, the specimens we received were soggy and ridden with small worms, and hardly lived up to the idealized expectation I had developed through reading, and the testimony of travelers to Europe. My hopes were confirmed, however, that chilly autumn day.

After driving for hours in the foothills of the Alps in search of an *osteria* whose whereabouts my Italian friend only vaguely remembered, we arrived, hungry and tired, at the door of an unassuming tufa stone building. Inside, the smell of a wood fire emanated from a massive hearth, which dominated the otherwise spare room furnished with long tables and re-cast church pews. Within the hearth, which accommodated both grills and spits, joints of game and small birds turned in front of the fire. Below the birds was a long metal tray propped up on either end by bricks and set against the warmth of the hearth, embers, and ash. There, glistening brown and buff-colored porcini caps collected the juices of the turning birds and the smoke of the fire. Before looking at the menu (which never was offered), we had chosen our dinner. Besides the birds from the spit and a platter of porcini, we ate *bresaola* (beef cured in the open mountain air), sliced grilled polenta with a stew of snails, and drank *amarone*, the rich and deeply tinted wine of Valpolicella.

Although the entire meal left me with a vivid impression, what stands out are those porcini mushrooms—their lingering, nutty flavor mixed with sage and garlic from the basted birds, their firm and meaty texture, and the aroma of smoldering oak. It is hardly sufficient to describe these qualities alone. That plate of mushrooms conveyed a much larger picture—the woodsy perfume of the surrounding hills and the taste of the earth in perfect evocation of a fall evening.

Wild mushrooms are a great gift of nature and far superior in their diversity, flavor, and texture to the few cultivated varieties available. Wild mushrooms are both very fragile and perishable. Encountering them in prime condition has been, until fairly recently, a privilege of knowledgeable hunters and mycologists. In California, the commercial market for wild mushrooms, which grow from Santa Cruz to points inland and along the Coast north to Oregon and Washington states, has grown dramatically in the past five years, together with a growing interest in natural and uncultivated foods. In Berkeley markets, where before only the common white button mushrooms were available, piles of golden chanterelles (*Cantharellus cibarius*), horns of plenty (*Craterellus cornucopioides*), boletes (*Boletus edulis*), matsutake (*Armillaria caligata*), and hedgehog mushrooms (*Dentinum repandum* and *Dentinum umbilicatum*) appear in the fall and winter, and morels (*Morchella esculenta*) in the spring. Our primary source, Jeff Hvid, an experienced and conscientious mushroom collector, brings us, in addition to the varieties that appear in the market, shaggy parasols (*Lepiota rachodes*), bluets (*Clitocybe nuda*), suillus (*Suillus pungens*), and fairy-ring mushrooms (*Marasmius oreades*).

The flavor and condition of wild mushrooms is subject to the great variations of climate and habitat. Rainfall, temperature, and dry periods following the rain are critical factors that influence the success or failure of the season for collectors. Water comprises the greater part of a mushroom's substance and allows it to reach maturity. Too much rain discourages growth and spoils the fruit that has already appeared. In general, the ideal time for collecting, or buying wild mushrooms in the market, is after the first rains in the cooling autumn, particularly if followed by periods that are warmer and drier. It is at this time that a number of edible varieties appear in profusion, golden chanterelles and boletes being the most common. The warming trends in the spring and early summer along with damp weather summons the second group of species, among them the morels, shaggy parasols, and fairy-ring mushrooms.

Wild mushrooms should be consumed as close to the time of harvesting as possible. Although they don't lose flavor if stored for a brief period, they will dry out some and their fresh, earthy scent dissipates. If you buy them in the market, choose mushrooms that are as dry as possible but not dessicated, firm, unbruised, with good color, and with no signs of deterioration such as dark spots, soft areas, or an unpleasantly moldy smell. If you are buying boletes, check the stems and caps carefully. If the stems are soft, it is a good indication that the mushroom was picked too late, and it will have a cottony texture or be infested with bugs. If the caps are slimy and the spongy pores under the cap are discolored, the mushroom is well on its way to decay. Chanterelles come up throughout the fall and winter, weather permitting. In rainy conditions this mushroom can take on several times its weight in water. Although the body of the mushroom may be in fair condition with deep golden color, the mushroom itself is likely to taste weak. Mushrooms that have absorbed a lot of water will appear large, weigh heavily, and are best avoided.

Wild mushrooms should never be washed under water to remove the dirt or leaves clinging to them, or they will become soggy and diluted in flavor. Handling them gently, brush the caps and stems with a small vegetable brush or towel. If there are any particularly soiled spots, implanted dirt, leaves, sand, or pine needles, cut or scrape them away with a knife. If you need to store wild mushrooms before cooking, do not clean them. Place them in a brown paper bag or a cardboard box with a top and store in a cool cellar or in the refrigerator.

Generally speaking, it is rare to find more than two of the wild varieties in the market. It is only occasionally, even in the restaurant, that we offer more than two or three varieties in the course of a meal. The limited, unpredictable, and climate-contingent availability of wild mushrooms has led us to better appreciation and use of each variety.

Boletus edulis, which the Italians call *porcini* (meaning "little pigs" in reference to their fat stems and stout caps) and the French call *cèpes*, are known locally as boletes (this term actually can include several different members of the family of *Boletus*, of which there are at least five other edibles) and set themselves apart from the more fragile varieties of wild mushrooms. A bolete, picked young, at its prime, is very firm and solid all the way through, with tight white pores under the cap. Boletes in this condition are ideal for eating raw, although only in small quantities, as some people are not able to digest raw mushrooms very well.

The appearance of young boletes often corresponds with the arrival of white truffles from Italy. We make a salad in the restaurant that consists of paper-thin slices of raw boletes, hearts of fennel, shavings of Parmesan, and white truffle dressed with olive oil, lemon juice, salt and pepper (see page 107). This is one of the most harmonious combinations I know of and beautiful to look at as well.

Boletes are never better than when cooked at the hearth on a grill over wood embers or below a turning spit where their flavor is enhanced by the smoke of a wood fire. For grilling there are several options: Cut the mushrooms lengthwise into thick slices about ⅜ inch thick, brush them with olive oil, and salt and pepper them lightly on both sides. Grill to a golden brown, sprinkle with a mixture of finely chopped parsley and garlic, and serve while still warm with a flask of your best olive oil on the table. If the cap is particularly large and extends far beyond the stem on either side, cut the cap at the top of the stem so that it rests flat. Season and grill the cap as is, or make deep little slits and stud the cap with very thin slices of garlic. Grill it slowly on both sides. Cut and grill the stem as mentioned above. Although grilling is the preferred method of cooking boletes at the restaurant, they can be sautéed, baked, or cooked as a moist little stew in a parchment package (see page 124). If you decide to sauté the mushrooms, do so over a gentle heat and take care not to brown the cut surfaces of the mushrooms. Remove them from the heat before the juices they release entirely evaporate.

Most wild mushrooms give off a quantity of water when cooked. With few exceptions, such as morels and a freak late-summer crop of rock-hard chanterelles from our north coast, most mushrooms never require additional moisture to cook properly. Chanterelles, horns of plenty, hedgehog, and shaggy parasols are delicious cooked in their own juices. Slice the mushrooms and add them to melted butter or olive oil in a sauté pan and lightly salt and pepper them. Rather than pouring off the liquid they release (which can be considerable, particularly in the wet season), allow it to reduce around the mushrooms until there is none left in the pan. During this time it is not necessary to stir the mushrooms, which causes the more fragile varieties to break into pieces. At this point the mushrooms are cooked enough. This depends on the variety—some may require a further drying-out period or browning in the pan to improve their texture and concentrate their flavor. During this final cooking add any other seasonings to the mushrooms, such as garlic and diced shallots, lemon juice or vinegar, and finally, just before service, chopped fresh herbs. Chanterelles develop a nutty flavor if allowed to brown slowly in the pan. Hedgehog mushrooms, on the other hand, are delicate and perhaps best served after the released moisture has evaporated and has been reabsorbed. Horns of plenty do not respond well to browning; because of their jet-black color it is virtually impossible to gauge their progress and they take on an unpleasant aroma when overcooked. Browning accentuates the already quite strong flavor of shaggy parasols; the cooking should be stopped before they take on color.

There are numerous uses for wild mushrooms in a menu. The three most common winter mushrooms, chanterelles, hedgehogs, and horns of plenty, by themselves or in combination with one another, are often served in the restaurant sautéed or baked with bread crumbs, herbs, and garlic beside roasted meats and poultry. They make a savory stuffing for pasta, both ravioli and lasagna, or can serve as the basis for risotti, *veloutés*, or as a garnish for consommé. Wild mushrooms are delicious sautéed, finished with a little cream and served on toast; or tossed in olive oil and vinegar or lemon juice and presented as an appetizer; or as an addition to warm salad.

Several types of wild mushrooms are available dried. Boletes and morels are the most common varieties and are best suited to this process. Dried mushrooms are used in infusions to impart their character to soups, sauces, and broth. Once the mushrooms have given up their flavor to the surrounding liquid, they are spent and should be removed unless their presence would go unnoticed (in a dense meat sauce, for instance). Dried mushrooms are a good pantry staple and can be used to boost a broth that is thin or pale, give added support to meat-based pasta sauces, and add depth to braises.

Cèpes Baked in Parchment

The best way I know to capture the flavors and juices of meat, fish, fowl, and vegetables is to cook them in parchment. Parchment cooking happens very quickly as the package is placed directly on the oven hearth or on a preheated baking pan. This direct heat and the steam trapped inside the envelope penetrate the food rapidly. Because the package is sealed, none of the aroma or moisture escapes, and the food inside bakes in its own juices.

Fresh cèpes (*Boletus edulis*) are the most succulent of all the wild mushrooms. To find them soon after they have fruited, in firm condition and uninfested by worms, is a cause for celebration. Their long-lingering nutty flavor and fine meaty texture are enough to suggest a meal in itself. One of the most delicious ways to cook them is to grill thick slices of them over an oak fire and serve them simply, with salt, pepper, and a flask of fruity olive oil on the table. This recipe was developed as an accompaniment to spit-roasted chicken. Since the mushrooms are sliced very thin, they release more of their juices and create a little stew inside the parchment package.

3 fresh cèpes (8 ounces)
2 tablespoons unsalted butter
1 shallot (1 ounce), minced
2 ounces pancetta, very thinly sliced, cut into ½-inch pieces
¼ cup water
1 clove garlic, finely minced
Scant teaspoon of lemon juice
¼ teaspoon salt
⅛ teaspoon freshly ground pepper
2 teaspoons extra virgin olive oil
¼ teaspoon chopped fresh thyme
4 sheets of baking parchment paper 16 inches long by 12 inches wide

With a small brush or towel, remove any dirt from the caps and stems and cut away the pine needles if any are imbedded in the base of the mushrooms. Slice the cèpes as thin as possible lengthwise (a mandoline is a very useful tool) and place them in a bowl. Melt the butter in a small pan, add the shallot, and cook for 1 minute. Add the pancetta and water and cook over medium heat for 2 minutes. Remove from the heat and add the garlic and lemon juice.

Season the mushrooms with the salt, pepper, and olive oil. Pour the butter-pancetta-garlic sauce over the cèpes and mix gently with your hands. Preheat the oven to 500°F.

To make the packages: Fold each sheet of parchment paper in half lengthwise. Open one sheet out and place one quarter of the mushroom mixture in the middle of half of the sheet. Close the other half of paper over the mushrooms and turn the folded edge toward you. Beginning in either corner make tightly creased, overlapping folds to form a well-sealed half circle. The folds should end 1 to 1½ inches from the mixture inside so that the steam can expand and the package will puff nicely. When you reach the last fold complete the package by twisting the corner. Make packages with the remaining mushrooms in the same manner.

Ten minutes before cooking the mushrooms, place a baking pan large enough to hold the packages in the oven. Put the packages directly on the hot pan and check them after 3 minutes. The mushrooms will cook in 3 to 5 minutes. The parchment will have puffed up and browned nicely. Transfer the packages to individual plates and rush them to the dining room before they deflate.

Chanterelle Custard

For 4

This rich custard enhances the flavors of unsauced roast chicken or grilled paillards of veal. Although the recipe calls for chanterelles, any wild mushroom or combination of mushrooms may be used. The mushrooms should be well seasoned and as dry as possible so that their moisture will not interfere with the balance of the egg and cream in the custard. See introduction to Wild Mushrooms, page 119.

For the mushroom sauté:
2 tablespoons unsalted butter
3½ cups chanterelles (8 ounces), thinly sliced
Salt and pepper
1 shallot (1 ounce), minced
1 small clove garlic, minced
½ teaspoon chopped fresh thyme leaves

Melt the butter in a 10-inch sauté pan, add the chanterelles, and season with salt and pepper. Cook the mushrooms at a simmer until the released juices are reduced and evaporated. Add the shallot, garlic, and thyme and continue to sauté the mushrooms for 5 minutes. Remove the pan from the heat and transfer the mushroom mixture to a plate to cool.

For the custard:
1 whole egg and 1 egg yolk
1 cup heavy cream
⅛ teaspoon salt
Pinch black pepper
Pinch freshly grated nutmeg
Butter for ramekins

Preheat the oven to 350°F.

Whisk together the eggs and the cream with the salt, pepper, and nutmeg until just mixed. Add the mushrooms and stir well.

Butter 4 ramekins and evenly divide the custard mixture among them. Place the ramekins in a baking dish. Pour hot water into the baking dish to reach halfway up the ramekins. Place the dish in the oven and bake for 35 minutes, or until the custards are firm in the center and brown on top.

Remove the custards from the oven, take them out of the water bath, and let cool at room temperature for 10 minutes. Run a knife around the inside edge of the ramekins, jiggle each ramekin from side to side, invert onto one hand, and carefully remove the custard. Set each custard, browned side up, on a warm dinner plate.

Morels Baked with Bread Crumbs, Garlic, and Parsley

For 4

The morel is a distinctively shaped wild mushroom that grows abundantly in the Pacific Northwest and is harvested in the spring. The gray-brown or beige-colored heads are roughly conical, chambered, and marked by wrinkled ridges. Morels contain less water than other varieties of wild mushrooms and therefore require liquid when cooked. Morels are superb in combination with meat or poultry juices or added to a sauce; their sturdy texture absorbs flavors without entirely surrendering their own. In this recipe morels are stewed briefly with shallot, garlic, and a little water to encourage the release of their juices, then are mixed with herbs and bread crumbs and put into a baking dish. Baking concentrates the morels' flavor. Serve the mushrooms with veal or beef roasts.

3/4 cup fresh sourdough bread crumbs
3½ tablespoons unsalted butter
1 shallot (1 ounce), finely diced
8 ounces morels, large ones cut in half
3 cloves garlic, finely diced
Salt and pepper
3 tablespoons water, or meat or poultry juices
½ tablespoon chopped fresh parsley
1 teaspoon chopped fresh thyme

Preheat the oven to 350°F.

Put the bread crumbs in a bowl. Melt 1½ tablespoons of the butter, pour it over the bread crumbs, and toss until the crumbs are well coated.

Melt the remaining butter in a sauté pan, add the shallot, morels, and garlic. Salt and pepper the mushrooms lightly, add the water to the pan, bring to a simmer, cover, and cook gently for 6 minutes. Remove the cover. The mushrooms will have released their juices. Stir in the herbs. Pour the mixture into a small baking dish just large enough to contain the mushrooms in an even layer. Cover with the bread crumbs and bake for 30 to 40 minutes, or until the crumbs are well browned. Serve immediately.

Bread and Onion Soup with Red Wine

For 6

Bread soups are a seasonal reminder on the menus at Chez Panisse, an indication that summer with its lighter fare has passed. Here is a substantial, cold-weather soup that is most satisfying when eaten in the winter months. Perhaps it is the deep color and the savory sweetness the onions and wine confer on the broth, or the cooking process itself—at first, a slow softening and caramelization of the onions, later a gentle simmer—that makes the soup so appropriate in a darker, more austere season.

The recipe that follows is a basic model for a number of variations, which differ in small details: the choice of cooking fat, the method of caramelizing the onions, the addition of other ingredients. The use of butter, olive oil, and animal fats, such as rendered duck fat or foie gras, will noticeably affect the flavors of this soup. The most richly flavored version is one made with onions (wine omitted) fried crisp in rendered duck fat and layered with toasted bread and slices of butternut squash. You may wish to experiment with different fats for different variations.

The wine and even the broth can be substituted with water in this recipe, particularly if you have fresh onions and flavorful bread. But I much prefer the soup if it is made with poultry or meat broth. Either way, it is a sturdy counterpart to muscular wines, both red and white.

5 tablespoons olive oil
3 pounds yellow onions, thinly sliced
½ teaspoon salt
¼ teaspoon dry thyme
5 slices levain bread (8 ounces), or other sturdy sourdough bread (see page 218 for a
*   description of levain bread)*
1 cup fruity red wine
4 cups beef broth (see page 427)
Freshly ground black pepper
1 clove garlic
3 tablespoons freshly grated Parmesan cheese

Preheat the oven to 375°F.

Warm 3 tablespoons of the olive oil in a heavy-bottomed casserole or crockery pot large enough to contain the sliced onions. Add the onions, salt, and thyme and stir well to coat the onions with the oil. Adjust the heat to low so that the onions sizzle gently. Cook them slowly for 1 hour, stirring occasionally.

In the meantime, brush the bread slices with the remaining 2 tablespoons olive oil, lay them on a baking tray, and bake in the oven for 20 minutes, or until they are dried out and lightly toasted.

By now, the onions will have reduced in volume considerably, softened, and browned lightly. Add the wine and scrape up any brown bits on the bottom or sides of the pan. Stir in the beef broth and pepper the mixture liberally.

Rub the bread slices with the garlic clove. Break up the bread and lay half of it into a baking dish (8 by 10 by 2 inches) and cover the bread with a thick layer of onions, removed with a slotted spoon. Set 3 cups of the onion broth aside. Ladle about ½ of the remaining onion broth over the bread slices and sprinkle 1 tablespoon of the Parmesan cheese over the layer. Form another layer using the remaining bread, onions, broth, and cheese. Bake in the oven for about 1 hour, until the broth has nearly all been absorbed and the cheese on top has formed a gratin. Divide the soup among six wide warmed bowls, keeping the crusty surface intact. Heat the reserved onion broth, pour about ½ cup around each serving and serve.

Sugar Snap Peas with Brown Butter and Sage

For 4

Very fresh sugar snap peas are firm and refreshingly sweet. The whole pod is edible and need not be shucked for the peas alone. This very simple recipe takes minutes to prepare. The flavor of sage and peas is a natural combination. The sage leaves aromatize the butter, which is allowed to brown as the peas quickly sauté. Do not overcook the peas. Sauté them until they surrender their fresh, watery crispness but are still crunchy. Serve with roast chicken, veal, or grilled fish.

2 tablespoons unsalted butter
16 sage leaves
8 ounces sugar snap peas, strings removed
Salt and pepper

Melt the butter in a sauté pan. Add the sage leaves and raise the heat. When the butter begins to brown, toss in the snap peas, add salt and pepper to taste, and sauté them over brisk (high) heat for about 3 minutes, stirring and turning them all the while.

Pimiento Soup with Fried Polenta

For 8

Fresh pimientos are relatively uncommon in the market because most are grown for the purpose of canning. The common variety of pimientos is distinguishable from other peppers in that it is red skinned (the flesh itself is crimson), has a thicker flesh, and a heart-shaped form that tapers to a point away from the stem. Fully ripe pimientos are very sweet and slightly piquant. Although not generally hot, they retain some of the spicy flavor characteristics of hot chiles. Choose peppers that are bright red, firm, slightly fragrant, and have smooth, unwrinkled skin.

Pimientos make a smooth-textured, rich, aromatic soup which harmonizes well with the flavor of corn. Grilling the pimientos will greatly enhance the soup. Stewing them produces a more refined result, with a singular flavor but one that is less interesting.

Polenta, cooked until thick, cooled, then cut into sticks and deep-fried until crisp, garnishes this soup. Use only coarse cornmeal, identifiable as "polenta" in specialty food shops or Italian delicatessens. Generally, polenta requires twenty-five minutes to cook sufficiently. In this recipe, however, the cornmeal needs only to soften and form a stiff porridge, since it subsequently will be quickly deep-fried.

Prepare a charcoal fire to grill the pimientos. While it is burning down, make the polenta.

For the polenta:
3 cups water
¼ teaspoon salt
1 cup coarse cornmeal

Prepare the polenta: Lightly oil the sides and bottom of a 10- by 8-inch baking dish. It is preferable to use a deep, heavy-bottomed pot in which to make the polenta; it has a tendency to sputter and stick. In the pot, bring the water to a rolling boil over high heat, add the salt, and whisk in the cornmeal, little by little. Reduce the heat and let the cornmeal bubble gently. After 3 minutes it will thicken considerably. It is important to stir at this point so that the polenta does not stick. Continue to cook the mixture for another 4 minutes, stirring often, until the consistency is stiff and somewhat dry. Immediately transfer the polenta to the oiled baking dish, smoothing it to cover the bottom of the dish in a thick, even layer. Let the polenta stand for 5 minutes, then cover the dish, and refrigerate for 1 hour, or until very firm.

For the soup:
2 pounds pimientos
3 tablespoons unsalted butter
2 yellow onions (12 ounces), diced
1 cup water
4 cups chicken broth (see page 426)
Salt and pepper
Balsamic vinegar

Prepare the soup: When the fire is very hot, rake it out and grill the pimientos whole, stems intact, until their skins blister and char very slightly. Turn them over and grill until evenly charred. Transfer the pimientos to a plastic bag or a container with a tight-fitting lid and let them steam for 20 minutes which makes it easier to skin them. Remove the pimientos and peel away as much of the charred skin as possible. Do not rinse the pimientos under water. Cut the pimientos in half and remove the seeds and stems.

Melt the butter in a 6-quart pot and cook the onions gently, without letting them brown, for 10 minutes. Add the pimientos and the water and stew the onions and pimientos together for 10 minutes, uncovered. Add the stock, bring to a boil, and reduce the heat. Simmer for 20 minutes.

While the soup is cooking, prepare the garnish: Remove the polenta from the refrigerator. Invert the baking dish onto a cutting board and cut the polenta into short sticks approximately ½ inch wide and 2 inches long. Heat 3 cups neutral-flavored oil, such as peanut or vegetable oil, in a 10-inch cast-iron skillet until it sizzles when you dip a piece of polenta into it. Carefully add the polenta sticks to the hot oil and deep-fry them, adjusting the heat to maintain an even temperature. The sticks will stick together. Do not stir or they will break apart. Let the sticks brown evenly on one side, then, with a pair of tongs, carefully turn the mass over to brown on the other side. When the polenta has turned a rich brown all over, remove it from the oil and let it drain on a towel-lined plate. Let cool slightly, then separate the sticks.

Transfer the soup in batches to a blender and purée each batch for 2 minutes. Pass the puréed soup through a medium-fine sieve into another pot. If the soup appears too thick, thin it with water so that it pours in a smooth stream and is not at all heavy. Season the soup to taste with salt, pepper, and a little balsamic vinegar. Serve the soup in warm bowls and garnish each bowl with several polenta sticks. Serve those that are left over in a separate bowl.

Potato and Black Truffle Croquettes

Large Russet potatoes, boiled, mashed coarse, and bound with egg yolk, make a light, fluffy mixture for frying. The classic method of combining mashed potatoes with cream puff dough (*pâte à chou*) is not necessary. This mixture, with fewer ingredients, has a texture and flavor that is more plainly potatolike. The croquettes are an excellent vehicle for the aroma of the black truffle, which is sealed inside the fried golden crust.

After boiling the potatoes, do not rinse them to cool them off. Allow them to drain in a colander and to dry out in the steam they release. For a varied texture, break the potatoes up coarsely with a fork and keep the mashing to a minimum. Before the potatoes are entirely broken up, add the egg yolks, so that the mixing occurs at the same time. Do not overmix.

There are two options for coating the mixture, in bread crumbs or flour. Flour creates a more thorough seal, while bread crumbs make a crisper and more interesting crust.

Serve the croquettes with roasted or grilled meats.

3 quarts water
2¾ teaspoons salt
2 large Russet potatoes (1 pound, 4 ounces), peeled, cut into chunks
3 egg yolks
1 black truffle (about 1 ounce), pounded to a coarse paste in a mortar
Freshly ground pepper
1½ cups fresh bread crumbs
Vegetable or neutral-flavored peanut oil for frying

Bring the water and 2 teaspoons of the salt to a boil. Add the potatoes and boil them for 15 minutes, or until fork-tender. Drain the potatoes in a colander and allow them to cool and dry out. Transfer the potatoes to a bowl and with a fork break them up roughly, without mashing. Add the remaining ¾ teaspoon salt, the egg yolks, black truffle, and a little freshly ground pepper. Stir the mixture briefly to combine and to further break up the potatoes. Taste the mixture for salt and correct it if necessary to your taste.

Spread half of the bread crumbs in a thick layer about 8 inches long on a wide counter, chopping block, or kitchen table. Spoon all of the potatoes on top of the bread crumbs in a rough log form. Sprinkle the remaining bread crumbs on top of the potatoes, so that when you begin to form the croquettes they won't stick to your hands. Compact the mixture slightly on all sides. Roll it out, like cookie dough, with a back-and-forth motion as you move your hands out from the center until you have formed a long cylinder about 1 inch thick. (You may wish to divide the mixture in half and roll two separate times if space does not permit.) Cut the cylinder into 2-inch pieces and roll each piece individually to reduce its size slightly and make sure it is coated with crumbs. At this point the croquettes can be refrigerated until ready to deep-fry.

Put about 2 inches of oil in a 12-inch cast-iron pan and bring the temperature to 350°F. Gently place 12 croquettes in the pan, and cook 1 to 1½ minutes, until golden brown. Allow the oil to return to 350°F before cooking the next batch. Transfer to a large plate lined with paper towels and hold those already fried in a warm oven. Serve immediately.

Purée of New Potatoes and Green Garlic

For 6

The flavor of green garlic stands out very clearly in this simple purée, which goes well with saucy roasted beef, veal, or pork as well as braised lamb shanks or shoulders. The garlic is stewed with diced new potatoes, puréed, seasoned with a little white wine vinegar, and finished with cream. The purée may be made ahead and rewarmed, or held in a covered baking dish in the oven until you are ready to serve it. Made with less cream and mixed with grated Parmesan cheese, this purée also makes a fine stuffing for ravioli.

To prepare the garlic for stewing, cut away the roots and dark green leaves of each plant. Remove the outer skin. Cut the garlic at the point at which the stem begins to turn dark green, leaving only the white and pale green part.

4 tablespoons unsalted butter
8 to 10 new red potatoes, peeled (1 pound, 8 ounces), diced
24 green garlic plants, white to pale green part only (6 ounces), sliced
1 cup water
½ cup heavy cream
½ teaspoon salt
¼ teaspoon freshly ground pepper
1 teaspoon white wine vinegar

Melt the butter in a 3-quart noncorroding saucepan. Add the potatoes, garlic, and water. Bring to a simmer, cover, and cook slowly for 30 minutes, until the potatoes are very soft.

Pass the potatoes and garlic through the finest blade of a food mill into a pan. Warm the cream and stir it into the purée with the salt, pepper, and vinegar. Serve the purée while it is hot, or keep it warm in a covered baking dish in the oven.

Potatoes and Onions Roasted with Vinegar and Thyme

For 4

Although they are good next to just about any roasted or grilled meat and poultry, I like to serve these potatoes and onions with braised dishes. The potatoes are half peeled, leaving a spiraling band of skin attached. This not only makes them look appealing, but allows the vinegar to penetrate them during their slow roast. If they are to brown evenly, it is important to turn the potatoes and onions (about every thirty minutes, and more frequently during the last half hour) to coat them with the vinegar and butter.

8 white (the size of a golf ball) boiling onions (9 ounces)
12 small (the size of a golf ball) red potatoes (1 pound)
2 tablespoons unsalted butter
3 tablespoons balsamic vinegar
½ teaspoon salt
Freshly ground pepper
6 sprigs thyme

Preheat the oven to 350°F.

Peel the onions. Starting at the top of each potato, pare away a ¼-inch-thick band of the skin, leaving half of it in place. Put the onions and potatoes in a baking dish just large enough to hold them. Melt the butter and pour it and the vinegar over the potatoes and onions. Add salt and pepper and mix until they are coated. Bury the thyme sprigs in the vegetables and cover the dish with foil. Bake in the oven for 2 hours, stirring the vegetables each half hour to recoat them. Be sure to cover them after stirring. When done, the onions and potatoes should be a deep brown color.

Potatoes Cooked in the Coals

For 4

This is one of my favorite ways to cook new potatoes. Enclose them in heavy aluminum foil with a thick slice of bacon, garlic cloves, a little thyme and a bay leaf, some butter or olive oil, and set them on hot embers in a corner of the fireplace. If the embers are glaringly hot, cover them with a layer of ash about ¼ inch thick. This keeps the potatoes from blackening on the bottom. (This package is also a fine way of trapping the aroma of the black truffle, which potatoes particularly enjoy.) A little water added to the package prevents the bottom from burning and creates steam, which helps the potatoes cook.

There is a certain comforting pleasure in cooking one's food on the open hearth. Sealed as they are against any smoke penetration, the potatoes are blind to the source of heat and cook simply, as they would if placed on the floor of the oven. Yet the presentation of the package, sealed like a Christmas gift and dusted with ash, never fails to elicit surprise and delight when it is opened at the table and its aromas escape in a glorious ascension of steam.

1 pound small new potatoes (about 1 inch in diameter), skins left on, or larger potatoes, cut 1 inch thick
4 cloves garlic, sliced
2 tablespoons unsalted butter, melted
Salt and pepper
¼ cup water
4 to 5 leafy sprigs thyme
1 bay leaf
2-ounce slice of lean slab bacon, rind left on

Toss the potatoes and garlic in a bowl in the butter, and salt and pepper them generously. Cut two pieces of heavy aluminum foil about 20 inches long and 12 inches wide. Set one on top of the other, forming a double thickness, and pour the potatoes and garlic in the middle of the foil. Press the edges of the foil up around the potatoes and pour the water over them. Place the thyme sprigs, bay leaf, and bacon on top and seal the package tightly.

Set the foil package on a bed of coals in the fireplace. If the coals are searing hot, cover them as described above. The potatoes should take about 40 to 50 minutes to cook. During this time, check them. If you hear a violent sputtering, the fire is too hot. Cover the bed with more ash to insulate the package from the direct heat. Since you will not be able to test the potatoes you will have to rely upon your ears and nose to tell you that they are done. Listen for a gentle sizzling sound, and if it is accompanied by the aroma of baked potatoes mingled with bacon and thyme, the package is ready to serve. Alternatively, the potatoes may be cooked directly on the floor of a preheated 350°F oven, in which case they will be ready in 45 minutes.

Set the package on a platter and open it at the table. Let the potatoes cool slightly, turn them over gently with a spoon to coat them with the juices in the bottom of the package, and serve them with a small piece of bacon and some of the garlic slices.

Straw Potato Cake

For 6

Straw potato cake is a frequent accompaniment to meat, fish, and fowl on the nightly menus at Chez Panisse. With the more unusual offerings at the restaurant, or with foods the public is generally predisposed to dislike—variety meats, for instance—the reassuring, familiar presence of these potatoes works a kind of magic, dissolving bias, providing encouragement.

Straw potatoes are best cut on the mandoline to resemble straw. The strips are packed into a seasoned sauté or omelet pan and cooked on both sides to form a well-browned, tangled surface. The interior of the cake is soft and yielding; depending on the condition of the potato the texture can be almost creamy. It is the combination of a browned, crisp surface with a tender layer beneath that makes these potatoes so appealing.

Straw potatoes can carry a variety of flavors in a sauce, as a complement to certain foods, such as sautéed wild mushrooms or grilled quail, or as an element of contrast in a composed salad. Or the cake can be the entire focus of a dish. One of the most special appetizers served in the restaurant is an individual straw potato cake garnished with caviar, crème fraîche, and a scattering of chives.

Large Russet potatoes are perfect for this dish. It is the quality of the starch in this larger, more-developed potato that accounts for the crisp caramelized surface and for the potatoes locking together in a solid mass. A mandoline with the julienne blade in place is the most effective tool for cutting the potatoes. If you do not own a mandoline, cut the potatoes by hand. First peel them, cut them lengthwise into thin slices about ⅛ inch thick, stack a few slices at a time, and cut them into strips about ⅛ inch wide. Do not shred the potatoes on a box grater, in a food processor, or with a hand-held rotary grater. Shredded potatoes produce a cake that is much more compact and less sharply defined in texture.

It is critical that the cut potatoes be thoroughly rinsed in several changes of cold water to remove excess starch, which gives them a sticky, glutinous texture. Following the rinsing, the potatoes should be dried thoroughly in a lettuce spinner or in towels. Wet potatoes will not brown but steam in the pan. It is also important that you choose the right pan. For best results use a 10-inch steel sauté pan or well-seasoned steel omelet pan. It is hard to heat pans larger than 10 inches evenly on the small burners of a home stove.

Straw potatoes are delicious with the addition of rosemary or thyme or sliced chives or green onions, which can be sprinkled over the potatoes as you pack the pan. Wild mushrooms, cooked until dry and nearly crisp, or browned shallots or onions can be sandwiched between the potato layers and make another good accompaniment to roasts.

2 large Russet potatoes (1 pound, 4 ounces)
3½ tablespoons clarified butter
½ teaspoon salt
Freshly ground pepper

Peel the potatoes and cut them lengthwise into ⅛-inch julienne strips by hand or on a mandoline. Put the cut potatoes in a large bowl and pour about 2 quarts cold water over them. Stir the potatoes with your hands. The water will appear milky. Drain the potatoes into a colander. Rinse the bowl of any starch in the bottom and repeat the process of rinsing, stirring, and pouring off the water three more times, or until the water around the potatoes is absolutely clear. Drain the potatoes and dry them in a lettuce spinner or roll them up in towels until they are very dry.

Preheat an omelet or sauté pan over low heat for several minutes. Add 2½ tablespoons of the clarified butter, raise the heat slightly, and warm the pan until a piece of potato sizzles when put in touch with the butter. Spread half the potatoes over the bottom of the pan in an even layer. Sprinkle the potatoes with ¼ teaspoon of the salt and grind fresh pepper over them. Spread the remaining potatoes over the first layer and season with the remaining salt and pepper. The pan will appear very full. Don't worry, the potatoes will settle into the pan as they cook. With the flat lid of a pan roughly the same size as the bottom of the pan, press down on the cake lightly so that the potatoes are in even contact with the bottom of the pan. Cook the cake over medium heat—you should hear a gentle sizzling and steaming sound—for 10 to 12 minutes. Several times during this period agitate the cake: Hold the handle of the pan and make a sideways jerking motion in one direction. This assures that the cake will cook evenly, as there are often cool spots in the pan. Also make sure that the pan is centered over the flame.

The cake is ready to turn when the edges are browned and the aroma is nutty. Move the pan back and forth. The potatoes on the bottom should appear as a solid mass. If you are uncertain that the cake is browned, lift a corner with a spoon or spatula. It should reveal a deep mahogany color. To flip the cake, place a flat lid over the pan and invert the pan. Carefully slide the cake back into the pan. Drizzle the remaining 1 tablespoon clarified butter around the edge of the cake and tilt the pan up and back so that the butter is distributed over the bottom of the pan. With a spoon, turn the ragged edges under so that the cake is a tidy, rounded shape. Cook the cake for 10 to 12 minutes on the second side. When well browned, slide the cake onto a cutting board and slice it into six portions. Serve immediately.

Spinach Soup

This is one of the simplest and most economical soups I know of, and it takes very little time to make. The preparation has been designed to maintain the intense green color and fresh flavor of spinach. Curly Bloomsdale spinach produces a soup with a meaty flavor, not undesirable, but not as clean a flavor as the flat-leaf varieties. Garnish the soup with Garlic Butter or swirls of crème fraîche thinned to the consistency of the soup and chopped nasturtium petals. The soup is perhaps most appealing with grated Parmesan, small buttered garlic croutons, and extra virgin olive oil drizzled over the surface. Puréed spinach will turn a dull army green color within twenty minutes, so this soup should be blended, seasoned, and served immediately.

4 tablespoons unsalted butter
5 ¼ cups water
1 large carrot (4 ounces), diced
1 stalk of celery (2 ½ ounces), diced
1 medium yellow onion (6 ounces), diced
3 bunches of spinach (1 pound, 2 ounces), de-stemmed, washed, and drained
Salt and pepper

Melt the butter in a wide stainless-steel pot (at least 5-quart capacity). Add ¾ cup water and the carrot, celery, and onion. Cook at a low simmer, covered, for 20 minutes.

Add the remaining 4 ½ cups water and bring to a boil. Add the spinach and cook over high heat for 1 minute, stirring until all of the spinach is well wilted. Do not cover the pot: Volatile acids, which are released when the vegetable is heated, will condense on the lid, fall back into the pot, and cause discoloration. Purée the entire mixture thoroughly in a blender, do not sieve, and transfer the soup immediately to a hot tureen. Season with salt and pepper to taste, garnish as desired, and serve immediately.

Grilled Tomato Croutons with Red Onion Vinaigrette, Anchovies, and Fresh Basil

4 large croutons

This dish is a celebration of the tomato and should be attempted only at the peak of the season in the summer, when tomatoes are sweet, full of flavor, and not at all watery.

An extravagant variation of this simple dish eliminates the anchovies but adds sliced lobster meat, first tossed in a little of the vinaigrette, then piled on top of the tomatoes.

For the vinaigrette:
½ small sweet red onion (2½ ounces), minced
2 small cloves garlic, minced
Large pinch salt
Pinch pepper
2 tablespoons fruity red wine vinegar
3 tablespoons extra virgin olive oil
16 fresh basil leaves

8 medium tomatoes
Salt and pepper
4 large slices of sourdough bread, each ⅓ inch thick
Olive oil
1 large clove garlic, peeled
12 salt-packed anchovy filets, soaked in several changes of cold water for 15 minutes, drained, patted dry, drizzled with olive oil

Prepare a charcoal or wood fire.

Prepare the vinaigrette: Combine the onion, garlic, salt, pepper, and vinegar. Let stand for 10 minutes. Stir in the olive oil. Mince half the basil coarse and add it to the vinaigrette.

Core the tomatoes and cut them crosswise into slices 1 inch thick. Lightly salt and pepper both sides. Brush the sourdough slices with olive oil.

When the fire has burned down to moderately hot, grill the tomatoes on one side only. Do not turn them: they will be soft and difficult to handle. Allow them to cook until they begin to bubble slightly and are soft to the touch throughout. While the tomatoes are cooking, grill the bread to a golden brown on both sides. Rub the bread with the peeled garlic and arrange two grilled tomatoes on each slice. With a knife, break up the tomatoes on the bread and spread them out to cover the crouton. Arrange the anchovies, three per crouton, over the tomatoes and spoon the vinaigrette on top. Mince the remaining basil. Sprinkle it liberally over the croutons and serve immediately while the croutons are still warm.

Tomato, Green Garlic, and Herb Soup

For 4

Make this simple and comforting soup with ripe tomatoes, green garlic, and whatever herbs are in the garden—basil is delicious, as is oregano, parsley, or thyme. Besides being served as a soup, the broth is excellent for poaching fish (substitute water or fish broth) such as halibut, salmon, or cod. Serve the fish in a bowl with some of the tomato and garlic broth around it, a slice of lime, and chopped basil or coriander leaves—it makes a light and clean-tasting course.

Serve the soup with slices of sourdough bread that have been buttered and sprinkled with Parmesan and baked.

15 green garlic plants (12 ounces)
2 tablespoons extra virgin olive oil
Salt and pepper
1 cup water
4 ripe tomatoes (1 pound, 4 ounces), peeled, seeded, diced, juice strained and reserved
3 cups chicken broth (see page 426)
Red wine vinegar
2 tablespoons chopped fresh parsley, oregano, or thyme

Trim away the roots of the garlic plants and cut the shoot where it begins to open out into dark green leaves. Remove one layer of the outer skin of the shoot. Slice the garlic in half lengthwise, then cut it into small pieces.

Combine the garlic and olive oil in a 3-quart noncorroding saucepan. Salt and pepper it, pour over the water, and bring to a simmer. Cover the pan and cook for 20 minutes. Add the tomatoes and broth, bring to a simmer, and cook for 10 minutes. Season the soup to your liking with salt, pepper, and a teaspoon or more of red wine vinegar. Stir in the herb of choice and serve.

Ratatouille

Ratatouille can be considered a sauté, rather than a vegetable stew. It is, in fact, much improved by this method of cooking as each vegetable contributes not only its own flavor, but its own distinct texture, resulting in a more lively, less uniform combination. Onions, peppers, and squash are separately sautéed until each is thoroughly browned. Eggplant, because it tends to absorb too much oil, is baked. The vegetables are then combined with raw tomatoes and cooked for a short time to let the juices mingle. The whole is then cooled and seasoned with herbs, capers, olives, and extra virgin olive oil. The process is really only a series of simple steps, and the only equipment needed is a wide 5-quart saucepot, a baking dish, and a bowl.

Ratatouille is best served cold, with grilled bread and anchovies, or as an accompaniment to grilled meats, particularly lamb and poultry. It is also wonderful warm in an omelet. If refrigerated, ratatouille will keep for several days and will actually improve in flavor.

Salt and pepper
4 Japanese eggplants (10 ounces), skin left on, sliced ¼ inch thick
½ cup pure olive oil
¼ cup water
1 large yellow onion (10 ounces), sliced
4 bell peppers (14 ounces), mixed colors, cut into ¼-inch strips
2 tablespoons fruity red wine vinegar
4 mixed green and yellow squashes (12 ounces), such as zucchini, crookneck, or scallopine, sliced crosswise ¼ inch thick
4 medium yellow and red tomatoes (1 pound), peeled, seeded, diced, juice discarded
1 tablespoon capers, rinsed and drained
2 tablespoons pitted green or Niçoise olives, chopped
2 tablespoons chopped fresh Italian parsley
1 tablespoon chopped fresh basil
2 cloves garlic, minced
Extra virgin olive oil

Preheat the oven to 400°F.

Salt and pepper the eggplant lightly and toss in a bowl with 3 tablespoons of the olive oil. Transfer to a baking dish just large enough to contain it and add the water. Cover and bake for about 40 minutes, or until soft to the touch.

While the eggplant is cooking, sauté the sliced onion in a large saucepot in 3 tablespoons of the remaining olive oil until it softens and begins to brown lightly. Add the peppers, season with salt and pepper, and cook over high heat, stirring often until the peppers are cooked through and both the onions and peppers are well browned. Add the vinegar and cook 1 minute. Transfer the mixture to a bowl. Add the remaining 2 tablespoons olive oil to the saucepot and in it sauté the squashes. Turn them carefully so that both sides are a dark brown, then put them in the bowl with the onions and peppers.

Remove the eggplant from the oven and combine it with the other vegetables. Discard any liquid left in the baking dish. Put all of the vegetables back in the saucepot and add the tomatoes. At this point the vegetables should not be stirred any more than is necessary or they will break up and spoil the presentation. Bring to a simmer and cook over medium-high heat for 2 minutes. Ratatouille should not be swimming in its own juice. If the vegetables appear too juicy, pour the excess liquid into a sauté pan and reduce it until it thickens. Then pour it back over the vegetables. Remove the pot from the heat and let the ratatouille cool. Then add the capers, chopped olives, parsley, basil, and garlic. Correct the seasoning, if necessary, with more red wine vinegar, salt, and pepper. Before serving, drizzle a little extra virgin olive oil over each portion.

Grilled Late-Season Tomato Soup with Bacon, Garlic, and Croutons

For 6

This is not a light summer soup, but a hearty stew of ripe tomatoes with flavors that are suggestive of winter. The soup is made with the last tomatoes of the season—those that have benefited from the hot August sun and infrequent watering—fruit that is deep-colored and sweet and rich in flavor. Choose tomato varieties such as beefsteak that are meaty and full of juice. Sauce or stuffing varieties will not give off enough liquid. If you grow your own tomatoes, resist the temptation to water the plants or pull them out of the ground if they still have fruit. Even though the vines appear wilted and discolored, allow the fruit to ripen to its fullest, then make this soup.

8 large tomatoes (2½ pounds)
2 leeks (7 ounces), diced
1 medium yellow onion (8 ounces), diced
6 cloves garlic, sliced
2 tablespoons olive oil
2¼ cups flavorful chicken broth (see page 426), heated
2 ounces thinly sliced smoked bacon
½ cup dry red wine
⅛ teaspoon ground cayenne
½ teaspoon red wine vinegar
¼ teaspoon salt
6 slices of sourdough bread, each cut ½ inch thick, brushed with olive oil
1 whole clove garlic, peeled

Prepare a wood or charcoal fire.

Grill the tomatoes whole, without coring them, over a moderately hot wood fire. Allow them to take as much smoke as possible and let their skins get fairly dark. The tomatoes should feel soft all over. Provided the skin remains intact, they will begin to bubble and release little puffs of steam, an indication that heat has penetrated to the center. Carefully transfer the tomatoes to a platter and let them cool.

While the tomatoes are grilling, in a soup pot sweat the leeks, onion, and garlic in the olive oil, covered, until they release their juices and begin to soften. Remove the lid, raise the heat, and let brown. Pour the hot chicken broth over the vegetables, heat to just under the boiling point, and turn off the heat. Cover the pot.

Over a bowl, remove the cores and as much of the skin as possible from the tomatoes. Break the tomatoes up into rough pieces by hand and let the juice and pulp fall into the bowl. Add the tomatoes and their juice to the pot. Slice the bacon crosswise into small pieces. In a small pan, simmer the bacon and red wine together for 5 minutes, then add to the soup. Add the cayenne, vinegar, and salt, and turn the heat on very low.

While the soup is warming, grill the bread over the wood fire until it is nicely browned on both sides. Rub the bread on one side with the garlic clove. Put one slice of the bread in each warm bowl and ladle the hot soup over it. Serve immediately.

Chilled Red and Yellow Tomato Soups with Peppers, Cucumbers, Onions, and Basil

For 6

This double soup is beautiful to look at, brilliant in color, and evocative of summer. The red tomato soup and the yellow tomato soup are presented side by side in the same bowl, and the flavor, acidity, and colors of each tomato remain distinct.

Chilled soups are meant to be refreshing and should be served by themselves on hot days. Similarly, they can be thought of as relief between two heavier hot courses, in which case weather is not important. In making these soups be careful when extracting the juice from the tomatoes. Never use a blender or food processor to purée the tomatoes—when the juice and pulp are agitated and become aerated, a stiff, pale foam forms, which will not go away unless heated, and then the soup will be ruined.

Make this soup only in summer. Choose tomatoes that are very ripe, sweet, and full of juice; those that are almost bursting out of their skins are best. Unripe, out-of-season tomatoes make a soup that is flavorless, overly acidic, or bland.

12 very ripe red tomatoes (2½ pounds)
12 very ripe yellow tomatoes (2½ pounds)
⅓ of an English cucumber (2½ ounces), peeled, cut into ⅛-inch dice
1 small red onion (4 ounces), root end removed, cut into ⅛-inch dice
½ red bell pepper (2½ ounces), de-stemmed, seeded, cut into ⅛-inch dice
⅛ teaspoon ground cayenne
2 teaspoons balsamic vinegar
½ teaspoon salt
¼ teaspoon freshly ground pepper
2 tablespoons chopped fresh basil

Cut the red tomatoes, then the yellow tomatoes, into ½-inch dice and put into separate bowls. With your hands, squeeze the tomatoes to release as much juice as possible. Keeping the red and yellow tomatoes separate, pass the juice and pulp through a stainless-steel sieve into noncorroding containers. Push as much of the juice and pulp through as possible. A food mill fitted with a medium blade (one smaller than the seeds) should be used. Turn the mill slowly, exerting a downward pressure.

The consistency of the juiced tomatoes will vary, depending on the ripeness and variety of the tomatoes. Both soups should be slightly thicker than heavy cream and their consistencies, if too heavy, should be equalized with a little cold water. To keep the soups separate in the bowl, similar consistencies are critical.

Mix the diced cucumber, onion, and pepper together, divide the mixture in half, and add half to each soup. To *each* soup, add ¹⁄₁₆ teaspoon cayenne, 1 teaspoon balsamic vinegar, ¼ teaspoon salt, ⅛ teaspoon freshly ground pepper, and 1 tablespoon chopped fresh basil. Place each container of soup in another larger bowl, and pack ice around it. Pour water over the ice and refrigerate. At the same time, put six soup bowls in the refrigerator to chill. It is best to serve this soup at 40°F, 1½ to 2 hours after it has been made. (It is at this point that the diced vegetables give their flavor over to the soup and blend and harmonize with the tomatoes.)

Use two ladles, one in each hand, to serve the soup. Scoop up equal amounts of each soup (figure ½ cup per ladle) and simultaneously pour it into each half of each chilled bowl. The soups should meet in the middle.

Black Truffle Puddings

For 6, as a first or second course

The technique for making these puddings is almost identical to that of a soufflé. A somewhat stiffer white sauce is flavored with cheese, scented with black truffle, bound with egg yolks, and leavened with stiffly beaten egg whites. The airy mixture is cooked until firm all the way through. It is then removed from the oven, unmolded, allowed to sink, and baked in the oven a second time in a bath of cream to puff and form a gratin. The first cooking can be carried out well in advance; in a meal of several courses, this simplifies considerably the number of last-minute maneuvers, as the puddings need only to brown in the oven. If you have extra black truffle, slice it into the cream before you bake the puddings the second time.

This pudding can also be made with white truffle. Rather than adding more of it to the cream, slice the raw truffle directly over each serving at the table; in this way, its full perfume will be released.

2 tablespoons unsalted butter
1 cup milk
3 tablespoons all-purpose flour
1 black truffle (1 ounce)
⅔ cup grated Swiss Gruyère cheese
4 tablespoons finely grated fresh Parmesan cheese
3 large eggs, separated
⅛ teaspoon salt
Pinch nutmeg
Freshly ground pepper
Butter for the ramekins
¾ cup heavy cream

Preheat the oven to 350°F.

Melt the butter in a 1½-quart saucepan. Add the milk and heat it to luke-warm. Add the flour, little by little, stirring all the time to prevent it from forming lumps. Over medium heat cook the mixture, continuing to stir, for 3 to 4 minutes, until it thickens. Transfer the roux immediately to a larger bowl. Pound the truffle to a coarse paste in a mortar. Add it, the Gruyère, and 1 tablespoon of the Parmesan cheese to the roux. When thoroughly cool, add the egg yolks, salt, nutmeg, a little pepper, and stir well.

Butter six 4-ounce ramekins and use about 1½ tablespoons of the Parmesan to dust the insides of the molds. Whip the egg whites to stiff peaks and fold them into the base thoroughly, but delicately, to keep the mixture light. Spoon the mixture into the ramekins until they are three-quarters full. Sprinkle the remaining Parmesan on top of the puddings and set them in a baking dish. Add hot water to the dish to reach halfway up the sides of the ramekins and bake on the middle rack of the oven for 25 minutes, or until the puddings are set all the way through and lightly browned. Remove from the water bath and let the puddings cool for 15 minutes.

Run a sharp knife around the edge of each ramekin and invert the pudding into your other hand with several sharp downward motions. Set the puddings right side up in a small baking dish or oval gratin just large enough to contain them but do not let them touch. Pour the cream over the puddings, sprinkle the remaining Parmesan around them in the cream, and return to the oven for 20 minutes, until they are nicely browned. Serve immediately, each on a small warm plate with a few teaspoons of the cream from the dish.

Black Truffle Soup

For 4

The truffle is an aroma, unmistakable and penetrating. Because of its rarity and cost, the amount called for in any one preparation is a major consideration. Yet, it is difficult to quantify the strength of a truffle and to predict its effect, particularly when used in an infusion or to perfume foods. Where, for instance, adding or subtracting a teaspoon more salt or spice to a dish results in a very noticeable difference, the effects of altering the quantity of truffle is more elusive. Learning to cook with truffles is a matter of practice and, with time, one begins to recognize their qualities and use them judiciously.

Texture, raw or cooked, is not a high point in the appreciation of truffles. Pounding black truffles in a mortar puts them to maximum use and is recommended if you only have a small amount. Adding truffles in this form allows the potent aroma to be widely dispersed in sauces, vinaigrettes, marinades, and composed salads. Or, the truffle can be sliced into baked dishes and braises or cut into small spikes and used to stud meats and poultry for roasting.

In this soup the flavor of black truffle predominates and the other vegetables provide a soft background. For those not acquainted with its aroma, folklore, and mystique, the truffle is merely an expensive oddity. However, if curiosity exceeds bias, this soup is a simple and persuasive introduction.

2 tablespoons unsalted butter
¾ cup finely diced celery root (3 ounces)
¼ cup leek (2 ounces), white part only, thinly sliced
¼ cup chopped parsnip (1 ounce), woody core cut away
2 small red potatoes (4 ounces), finely diced
1 sprig fresh thyme
¾ teaspoon salt
⅔ cup water
3 cups chicken broth (see page 426)
1 black truffle (1 to 1½ ounces)
½ cup heavy cream
Freshly ground pepper

Melt the butter in a 3-quart noncorrosive saucepan. Add the celery root, leek, parsnip, potatoes, thyme, ¼ teaspoon salt, and water. Bring to a simmer, cover, and cook for 15 minutes, or until there is very little water left in the pan. Add the chicken broth, return to a simmer, and cook, covered, for 15 minutes.

148   VEGETABLES

Transfer the mixture to a blender and purée it for 1½ minutes. Pass the soup through a fine sieve into a clean saucepan. Brush or scrape away any dirt from the surface of the truffle and pound the truffle to a coarse paste in a mortar. Add to the soup. Add the cream, the remaining ½ teaspoon salt, and grind pepper over the top. Stir the soup to combine all the ingredients, heat it gently, and serve.

Garden Salad

Garden salad is ever present in the menus at Chez Panisse and means something quite different from what most expect of a plate of lettuces. Modeled after the grand variety of young salads (both wild and cultivated) mounded in baskets in the marketplaces of Italy, where it is called *misticanza de taglio* and in France, *mesclun*, our own mix includes numerous different lettuces chosen for their shapes, color, and mild, spicy, or delicate flavor.

When picked young, lettuces nearly resemble herbs; their virgin flavors, although softer, are sharply defined. Transferred immediately from garden to table they carry a lovely grassy scent. Garden lettuces, by themselves or in composed salads, are light, refreshing, and cleansing.

Lettuces are by far the simplest crop to grow in the garden. Requiring no special soil or extravagance of space, a mixture of seeds may be quickly broadcast and will be ready for harvesting, in fair weather, in a little over a month's time. For a continual supply it is wise to divide a smallish patch (6 feet by 4 feet) in two and make staggered plantings on each half according to the rate of growth. A cool spot in the garden is the best place to grow lettuces and plenty of water will keep them green and tender. Too much sun causes precocious growth (dry soil usually accompanies this problem), which results in spindly plants, bleached-out colors, tough leaves, and bitter flavors. The best time of year for salad-growing is in the cooler, darker months, before frost, when shorter days impassion colors of each variety. Red lettuces, in particular the Italian chicories, as well as loose-leaf varieties, are stunning in these months. Damp or cooler soil causes the plants to grow more slowly, a condition they appear to enjoy if their deep tints, concentrated flavor, and squat, sturdy appearance are any indication.

To grow your own mixture of lettuces, combine a variety of seeds for sowing.

Equal quantities of red, green, and spicy varieties (see descriptions below) will provide fanciful salads. You may also wish to include plants in your garden that yield edible blossoms, such as nasturtiums, borage, violets, mustard, and hollyhocks. Calendula, roses, and johnny jump-ups are dull to taste, but visually exciting. Edible blossoms contribute pleasing nuances of flavor to a salad. Cut and jumbled, and strewn like confetti, they add whimsy and sparkle.

First-picked tender leaves are perhaps best dressed just with soft extra virgin olive oil, salt, and pepper. At this stage they are most fragile and likely to be overwhelmed by vinegar. Dress sturdier leaves in vinaigrette or a light, lemony cream dressing. It would be impossible to give precise instructions for a vinaigrette that would ensure consistent results. Both vinegar and olive oil are much too variable. Furthermore, salad lettuces require adjustments of the quantity and character of the vinaigrette according to the stage at which they are picked. Generally speaking, three to four tablespoons of vinaigrette will dress two large handfuls of mixed lettuces.

To make vinaigrette, begin with finely diced shallots. Pour good vinegar over them and allow them to stand for a half hour or so, if time permits; this draws out the flavor of the shallots. Dissolve a little salt in the vinegar, pepper the mixture, and stir in extra virgin olive oil to your taste. If you like the flavor of garlic, you may wish to smash a piece and let it soak with the shallots. I prefer a vinaigrette on the tart side, but not so much so that it leaves a bite in the back of the throat. Dress the lettuces lightly and immediately before you serve them. Never should the dressing weight the lettuces or coat them unctuously. Often you may need to correct the seasonings with a dash more vinegar, a pinch of salt, or a little more oil after you have tossed the lettuces.

Considering the types of lettuces, I think of four categories: head lettuces, loose-leaf or cutting lettuces, those that are spicy, and the longer growing Italian chicories. Include lettuces from each of these categories in your mix, if possible. Names and the descriptions of varieties that appear in our nightly salad at Chez Panisse at various times throughout the year are listed below.

Head Lettuces

This type of lettuce comes in a wide range of colors and forms smallish heads with loosely gathered leaves. The leaves tend to be fine, smooth, and fragile. Any of these may be grown as seedling crops or left in the ground to mature and form heads. The hearts of head lettuce are delicious in summer, when loose-leaf varieties tend to get spindly or slightly bitter from the warmer, sunnier conditions. The heart of a head lettuce is shielded by the outer leaves and develops a pale green to yellow color and crisp texture.

MARVEILLE DE QUATRE SAISON: tender butter head lettuce with magenta-colored outer leaves and pale green center. It grows year round in fair weather climates and is slow to bolt.

PERELLA RED: open-leaf butter head. Round leaves in variegated shades of red and green. Steady, hardy growth in fall, spring, and early summer.

PERELLA GREEN: similar to Perella red but clear green in color.

ROUGETTE DU MIDI: smallish open-leaf butter head with bronze-colored leaves for fall, winter, and spring plantings.

TROCODERO: light green color tinged with red. Thrives in wet, cool weather.

COS OR ROMAINE: this lettuce forms an upright head, which may be tight or loose. Colors vary in shades of deep red to bronze, light to dark green. Textures vary from fine to sturdy and crunchy upon maturity.

PARIS WHITE COS: tightly folded upright leaves, medium green with a greenish white interior.

CRAQUANTE D'AVIGNON: crunchy deep green leaves.

DE FRONTIGNAN ROMAINE: hearty heads with bright green color.

DE MORGES BRUAN: bronze-colored, loose heads with thin ribs.

ROMAINE ROUGE D'HIVER: broad, flat leaves, bronze to deep red in color.

Loose-leaf or Cutting Lettuce

The growth pattern of this type of lettuce is open; heads do not form. Loose-leaf lettuces are slower to go to seed than other types and thus useful over a long period. They can be planted intensively since many grow up before out, and lend themselves well to "cut and come again" gardening, which describes the happy ability of a plant to resprout once it has been cut. In the case of salad lettuces, this characteristic turns a mere handful of seeds into an abundant harvest. Loose-leaf lettuces come in a wide variety of leaf sizes, shapes, colors, textures, and tastes.

LOLLO BIONDO: ruffled, bright green leaves.

LOLLO ROSSO: ruffled, magenta leaves with light green base. Both the Biondo and Rosso are best in spring and fall.

GREEN OAKLEAF: deeply indented green leaves.

RED OAKLEAF: indented leaves and brilliant red color that deepens in the sun.

RED SALAD BOWL: fragile, lobed leaves of unusual beauty, cast with deep-red color.

GREEN ICE: glossy, dark green color on fringed leaves.

MÂCHE OR LAMB'S LETTUCE: deep green, glossy leaves, forms small rosettes.

TANGO: deeply cut, vivid green, pointed leaves with a tangy flavor.

RED SAILS: bronze to red-colored, ruffled leaves.

RUBY: bright green, frilled leaves shaded with intense red color.

Spicy Lettuces

Although there are distinctions between the domesticated cousins of wild rocket (*Eruca sativa*)—variously called arugula, roquette, ruchetta, and rucola—their flavors are almost identical. They differ in the configuration of the leaves and in their depth of pungency. ROCKET is potently aromatic with warm, penetrating, peppery flavors. Rocket grows very quickly and will be the first of your seeds to germinate; in fair climates the seedlings break the soil in as little as a week's time. Seedling rocket is mild and develops in pungency as it grows hardier. Quick to bolt, the flowers of rocket are a fine addition to salads, somewhat sweeter than the leaves and reminiscent of their bite. A salad of rocket alone complements the flavor of grilled pigeon, lamb, or beef, while a few leaves is enough to hail its presence in a bowl of mixed lettuces.

BURNET SALAD: not really a salad at all, but a small plant with spindly stems and small leaves that contribute a cucumberlike flavor.

GARDEN CRESS (*Lebidium sativum*): curly loose leaves resembling immature parsley with a peppery, hot flavor. Resembles a somewhat more concentrated neighbor of watercress (*Nasturtium officinale*), which is also a good addition.

CHERVIL, BASIL, MINT: classified as herbs, these fall into the softer category of herbal flavors. Each adds a cool spiciness and perks attention.

Chicories

The chicories are most notable for their bitter flavor, which is more or less pronounced at various stages of maturity and also depends upon cultivation techniques. More often than not the chicories are blanched, that is, covered or otherwise deprived of sunlight, which causes them to whiten or fade and mitigates their harsh bitterness. The most common chicories for use in salads are the curly types called CHICOREE FRISÉE, the best of which we have found to be FINE LOUVIERS (finely curled, indented leaves with thin ribs) and FINE MARAÎCHÈRE (similar to Fine Louviers but with softer green color).

ESCAROLE is another delicious addition, particularly the butter-colored centers of blanched heads, which bear a delicate fragrance of newmown grass. The chicories also include the Italian radicchios and BELGIAN ENDIVE, also called Witloof chicory. Both of these are nearly impalatable if the whole leaves are served in their young, green stages. If cut, however, into fine ribbons and dressed liberally with good red wine vinegar, olive oil, and thinly sliced red onion, their strong astringency recedes, as the thin-strand cut permits a more thorough coating of vinaigrette.

I plant my own radicchios in early summer for fall and winter harvest. Shorter, darker days cause the heads, which first appear loose and leafy, to squat and darken dramatically. The leaves themselves grow rounder and develop a glossy heft. Be patient with your radicchio; simply cut it back when it becomes too invasive. It will continue to resprout. Rather than blanching radicchio, I prefer to leave it to the scanty sunlight and cold soil of winter. While it is still markedly bitter, there is no lettuce that expresses itself in more passionate tones. Coming upon heads of radicchio in the fading light of a winter day is startling as they resemble deep-red roses nestled in the ground.

RADICCHIO DI VERONA: forms small clusters of round leaves of deep-red color.

RADICCHIO DI TREVISO: long tapering head with wide-ribbed leaves.

RADICCHIO VARIEGATO DI CASTELFRANCO: green to yellow leaves flecked with red.

Blanching Belgian endive is no secret and can be accomplished *in situ* in fair weather climates or in a basement or garage. Descriptions of the blanching technique for radicchios as well may be found in *The Salad Garden* by Joy Larkcom (New York: Viking Press, 1984), an excellent gardener's guide which includes many illustrations and photographs of international lettuce varieties.

Mail-order Sources of Domestic and International Seeds

Le Marché Seeds International
P.O. Box 566
Dixon, California 95620

Nichols Garden Nursery
1190 North Pacific Highway
Albany, Oregon 97321

Johnny's Selected Seeds
305 Foss Hill Road
Albion, Maine 04910

W. Atlee Burpee Company
300 Park Avenue
Warminster, Pennsylvania 18991

Apples Baked with Orange and Riesling

These apples are a highly spiced accompaniment to rich meats, such as roast pork; or they can be scattered with raisins or dried currants and served with crème fraîche as a dessert. The advantage of baking the apples rather than cooking them on the top of the stove is that they keep their shape and thus make a nicer presentation. The cooking time will vary according to the type of baking pan you use—crockery dishes warm up much more slowly than metal or glass. The apples should cook gently, otherwise they turn to mush; check them after thirty minutes and continue to monitor their progress until they are soft. Handle them gently when removing them from the baking dish.

1½ cups freshly squeezed orange juice
¾ cup dry Riesling
5 tablespoons brown sugar
Zest of 1 orange, grated
⅛ teaspoon ground cinnamon
1/16 teaspoon ground cloves
⅛ teaspoon ground ginger
¼ teaspoon anise seed, cracked
8 Pippin apples (3 pounds, 8 ounces), cored, peeled with a sharp paring knife, cut into eighths

Preheat the oven to 350° F.

Combine the orange juice, Riesling, sugar, orange zest, and spices in a bowl large enough to hold the apples. Whisk the mixture to dissolve the sugar. Add the apples and toss them. Pour the apples and spices out into a 16- by 8-inch baking dish, add any juice left in the bowl to the dish, cover with foil, and bake for 30 to 45 minutes, or until the apples are just soft throughout but remain intact. Remove from the oven and let the apples cool in their juices.

Citrus Fruit Salad

Citrus fruits of all kinds are available in the winter months of January and February, and are at their peak at this time. In the winter months, as an alternative to the garden lettuces on the menu at the restaurant, we serve citrus fruits splashed with very cold Champagne or dressed in a vinaigrette based on the combined juices of the various fruits. The mixture might include sections of pink grapefruit and thin slices of lime, Meyer lemon, tangerines, and various oranges. Blood oranges are a particularly colorful contribution to this salad and give it an exotic appeal. A number of years ago our supply of blood oranges came from Sicily, where they are grown in great number. Since that time, local demand has increased and they are now available from late January through the early spring from California growers.

When choosing citrus fruits, look for the ripest fruit—deeply colored, neither hard nor thick skinned, and heavy for their size. If blood oranges are available, select those with red blushed skin; this is usually an indication that the pulp will be suffused with color.

When assembling this salad, slice the most acidic fruits (the lemons and limes) into very thin slices so that their sourness is not overwhelming, and arrange them adjacent to sweet fruits. This salad is particularly refreshing after a rich braised or roasted course. Omit the olives and splash with Champagne and this salad can also serve as a dessert.

3 blood oranges (14 ounces)
1 pink grapefruit (1 pound)
1 lime (2½ ounces)
1 navel orange (5 ounces)
2 tangerines (5 ounces)
1 Meyer lemon (3 ounces)

For the vinaigrette:
¼ cup juice from the citrus trimmings
1 teaspoon balsamic vinegar
⅛ teaspoon salt
½ teaspoon chopped fresh oregano
2 tablespoons extra virgin olive oil
½ cup small salt-cured Italian olives

Chill the citrus fruits thoroughly.

Cut the skin and pith away from all of the citrus fruits with a sharp serrated knife so that only the pulp remains. Do not discard the skins as they contain some pulp and juice, which will be squeezed out and used in the vinaigrette. Slice the fruit and arrange it loosely on individual plates or on a large platter. Chill the fruit again.

Prepare the vinaigrette: Squeeze the skins of the various fruits to obtain ¼ cup mixed juice. Combine the juice with the vinegar, salt, a little freshly ground pepper, and ¼ teaspoon of the oregano. Whisk in the olive oil. Adjust the vinaigrette for more vinegar if necessary.

Dress the olives with about 1 tablespoon of the vinaigrette and scatter them over the sliced fruit. Spoon the remaining vinaigrette over the fruit and serve very cold.

Fall Fruit Salad with Warm Goat Cheese and Herb Toast

For 4

This salad makes a fanciful first course and is a fine opportunity to present together the typical fruits of early fall—figs, pears, Muscat grapes, and pomegranates. Montrachet goat cheese is generally sold in cylindrical logs that are approximately 6 inches long. The cheese has a tendency to crumble, so it is best cut with a knife that has first been dipped in hot water.

2 tablespoons extra virgin olive oil
¾ cup coarse sourdough bread crumbs
Four 2-ounce slices Montrachet goat cheese, each cut ½ inch thick

Put 1 tablespoon of the olive oil in a sauté pan. Add the bread crumbs and stir them well until they are coated with the oil. Turn on the heat and fry the crumbs over low heat for about 8 minutes, turning them over often until they are golden brown. Transfer the crumbs to a plate.

Put the remaining 1 tablespoon oil in a bowl. Dip each slice of cheese in the oil, coating the surfaces. Then roll each slice in the fried crumbs. Use your hands to press the crumbs onto all sides of the cheese so that the slices are well covered and place on a small baking sheet.

Preheat the oven to 350°F.

For the vinaigrette for the fruit: makes ⅓ cup
1 small sweet pomegranate, juiced to yield ¼ cup
¾ teaspoon balsamic vinegar
1 teaspoon olive oil
1 teaspoon walnut oil
Salt and pepper

Combine the pomegranate juice, the vinegar, and the oils, and season with salt and pepper to taste. Next, prepare the herb butter for the toast:

¼ teaspoon chopped fresh oregano
¼ teaspoon chopped fresh thyme
⅛ teaspoon chopped fresh rosemary
2 tablespoons unsalted butter, softened
Black pepper
1 sourdough baguette

Mix the herbs with the butter and season with a little freshly ground black pepper. Slice the baguette crosswise at an angle to produce croutons that are oval in shape and approximately 3 inches long. Just before serving, prepare the fruit:

¼ cup pomegranate seeds
4 ripe figs
12 large Muscat grapes (1 cup)
1 large ripe French Butter or Comice pear

Prepare the grapes and pears at the last moment because both will gradually turn brown when exposed to the air. Extract the seeds from the pomegranate. Cut the figs into 6 segments each. Next peel the grapes and halve and seed them. Peel the pear, core it, and slice it thin. Distribute the pear slices among 4 plates.

Put the goat cheese into the oven and bake it for 8 minutes, or until just soft throughout.

While the goat cheese is baking, toast the baguette croutons and spread herb butter on each warm slice. Arrange the other fruits on top of the pears, leaving room for both the cheese and toast. Spoon a little vinaigrette over the fruits. Transfer the cheeses to the plates, garnish with 2 croutons apiece, and serve immediately.

Spiced Quince

Raw quinces are unpalatable. Their flesh is highly astringent and it is necessary to cook them in a concentrated sugar syrup to temper this quality. Ripe quinces are yellow skinned and have an irresistible pineapple-like fragrance, which, unfortunately, is lost in cooking. There is perhaps no other fruit that is so altered during the process: The very pigment of the quince changes from pale yellow to a deep rose-amber color. (This color, by the way, indicates doneness.) Quinces should not be stirred while cooking or they will break apart. The poaching liquid derived from cooking quinces when reduced makes an excellent clear glaze for pear and apple tarts, so do not discard it. Store in a sealed jar in the refrigerator.

In the restaurant, we have found that quinces are better served in combination with fruits such as pears or apples. Alone, their unique flavor is not to everyone's liking. Use spiced quinces as part of a winter fruit compote, with poached pears for instance, or combine them with Apples Baked with Orange and Riesling and serve as an accompaniment to roast pork.

1 ⅔ cups sugar
4 cups water
4 quinces (2 pounds, 4 ounces), quartered, cored, peeled with a sharp paring knife,
*   sliced into ½-inch segments*
3-inch piece of vanilla bean
4 whole allspice berries
4 whole cloves
2-inch piece of whole cinnamon

In a heavy 3-quart saucepot dissolve the sugar in the water. Add the quinces, vanilla bean, and spices. Bring to a low simmer and cook, covered, for 2 hours and 15 minutes. Let the quinces cool in the poaching liquid. Refrigerated in the liquid, they will keep for up to 5 days.

Risotto
and
Pasta

Risotto

Risotto with Tomatoes, Shrimp, Garlic, and Parsley

Saffron Risotto

Smoked Pigeon Risotto with Grilled Red Onions and Chard

Wild Mushroom Risotto

Basic Pasta

Ravioli of Chicken, Pancetta, and Browned Garlic, with Rosemary Oil

Lasagna of Eggplant, Tomato, and Basil

Pasta with Giblet Sauce

Lobster Raviolis

Rosemary Noodles with Pigeon Essences

Pumpkin Tortelli with Brown Butter and Sage

Tortellini of Veal, Ricotta, Spinach, and Parmesan

Pan-Fried Bay Scallops and Saffron Pasta with Parsley and Garlic

Pasta with Sweetbreads, Mirepoix, Cream, and Thyme

Risotto

Risotto is like a great simmering stew, where a number of elements surrender their individual identity to the greater purpose of a unified flavor. I don't mean that the individual ingredients of a risotto ought to be indistinguishable, but that they are subordinate to the overall effect.

The Italian menu places risotto, like pasta, as a *primo piatto*, that is, served after the appetizer and before the meat, poultry, or fish course. To my mind, risotto constitutes a substantial course and should be preceded and followed by lighter fare. It can also stand by itself and then be followed by a salad and dessert. Although I cannot resist making it year round, risotto is a cozy, cool-weather food and stands alongside braises and other long-cooked dishes, which are most appropriately served in fall and winter.

The possible ingredients for making risotto are limitless, although it tastes best when the number is kept to a minimum and each is harmonious with the others. Risotto can be a medium for capturing one specific flavor—pigeon, or wild mushrooms, or the taste of the sea. Enhance a pigeon risotto, for instance, with braised chard and roasted onions, or smoked bacon and wild thyme, or raspberries and bitter chicory. I think of risotto, whether simple or complex, as the focus and elaboration of one flavor rather than the juxtaposition of many.

Inspiration for making a risotto can come from unexpected sources—leftover portions of braised, roasted, or grilled meat and poultry, or extra vegetables that by themselves would not constitute a substantial course. When the cupboard is bare, a risotto can be a very simple combination of meat or poultry broth, butter, and Parmesan cheese. Risotto can also be a celebration of a particular seasonal food—the first wild mushrooms, white truffles, or tender spring vegetables such as artichokes, asparagus, and peas.

There are four grades of rice in Italy—*comune, semi-fino, fino, superfino*—and they vary according to grain size, color, and consistency. Superfino Arborio is the grade used most frequently to make excellent risotto, and the type commonly exported to this country. Superfino Arborio has the longest, fattest grain, the characteristic white kernel in the center, and a great capacity to absorb liquid. Arborio rice is essential to risotto for its absorption capacity, and for the starch it releases in cooking, which accounts for the creamy consistency of the dish. Other types of rice cannot be substituted successfully.

Rice, like any other grain, can deteriorate over time and easily absorbs odors if left open to the air. It should be used soon after being opened or stored in an airtight container. Most Arborio rice is packed in clear bags and can be examined. The rice should not contain many broken or blunted grains and should have a fine pearl to light ivory color. Another indication of the quality of the rice is its fragrance, which should never be stale.

The most important aspect of making a risotto is the quality and character of the broth used, as it provides a foundation of flavor and is the unifying element of the dish. The broth is usually derived from the main ingredient of the risotto—in the case of poultry, the carcasses of the birds; with meat or fish, the bones and trimmings. The broth should be richly flavored but never salty or over-reduced. To assure this in the restaurant, we use double broths rather than reductions. A double broth is made with bones and trimmings or carcasses of poultry, meat, or fish that have been moistened with previously made broth instead of water. We keep two generic broths on hand, chicken and beef. We then flavor these broths with more bones and trimmings appropriate to the preparation.

The broth used in making risotto should reflect the other elements of the dish. Fish broth is used for seafood risotti. For those involving vegetables, light poultry broth or vegetable *fumet* is suitable. Turkey broth made from the backs, necks, wings, and giblets is the most flavorful of all the poultry broths and the one I prefer to use in making unadorned risotti flavored with saffron or simply butter and Parmesan.

Begin by choosing a heavy pot—saucepots or casseroles made of laminated metal with a stainless-steel interior are ideal. The pot should suit the quantity of risotto you plan to make: risotto for 4 to 6 persons can be managed in a 2-quart saucepot; risotto for up to 12 persons can be made in a 6-quart pot. Bear in mind that risotto swells in volume: all additions included, up to 4 times its original volume. The pot used should have sides at least 4 inches high with a surface area that is not too wide, which would cause a too-rapid evaporation of the broth.

Assemble all your ingredients ahead of time so that you can tend the pot as it cooks. Most all risotti are started in the same way. Onions, shallots, or other aromatic vegetables and seasonings are cooked for a brief period in hot oil or butter until they soften and their flavor is released. The rice is then added to the hot oil and stirred. It is not necessary to brown the rice, only to coat it with the hot oil, which causes some of the surface starch to break down. Beyond softening the grains of rice and preparing them for the subsequent additions of broth, the starch released by the rice and vegetables, particularly the onions, plays a vital role in determining the creamy texture at the end.

A small amount of wine or hot broth is then added while the pot is stirred, which causes the rice and vegetables to sputter violently. Then enough broth is added to just cover the rice, and the heat is reduced to a gentle simmer. The rice and broth should bubble gently throughout the cooking. Cooking over too high a heat interrupts the slow, even absorption and causes the grains to bloat and go soft. The broth around the vegetables and rice will thicken slightly, evidence of the emulsion forming by the release of starch.

With this primary stage of the cooking completed, the next step is to add small increments of broth, keeping it at a level just above the rice. Maintain the emulsion that appears after the first addition throughout the cooking by never adding too much broth at one time. Stir the pot frequently. The rice tends to sink to the bottom, pushing broth to the top, making it appear more moist than it actually is. Besides preventing sticking, stirring will reveal the actual amount of broth. Never allow the rice to go dry. Keep it loose and submerged so that it absorbs evenly.

After 15 minutes of simmering, the risotto is in its final stage and care must be taken in judging the amount of broth required to finish cooking. This is not always a simple matter as the solid additions (meat, poultry, shellfish, or vegetables) that release some liquid into the pot are also added at this time. Make the solid additions after the last broth addition has reduced and been absorbed. At the point at which you would then add more broth, add the solids instead, stir, and look to see what liquids they contribute before adjusting with broth. Precaution must also be taken if the solids are not hot. The temperature of the rice and broth can be brought down dramatically and this interferes with absorption. Maintain a simmer by raising the heat.

With few exceptions, the solid additions are precooked and simply warmed in the hot rice in this final stage. The advantage of this is a simplification of the tasks demanded at this point. The cook doesn't have to be concerned with coordinating the finishing of the rice with correctly cooking any additions, and it ensures that the additions will not overcook or dissipate their flavor in the rice. Furthermore, the final stage of cooking risotto—achieving the desired consistency and texture—is not always a matter of predictable timing. Some risotti, particularly those made with ingredients that cook very rapidly (small shrimp or peas, for instance) are marred by even a 30-second error in judgment.

Finishing the rice involves gauging the proper consistency (it should be slightly chewy, never hard in the center), enriching the risotto with butter, correcting the seasoning, and allowing the liquid to reduce until rice and sauce are unified. The goal is to bring about a marriage of rice and broth. The rice should be coated and in proportion to the sauce so that it is nearly pourable; the sauce should be reduced to the point that it doesn't separate from the rice. The challenge in cooking risotto lies in simultaneously bringing about these final refinements—a little more broth, a bit more butter, raising the heat to hasten the reduction, adding a dash of vinegar. The adjustments can be numerous or few depending on the state of the risotto near the end.

There is one point at which risotto is done: when all elements conspire in a union of flavor, texture, and consistency, a timeless moment in cooking, one that can be shared if you serve the dish immediately.

Risotto with Tomatoes, Shrimp, Garlic, and Parsley

6 large servings

Most of the preparation for this risotto resides in making a flavorful fish broth. You will note that the shrimp are not added until the last minute and are intended to retain their flavor and juice rather than render them to the rice. The quality of the broth is crucial in providing a foundation for this dish and should be rich in flavor—thus the use of chicken stock instead of water. The chicken flavor will subside with the addition of fish bones and seasonings, yet contributes invaluably to the strength of the reduction. If the final broth is not strong or satisfying enough to sip by itself, it will not do much more for this risotto.

For the fish broth:
¼ cup pure olive oil
3 pounds rock cod carcasses, head included, cleaned, gills removed, cut into pieces with a cleaver
1 cup dry white wine (such as Muscadet, Sancerre, or Sauvignon Blanc)
2 quarts flavorful chicken broth (see page 426)
2 carrots (7 ounces), finely diced
½ large stalk of celery (2 ounces), finely diced
1 medium onion (8 ounces), finely diced
Optional: 1 stalk of fresh lemon grass (1 ounce), thinly sliced
1 head of garlic, unpeeled, split in half
Pinch saffron threads
3 bay leaves
6 sprigs lemon thyme
3 sprigs Italian parsley
1 tablespoon Champagne vinegar

1 pound small shrimp in their shells

Prepare the fish broth: Warm the olive oil in a large saucepot or casserole (minimum 6-quart capacity). Add the carcasses and cook the fish gently for 5 minutes, turning often until all sides have been exposed to the heat and the aroma is released. Add the wine and stir well to release any bits of fish or bones that have stuck to the pot. Pour the chicken stock into the pot and heat to just under a boil. Hold it there for 5 minutes and skim off the brownish-white foam that rises to the surface.

Add the carrots, celery, onion, lemon grass, garlic, saffron, herbs, and the vinegar. Make sure all the ingredients are well covered in the liquid. Simmer the broth for 30 minutes.

While the broth is cooking, peel the shrimp, reserving the shells. Transfer the shrimp to a plate and put in the refrigerator. So that their flavor remains clean in the broth, add the shells to the fish broth during the last 10 minutes of cooking time. Remove the broth from the heat and pour it through a large, medium-fine sieve into another pot. Gently press on the contents of the sieve to extract as much of the liquid as possible. Discard the solids.

For the risotto:
4 tomatoes (approximately 1 pound, 5 ounces), peeled, seeded, diced, juice strained of
*   seeds and reserved*
4 tablespoons unsalted butter
³/₄ cup finely diced onion (3 ounces)
1¼ cups Arborio rice
½ teaspoon salt
¼ teaspoon freshly ground pepper
1 tablespoon balsamic vinegar
2 cloves garlic, finely minced
¹/₁₆ teaspoon ground cayenne
2 tablespoons pure olive oil
⅛ teaspoon fennel seed, powdered
2 tablespoons chopped fresh parsley

Prepare the risotto: Add the strained tomato juice to the fish broth, put on the stove, and bring to a simmer. Melt 2 tablespoons of the butter in a wide 6-quart casserole or saucepot, add the onion, and cook over medium heat for 5 minutes, stirring so that the onion does not brown. Add the rice and continue cooking for 3 minutes, stirring often to keep the rice from sticking to the bottom of the pot. The onion will begin to brown lightly and the rice will smell nutty and toasted. Do not let the rice brown. Add 2 cups of the simmering fish broth. The rice and onions will sizzle violently and release steam. Stir the onion and rice and immediately reduce the heat so that the rice bubbles gently over its surface. Check the rice at 2-minute intervals and, as the liquid reduces and is absorbed, add another ½ cup broth. The rice should be kept barely submerged and the liquid surrounding it, now thickened by the release of starch from the rice, should not be watered down by the addition of too much broth at once. Maintaining an emulsified reduction is crucial in achieving the right consistency where rice and broth do not separate.

After 15 minutes of cooking, the rice will be nearly done. Continue to simmer it gently. Instead of adding more broth to the pot, warm the tomatoes in a sauté pan for 1 minute with ¼ teaspoon salt, ⅛ teaspoon pepper, the balsamic vinegar, and minced garlic, and add them to the risotto. Add the remaining 2 tablespoons unsalted butter and the cayenne and raise the heat a little.

The last 5 to 7 minutes of cooking are critical—the rice should have enough liquid from the tomatoes and broth to finish cooking. Monitor the rice closely at this point. Taste the rice for texture several times in the next minutes. It should not be crunchy, but slightly chewy. If you taste any hardness in the rice, continue to cook it, adjusting with small amounts of fish broth as the rice continues to absorb it. Allow the sauce around the rice to thicken to the point that it clings to the rice but not so much that the rice becomes heavy or sticky. Ideally the rice should be quite saucy, but the reduction should ensure that the rice and sauce are one.

In the last 2 minutes of cooking, quickly sauté the shrimp in the olive oil, season them with ¼ teaspoon salt, the fennel, and ⅛ teaspoon freshly ground pepper until they just color. Add the shrimp directly to the risotto and cook 1 minute. If the risotto is a little dry, not saucy, add a little more broth and stir well. Add the chopped parsley and serve the risotto in wide, flat, warmed bowls.

Saffron Risotto

This risotto represents my fondest and most vivid childhood memory of food. It is associated with the holidays, particularly Thanksgiving and Christmas, and was prepared by my grandmother, whose visits to our home were an eagerly awaited event. Until I traveled to Italy, risotto always meant one thing—to my child's eye, an enormous cauldron of golden rice and the mingled fragrance of saffron, poultry broth, butter, and Parmesan cheese, a dish that our family would literally fight over. To me, this was the most delicious food imaginable, and when I left home I sought to re-create the taste I remembered. Of course, I repeatedly questioned my grandmother about the ingredients and the process involved, but her instructions were sketchy, as is always the case with Italian grandmothers when asked to give a recipe. Nevertheless, enticed with some new bit of information she supplied about salt pork or dry porcini or the kind and quality of broth, I continued to try to make her risotto. After several futile attempts I concluded that I could not match her instinct for this dish and that a mysterious alchemy was involved, the same that accounted for the sugar-sweet carrots she pulled from her garden, and the haunting smell of anise cookies that lingered in her small house.

Although nothing can supplant the taste memory of that dish, I am now perhaps closer than I have ever been to re-creating it. I am at least certain of what went into it. The addition of shaved white truffles in this recipe is optional. I mention it only because this rice provides a wonderful foil for that unique flavor. It did not occur in my grandmother's version and I apologize to the rest of my family for gilding the lily.

1 tablespoon olive oil
1 small yellow onion, finely diced
1 cup Arborio rice
Large pinch saffron threads (about ¼ teaspoon)
1½ ounces pancetta, thinly sliced, diced
2 large slices of dry porcini
¼ teaspoon salt
4 cups hot turkey broth (see page 426)
4 tablespoons unsalted butter
½ cup freshly grated Reggiano Parmigiano cheese
Optional: 1 fresh white truffle (1½ ounces)

Warm the olive oil in a heavy, 2-quart saucepot. Add the onion and sauté over medium-high heat for 4 minutes, until it begins to color lightly. Add the rice, the saffron, and pancetta and cook for another 3 minutes, stirring often to prevent the rice from sticking to the bottom, and to make sure it is coated with hot oil. Add the porcini and the salt and about 1½ cups hot broth, enough to just barely cover the rice. Stir the pot well to combine all the ingredients, reduce the heat, and simmer gently. At this point, the rice should be surrounded by broth so that as it begins to absorb the liquid it does so evenly.

As the rice absorbs the broth, continue to add more broth in ¼-cup amounts, keeping the heat at a constant simmer. Stir the pot often and continue to add the broth, keeping the level just above the rice.

After 15 minutes, the rice will lose most of its hard-kernel quality, but will still be firm in the middle. Stir in the butter. In the next 3 to 5 minutes the rice will finish cooking. Taste the rice for texture and seasoning and correct it for salt and pepper, if necessary. If the rice still feels firm and has absorbed most of the liquid in the pot, add a little more broth. If too much broth is added in the last few minutes, the rice and broth will separate. Too little broth and the rice becomes heavy and sticky. Stir in 2 tablespoons of the Parmesan just before serving and sprinkle the remaining cheese over each portion at the table. Shave the truffle, if used, over the top of each serving.

Smoked Pigeon Risotto
with Grilled Red Onions and Chard

This is a risotto with smoky flavors. Both the sweet red onion and the pigeons, which form the base of the risotto, are first cooked on the charcoal grill. After they have browned all over, the pigeons are covered, which traps the smoke that then permeates them. When the pigeons are sufficiently smoked, the meat is removed from the bone and the carcasses are chopped and added to a previously made poultry broth, which focuses and further concentrates its flavor.

The addition of greens contrasts nicely with the rich flavor of pigeon. In this recipe, chard is used; however, other versions might include bitter greens, such as escarole and radicchio, or in heartier variations for the winter months, cabbage and beans or stewed wild mushrooms.

To cook the pigeons you will need a gentle charcoal fire. The fat of pigeon, contained in the skin, will very likely flare up if the fire is too hot—this, together with even a moment's inattention, will make the birds go up in a blaze. Grill the onion first while the coals are medium hot; then let them burn down and adjust them so that they rest in an even bed about 3 to 4 inches below the surface of the grill. The coals should feel hot but not so much so that you can't hold your hand just above the grill.

A barbecue with a tight-fitting cover is ideal for smoking the pigeons. Otherwise they can be covered with a deep roasting pan or a dome of heavyweight foil secured by small rocks at the edges of the grill.

You may prepare the pigeons, onion, and broth well ahead of time. Even so, making this risotto is a rather lengthy process.

2 fresh pigeons (about 2 pounds), heads and feet cut off and discarded
Salt and pepper
1 large red onion (10 ounces), peeled, sliced into ¼-inch-thick rounds
3 tablespoons pure olive oil
6 cups poultry broth (see page 426)
4 ounces red chard leaves, coarsely sliced
1½ cups Arborio rice
3 tablespoons unsalted butter
1 teaspoon balsamic vinegar
1 teaspoon chopped fresh savory
3 tablespoons freshly grated Parmesan cheese

Prepare a charcoal or wood fire.

Cut off the neck and the wings of the pigeons at the first joint. Remove the skin from the necks and discard it. Salt and pepper the birds all over and set aside for grilling, with the wings and neck. Brush both sides of the onion slices with 1 tablespoon of the olive oil, add salt and pepper to taste, and grill them on a medium-hot fire for 4 to 5 minutes on each side, or until they go limp and take on light grill marks. Remove the onions and allow the fire to burn down as described above. Place the whole pigeons, with the necks and wings, on the grill (you should soon hear a gentle sizzle) and cook them on all 4 sides about 6 minutes per side, or until lightly browned. Turn the pigeons upright, cover them (if you have a barbecue with a lid, open the air vents slightly or poke holes in the foil covering so as not to smother the fire) and smoke them for 20 minutes more. Remove the pigeons from the grill and let them cool until they can be handled.

Remove the breast meat and legs of each pigeon, picking off as much meat as possible. Chop the carcasses, necks, and wings into small bits with a large heavy knife or cleaver. Combine the poultry broth and the chopped carcasses in a pot, bring to a simmer, and cook for 45 minutes.

While the broth simmers, remove the skin from the breast meat and legs and set it aside. Tear the pigeon meat into shreds, and add to the broth along with any bones. Strain the pigeon broth into another pot, pressing hard on the solids to extract as much flavor as possible. Chop the onions into coarse bits and finely chop the pigeon skin.

Add 1 tablespoon of the olive oil to a heavy 6-quart noncorroding saucepot, warm it, and toss in the chard. Salt and pepper the chard and cook it for 2 minutes, stirring often, until it is just wilted. Remove the chard to a chopping block.

Prepare the risotto: While the saucepot is still hot, add the chopped pigeon skin and the remaining 1 tablespoon olive oil. Allow the skin to render some of its fat over medium heat for about 1 minute. Add the rice and warm it for 3 minutes, stirring often to prevent it from sticking to the bottom of the pot. Stir in the chopped onion and the chard. Begin adding broth, little by little. Maintain the level of the broth just above the rice, gently simmer and add broth when the level begins to drop, but before the previously added amount has been completely absorbed. Stir the rice before and after each addition. After the rice has simmered for 15 minutes, add the shredded pigeon meat (the rice will take about 20 minutes altogether). In the last minutes, stir in the butter and balsamic vinegar, correct the rice to your taste with salt, and generously pepper it. The consistency of the rice should be nearly pourable, yet the rice and broth should not separate. Stir in the savory, sprinkle the risotto with the Parmesan cheese, and serve immediately.

Wild Mushroom Risotto

Make this dish in the autumn, when wild mushrooms become available in the market. The more variety the better; each will contribute its particular earthy scent, color, and texture. If only one type is available, that is fine too. Refer to the technique for making risotto as described on page 164. It is worth emphasizing that the quality of the broth is essential to the flavor of any risotto, but particularly this one, since there are few elements—shallots, a little pancetta, wine, which adds a subtle acidity, broth, and mushrooms. I prefer to add the mushrooms toward the end of the cooking so their flavors do not dissipate. It is difficult to give an accurate raw weight measurement for the amount of mushrooms required. Depending on the type of mushroom and amount of moisture they contain (particularly the chanterelles) raw weight varies enormously. Bear in mind that you will need roughly 1½ to 2 cups sliced, cooked mushrooms to make four large portions of risotto.

Broth made from richly flavored fowl, such as turkey, remains the best choice. It is wise to flavor the broth with some dried mushrooms (boletes) so that the rice will begin to absorb mushroom flavors from the start.

Resist the temptation to use cheese on this risotto; it competes strongly, and unfavorably, with the flavors of the mushrooms.

4 to 6 cups raw wild mushrooms (chanterelles, horns of plenty, dentinum, boletes; see
  introduction to wild mushrooms, page 119)
8 tablespoons unsalted butter
Salt and pepper
2 shallots (2 ounces), finely diced
1½ cups Arborio rice
2 ounces pancetta, diced
1 cup dry white wine
1½ quarts turkey or chicken broth (see page 426)
1 tablespoon chopped fresh Italian parsley
1 teaspoon chopped fresh thyme

Brush off any dirt from the mushrooms with a small vegetable brush. Use a knife to cut away any implanted dirt. Slice the mushrooms. Melt 2 tablespoons of the butter in a sauté pan, add the mushrooms, salt and pepper them, and cook for 8 to 15 minutes (this depends on how much moisture they contain) until nearly all of the liquid they release has evaporated. You should end up with approximately 2 cups mushrooms. Set aside.

Melt 2 more tablespoons of the butter in a 6-quart noncorroding pot. Add the shallots and let them soften over medium heat for 2 minutes. Add the rice and the pancetta and cook for 3 minutes, stirring often. Do not allow the rice to brown. Stir in the wine and allow it to nearly evaporate. Then begin making the broth additions. Add only enough broth to maintain the level just above the rice. Maintain a gentle simmer and add broth when the level begins to drop, but before the previously added amount has been entirely absorbed. Stir the rice often, before and after each addition.

After 15 minutes, raise the heat and add the mushrooms. Readjust the heat so that the rice simmers. Cook for about 5 minutes more. During the final cooking, make broth additions judiciously and taste the rice frequently to gauge its progress. When it is nearly done (chewy but not firm in the center) stir in the remaining 4 tablespoons butter and make any final corrections of salt and pepper. The risotto should be unified so that the sauce does not separate from the rice, but should not be so reduced that the rice becomes thick. The consistency should be nearly pourable. Stir in the fresh herbs and serve in warm bowls.

Basic Pasta

For 2 main course servings, or 3 to 4 first course servings

1 cup all-purpose unbleached flour
1 whole large egg, as fresh as possible
Water

Making pasta is simply a matter of combining flour with egg and water and kneading the mass to an elastic consistency. This can be done mechanically, with a mixer or food processor, or by hand. I like the hand method as it allows for the most control. You can feel the dough, its progress and formation, and participate more actively and enjoyably in the process. There is really no substitute for the hands-on technique and I believe any use of machines should be preceded by numerous batches of hand-worked dough. In this way, the cook will develop a sensitivity and understanding of the variables involved, and this will carry over if the exigencies of time or quantity call for the use of a machine. Machines, of course, greatly accelerate the process of combining dough and kneading it, an "improvement" that has no detrimental effect on the dough per se. Large amounts of flour, containing more than 3 to 4 cups are, in fact, better handled in a mixer. Pasta dough is not at all as pliable as bread dough, and kneading a large amount of it by hand to the right consistency requires strength so that the dough is not underworked.

The goal of pasta making is to produce a noodle with a fine texture but sturdy structure that is not subordinated when combined with sauce. Pasta should be a lively collaborator rather than a mere vehicle for the sauce, as pleasing with simple, lean flavors as it is with richer and more complex ones.

The two most important aspects of making pasta are judging the correct amount of moisture in the dough and kneading it. Water activates gluten formation—the structural network of the dough that lengthens when it is kneaded and expands when it is rolled. A dough with too little moisture is too stiff to knead or combine. Too wet a dough produces pasta that is slack, sticky, and flabby when cooked. The goal then is to form a dough that contains enough moisture to combine evenly, and upon being kneaded, becomes firm and elastic but never wet and sticky. On any given day variables such as humidity, temperature, and the gluten content of the flour will require adjustments to the amount of water added. This is why I call for a nonspecific amount of water in the ingredients list.

I prefer to mix batches of pasta dough in a large, wide bread bowl at least until the ingredients have, through preliminary kneading, come together to form a rough mass. This way there is hardly any clean-up and no waste. Put the flour

RISOTTO AND PASTA 177

in a bowl, make a well in the center, and add the egg. With a fork, stir the egg. Gradually begin to bring the flour into the center. Mix until the flour absorbs the egg. The texture at this point will appear dry and crumbly. With your hands, scrape the dough from the fork and begin kneading the dough with a pushing and squeezing motion. It is at this point you may need to add water (a teaspoon at a time) if the dough is altogether resistant or excessively crumbly. Continue kneading for several minutes until the dough forms into a rough mass.

As a general rule, err in the direction of the dough being more dry than wet. It should contain just enough moisture to bring the flour together. If some crumbling occurs in the initial stages, push the bits of dough back into the bowl. Resist the temptation to add more water, and continue to knead. Continue pushing, squeezing, and folding the dough back on itself. The purpose of kneading the dough is to make it evenly moist throughout and to develop the gluten structure.

After 10 to 15 minutes of kneading, the dough will lose its ragged aspect and have a smooth, integrated appearance and feel. Wrap the pasta in plastic so that no moisture can evaporate and allow it to relax for 45 minutes. During this time the hydration process will continue and the dough will feel more evenly moist than at any point during the kneading. It is not critical that the dough be used right away. At this point, it can also be refrigerated, wrapped tightly, for up to 8 hours. If held this long, however, re-knead the dough for 3 to 5 minutes before rolling.

Options for rolling and cutting the dough are similar to those for kneading. Rolling dough by hand requires a large work surface and a vigorous, concentrated effort as pasta dough is resilient.

I prefer to use a small hand-operated pasta machine, which is capable of evenly sheeting the dough to a thin transparency or into a thicker more textured noodle. The dough is formed into a rectangle (roughly 4 by 4 inches) and flattened to a thickness that the machine, at its widest setting, will accept without strain. The dough is then rolled through the progressively narrower settings of the rollers until the desired thinness is achieved. If the dough feels a bit too wet at this point, it can be corrected with a liberal dusting of flour before rolling.

As the dough is rolled, it will lengthen. Long ribbons are easier to handle if they are cut into manageable lengths. When the final thinness has been achieved, cut the dough into 12-inch lengths as it leaves the machine, dust it with flour, and set it aside in slightly overlapping stacks.

Cutting the dough is easily accomplished by hand and produces noodles with an individual, less uniform appearance than machine-cut noodles. Flour one sheet at a time; semolina flour is milled to a coarser texture and is ideal for dusting noodles so that they separate readily and roll it up lengthwise. Then cut the roll to whatever thickness of noodle you desire.

If not used right away, noodles should be stored on a floured plate, covered with a towel or plastic wrap, in the refrigerator. Stored in this way they will keep for several days.

Ravioli

The technique for making dough for stuffed pasta, such as ravioli and tortelli, is the same as that for cut pasta. It is helpful, however, to make a dough that is slightly moister. Adding a little more water will help in sealing the edges of the stuffed pasta and aid in preventing any cracking of the dough, which can dry out in the period between rolling and filling.

To make raviolis: Roll the dough to a thin, almost transparent ribbon that is roughly 5½ inches wide and 15 inches long. Work with only half the dough at a time so that it doesn't dry out. Store the rolled sheets, ready to fill, unfloured, and slightly overlapping so they don't stick, under a towel. Set a sheet of dough in front of you. Along the length of the dough, place a scant tablespoon of filling in a neat ball 1 inch from the bottom and side edges, and 1 inch apart. Have ready a small bowl of water. With your finger, moisten the bottom edge and the spaces between the raviolis. (An atomizer is a quicker way of accomplishing this—direct a fine mist over a surface of the sheet and filling.) With both hands, fold the top portion of the sheet over the raviolis so that the top edge meets the bottom evenly. With your hands spread out flat, the forefingers opposing one another, and thumbs at right angles to the forefingers, flatten and seal the spaces between each ravioli as close as possible to the stuffing, expelling any pockets of air at the unsealed end. Press the bottom and top edges together so that they seal. Use a zigzag ravioli wheel to cut out the raviolis. Cut directly through the sealed sheets, about ⅜ inch from the filling, creating squares that are 2½ inches wide. Check all sides for a good seal. If the edges are unsealed at any place, moisten your fingers and press them tightly back together. Set the raviolis in one layer on the floured plates and store in the refrigerator until ready to use.

Tortelli and Tortellini

To make tortelli: Roll out a sheet of dough 4 inches wide and 24 inches long. With a round cutter 3¼ inches in diameter, cut out rounds of dough. Place a heaping teaspoon of the filling, formed into a ball, just below the diameter line, leaving ½ inch at the bottom edge. Moisten the edge of the lower half of the round of dough, fold the top edge over the filling so that it meets the bottom edge evenly, and press firmly. With the thumb and forefingers of both hands, grasp the corners of the sealed edges. Join them, overlapping slightly, and press them firmly together, curving the tortelli around your forefinger at the same time. Turn the edges up so that the tortelli resemble little hats with the brim up.

To make tortellini: Cut the rounds 2 inches in diameter, put ½ teaspoon of filling just below the diameter line, leaving ⅜ inch for the edge. Seal and form tortellini as described above.

Ravioli of Chicken, Pancetta, and Browned Garlic, with Rosemary Oil

30 raviolis, for 6

1 recipe Basic Pasta (see page 177)
For the filling:
3 chicken legs (about 1¾ pounds)
1 tablespoon plus 1 teaspoon fresh rosemary
2 large cloves garlic, thinly sliced
4 ounces pancetta, thinly sliced, minced
¼ teaspoon freshly ground pepper
Freshly grated Parmesan cheese

For the rosemary oil:
6 tablespoons extra virgin olive oil
6 small sprigs rosemary
3 whole cloves garlic, peeled

Make the pasta, wrap it, and set it aside to rest.

Prepare the filling: Salt and pepper the chicken legs and place them, skin side down, in a 12-inch cast-iron pan or skillet. Sprinkle 1 tablespoon of the rosemary leaves over the chicken. Cook the chicken over low heat for 20 minutes, or until the skin is very brown and crisp. Turn the chicken over and cook it for another 20 minutes. Transfer the legs to a plate to cool and pour off the rendered fat in the pan, leaving only a coating.

While the pan is still hot, add the sliced garlic and brown lightly over low heat. With a wooden spoon loosen the bits of chicken adhering to the bottom. Add the pancetta and the remaining 1 teaspoon rosemary. Cook for 2 minutes and transfer to a bowl.

When the chicken is cool enough to handle, remove the skin and set it aside. Working over the bowl containing the pancetta, pull the meat from the bones and let any juices fall in the bowl. Add any juices that have collected on the plate to the bowl. On a cutting board, chop the chicken skin into small bits. Chop the pancetta mixture and chicken meat to a fairly fine, ⅛-inch forcemeat. Add the freshly ground pepper and correct the filling for salt if necessary.

Make raviolis following the directions on page 179 and set them aside on a floured plate.

To make the rosemary oil: In a small saucepan warm the olive oil, rosemary, and garlic. Let it sizzle gently for 2 minutes and turn off the heat. Let the rosemary oil sit until you are ready to use it.

Bring a large pot of water to the boil, salted 3 tablespoons to the gallon. Cook the raviolis for 4 to 5 minutes. The raviolis will float and be tender at the edges. Drain well, and serve them 5 per person on warm plates. Drizzle ½ tablespoon of the rosemary oil over each serving and sprinkle with Parmesan cheese.

Lasagna of Eggplant, Tomato, and Basil

8 to 10 servings

I think of lasagna as a dish naturally suited to improvisation, expressing typical Italian exuberance in the kitchen. Lasagna is a comfortable, filling dish that combines pasta, sauce, and other ingredients to make a meal by itself. The possibilities for lasagna are endless. Variations might include assorted wild mushrooms set upon layers of noodles and béchamel sauce; or a stew of sliced sausages, onions, and greens, with tomato sauce; or chopped veal cooked with onions and herbs, then mixed with chopped calf's brains (which enrich and lighten the layers), spinach, and Parmesan and moistened with a Marsala-flavored béchamel. The elements that make up the layers of a lasagna must be well seasoned and each layer, particularly if there are many, must not be too thick; otherwise, the whole will be too heavy and the noodles—after all, this is pasta—will be lost.

This recipe is a light, meatless lasagna that features tomato, basil, and eggplant. It can be made a day ahead and covered and refrigerated until you are ready to finish it in the oven.

Basic Pasta, using 2 cups flour and 2 eggs (see page 177)
3 globe eggplants (3 pounds)
4 tablespoons pure olive oil
Salt and pepper
Water
1 pound mozzarella cheese
3 cups Tomato Sauce (see page 338)
3/4 cup loosely packed coarsely chopped fresh basil
3/8 cup freshly grated Parmesan cheese

Preheat the oven to 400°F. Make the pasta, wrap it up, and set it aside to rest for at least 45 minutes.

In the meantime, peel the eggplants and slice them into round pieces ¼ inch thick. Brush both sides of the slices lightly with the olive oil, salt and pepper them, and place them in overlapping rows on several baking pans. Add enough water to the pans to just cover the bottom. (This creates steam, which will keep the eggplants moist and help them to cook quickly.) Cover the pans with foil and bake the eggplants for 30 minutes, until they yield easily to the tip of a knife. When the eggplant is done, pour off the liquid in the pan and allow the eggplant to cool. Press the slices gently between the palms of your hand to remove excess water (otherwise the lasagna will be soggy) and pat the slices dry with paper towels. Slice the mozzarella as thin as possible.

Roll out the pasta dough, but not too thin (several times through the next-to-last setting on the machine is about right), and cut it into roughly 5-inch squares. Bring a large pot of water to the boil and in it cook three or four squares of pasta at a time, leaving each in the water for about 45 seconds, so that it is still somewhat firm to the bite. Have a pot of cold water next to the stove. Refresh the cooked dough squares in it a moment and transfer them to a large towel spread out upon the counter. (The most efficient method to prepare the dough is to have two people involved—one cooking the pasta, the other putting the lasagna together. If you are alone, you may wish to cook the dough squares as you need them, otherwise the preparation of this dish may present a space problem.)

Preheat the oven to 350°F. To assemble the lasagna: You will need a baking pan, roughly 16 by 9½ by 2 inches. Spread about ½ cup of the tomato sauce over the bottom of the pan. Set squares of the dough in the pan, slightly overlapping. Arrange eggplant slices side by side in an even layer over the dough, spoon a little sauce on each slice, sprinkle with basil and Parmesan, and top with slices of mozzarella to complete the first layer. Begin the next layer with a layer of pasta followed by sauce, then eggplant, and repeat what you did from the first layer. Repeat the second layer, to form three layers in all. To finish the top, arrange a layer of pasta, spoon ½ cup of the sauce over it, sprinkle with basil and Parmesan, and cover with slices of mozzarella. Dab each slice of cheese with sauce and bake the lasagna in the oven for 50 minutes. Let stand 5 minutes before serving.

Pasta with Giblet Sauce

4 large servings

Giblets are the heart, gizzard, and liver of poultry and are usually found wrapped together inside the cavity of the chicken or turkey. They are an inexpensive source of flavor and richly characteristic of the bird. This recipe uses hearts and gizzards only. They are generally available in shops that sell large quantities of poultry. Chinese markets are also a good source for duck, pigeon, and chicken giblets. All grain-eating birds have gizzards, a special digestive organ that breaks down the bird's feed. The gizzard has two dense lobes held together by a thick, tough membrane that must be cut away. The gizzards and hearts of small birds also can be used in this recipe; however, it is wiser to choose those from larger birds—the gizzard, in particular, is more substantial—and it is simpler to remove the lobes.

To make the sauce, the hearts and gizzards are first browned, then combined with diced vegetables, moistened, and braised until tender. Then they are finely chopped, remoistened with poultry broth (red wine is another option), and enriched with a little butter. Besides pasta, this sauce is delicious on grilled polenta or in risotti (after chopping the giblets do not remoisten them) and can be used to compound the flavor of stuffings and pan sauces for roasted birds.

This recipe yields 3 cups giblet sauce. You will need only half for four portions of pasta. The remainder will keep well for three to four days if wrapped tightly and stored in the refrigerator.

Basic Pasta, using 2 cups flour and 2 eggs (see page 177)
2 pounds chicken or duck gizzards and hearts (in approximately equal proportion)
2 tablespoons pure olive oil
Salt and pepper
1 large carrot (4 ounces), finely diced
½ large stalk of celery (2 ounces), finely diced
1 small yellow onion (5 ounces), finely diced
3⅓ cups poultry broth (see page 426)
5 tablespoons unsalted butter
Freshly grated Parmesan cheese

Make the pasta, wrap it up, and set it aside to rest.

Cut the hearts in half. Position the gizzards so that the rounded lobes are facing up, the connective membrane on the cutting board. Cut the red lobes away from the bluish-white skin to which they are attached. Warm the olive oil in a 10-inch pot with a 3-quart capacity. Add the gizzards and hearts, salt and pepper them, and raise the heat. The hearts and gizzards will release their juices. Allow these juices to reduce and evaporate. This takes 5 to 8 minutes. Lower the heat so that the pot hisses gently and cook them until they are browned well all over, about 20 minutes, stirring often to expose all sides to the heat.

Stir in the vegetables and cook another 8 to 10 minutes, until the vegetables have softened. Add ½ cup of the poultry broth and scrape up any bits adhering to the bottom of the pan. Add 2½ cups more broth, bring to a simmer, and cook

for 1 hour, until the broth has nearly all evaporated. Taste the gizzards; they should be tender yet slightly chewy. Turn the gizzards and hearts out onto a cutting board and chop them into an evenly fine mass of small bits.

Put a pot of water on for cooking the pasta. Roll out the pasta, cut the sheets into 8-inch lengths, and flour them on both sides. Roll up each piece of pasta and cut it into noodles ½ inch wide. Transfer half the minced giblets to a saucepan. Store the remaining giblets, tightly wrapped, in the refrigerator. Add the remaining ⅓ cup poultry broth to the giblets and adjust the heat so that the mixture bubbles. Stir in the butter, then reduce the sauce for 3 to 4 minutes, until the brothy portion is thickened slightly. Adjust the seasoning with salt and pepper.

Cook the noodles and toss them with the hot sauce. Serve with the Parmesan.

Lobster Raviolis

Thirty 2-inch raviolis, for 6

This recipe uses the whole lobster: Chop the tail and claw meat for the filling. The tomalley, roe, if any, and the head section are used to make the sauce. Seafood with a rich full flavor, such as lobster or sea scallops, need little else but butter, lemon, and herbs to make a stuffing for ravioli. The spare ingredients give these raviolis a simple, direct appeal; however, the price of lobster makes them an extravagance. At home, lobster raviolis are perhaps best served on special occasions, a birthday or New Year's Eve. If you make these raviolis in the summer and have access to lemon basil, you will find it to be particularly well suited to the flavor of lobster. In the winter, when basil is out of season, fresh chervil is a fine substitute.

1 recipe Basic Pasta (see page 177)

For the filling:
Two 1½-pound live lobsters (13½ ounces meat)
10 tablespoons unsalted butter, very well softened
Juice of 1 small lemon
Zest of ½ lemon
20 very fresh basil leaves, chopped

Make the pasta, wrap it up, and set it aside to rest.

Prepare the filling: Place each lobster belly down on a cutting board and insert a knife just above the tail and cut through the head section (see page 33 about live lobsters). Twist off the tail, pull off the claws, and set aside. Using both hands, split open the abdominal section and remove the sand sac. Rinse out the abdominal shell and head, and with a cleaver hack it into small pieces to make the sauce. Reserve the liquid from the lobster, along with the green tomalley (liver) and the roe, if any, and pass them through a medium sieve into a bowl. Reserve for finishing the sauce.

In a pot of boiling salted water cook the lobster tails and claws for 5 minutes. Drain and cool the lobster, crack the shells, and remove the meat. Save the shells for the sauce. Make a shallow cut down the top side of the middle of the tails and remove the lower portion of the digestive tract, which will appear as a yellow to green strand. Cut the claws in half and remove the claw meat. Dice the meat finely. In a bowl mix well with the other filling ingredients. Figure a scant tablespoon of filling for each ravioli.

Make raviolis following the directions on page 179 and set them aside on a floured plate.

For the sauce:
5 tablespoons unsalted butter
2 shallots (2 ounces), diced
1 carrot (3 ounces), diced
1 small stalk of celery, from the inner stalk (1 ounce), diced
1 small tomato
¼ red bell pepper (1½ ounces), diced
2 cloves garlic, sliced
3 sprigs fresh thyme
1 sprig parsley
1 bay leaf
5 cups water
1¼ cups heavy cream
1 teaspoon lemon juice
2 tablespoons chopped fresh basil

Prepare the sauce: Melt 3 tablespoons of the butter in a large saucepan, add the vegetables, garlic, and herbs, and cook slowly for 15 minutes. Raise the heat and add the reserved lobster carcasses. Turn the shells and stir for 5 minutes, until they have taken on color. Add the water and bring to the boil. Reduce and simmer for 15 minutes, without skimming the pot. Strain the lobster broth through a sieve into a wide sauté pan and reduce over high heat by half.

Stir in the heavy cream and lemon juice and reduce until the sauce thickens slightly and about 1 cup liquid remains. Over high heat, whisk in the remaining 2 tablespoons butter. Stir in the sieved roe and tomalley, remove from the heat, and pass the sauce through a fine sieve into a clean sauté pan. Warm the sauce without allowing it to bubble or reduce.

Bring a large pot of water to a boil, salted at 3 tablespoons per gallon. Cook for 4 minutes until the raviolis float and the edges are tender. Drain well, and add them to the sauce, turning them over gently so that they are coated. Arrange on warm plates and spoon the sauce around them. Sprinkle the basil over each portion.

Rosemary Noodles with Pigeon Essences

4 small servings

This pasta captures the essential flavor of charcoal-grilled pigeon and is otherwise unadorned. The whole pigeon is used to make a richly flavored reduction to sauce the noodles. The hearts and giblets of the birds are cooked separately and stirred into the sauce just before the pasta is added. So the liver does not overcook, it is added at the last moment.

This pasta was conceived in the context of a long menu with many courses. It belongs to a category of dishes, like consommé and certain soufflés, that are meant to be savored for their flavor, rather than consumed in quantity. Because it is rich, the portions should be small.

1 recipe Basic Pasta using 1 cup flour and 1 egg, and 1 tablespoon finely chopped rosemary (see page 177)
4 pigeons, with hearts, livers, and giblets
1 tablespoon olive oil
2 shallots, minced
2 ounces pancetta, diced
2 cloves garlic, finely sliced
4 cups chicken broth (see page 426)
4 cups beef broth (see page 427)
Salt and pepper
4 tablespoons unsalted butter
¼ cup freshly grated Parmesan cheese

Make the rosemary noodles.

Prepare a wood or charcoal fire. Remove the head and feet from the pigeons, but leave the necks on. Trim the giblets of surrounding and connective tissue. Separate the livers and remove any small bits of fat.

In a skillet, sauté the hearts and giblets in the olive oil over medium-high heat, stirring often so that they don't stick, until they are very brown all over. Add the shallots and cook for 5 minutes. Add the pancetta and the garlic. Reduce the heat and cook slowly for 10 minutes (without browning the pancetta and garlic), stirring often. In this time the hearts and giblets will have cooked to the well-done stage and will be very firm to the touch. Remove the mixture from the heat and transfer to a cutting board.

While the skillet is still hot, add the livers and cook them gently over very low heat. (Cooking livers correctly requires an increased attention on the part of the cook, as heat penetrates liver quickly. Do not leave the pan.) Turn the livers as soon as the edges begin to lighten in color and touch them frequently to test for doneness (get the feel of how soft the livers are when they are raw and how the texture changes as they are heated). When the livers are just firm in the center, remove them immediately from the pan and set aside on a cool plate. Chop the hearts and giblets, pancetta, and garlic into small bits and reserve in a bowl.

Return to the fire. Rake it out evenly and allow it to burn medium hot. If the fire is too hot, the results can be disastrous as the fat in the pigeon skin is very flammable. Before grilling the pigeons, it will be helpful to turn the wing joints under the neck. Grilling will take approximately ½ hour. Allow the pigeons to take as much smoke as possible (they should not be covered while cooking, however), brown the skin to a mahogany color, and render the fat. The pigeons will need to be turned frequently to insure that all portions cook evenly. Start them on their backs, then turn them breast side down. When the breast is brown, turn the pigeons on their sides propping one against the other so they do not fall over. Finish browning the last side.

Remove the pigeons from the grill, holding them flat so the juices in the cavity do not run out. Tip the birds, legs down, over a bowl to catch the juices, then transfer the birds to a heavy, wide cutting board. With a cleaver, chop them into very small pieces, making sure to crack all the bones. Transfer the chopped pieces to a saucepot and add the chicken and beef broth. Bring to just under the boil, skim, and simmer for 1 hour.

Sieve the broth through a heavy conical sieve into another pot. Use a pestle to push and pound through as much pigeon meat and marrow as possible, a little at a time. Alternatively, a food mill fitted with a medium blade can be used. This is a tedious process, but the more thoroughly it is done, the richer and more flavorful the sauce.

Put a large pot of water on to boil for the pasta.

To finish: Return the pigeon broth to the heat and reduce it to 2 cups. Add the chopped hearts, giblets, a large pinch of freshly ground pepper, and the butter to the reduced broth. Check the sauce for salt. Simmer until the butter is melted and stir well. Coarsely chop the reserved cooked livers.

Cook the noodles and drain them well. Add the noodles to the sauce with the chopped livers. Toss well. Transfer the noodles to a heated platter or to small bowls, distributing the sauce equally. Sprinkle lightly with the grated Parmesan and serve immediately.

Pumpkin Tortelli with Brown Butter and Sage

30 tortelli, for 6

Baked pumpkin, with the addition of brown butter, sage, and crumbled Italian almond cookies, makes an unusual, sweet-savory stuffing for pasta. They are fine by themselves but we have also served them alongside roasted fowl with a sauce made from the bird giblets.

One small pumpkin weighing about 5 pounds will provide enough stuffing for 60 to 75 tortelli. If less than this is desired, the finished stuffing can be reserved and served as a vegetable accompaniment at another meal. Unseasoned cooked pumpkin pulp can be used to make pumpkin bread or pie.

For the filling:
1 small pumpkin
2½ tablespoons unsalted butter
10 sage leaves
1 Amaretto di Saronno cookie, pounded to a powder in a mortar
1 tablespoon brown sugar
¼ teaspoon salt
⅛ teaspoon freshly ground pepper

1 recipe Basic Pasta (see page 177)

For the sauce:
2 cups chicken broth (see page 426)
8 small sage leaves
1½ tablespoons Marsala
5 tablespoons unsalted butter

Preheat the oven to 375°F.

Prepare the filling: Split the pumpkin in half and invert it, cut ends down, on an oiled baking sheet. Bake the pumpkin for 1 hour, or until the flesh is soft. Scoop out the pumpkin flesh, and measure 1¾ cups and reserve the rest. Transfer the pumpkin to a sauté pan. Over medium heat dry out the pumpkin for 5 to 10 minutes, stirring often so that it does not stick and until it exudes no water.

Brown the butter in a small saucepan with the sage, allowing the sage to fry in the butter. Strain the butter through a coarse sieve to catch the sage leaves, but allow the brown solids to pass through. Pour the butter over the pumpkin and mix well. Set aside the sage leaves. Transfer the pumpkin to a bowl to cool.

Chop the sage leaves and add them to the pumpkin with the ground cookie, sugar, salt, and pepper. The mixture should be slightly sweet. If it is not, add a little more sugar.

Make tortelli, allowing ½ tablespoon filling for each, following the directions on page 179.

Put a large pot of water on to boil for the tortelli.

Prepare the sauce: Pour the chicken broth into a 10-inch sauté pan and add the sage leaves. Reduce the broth by half. Add the Marsala, raise the heat, and whisk in the butter. Reduce the sauce until it thickens slightly and ¾ cup remains.

Keep the sauce warm. Salt the water and in it cook the tortelli for 4 to 5 minutes, drain them well, and add them to the warm sauce. Stir the tortelli carefully in the sauce until they are well coated. Serve on warm plates and spoon 2 tablespoons of the sauce over each serving.

Tortellini of Veal, Ricotta, Spinach, and Parmesan

72 tortellini, for 12

The stuffing for these tortellini is a delicately flavored mixture of lean veal, pancetta, spinach, ricotta, and Parmesan. Poached beef brain is added to enrich the mixture and contributes a creamy texture. There are several options for serving this pasta: in a full-bodied broth such as one made with turkey or veal; tossed in butter; or drizzled with extra virgin olive oil and sprinkled with Parmesan. A sauce of fresh porcini mushrooms, sliced thin and stewed in butter with a rosemary sprig, makes for a perfect union of flavors. When the mushrooms have softened, add a little poultry or veal broth, a bit more butter, and reduce to a saucy consistency before tossing with the tortellini.

When making tortellini, or any stuffed pasta, make the dough a little more moist than for cut pasta and allow it to rest and hydrate thoroughly before rolling. A slightly softer dough will insure that the edges seal tightly and the dough will stretch around the stuffing without tearing. When rolling the dough with the machine, remember to work with one sheet at a time and keep the remainder of the dough under a towel so that it does not dry out.

Basic Pasta using 3 cups flour and 3 eggs (see page 177)
1 large bunch spinach, leaves removed to yield 6 ounces, washed
Salt
2 bay leaves
4 ounces beef brains, rinsed under cold water
1 tablespoon pure olive oil
2 shallots (2 ounces), finely diced
2 ounces pancetta, sliced thin, diced
1 clove garlic, finely chopped
8 ounces lean veal from the shoulder or leg, fat and sinew removed
⅔ cup whole-milk ricotta
1 egg
⅛ teaspoon freshly grated nutmeg
½ teaspoon salt
Freshly ground pepper
3 tablespoons freshly grated Parmesan cheese
Butter, about 2 tablespoons per serving

Make the pasta, adding a little more water than for cut pasta, to produce a pliable dough. Wrap in plastic wrap and let rest about 1 hour before making the tortellini.

Parboil the spinach leaves for 2 minutes. Pour the spinach out into a colander and run cold water over it to cool it. Set a small pot of water (1 quart) with 1 teaspoon salt and the bay leaves to boil. Plunge in the brains and simmer gently for 15 minutes. Transfer the brains to a plate to cool. Form the spinach into a ball and, using your hands, squeeze out as much water as possible until the spinach is nearly dry, and set it aside.

Heat the olive oil in a small sauté pan, add the shallots, and cook them for 3 minutes. Add the pancetta and garlic and cook another 3 minutes, until the pancetta renders some of its fat and softens. Turn the mixture out onto a cutting board to cool. In the meantime, slice the veal thin, cut it into thin strips, then dice it.

Combine the diced veal and shallot-pancetta-garlic mixture in one pile and chop very fine with a heavy knife or cleaver, turning the mixture over upon itself with the blade of the knife. Transfer to a bowl. Chop the spinach and the brains to a similarly fine consistency and combine with the veal. Add the ricotta, egg, and seasonings and mix thoroughly. Refrigerate the stuffing until you are ready to make the tortellini.

Make tortellini following the directions on page 180. To cook them, bring a large 6-quart pot of salted water to the boil. Add the tortellini and cook for about 5 minutes. (Unless you have a very large pot, it is wise to cook half at a time.) Remove the tortellini with a flat wire strainer, toss them gently in butter (about 2 tablespoons per serving of 6), sprinkle lightly with Parmesan, and serve.

Pan-Fried Bay Scallops and Saffron Pasta with Parsley and Garlic

4 hors d'oeuvre or second course servings

The elements of this dish are meant to accompany one another—not meld— and so are assembled separately on the plate. Bay scallops are an autumn East Coast delicacy, with a clean, rich flavor and incomparable sweetness and tenderness. Breaded and pan fried, they require little more than a wedge of lemon. They are also superb with parsley and garlic, which is made here into a type of pesto that adds a fresh flavor to the noodles.

For the saffron pasta:
1 large pinch saffron
1 tablespoon hot water
1 egg yolk
1⅛ cups all-purpose flour

1 egg, beaten
8 ounces bay scallops
¾ cup fresh sourdough bread crumbs
1 small clove garlic
1 cup finely chopped fresh Italian parsley
Zest of ⅓ lemon
5 tablespoons unsalted butter
Pinch of salt and pepper
3 tablespoons clarified butter

Prepare the saffron pasta: Dissolve the saffron in the hot water and let it stand for 5 to 7 minutes. Strain the water through a fine sieve into a bowl, pushing on the threads with the back of a spoon to extract as much of the saffron as possible. Combine the saffron water and egg yolk with the flour to make pasta as described on page 177. When the pasta has rested, roll it thin and cut it into noodles ¹⁄₁₆ inch wide.

Next, bread the scallops: Beat the egg in a bowl, add the scallops, and coat them with the egg. Bread the scallops, one at a time, in the crumbs and lay them on a plate.

Put a pot of water on to boil for the pasta and put four plates above the stove or in a low oven to warm. In a mortar, smash the garlic little by little. Add the parsley and lemon zest and work it to a paste. Melt 2 tablespoons butter, stir it into the parsley mixture, and season with the salt and pepper.

Pour the clarified butter into a 12-inch cast-iron pan or a similar size skillet (one that will hold the scallops in a single layer) and warm it. When a bread crumb sizzles in the butter and the pasta water is boiling, add the breaded scallops to the pan. Cook the noodles at the same time as the scallops. Make sure the heat is high enough under the scallops or the crumbs will go soggy and will not brown. Turn the scallops in the pan to assure that all sides are brown. Meanwhile, test the noodles and have a bowl ready with the remaining 3 tablespoons butter in it. When the scallops are cooked, transfer them to a paper towel-lined plate to drain. Toss the saffron noodles in the butter and serve on the warmed plates. Arrange the scallops next to the pasta with about a teaspoon of the parsley paste on each plate.

Pasta with Sweetbreads, Mirepoix, Cream, and Thyme

For 4

Sweetbreads are the thymus and pancreas glands of a calf, which are lobe shaped—one long and flat, the other more rounded. They are quite common at well-stocked meat counters. Lamb sweetbreads are also sold by some butchers, by special order. Sweetbreads are perhaps the most delicately flavored of all the variety meats and require two separate cooking operations after having been thoroughly rinsed. The first is a long, gentle simmer with aromatic vegetables and herbs to make the sweetbreads tender. Then the thin elastic membrane, which covers the sweetbreads, needs to be peeled off. The sweetbreads are then ready to be finished and sauced.

1 recipe Basic Pasta (see page 177)
1 pound veal sweetbreads
1 small carrot (3 ounces)
¼ large stalk of celery (1 ounce)
½ medium onion (4 ounces)
1 bay leaf
Salt and pepper
Mirepoix:
  ½ small carrot (1 ounce), finely diced
  ¼ large stalk of celery (1 ounce), finely diced
  ½ small yellow onion (2 ounces), finely diced
2 tablespoons unsalted butter
¼ cup water
3 branches thyme
2 tablespoons clarified butter
½ cup heavy cream
1 tablespoon Dijon mustard
½ cup chicken broth (see page 426)
Juice of ⅛ lemon (1 teaspoon)
½ teaspoon chopped fresh thyme
½ teaspoon chopped fresh parsley
¼ cup fresh sliced chives

Make the pasta dough, wrap it, and set it aside to rest.

Rinse the sweetbreads in several changes of cold water to remove the blood and put them in a pot with enough water to cover well. Add the carrot, celery, onion, bay leaf, and ½ tablespoon salt. Bring to the boil, skim, and simmer, covered, for 1 hour and 15 minutes, or until the sweetbreads are soft and no longer resilient. Remove the sweetbreads from the pot, transfer to a colander, and let them cool. Discard the carrot, celery, onion, and bay leaf.

When the sweetbreads have cooked for 45 minutes, roll out the pasta dough and cut it into tagliolini (¼-inch-wide noodles).

In a pot, stew the mirepoix with the unsalted butter, water, thyme branches, and a pinch each of salt and pepper for about 10 minutes, or until the water evaporates.

Put a large pot of water on to boil for the pasta. Peel the sweetbreads. This is best done with your fingers, like peeling fruit. If the tough membrane is thoroughly removed, the sweetbreads will have a fine, delicate texture. Separate them into small pieces. In a 10-inch sauté pan cook the sweetbreads in the clarified butter, stirring often so they do not stick, until they are well browned and crispy all over. Remove the sweetbreads from the pan and transfer to a plate. Drain off the butter in the pan and discard it. Add the stewed mirepoix to the sauté pan and allow it to brown lightly. In the meantime, mix together the cream and Dijon mustard in a small bowl until well combined. When the mirepoix is lightly browned, add the chicken broth and bring to the boil. Then add the mustard-cream and bring it to the boil again. Reduce over high heat for approximately 1½ minutes, being careful not to let the mixture boil over. Bubbles will appear all over the surface, the cream and stock will thicken slightly and deepen in color. The goal is to achieve a consistency that is neither too thin (if so, it will not coat the pasta), nor too thick (which will make the noodles sticky and heavy); these are common pitfalls with cream-based sauces. The reduction time will vary: If a pan with more surface area is used, reduction will occur more quickly. It will also be affected by how much heat is applied—the higher the heat the faster the reduction.

When the sauce has reduced to the proper consistency, turn off the heat. Add the lemon juice, sweetbreads, chopped thyme, and parsley. Cook the pasta and drain it well, reserving a little of the water. Add the pasta to the sauce, stirring well so that the sauce coats the noodles. After stirring the pasta, there should be a surplus of sauce. If not, and the pasta appears sticky or heavy, it is an indication that the sauce was too reduced. In this case, add a little of the water in which the pasta cooked and continue to stir. Serve the pasta immediately in warmed wide bowls and garnish with the chopped chives.

Bread

Bread
Country Bread
Spontaneously Leavened Sourdough Bread
Levain Bread

Bread

While traveling through the small towns of Italy, where bakers still practice traditional methods, I saw that the flavor and character of bread has not been irretrievably lost to modern methods and that fully satisfying bread may be available to those willing to make it from scratch. Spontaneously leavened bread declares a personality and embodies a presence. I remember an Italian baker outside of Prato who referred to a loaf he had been making for twenty years (handed down by his father) as "the wise old man." Bread is similar to wine in that it is often understood to evoke something larger than itself, the regional soil, the character of the place and people who make and eat it.

Although spontaneously leavened bread may not be immediately discernible at first glance, its flavor and texture are a dead giveaway. They are characterized by long, lingering flavors, sophisticated yet down to earth, easy digestibility, and a keeping quality that is much longer than modern breads. The bread I strive for and most favor has a rustic, handmade quality, a crust that is sturdy and well browned, a certain weight without heaviness, a crumb that displays an interesting irregularity of small and large holes, a chewy, resilient texture, and bright, grainy flavors that make it satisfying all by itself.

So much of the mystery of spontaneously leavened bread, and the subject of starters (the culture of "wild" yeasts and bacteria that is introduced to the bread dough) can be attributed to the fact that the various strains of microorganisms cannot be seen or defined by the baker. Much like winemaking or cheesemaking, traditional breadmaking is a form of artisanry adapted to the variations of climate and environment, and the special flavor and character of the bread are a reflection of these factors. Although traditional bakers could not actually see what their bread contained, they developed a keen awareness of it through repetition, trial and error, and close observation. By making bread regularly, they understood the subtleties of fermentation, the character and particular demands of their starters, the ways in which more or less water, salt, or fat altered the crumb or crust, and the rhythms of the baking cycle. Before the development of commercial yeast, bakers were necessarily more intuitive practitioners.

Commercial yeast, a relatively recent phenomenon considering the long history of leavened bread, is an isolated strain that makes it easy for anyone to make bread with a high degree of consistency in a short period of time. Yet these merits must be weighed against a weaker and less interesting uniformity of flavor when compared to breads made with traditional leavens. Commercial yeast is vigorous and tyrannical, crowding out its wilder competition—airborne yeasts and bacteria that leave stronger, more distinctive characteristics in the bread. Yeasts, the microorganisms responsible for leavening bread, are ubiquitous in our environment and are naturally present on untainted grains that are milled to make flour. Wild yeasts may appear to act unpredictably until you understand them and learn to coax them to act in accordance with the bread you have in mind. This is a cooperative effort; the yeasts and other organisms have their own life rhythms and are sensitive to the variables of temperature and time. Working with spontaneous leavens is a commitment, not so much of time (the manipulations involved in keeping it healthy are brief and simple) but of consistent and regular attention. The culture you keep requires care and feeding to keep it growing. Without regular attention your starter culture may not die, but it is likely that a pattern of neglect will mean spending more time restoring its vigor. Using a starter that is less than vigorous to make bread will yield loaves that are unpredictable and disappointing. When making bread with spontaneous leavens, first, discover the condition in which the starter culture thrives. Second, develop a recipe in cooperation with the starter that satisfies your particular preferences for bread—its flavor, crust, color, and weight.

Although it is known that yeasts are all around us, this isn't much help when it comes to actually making spontaneously leavened bread. Indeed, this fact only contributes to mysterious notions about the process, and the baker as alchemist. How are yeasts trapped and how can one be sure of the efficacy of the strain? A common recipe for bread starters instructs that flour be mixed with water and left out in the open air with the hope that leavening yeasts would light upon it, thereby activating the dough and initiating the starter. The idea of trapping yeast is not the point. Yeasts are naturally present on the grains milled to make flour, in the same way that organisms that make wine live naturally on the skins of grapes. That yeast would gravitate toward a favorite food source (the sugars present in grains) is logical. That flour contains exactly what is needed to eventually become bread is a wonderful coincidence of nature.

There are other sources of wild yeasts besides grain. Steve Sullivan, who operates the Acme Bread Company and is Chez Panisse's first baker (we still serve his bread nightly), attributes the particular character of his levain bread to a starter he inoculated with wine grapes. (See the description of this process and his recipe on page 218).

Fermentation, the signal of yeast and bacterial activity, is encouraged by providing three essential conditions: a moist environment, consistent temperatures in an optimal range (too high and the bacterial population takes over, producing acid which sours the starter excessively; too low and yeast becomes dormant), and a regular replenishment of flour and fresh water, which provides a source of food. Assuming that all ingredients are pure, fermentation is inevitable. The traditional method of maintaining the starter culture is to make it part of the breadmaking process: A portion of the bread dough, or sponge (a preliminary mixture of the starter culture with water and a portion of the total flour in the formula), is held back before salt is added, and used as the basis for the next batch of bread. This fulfills two functions: the starter culture, mixed together with new flour and water, is given fresh nutrients, and the bread cycle is regenerated. The regular cycle of use and replenishment, where nothing is wasted or extraneous, is a recurrent theme in breadmaking.

Developing a bread recipe involves an understanding of the effect of the various ingredients, then working from what is known to an educated guess about proportions. It is important that you have in mind an idea of the kind of bread you would like to make. You may even begin by noticing what it is you like or dislike about the bread that you are able to buy. You may wish, for instance, to have your own bread be darker with more of the flavor of the whole grain, or to be lighter with a more crunchy crust, more or less sour, and shaped differently.

Having experimented with spontaneous leaven, I have discovered that it is perhaps more helpful and less frustrating from the standpoint of learning about the principles of breadmaking to begin by making bread with commercial yeast, which acts quickly and predictably. Once you have discovered your preferences, isolate a particular loaf and analyze the formula. What is the process, the proportion of flour to water, how much salt? The success of any bread depends upon the interplay of specific ingredients and proportions. Although it is not probable that the same formula would apply to a bread made with a spontaneous leaven, you will most likely gain a reference point. It may require some detective work to correct a fault or change the character of your bread. Inevitably this will lead you to understand bread as a simultaneity of reactions and conditions, each one dependent upon the other.

Bread's Basic Ingredients

I prefer to use unbleached flours that are milled from organically grown grains. These are generally available in natural food stores (see page 211 for sources of untreated flours and grains). Untreated flour is nutritious and wholesome. If you are making spontaneously leavened bread, untreated flour is a must since you are relying upon the flour to contain a healthy population of organisms to leaven and flavor your bread. Grains treated with pesticides or those that have been bleached after milling are less likely to contain the necessary organisms.

This applies to both white flour and whole grain flours. When white flour is called for, use organic unbleached white flour, which contains a high protein or gluten content (around 13 percent). Unless you are making a quantity of bread each week, buy your flour as you need it and store it in airtight containers. Flour is perishable—whole grain flours milled from wheat berries or rye are particularly subject to rancidity as they contain more of the natural oils of the grain. It is best to purchase small quantities and store them refrigerated. When you purchase flours, sample them first. They should smell clean and taste bright without a trace of bitterness. If you become an avid baker, you may consider purchasing a home mill so that you can be assured of the freshness of your flour (see page 211).

The quality of the water you use in breadmaking should not be underestimated. In general, water that is suitable for drinking is suitable for breadkmaking, and it should neither be too hard nor soft, nor should it contain a high concentration of chlorine. Use the purest water you can find but never use distilled water (the softest water of all). If you distrust the quality of your water, or if its taste and odor make you suspicious, you may consider purchasing mountain spring water. Otherwise, boil it first and use it after it is cooled.

If you are using commercial yeast, you will encounter it in two forms—fresh compressed yeast, also called cake yeast, and dehydrated granules, called active dry yeast. Both are strains of *Saccharomyces cerevisiae* and are very reliable when it comes to raising bread. I prefer to use active dry yeast because it is less perishable and can be bought in bulk at substantial savings. Avoid fast-acting yeasts— they produce quick-risen breads with little flavor and interest. Store your yeast in tight containers in a cool place as far away as possible from exposure to warmth, moisture, or air. In this way it will maintain its potency for several months. The cell walls of dried yeast are fragile and are most readily restored in warm water. If the water is too cool, cell contents can leak out, damaging the yeast. If the water is too hot, the yeast will die. Follow the manufacturer's directions explicitly for reactivating the yeast from its dormant state. Ask to see the instructions on the label if you buy it in bulk.

Salt is another basic breadmaking ingredient. Most salt that is available contains additives, which prevent it from forming lumps, and so-called "free-flowing" agents. Although these additives do not affect breadmaking in any observable way, it is questionable whether they are really necessary. You can avoid them by purchasing additive-free salt, which will not cake up if you keep it in a sealed container. Finely ground imported sea salt is another option, the virtues of which are its higher mineral content and a more potent flavor. Salt strengthens the gluten and regulates the activity of the yeast. With certain precautions it is possible to make saltless bread (the dough rises quickly, and must be watched carefully so that it doesn't overferment), while too much salt inhibits fermentation and causes the loaf to expand poorly.

Notes on Method of Making Bread

Yeasts and other microorganisms are the mother of the bread and play a major role in determining its characteristics; good bread is also a harmony—balanced ingredients carefully manipulated in the context of regulated time and temperature. Through repetition of a basic recipe you will learn the demands of your bread and how it can change in subtle ways from day to day depending upon your manipulations. If you set out to develop your own bread from a spontaneous leaven it is particularly important to keep a record of your formula and the results. (See page 209 for a system of evaluation for your bread.) It is also wise to have a few simple tools, namely a large ceramic bread bowl, plastic dough scraper with one side rounded for scraping the inner contours of the bowl, and a large metal spoon.

First list your proportions. Measure carefully. Professional bakers weigh everything, which is certainly the most accurate method of measuring, particularly as applied to starters that expand in volume and not in weight during fermentation. Furthermore, the milling of flour is variable as is the degree to which the flour has been compacted in storage. Volume measurement of flour is not reliable. Thus the recipes that follow call for measurements of flour in pounds and ounces.

Room temperature (70°F to 75°F) is ideal for making bread. Except for yeast, which is dissolved at a warmer temperature, the ingredients should be at room temperature before you mix the dough. To gain control from the very start, professional bakers generally take an average of room, water, and flour temperature, and adjust accordingly to bring the mixture into the optimal range. If you keep your flour in a cool larder and your work space is similarly cool, it may be necessary to use warmer water. If your kitchen is hot, you can correct by adding cooler water. When beginning to make bread it is wise to purchase a rapid-response thermometer and to take the temperature of the work room, the flour, and water. With practice you will be able to determine this by feel. Until you gain the sense, use this simple calculation: add the temperature of the flour, water, and room and divide by three; if the outcome is in the 70°F to 75°F range, proceed to mix the dough. Otherwise, adjust the temperature of the water (this is easier than warming or cooling the flour).

There are a number of different ways in which a bread dough can be mixed, and it is well worth experimenting to develop new possibilities in your bread-making. A "straight" dough is one in which all of the ingredients in the formula are mixed together from the start. First, dissolve the yeast in warm water in the bread bowl. Then add the rest of the water called for in the formula. If you are working with a natural starter, break it up in the water. Then add the flour and lastly the salt. Never add salt while the yeast is dissolving or you will damage it. When all the flour has been incorporated, dig in with your hands. Bring the mixture together in a shaggy mass, turn it out onto a floured board, and begin kneading.

Straight doughs, though perhaps the simplest method for home bakers, offer less flexibility as compared to the "sponge" dough method. A sponge is a portion of the ingredients—flour, water, yeast or starter, and most often, salt—that has been allowed to ferment ahead of time. When the rest of the ingredients are added later the mixture is called a sponge dough. Once mixed, a straight dough will eventually ripen and be ready for baking. Working with a sponge, however, one can either use it right away or wait a while, since it does not comprise the entire formula. The sponge method produces some of the best and most flavorful breads and is quite practical if your schedule is demanding or erratic. The usual long fermentation of the sponge contributes flavor to the bread and increases its keeping quality. The sponge method can be adapted to almost any bread recipe by setting aside one half or slightly more of the total flour, yeast, and enough of the water to bring the dough together in a moist (never wet) but slightly stiff consistency, and to allow it to ferment for a period of 3 to 24 hours. The longer the fermentation period, the cooler the temperature should be. Remember, the higher the temperature the more active yeast becomes. (I usually leave the sponge overnight in a cool spot in the house—around 50°F—or in the refrigerator. If you decide to ferment the sponge for half this time, do so at room temperature. Longer fermented sponges also require less yeast since during this time yeast will reproduce and multiply.)

You may also wish to vary the point at which you add salt. Some bakers favor the delayed salt process for certain breads. In its absence, fermentation will proceed more vigorously. It is wise with an overnight or day-long process to include some of the salt in the formula so that there is some check on fermentation and your bread dough does not deteriorate.

Kneading develops and lengthens the gluten in the flour and creates a resilient fabric that will readily expand upon release of carbon dioxide, which is expelled by the yeast during fermentation. Besides forming the gluten network, kneading helps incorporate air, which makes the dough stronger and encourages the bonding of proteins into gluten. I like to mix and knead bread by hand as it affords the opportunity of being that much closer to the process and for gaining a sensitivity to the feel of the bread. Kneading may make you breathe hard, but will inform you at the same time of the progress of the dough. Kneading will bring you a sense of satisfaction in having molded the bread yourself.

A slow, cool, fermentation period contributes to the flavor of bread, and also appears to be related to the keeping quality of the finished loaf. I think of the fermentation period of bread somewhat like marinating. The bread dough is conditioned and flavored by the by-products of its own fermentation; the longer the fermentation the better the flavor. Cool temperatures are usually recommended so that yeast and bacterial activity are kept under control. Although most breads made with commercial yeast will be ready to bake in relatively shorter periods of time, you may wish to allow your dough to ferment overnight in a cool spot (50°F to 60°F). Prolonged doughs should be deflated and kneaded briefly throughout their cool fermentation period, when they appear fully expanded. Punching down a dough after rising invigorates the leavening organisms by moving them to new sources of food and oxygen. A dough will stop rising when yeast uses up the nourishment in its immediate environment. Furthermore, alcohol, which is another by-product of yeast fermentation, is released and allowed to evaporate. A strongly alcoholic dough is harmful to the yeast and gives bread an unpleasant aroma.

When the bread dough is fermented long enough and has flavored and conditioned itself sufficiently, it is said to be ripe and is ready for shaping and a final rise, but not always—some breads go directly from their slow first rising to the oven—levain bread, for instance. The gluten is at its most elastic and in the best condition for expanding with the release of gas produced by the yeast. Ripe dough produces the best bread, with good volume, color, and flavor, and it will last longer in your cupboard as well.

Before its final rise the bread dough must be shaped. The purpose of shaping is to give the dough a well-arranged structure to encourage its expansion in the oven and to create a form for the bread that delights your eye. While shaping, the dough is thoroughly deflated and the gas that has collected within is expelled so the bread does not later contain gaping holes. I have had best results rolling up the dough, a method which is applicable to both long and round shapes. Lightly flour the work surface. Invert the dough onto the surface and deflate it with the palm of your hand. Don't stretch the dough at this point or handle it roughly or the gluten will tear. Press it out to a rough circle. To shape a round loaf, roll the dough up snugly into a rough cylinder. Turn it on end and roll it up again tightly. Turn the dough folded side down and round it with cupped hands until you have a smooth taut ball. Another method of shaping a round loaf is to place it (first rolled and formed into a taut ball) for its final rise in a basket lined with heavy, floured cloth, such as muslin. As the dough expands, it fills the basket and takes on its shape. The dough is placed in the basket smooth side down and later carefully inverted onto a baking peel and loaded in the oven. You may have to experiment some with the amount of dough and basket size until they fit.

For a longer loaf, follow the same process but instead of turning the dough on end and rolling it up again, allow it to rest about 5 minutes, then, placing your hands on the dough with fingers extended, press moderately and roll back and forth, gradually moving your hands apart until the loaf has extended to the length you want.

The final rise is usually carried out in a warmer temperature to encourage vigorous yeast activity. For the final rise, most professional bakers use a square metal container, called a proof box, which is temperature and humidity controlled. The proof box can be easily improvised at home. I use a sheet pan enclosed in a large, transparent plastic trash bag. The bag is gathered together, inflated by blowing into it, tied off, and set in a warm place. The bread is sealed from the air, stays moist without forming a skin, and warmth is trapped in. I enclose a thermometer to monitor the temperature of the final rise. The time necessary for the warm rising period will vary according to the particular loaf. Dough that is ready for baking will have at least doubled in size in the final rise. The dough may rise too far, in which case it will appear jiggly or flabby, evidence of gluten deterioration. Large blisters or bubbles usually accompany this symptom.

Bread that is fermented too long and that has been allowed to rise excessively will not achieve the full measure of its growth in the oven. This growth is called "oven spring" and refers to the dramatic increase in volume the loaf achieves about 15 minutes into the baking. Experimenting with the time of the final rise of your bread will produce dramatically different results—a half hour more or less can make a considerable difference. It is critical that you understand these limits and the potential of your bread at this finishing stage. Note the appearance of the dough, not only its volume, but its color and character (ripe, risen dough usually loses its glossiness), and touch it to get a sense of the condition of the gluten. Record your results. Soon you will be able to tell at a glance when the dough is ready for the oven.

Before the invention of the gas oven, bread was baked directly on the hearth in stone or brick ovens fueled by wood fires. There is still no substitute for this method. At the restaurant all of our pizzas are baked in a large brick oven that never cools down; by now it is seasoned with the smoke of burning oak, which is clearly detectable in the crusts of the pizzas and other foods we bake in it. I have two ovens at home, one is gas, and the other is outdoors and is made of a mixture of brick and refractory cement, sand and crushed rock. I fuel it with seasoned hardwood. In it I bake all my bread. Beyond the enhancement of wood and smoke, dense stone ovens provide a quality of heat that is altogether different from a gas oven. Baking in a stone oven provides heat that is more consistent, intense, and penetrating; dense brick on the hearth and walls holds the heat so that temperature fluctuation, as a result of opening the door to load the oven, or peering in to check the bread's progress, are quickly equalized. There are few things as simple and exciting as a crackling fire, the wafting, anticipatory aroma of burning wood (later captured in crust and crumb), the warm glow of coals, then steam and ash as you mop the hearth clean with water. Using a wood-fired oven for baking is perhaps less convenient, but is all the more beautiful and so will be your bread.

Some of the qualities of the stone oven can be improvised in your own oven at home. Placing quarry tiles or other flat ceramic bricks directly on the floor of the oven simulates the even, heat-retaining properties of a stone hearth, aids in the formation of a crust and in cooking the loaf through. Be certain you preheat your oven well before baking. A half hour to 45 minutes is necessary whether or not you use tiles on the bottom.

Introducing steam in the oven enhances the color, sheen, and crispness of the crust. Steam prevents a tight skin from forming on the outside of the loaf during "spring" time and thus allows for maximum expansion. Since moisture inhibits browning reactions, steam is introduced in the early stages of baking. The sheen that results from a steamy oven is due to surface starch that gelatinizes on the crust of the bread. In a gas oven the simplest way of steaming is to use a plastic spray bottle. Mist the oven before you load it with bread (be careful not to put out the pilot light) and three or four times more during the first 10 minutes of baking. Not all breads require steam to achieve good color and crumb quality. Wet doughs in particular release vapor as they cook, creating a steamy microclimate all by themselves.

The first indication that bread is done is its aroma, which changes from sweet, steamy, and yeasty during its initial period in the oven to the drier, pleasantly nutty aroma of browned grain. The common method of insuring that the interior of the bread is cooked is to tap it on the bottom and to listen for a hollow, resonant thud. You can verify this sound by checking the quality of the crumb when you later slice into the cooled loaf. Allow the bread to cool on an elevated rack so that air can circulate around it. Breads made from wet doughs that left the oven crisp will often soften during cooling with the release of steam from the center of the loaf. Putting the bread back in the oven a second time for another 10 minutes or so will restore the crunch of the crust.

Keeping freshly made bread around the house may be improbable—the temptation to eat it all at once is strong. Nevertheless, if you need to store it for a period, allow it to cool thoroughly and place it in a closed plastic bag, expelling as much air as possible before closing it off. This will lock in its moisture.

The following is a list of criteria that may be useful in evaluating your bread, as well as some remarks that may be helpful in troubleshooting disappointing results. When you learn to look closely at bread, you will look at its various qualities separately. However, it is important not to dwell on any one aspect, but to consider the whole so that you can develop an informed hunch about what to do differently the next time you bake. You may find, for instance, that a dull, disappointing crust color in one of your trials is accompanied by heaviness, a tight crumb, and a sour flavor. Consider these defects together, not separately, before setting out to correct the fault. Remember: Bread is an integrity, a simultaneity of reactions and conditions. If your bread has defects, try to solve the whole problem, not just a part of it.

Before and Through the Baking

First, list your proportions so that you can refer easily to your formula.
How much flour, water, yeast or starter, salt
"Straight" dough or "sponge" dough
How long kneaded
Dough temperature after kneading
Temperature of environment in which dough is put to rise
Length and number of rises
Dough punched down at . . . (list times)
Method of shaping
Temperature and length of final warm rise
Oven temperature
Steam introduced
Length of baking

After Baking

VOLUME: A loaf with poor volume probably didn't rise well. Lack of volume is related to a number of causes—old or soft (low gluten) flour; yeast that isn't fresh or that wasn't properly reconstituted (water too hot or cold); or damaged by direct contact with salt; inadequate rising period or final rising too cool; or insufficient kneading.

CRUST: Crust color should have a certain brightness in shades of warm gold to deeper tones of chestnut and foxy brown. Paleness, grayness, or dullness are usually associated with an overly risen loaf or one that has fermented too hot (or both) or oven temperatures that are too low. A heavy or tough crust can result from the same problem. If the color of the crust is uneven, it is a good idea to rotate the bread in the oven as most metal ovens have hot spots. If the crust is blistered, it may have risen too long, a common symptom of wet doughs left unattended in the final warm rise, or it may not have been deflated entirely when shaped.

SHAPE: If the dough bulges or rises uncontrollably in the oven, it is likely that it needed to be slashed or dimpled before baking to prevent a wild expansion of the loaf.

CRUMB: After you slice the bread, check the crumb. Are the holes small or large, tightly closed or open, irregular or of consistent size? Large holes result when the dough is not deflated sufficiently, or carelessly shaped and for other reasons such as an excessively long final rise. If the crumb is very airy and open, it is likely that the dough was too moist. If the crumb is uneven, dense in the center, or open outside, it was too cold before going into its final warm rise. If there are any hard spots in the crumb you may have damaged or dried out the dough by placing it too near a source of heat during the final rise, such as a pilot light on a gas-burning stove. You may also have incorporated hard bits of flour and water scraped up from the table during kneading. Or again, your dough may have fermented either too long or not long enough. Well-fermented bread will exhibit a crumb clarity, well-defined holes, and areas of near translucency where thin sheets of gluten have stretched and are fixed in place. A crumb should also feel slightly resilient, unless you are baking a moist bread enriched with fats. If the crumb is crumbly, it is likely that you added too much flour, kneaded too little, or overfermented the dough.

FLAVOR: Make some notes on the aroma and flavor of the bread. Overly fermented breads will taste cidery or like flat beer. A long-process bread that has not been punched down will smell alcoholic. If the bread is overly sour, your starter is probably the culprit. It may need to be given some attention before you bake again. If the bread is bland, you probably forgot, or need to increase, the amount of salt.

When a loaf of bread exhibits all the right qualities the word "bloom" is used to describe the unmistakable luster, a sum larger than the parts. Such a loaf, coaxed into being by knowing hands, is the baker's ineffable pleasure.

Giusto's is a large-scale operation that mills all its own flour, distributes a variety of grains, beans, edible seeds, leaveners, sweeteners, oils, and other items used in natural baking. Both conventionally grown and organically grown grains are sold, and products processed from the latter are so identified as "organically grown and processed" in accordance with Section 26569.11 of the California Health and Safety Code. Giusto's ships anywhere in the country. Their catalog is $1.00, upon request.

Giusto's
241 East Harris Avenue
South San Francisco, California 94080
(415) 873-6566

I personally own and can attest to the efficiency of an electric grain mill called Magic Mill III Plus. This machine mills, at low temperature, all grains and small dried beans into flour at the rate of 1.2 pounds per minute and has a texture dial, which allows the user to mill grains into coarse and fine flours. The grain mill may be purchased from distributors in your area to which the headquarters listed below would be happy to refer you. Otherwise you can purchase it directly. A brochure with pictures and specifications is available upon request.

Magic Mill, International Headquarters
1911 South 3850 West
Salt Lake City, Utah 84014
(801) 972-0707

Country Bread

When I developed this bread I had in mind a rustic country bread with a tasty brown crust, a regular, porous crumb, the flavor of whole grains, and a full, chewy bite. I begin with a starter made of a little yeast, water, and flour. This recipe gives several optional times for fermentation of the starter and the bread dough. The longer the fermentation periods, the more flavor and character the loaf will develop. Making this bread the first time is a two-day process, even if you opt for a shorter fermentation time for the starter and dough.

The proportions for the starter make four times more than is necessary for one loaf. I like to keep more of the starter on hand in case I bake more frequently than once a week, or in more quantity. Once the starter has fermented for at least 24 hours it will keep well for about 6 days, if covered tightly and left in the refrigerator. After this point it begins to take on a beery, bitter quality unless attended to: To keep your starter going, stir it several times a week to expel alcohol, and replace the amount you last removed to make bread. Make these replacements to the starter at least 24 hours before you make bread again to give them time to ferment. If you do not intend to make bread, and merely wish to refresh the starter, cut away and discard 4 ounces and replenish it with the amounts of flour and water described below.

The recipe makes about 1 pound of starter. For one loaf of bread you will need one-quarter of this amount, or 4 ounces. To replace the 4 ounces of starter you used to make the bread, soften the remaining starter with ¼ cup of water and stir in 2½ ounces bread flour. Use these proportions to replace the starter each time you bake. It should not be necessary to add more yeast to the starter if you use it frequently, since your original yeast will reproduce and multiply. If your starter appears sluggish (slow to bubble up, or expand when left at room temperature), add ⅛ teaspoon yeast with your next feeding: Warm the ¼ cup water to dissolve the yeast, then proceed as described above to replace the starter with 2½ ounces of flour.

For the starter:
½ cup water at 100°F
½ teaspoon active dry yeast
½ cup water at room temperature
10 ounces unbleached bread flour

Put the warm water in a small bowl and sprinkle the yeast over it. Let the yeast stand for 10 minutes. After this time the mixture should appear milky. If some of the yeast has not dissolved, stir the mixture with a clean spoon. Pour the yeast mixture into a larger bowl or crock, add the other half of the water, and mix in the flour until both are well combined in a stiff batter. Cover the bowl or crock tightly with plastic wrap and let stand at around 70°F for 24 to 72 hours. Then make the bread dough. After one day the starter will be bubbly and full of air. Stir it each day to invigorate the yeasts and expel alcohol.

For the bread dough:
¾ teaspoon active dry yeast
½ cup water at 100°F
1¼ cups water at room temperature
4 ounces of starter
1 pound unbleached bread flour
2½ ounces rye flour
2½ ounces whole wheat flour
2 teaspoons salt

In a bread bowl, dissolve the yeast in the warm water. Add the remaining water and the starter and using your hand, break it up in the water. Pour over the yeast mixture 15 ounces of the bread flour, the rye and wheat flours, and the salt. Mix the ingredients together by hand until you have formed a rough mass. Gather up all the flour or bits of dough sticking to the sides of the bowl (a plastic scraper is handy) and turn the dough out onto a floured work surface with ample space, about 2 feet square.

Dust the work surface and the top of the ball of dough with a little flour (use a portion of the remaining 1 ounce bread flour) and begin kneading the dough. It will feel very sticky and will adhere to your hands, but ignore this and dive in. Form the dough into a rough round. Plant yourself firmly in front of the work surface and begin pushing down and forward on the dough from the center out. Gather it up, and turn the extended portion back upon itself. Continue this motion of pushing down and forward and folding the dough over upon itself using quick motions. Rotate the dough slightly each time you bring it back upon itself and continue kneading with a rhythmic motion. Use your whole upper torso and lean into the dough (the level of the work area should not be too low—just below your navel is ideal) so as not to tire your arms. Add more flour to the work surface and the top of the dough as necessary, but use no more than the 1 ounce during the entire kneading process.

Every once in a while scrape up the dough adhering to the work surface and push it back into the mass. The reason for kneading is to extend and stretch the dough. If the dough shreds or tears you are working it too hard. Once all of the dusting flour has been incorporated, after about 5 minutes, continue to knead the dough for 10 minutes more, making the forward, backward, and rotating stroke about every 3 seconds. At the end of this time the dough will have lost most of its tackiness.

At this point there are two options. If you wish to have fresh-baked bread the same day, place the kneaded dough in an oiled bowl large enough for a triple expansion of the dough, cover it tightly with plastic wrap, and store it at warm room temperature, around 75°F for 3 to 3½ hours, or until the dough is tripled in volume.

Turn the risen dough out onto the work surface, deflate it, and then shape it into a round loaf as described on page 224. Place the dough in a basket or the middle of a baking pan, enclose in a large plastic bag (preferably clear, so that you can monitor the rising), inflate the bag by gathering it together at the open end and blowing air inside. Twist the end of the bag to hold the air and tighten a piece of string around the twisted end. Set the basket or baking pan in a warm place. An ideal temperature for the warm final rise is close to 100°F. You may wish to check this temperature by enclosing a thermometer in your improvised proof box. Let the bread rise for 1 hour, or until it has doubled in size, loses its glossy appearance, and is somewhat jiggly.

The second option is to allow the dough to triple in volume, then to punch it down and refrigerate it for 24 hours. Fermentation will proceed at a much slower rate; in the meantime, the dough will develop an added character and flavor. After the long, cool fermentation, allow the dough to return to room temperature (this takes about 3 hours), shape it, and give it the warm final rise described above.

To bake: Preheat the oven to 500°F, about 30 to 45 minutes before you intend to bake. Remove the plastic bag and sprinkle the top of the loaf with flour. Using your fingertips, make shallow impressions all over the surface to prevent the bread from bulging or rising up irregularly. Set the bread in the oven, reduce the heat immediately to 400°F, and bake the bread until it is crusty and dark brown, for about 45 to 50 minutes, or until it sounds hollow when rapped on the bottom. Cool the bread on a rack and if the crust loses its crispness in cooling, return it to the 400°F oven for 10 minutes.

Spontaneously Leavened Sourdough Bread

This loaf is, to my taste, fully gratifying—its sophisticated, tangy, lingering flavors are carried by a crumb that is chewy and unevenly porous. If you cut into the loaf before it cools entirely (a temptation you will hardly be able to resist) you will be privy to its mysterious and complex aroma reminiscent of grape must and dry grasses. The soulful character of this bread is due to a spontaneous leaven propagated from simple ingredients—water, flour, and potato.

It has long been known that boiled potato, as well as the water in which it has cooked, is an attractive food source for yeasts and other microorganisms beneficial to bread. Breads that use the potato, or its cooking water, as an ingredient have moist crumbs and fine crust color. Here the potato and cooking water provide a fertile medium in which a starter culture of leavening yeast and other microorganisms is generated. The potato encourages the vigorous growth of the wild yeasts and organisms present in the flour and air. With subsequent feedings and refreshings of the starter (flour and water only), the potato is eventually metabolized by these organisms. You will notice its ever-weakening presence in successive bakings: the crumb will lighten in color and will not bear as much moisture as it previously did, and the warm caramel tones of the earlier crusts will be supplanted by coarser, mat-brown hues. The power of the potato should not be underestimated—if, at some point later on, your starter has suffered from neglect and appears slow to bubble up or produces heavy bread, use the water in which potatoes have boiled to fertilize and restore its vigor.

As you have already gleaned, it takes some time for this bread to come into its own. Your role as baker is also one of nursemaid and it is necessary that you administer regular and patient care in the infancy of this bread. This is not a bread that can be fashioned in an afternoon. The starter must be coaxed and attended through a period of clumsiness (your first loaves may be heavy and contain cheesy aromas you might find distasteful) until its full powers develop and come into balance. Once established, however, the starter will require less of your time and can be refreshed at the same time you make bread (provided you do so on on a weekly basis). Each time you mix the bread dough a portion of the dough (10 ounces per loaf) is held back as the basis for future doughs.

If you have experience making bread with commercial yeast, you may be discouraged by the apparently sluggish pace at which this dough rises. It prefers to take its own sweet time. The 8 or more hours allotted the dough to rise results in a full fermentation of the loaf and a complete dispersion of the flavorful by-products of this activity throughout the crumb and crust. The warm final rising is critical to achieving a light, porous crumb.

Step One: Sourdough starter for 2 large loaves
2½ ounces peeled Russet potato, cut into small pieces
⅞ cup water
7½ ounces organic unbleached bread flour

Combine the potato and 1½ cups water in a small stainless-steel saucepan, bring to the boil, reduce to a simmer, and cook for 15 minutes, until the potato pieces are very soft. Pour the potatoes and the water into a clean 1½-quart glass or clear plastic container (so that you can observe the starter as it ferments). Mash the potatoes finely with a fork and allow the mixture to cool to room temperature. Stir in the flour gradually and work it until well combined in a stiff batter. Cover the container tightly with plastic wrap and store it at 70°F to 80°F.

Keep a notebook and record the time and date you set the starter; this will help you understand what you are working with. You will notice after 6 to 8 hours that the starter has lost its ivory color and has begun to gray. This is perfectly normal and is the result of air in contact with the potato in the starter. The starter often progresses to darker shades of gray, particularly on the surface. Liquid may rise to the surface as well. Don't be alarmed, simply stir the starter vigorously, cover it, and let it sit.

Taste the starter after 24 hours to monitor its progress. You should detect a flavor somewhat akin to mild white cheese. After 32 hours, you should notice small holes against the glass or plastic container, bubbles on the surface, and that the whole mixture has expanded. Stir the starter, re-cover it, and let it stand another 24 hours. By this time the mixture will be quite loose and nearly batter-like as a result of the breakdown of gluten by the microorganisms. Its taste will reveal a slight sourness, not entirely developed yet. Refresh the starter by stirring in 4 tablespoons water and 1¼ ounces of flour and let it stand for 48 hours more. By now the starter should smell pleasantly sour when you uncover it.

Now stir in 4 tablespoons water and 3 ounces flour. This will be the final addition before you make the dough. Continue to stir until all of the flour is incorporated and the mixture feels heavy and sticky. Let this mixture triple in volume; this takes about 8 hours.

You are now ready to make bread with the starter. If you don't make bread immediately, cover the starter tightly and refrigerate it. You should end up with 13 ounces starter, slightly more than needed to bake 2 loaves of bread. If you plan to bake 2 loaves at a time, you may wish to discard the extra 3 ounces (each loaf requires 5 ounces of starter) so that you will retain just as much as you will need, and weighing the starter twice each time you bake won't be necessary. Weighing a sticky starter can be messy.

If you don't bake bread on a weekly basis, you should nevertheless refresh your starter after 7 days with fresh water and flour. Remove the starter from the refrigerator and stir in ⅛ cup water and 1 ounce flour until well combined.

Step Two: Sponge
1⅛ cups water at 80°F
5 ounces of starter
8 ounces organic unbleached bread flour

Put the water in a bread bowl, add the starter, and break it up well by hand until the mixture resembles a cloudy slurry. Stir in the flour until well combined. Cover with plastic film and set in a warm (80°F) spot for 2 hours, then refrigerate the sponge for 12 to 24 hours.

Step Three: Mixing the dough
¼ cup water at 80°F
11 ounces organic unbleached bread flour
1 teaspoon salt

Remove the sponge from the refrigerator, add to it the water, and stir until the water has been absorbed. Pour 8 ounces of the flour into the bowl and stir until the mixture comes together in a shaggy mass. Cut away 5 ounces of this dough and reserve it as the starter for your next loaf. (If you plan to bake the next day, leave it out at room temperature for 2 hours, then refrigerate it; or, refrigerate it immediately.) Pour the remaining flour on the dough and the salt and begin kneading. Knead the dough (see page 205) for about 10 minutes, until it feels smooth and elastic, dusting it lightly in the first few minutes to reduce its stickiness. When poked, the dough should spring back.

Lightly oil the bread bowl; form the dough into a round and set it in the bowl to rise. Cover the top of the bowl tightly with plastic wrap and leave the dough at 80°F. for 3 hours, or until it has tripled in volume.

Turn the dough out onto a dry work surface, flatten it with the palm of your hand, and shape it (see page 206) into a long or round loaf. Set the loaf in a cloth-lined basket or on a baking pan with a thermometer and enclose the basket or pan in a large, clear plastic bag. Bring the open end together and inflate the bag by blowing into it. Tie off the bag and set the pan in a warm place, above the stove, for its warm final rising. The ideal temperature for the rise is around 100°F. Let the bread rise for 2 to 2 ½ hours, or until it triples in volume, expanding to 3 times its size after shaping.

To bake: Preheat the oven to 500°F. If the bread has risen in a basket, invert it onto a floured peel. Mist the top of the bread with water from an atomizer and set it directly on oven tiles. Otherwise, bake the bread directly on its pan—dust the top of the loaf with flour and mist it just before placing it in the oven. Immediately reduce the oven temperature to 400°F. The bread will take about 50 minutes to bake; in addition to its nicely browned, firm crust, when done it should emit a hollow resonant thud when rapped on the bottom. Cool on a rack.

Levain Bread

Two 2-pound loaves

This recipe was graciously donated by Steve Sullivan, Chez Panisse's first baker, who currently operates the Acme Bread Company in Berkeley. It is one of his most irresistible breads and we serve it nightly in the restaurant. In addition to its comforting presence on the table, we use it to make croutons, panades, stuffings, and crumbs. A thick slice, doused in olive oil, grilled over a wood fire, then rubbed with raw garlic is very satisfying. Wherever levain bread is used, it greatly enhances everything served with it. It is of incomparable flavor, with a bright graininess, mellow tang, and a chewy crumb and crust. Stored properly, levain bread keeps for an unusually long time. The following is Steve's commentary and recipe for levain bread:

In France, *pain au levain* refers to a range of breads leavened in an ongoing process with a piece of dough held back from a previous baking. The levain system is cyclical and self-renewing. The *pain au levain* that we make every day for the restaurant is a variation, wherein we maintain a separate starter dough of organic whole wheat flour and water. When we are about to mix a dough we take out the amount needed to leaven the mix and add it (as the recipe's "yeast," if you like) to the water, flour, and salt that make up the balance of the dough. We then refresh the starter by adding water and whole wheat flour to the remainder, mixing it by hand and allowing it to ferment and become active in the

warmth of the bakery. We have then produced the leavening for the next batch. The flavor, texture, aroma, the very look of the loaves develop an added dimension of character through the leisurely action of wild yeasts over the course of an exceptionally long fermentation and rising.

On our honeymoon, my wife, Susie, and I were fortunate to visit the Domaine Tempier in Bandol near Toulon. There we were taken in by the generous and spirited Peyraud family, who make the wines of Domaine Tempier. In our honor, I imagine, bread and baking became dominant conversational themes and one of the younger Peyrauds, Jean-Marie, I think, was musing on the similarities between the work of the winemaker and the baker. He suggested that I make a *levain*, wild yeast starter, capturing the yeasts present on fully ripened wine grapes in a good vineyard. The idea seemed to me simple and natural, so on our return home in October, which, in California, finds the grapes at their peak of ripeness, I made a starter using grapes from a friend's vineyards. The grapes I knew to be unsulfured. I wrapped them in cheesecloth, bashed them up a bit, and immersed them in a thin batter of tepid water and flour. Within five to six hours it was bubbling vigorously, and we have been leavening most of our breads with this levain ever since.

To make this bread, you will first have to make a natural starter. There are many ways to do it; I only suggest that you avoid methods that begin with commercial yeast. Otherwise, your starter will become too violently active and altogether unsatisfactory. If you are fortunate to be trying this at the right time of year and have access to a vineyard, you should certainly try to get grapes from an unsprayed, unsulfured vineyard. Or, you can try other organic fruits at the peak of their ripeness, or even unsulfured raisins, which I'm told can be used quite successfully.

Because this bread requires a long fermentation and rising period it is a good idea to plan ahead. The sponge-dough process used herein allows for some latitude. Ideally you should let the thin starter develop for 5 to 7 days before making bread.

Note: The sourdough starter for Spontaneously Leavened Sourdough Bread (see page 216) works very well in this recipe. Thin it with water until it is the consistency of pancake batter (pourable, but slightly thick), then proceed to step one in this recipe.

Step One: The starter
3 cups water at 80°F
1 pound organic unbleached bread flour
12 ounces unsulfured and unsprayed wine grapes

Wash a bowl or crock with a capacity of about 1½ quarts and rinse it out with boiling water. Add to it the 3 cups water and, little by little, whisk in the flour. Tie up the grapes (it is not necessary to de-stem them) in cheesecloth and gently squeeze them over the sink to break the skins. Plunge the grapes into the flour and water mixture and cover with plastic wrap. Place the bowl or crock in a warm place (80°F) and let it stand. You should expect some activity within 12 hours' time.

After 20 hours, the starter should be quite vigorous and, in addition to having expanded, will be full of bubbles and frothy on the surface. Although you could make bread at this point, it is better to allow the starter to develop a sourness for about 5 to 7 days. In the first few days of fermentation, it will smell like fresh cheese and as time goes on this will progress to a more sour, cidery aroma. As the starter matures, it will need some refreshment, that is, additions of fresh water and small amounts of flour. Check the consistency of the starter every 2 days. As it develops, its consistency will become thinner and looser. Stir in a small amount of room-temperature water and a little flour to restore it to its original batterlike texture. After 5 days, taste it. It should be pleasantly sour. Once your starter is active, you will need to thicken it up to the proper density with an organic whole wheat flour as described below.

1 cup active thin starter
5 ounces organic whole wheat flour

Pour the starter into a mixing bowl and add the whole wheat flour, stirring to make a solid yet pliable lump of dough. Leave this in a warm spot (80°F to 90°F) for 2 hours, then refrigerate for at least 6 hours, or until the day before baking. Check it the day after refrigeration even if you don't intend to use it then. It should have risen noticeably and be domed over on the top. This starter should be used within 4 days at this point.

Step Two: Sponge and starter refreshment
Starter
3 cups water at 80°F.
1½ pounds organic unbleached bread flour
1 teaspoon salt

Pour the water into a mixing bowl, break up ½ pound of the starter into the water, and stir it in thoroughly. Pour in the flour and salt and mix thoroughly with a spoon. At this stage it should be a bit too thick to use a whisk, yet much too thin to work by hand. Leave this mixture, covered, at 80°F to 90°F for 4 hours, then refrigerate it for 6 to 24 hours.

Refresh the levain starter at this point also: Put ½ cup of water (80°F) into a mixing bowl and break up the remaining ½ pound or so of starter into it. Then add 5 to 6 ounces whole wheat flour to make a firm, pliable lump of dough. Leave this in a warm spot for 2 hours, then refrigerate it for up to 7 days before your next baking, when you will start again at step two.

Step Three: Mixing the dough
Sponge
½ cup water at 80°F
1 pound, 14 ounces organic unbleached bread flour
4 teaspoons salt

Using a rubber scraper, empty the sponge into a large bowl and stir in the water. Put the bread flour on top of it, then the salt. The most efficient way to blend everything is to cut it all together with the edge of a large cook's spoon while rotating the bowl an inch or so with each stroke. After a minute or two of this, everything should be more or less combined into a stringy, shaggy mass. You can now reach under the dough with both hands and lift what unmixed flour remains onto the top of the dough, and fold the dough onto itself several times to work it in. It is convenient to knead it a bit *in* the bowl at this point to minimize the mess on your counter.

Now flour the counter lightly and turn the dough out of the bowl for kneading. About 7 to 10 minutes will be required, depending upon your vigor. If the dough seems to get too sticky to come up from your counter, throw down a little flour occasionally. If it seems inclined to come apart a bit (as sourdoughs can), you might want to divide the kneading into two stages and let it relax a few minutes in between. You should now have a smooth, firm, elastic dough that is lightly speckled with whole wheat. Clean out the mixing bowl, lightly oil it, and place the dough in it. Cover with plastic wrap and put it back in the warm spot (80°F to 90°F) for about 3½ hours, after which time it should have grown noticeably. There should be gas bubbles evident to the eye and to the touch throughout the dough.

Step Four: Shaping the loaves

This bread is traditionally shaped in cloth-lined baskets. You can improvise the baskets by using two 5- to 6-quart mixing bowls, each completely lined with thick, stiff cloth, such as muslin. Spread the cloths flat over the top of each bowl. Sprinkle the cloths with a thin, even layer of flour. Set the bowls at the side of the table, then lightly flour the table.

Turn the dough out, then divide it in half with a sharp knife or a dough scraper. Don't tear it as this will be damaging. Work each piece into a ball by folding and kneading several times more. Round the dough each time until you have a taut ball. It need not be absolutely round. While shaping, knock out most of the gas to rejuvenate the yeasts, but don't be too careful about it as the irregularity of texture is one of the great charms of this bread. Dust each dough ball lightly with flour, pick up by the ugliest part, which will become the bottom, and lower it onto the floured cloth across the top of each bowl. Put a piece of foil lightly over each loaf and leave them at room temperature (75°F to 80°F) for about 5 hours, or until the bread has grown about 75 percent in volume and feels soft, inflated, and only slightly resilient. Remember to preheat the oven (as described below) around the 4-hour mark so that it is ready when the bread has risen sufficiently.

Step Five: Baking the loaves

If your oven is large enough, the loaves may be baked at the same time, or they must be baked one at a time. Traditionally, this type of bread is baked directly upon a stone or brick hearth. To improvise a stone hearth, line the bottom shelf of your electric oven, or the floor of your gas oven with large quarry tiles. Place another rack on the top shelf 10 inches above the bottom shelf and on it put a wide, low, heavy pan to pour water into for humidifying the oven. You will also need a peel for loading the bread into the oven, long tongs, and an old kitchen towel for swabbing the tiles, a long-necked bottle, and a single-edged razor blade.

Forty-five minutes before baking, preheat the oven to 500°F. It is essential that the tiles and the water pan, as well as the air, get to 500°F.

There are several steps that must be performed in about 2 minutes at this stage, so please make sure that you have all of your equipment at hand and that you have thought through it a couple of times before beginning:

Rub the peel with flour and set it near the oven.

Put about 1 cup of hot water into the bottle and set it within easy reach of the oven.

Fold up the kitchen towel into a thick square, grab it with the long tongs, wet it under the tap, then mop the hot tiles with it.

Gently invert the bowl of dough onto the board. Remove the bowl and cloth.

Using the razor blade, slash a 6-inch square, ½ inch deep, into the top of the loaf. This must be done with quick, decisive strokes and must not be too large across or the loaf may flatten out instead of rising up in baking.

Open the oven, insert the peel with the bread on it into the oven. Touch the front of the peel to the tiles about 2 inches from the back of the oven, then jerk the peel quickly and smoothly away from the bread and out. Set the peel down immediately, pick up the bottle of water, and carefully empty it into the pan on the top shelf of the oven. Close the oven and lower the temperature to 400°F.

This loaf will take about 45 minutes to bake. If the oven is preheated properly and the oven door is open only a short time for loading, the oven temperature will not fall below 400°F. This constant temperature will allow the loaf to develop a thick, dark crust without danger of scorching. Please try to resist checking the loaf for at least 20 minutes: a consistent humidity and temperature are very important during the early baking. After the loaf has finished baking (rap it on the bottom and listen for a resonant thud), remove it from the oven and set it to cool on a wire rack. Reheat the oven to 500°F for 15 minutes and then bake the second loaf. It is an advantage of the long rising that this dough can wait an additional hour without over-rising as a 1-hour yeast bread would.

Meats and Poultry

Butterflied Filet of Beef with Herbs

Braised Tripe

Gratin of Tripe, Penne, and Cabbage

Marinated Veal Chops Grilled over an Oak Fire

Veal Meatballs with Artichokes, Tomatoes, Green Olives, and Sage

Lamb Salad with Garden Lettuces, Straw Potatoes, and Garlic Sauce

Lamb Shank Soup with Tomatoes and Shell Beans

Braised Lamb Shanks with Gratin of Flageolet Beans

Lamb Tartare

Lambs' Tongues with Herb Sauce

Roast Loin of Cured Pork

Braised Pork Shoulder with Tomatoes, Fennel, and Olives

Fresh Pork Sausages
Cotechino Sausage
Terrine of Pork
Prosciutto with Warm Wilted Greens

Roast Chicken
Spit Roasting
Chicken Breast Stuffed with Wild Mushrooms
Chicken Sausages
Steamed and Roasted Duck
Duck Legs Braised with Onions and Cabbage
Duck Liver Croutons
Pigeon
Roast Pigeon Salad
Roast Pigeon and Green Garlic Soup
Pigeon Marinated in Muscat Wine
Stuffed Quail
Rabbit Salad with Browned Shallots

Butterflied Filet of Beef with Herbs

For 4

The filet is probably the most tender of all cuts of beef, but it is less flavorful than those from the working muscles of the animal. In the restaurant, we are forever trying to introduce flavor to the filet by marinating or stuffing it, or choosing methods of cooking, such as spit-roasting or charcoal grilling.

A good way to prepare the filet is to cut it in such a way that its cylindrical form unrolls into a rough rectangular shape of even thickness. The surface of the meat is then patted with a layer of chopped fresh herbs and the filet is rolled up and tied. The roast is first browned on top of the stove, then finished in the oven. As the meat cooks, the herbs, which have been distributed over the inside of the roll, perfume the filet and display an attractive spiral pattern when the roast is sliced.

There are numerous other possible stuffings depending on the season. A mixture of finely diced carrots, celery, and onion cooked until soft and combined with chopped, blanched, smoked bacon adds considerably to the flavor of the meat, as do finely chopped wild mushrooms stewed in butter with diced shallots and garlic.

Filet of beef with just herbs is wonderful in the summer when you can include basil and serve it with colorful vegetables. Perhaps the most compatible vegetable accompaniment is a combination of sliced zucchini, tomatoes, and eggplant, set in overlapping rows on a bed of onions and peppers that have been stewed in olive oil, seasoned with chopped garlic and basil leaves, and baked until the vegetables soften and their flavors melt into one another. The roast is also fine as a cold leftover, with a salad of mixed lettuces or tomatoes vinaigrette and garlic mayonnaise.

The filet is a long tapering muscle attached to the underside of the loin and sirloin of beef. It is thought of in three sections: the head, the center—or heart—and the tapered tail section, also called the tip. The cut called for in this recipe is the center of the filet, uniformly cylindrical, about 2½ inches thick and 9½ inches long. It is cut out of the filet just below the head and just before the tail begins to taper. The center cut does not generally appear whole in butcher cases; it is divided into steaks and sold as tournedos or filets mignons. (You may have to make a special request or purchase the entire filet if you cannot convince your butcher to sell you this particular cut.) The filet is expensive if you buy it whole, considering that you will be paying for fat, about two thirds of its weight. If you do have to purchase the whole filet, the tail can be used for sautés. The head section, turned on the cut end and pounded to a thickness of 2 inches, makes a sublime chateaubriand for grilling.

To prepare a whole filet, all fat and sinew must be removed. Begin at the thick head of the filet and cut and lift the fat and veil-like membrane away. Remove the top layer of fat mostly by hand; cut only where it is necessary to free it from the meat. Pull away and cut off the "chain," the fatty, gristly strip of meat attached to one side of the filet (opposite the head). Cut away the thick clump of fat underneath the head. Next remove the "silverskin," the tightly adhering sinew covering the top of the filet: start at either end of the filet and cut right under the silverskin. Run the knife along the filet angling it upward against the silverskin, removing a strip at a time, until the filet is completely nude.

1 center cut of beef filet, trimmed of all fat and sinew (1 pound, 12 ounces)
Salt and pepper
2 tablespoons finely chopped fresh chervil
½ tablespoon finely chopped fresh thyme
3 tablespoons finely chopped fresh parsley
2 tablespoons thinly sliced chives
1 tablespoon vegetable oil

To open the filet: Position the meat vertically in front of you end to end. With a 10-inch chef's knife (or blade slightly longer than the meat) make a cut along the length of the filet ¾ inch from the edge and about 1¾ inches deep so that the uncut portion of the filet is about ¾ inch thick. Roll back the cut edge. To open the rest of the filet, make short sawing motions while exerting a sideways pressure with the knife at the same time. *Do not* cut downward and keep the knife perpendicular to the table. Maintain the ¾-inch thickness as the filet opens out. Follow the movement of the knife with your other hand, pressing down on the unrolled portion of the filet so that it doesn't stretch and tear. When the roast is unrolled, flatten it with the palm of your hand to even it out.

Preheat the oven to 350°F. Lightly salt and pepper the filet. Mix together the herbs and cover the surface of the meat with them in an even layer. Roll the meat up tightly and tie it snugly at 1-inch intervals.

Salt and pepper the roast on the outside. Add the vegetable oil to a 12-inch cast-iron pan and allow the pan to get very hot. Toss in a speck of water; it should pop and hiss angrily. Sear the meat on all sides. Use a pair of V-shaped tongs to turn the roll every minute. Do not let the filet rest for more than a minute on any one side in the pan—the filet is a soft cut that cooks very quickly. Transfer the meat to a baking pan and roast it in the oven for 15 minutes until it is medium rare. Allow the meat to rest in a warm place for 5 minutes and untie it before you slice it.

Braised Tripe

For 6

It is unfortunate that tripe, and variety meats in general, are ignored or dismissed in this country by almost everyone except the ethnic populations. If restaurant menus are any indication, the bias has grown to include nonprimal cuts of beef, veal, and lamb. Thus the door is closed on a rich and diverse resource. More often than not, braised tripe on the menu at Chez Panisse is met with stubborn resistance, but those daring enough to try it are won over by the melting texture and unusual marriage of flavor. A number of guests finish this dish with pleasant surprise and even request second helpings.

Tripe is a portion of the numerous stomachs of cud-chewing animals and is taken primarily from beef. Tripe from the first stomach is called blanket tripe for its smooth-textured surface. Honeycomb tripe, so named for its appearance, is from the second stomach of the animal. It is slightly more expensive but more desirable because it is comparatively less fatty, more uniform in thickness, and cooks in less time. The best and freshest tripe is generally available in ethnic markets where the demand is greatest. Tripe comes prewashed, scalded, and ready to cook. It must be cooked for a long while in a moist medium because of its stiff, rubbery texture. As it cooks, the tripe releases gelatin, which upon reduction slightly thickens the surrounding liquid.

For this dish the tripe is sliced very thin and combined with an almost equal amount of finely diced vegetables, tomatoes, and Italian bacon. The whole is then simmered in chicken broth for several hours. Finally, the flavors are smoothed and freshened with a little butter, parsley, and Parmesan cheese. It can be cooked several days in advance. If so, rewarm the tripe and make the final butter and parsley addition just before serving. We serve braised tripe in the restaurant as a second course, where pasta or soup generally appear, and recommend that Chianti be drunk with it.

1 pound, 8 ounces honeycomb tripe
2 tablespoons unsalted butter
1½ large stalks of celery (2½ ounces), cut into ⅛-inch dice
2 small carrots (5 ounces), cut into ⅛-inch dice
1 small yellow onion (5 ounces), cut into ⅛-inch dice
3 ounces pancetta, thinly sliced, diced
2 bay leaves
2 cups tomatoes, peeled, seeded, diced, the juice strained and reserved
3 large cloves garlic (1 ounce), thinly sliced
1 teaspoon salt
⅛ teaspoon ground cayenne
1 quart chicken broth (see page 426)

To finish:
2 tablespoons unsalted butter
3 tablespoons chopped fresh Italian parsley
Freshly ground pepper
Freshly grated Parmesan cheese

Rinse the tripe and cut it as thinly as possible (a sharp knife is crucial) into strips 2 to 3 inches long. Melt the butter in a 6-quart pot. Add the celery, carrots, onion, and pancetta and soften the vegetables over low heat for 5 minutes. Add the bay leaves, tomatoes, garlic, salt, cayenne, and tripe and stir well to combine. Pour in the strained tomato juice and the chicken broth, raise the heat, and bring slowly to the boil. Skim off the white froth that comes to the surface. Reduce to an even, gentle simmer, cover, and cook for 2 hours.

Remove the cover, raise the heat so that the tripe boils gently, and cook another 30 to 35 minutes, allowing the surrounding liquid to reduce until there is a little less liquid than tripe, and the two are combined in a thickened saucy blend. It is possible to overcook tripe—the cooking should be stopped when the texture is still distinct but there is no longer resistance when the tripe is bitten into. If the tripe is cooked before the amount of liquid in the pan has reduced and thickened sufficiently, remove it with a strainer and reduce the liquid by itself. Then return the tripe to the pot.

Just before serving, finish the braise: Stir in the butter and the parsley. Grind pepper liberally over the surface and serve in warmed bowls. Sprinkle Parmesan cheese over each portion and serve more of it in a small bowl at the table.

Gratin of Tripe, Penne, and Cabbage

For 6

Braised tripe can also be considered a long-simmered sauce for pasta. The tripe and its sauce coats the noodles and keeps them moist while it bakes under a crust of bread crumbs. This dish has rich, lingering flavors and is very pleasing with young, tart red wines.

2 quarts water
1¼ teaspoons salt
2 cups dry penne
½ yellow onion (3 ounces), finely diced
1 tablespoon pure olive oil
2 cups thinly sliced savoy cabbage
Freshly ground pepper
1½ cups sourdough bread crumbs
2 tablespoons unsalted butter, melted
2 cups Braised Tripe (½ recipe, see page 231)
4 tablespoons freshly grated Parmesan cheese

Preheat the oven to 375°F.

Bring the water to a boil, add 1 teaspoon of the salt and the penne, and cook for 8 minutes, or until the noodles lose their firmness but are still slightly chewy. Drain the noodles in a colander and cool them briefly under cold running water. (Do not soak the noodles.)

Brown the onion in the olive oil in a saucepot, add the cabbage, the remaining ¼ teaspoon salt, a little freshly ground pepper, and cook over medium heat for 8 minutes, stirring often until the cabbage is thoroughly wilted. Toss the bread crumbs with the melted butter, spread them out on a baking pan, and bake them for about 15 minutes to a golden brown.

Combine the noodles, braised tripe (if refrigerated, rewarm it as it will be firmly bound in its own gelatin), cabbage, and onion, and 2 tablespoons Parmesan cheese and stir them together. The mixture should be somewhat saucy and the noodles coated thoroughly. If not, add a little chicken broth or water to loosen the mixture and enough of the juices from the tripe to moisten the whole dish while it bakes. Turn the mixture out into a baking dish (8 by 10 by 2 inches) or oval gratin and dust the top with the remaining 2 tablespoons Parmesan cheese. Cover the top with the bread crumbs, bake for 30 minutes, and serve.

Marinated Veal Chops Grilled over an Oak Fire

For 4

While grilling a piece of meat is certainly no novelty, there are perhaps a few things left to be said about cooking over a live fire. The modern and relatively expedient fuel for the grill is charcoal, the best of which is produced by smothered combustion from wood. Charcoal, of course, eliminates the stage of burning that reduces wood to embers. As such, it is a great time saver, an economical and efficient fuel with good staying power compared to wood embers, which are more short-lived. Yet, whenever I have a good piece of meat I light a wood fire and let it slowly burn down to a thick bed of glowing embers. Wood embers lend quite a different aromatic quality to foods, somewhat softer and more perfumed with the burning resins of the wood. One of the most common hardwoods that makes excellent embers (fuel for the grill) is seasoned oak. Fruit woods such as fig, apple, cherry, or grape are equally suited. I do this kind of cooking in my fireplace since often there is a ready source of unspent embers that accumulate when the logs burn down. Grills that fit inside the fireplace can be bought, but you don't really need anything special. I use the grill from an outdoor barbecue and prop it up on bricks set to either side of the fireplace. There is no reason why you can't build a wood fire in your barbecue if it is sturdy and large enough.

There is a lot to say about veal, much of which is unpleasant because most of the veal that is available commercially, the pale white variety so highly esteemed by connoisseurs of the so-called milk-fed animals, is the result of practices that are questionable from the standpoint of humane animal husbandry and human health (see page 352).

The veal we use at Chez Panisse comes from Jamie and Rachel Nicoll who operate Summerfield Farm. You, too, can order directly from them, and their address is given below.

Summerfield Farm
SR4 Box 195-A
Brightwood, Virginia 22715
(703) 948-3100

Although some may argue that their veal more accurately resembles beef (its color is more red than white because the calves have access to pasturage; normally this concession is disallowed to commercial veal calves raised for their pale color), the meat is deliciously mild, yet long in flavor, and is as tender as veal from other sources. It has been raised in a healthy, humane manner, clean environment, and without unnecessary medication.

To make this recipe you will need four veal chops taken from the rack or rib portion of the animal. I prefer to cut them extra thick (about 1½ inches) and cook them slowly over the coals so that they take on the aroma of the burning wood. It is a good idea to leave the meat in the marinade for at least six hours for it to have any effect; overnight and it will penetrate still more fully.

4 veal chops (2 pounds), cut 1½ inches thick

For the marinade:
3 tablespoons extra virgin olive oil
1 shallot (1 ounce), finely diced
2 tablespoons rosemary leaves
4 cloves garlic, coarsely chopped
⅛ teaspoon star anise, pounded to a powder in a mortar
½ teaspoon cracked black pepper
3 bay leaves
1 tablespoon balsamic vinegar
½ cup dry white wine

Prepare the marinade: Warm the olive oil in a small saucepan. Add the shallot, rosemary, and garlic and let them sizzle gently for 2 minutes to awaken the flavors. Combine this mixture with the other ingredients and stir well. Arrange the chops in a baking dish that is slightly larger than all the chops and pour in the marinade. Place the rosemary leaves and garlic on top and under the meat, cover the dish, and let it stand at cool room temperature for 6 to 8 hours. Spoon the marinade frequently over the meat as it stands.

To grill the chops: Prepare a wood fire and when it has burned down, break it up and form a thick bed of embers. Position a grill about 4 inches from the bed and allow the flames to subside. You should not grill the chops while the fire is searing hot. Allow it to reduce in intensity so that when you hold your hand over the grill you feel a penetrating warmth. Grill the chops for about 8 minutes per side, rotating and adjusting them on each side during this time to brown them evenly. Brush them occasionally with the marinade. Serve the chops immediately, with Potatoes Cooked in the Coals.

Veal Meatballs with Artichokes, Tomatoes, Green Olives, and Sage

For 8

I could not fail to include in this book a favorite dish of mine: my mother's veal meatballs with artichokes, olives, and sage. My own version is slightly different; she used marinated artichokes and a type of green Spanish olive I can't find anymore. Although it doesn't taste quite the same, this recipe is in the same spirit. Ground veal is mixed with parsley, softened onions, eggs, Parmesan, and bread crumbs. The egg and bread crumbs stiffen the mixture slightly so that it doesn't come apart in the oven. The seasoned veal is formed into balls, browned, and set on a bed of onions. Fresh artichokes (the smallest buds without chokes, called "loose" artichokes), tomatoes, olives, and sage leaves are tossed with lemon juice and olive oil and strewn around the meat. The dish is moistened with broth and set in the oven to braise for an hour. Serve the meatballs and vegetables with fresh noodles tossed with butter and Parmesan.

5 tablespoons pure olive oil
3 medium yellow onions (22 ounces), finely diced
Salt
Freshly ground black pepper
2 pounds ground veal
2½ tablespoons finely chopped fresh parsley

3 tablespoons freshly grated Parmesan
3 large eggs
½ cup bread crumbs
15 small artichokes (2 pounds, 4 ounces)
12 ounces cherry tomatoes, peeled (or 2 large ripe tomatoes, peeled, seeded, diced)
4 cloves garlic, finely chopped
⅔ cup green olives, coarsely chopped
2 tablespoons coarsely chopped fresh sage leaves
2½ tablespoons lemon juice
¾ cup poultry broth (see page 426)

Warm 3 tablespoons of the olive oil in a sauté pan, add the onions, salt and pepper them lightly, and cook over moderate heat for 8 minutes, until they are softened. Do not let the onions brown. In the meantime, put the veal in a mixing bowl and add the parsley, Parmesan, eggs, and bread crumbs. Remove ⅓ cup of onions from the pan and add them to the bowl with the veal. Season the mixture with 1 teaspoon salt and ¼ teaspoon ground pepper and mix thoroughly. Form the veal into 16 meatballs, each weighing about 2 ounces, and set them aside on a plate.

Transfer the remaining onions to a large baking dish (16 by 8½ by 2 inches). Remove the outer leaves of the artichokes until you reach the pale green heart. Trim the pointed end, cut off the stem, and pare away the tough green portion surrounding the artichoke bottom. Cut the artichokes in quarters and place them in a bowl of acidulated water as you work.

Preheat the oven to 350°F. The next step is to brown the meat. Warm the remaining 2 tablespoons olive oil in a 12-inch cast-iron pan. When the oil is hot, add the meatballs and brown them all over lightly, allowing 1½ minutes per side (a pair of V-shaped tongs is handy for turning them). Set the browned meatballs in the baking dish on the bed of onions.

Drain the artichokes. Combine the artichokes with the tomatoes, garlic, olives, sage, and lemon juice. Season with ½ teaspoon salt and a grinding of pepper. Mix well and distribute the vegetables mixture around the meatballs. Pour the broth over the dish, cover tightly with foil, and bake in the oven for 1 hour. Transfer the meatballs and vegetables to a large heated platter, pour some of the juices over them, and serve.

Lamb Salad with Garden Lettuces, Straw Potatoes, and Garlic Sauce

This composed salad of mixed lettuces and wild mushrooms, sautéed lamb with anchovies and garlic sauce, and crispy straw potatoes is not based on, nor is it unified by the flavor of, any single ingredient. Rather, it is a combination of naturally harmonious flavors. It was Alice who introduced the idea of serving salads like these as a main course in the restaurant. Not only do they provide a full and varied course, but they reawaken the appetite. The tart, herbaceous flavors of lettuces vinaigrette blend very agreeably with meat juices and it is this feature that is perhaps most compelling about the dish as a whole. At home, I treat this salad as a complete meal in one dish. It makes a fine lunch or supper with a straightforward, light-bodied red or rosé wine and I follow it with a bowl of ripe fruit, such as Bartlett pears.

To my taste, potatoes cooked brown and crisp in clarified butter, whether *pommes Anna*, straw cakes, or roughly cubed, as well as garlic sauce, are indispensable to this salad. Depending on the season, the other elements can vary. Wild autumn mushrooms can be supplanted in the spring by small artichokes, peas, carrots, asparagus, or a variety of edible blossoms. Summer vegetables such as ripe tomatoes, grilled eggplant, red onions, and zucchini are delicious, yet more imposing accompaniments.

The loin of lamb is usually sold as chops in butcher shops. Uncut, it is a long, roughly rectangular muscle positioned just below the rib cage and is also known as the saddle. It includes the tenderloin—the thin, tapering muscle on the underside of the bone. It is considered a prime cut—the meat itself is very tender and free of gristle, sinew, and fat. Using this cut assures consistency and quality but it is expensive. The salad can also be made with a small cut from the leg or shoulder of lamb. Whichever cut you choose, time the cooking so the meat is still warm in the salad. If you use the leg, make sure you remove any fat from the roasting juices before adding them to the salad. There is nothing worse than the taste and waxy texture of congealed lamb fat.

½ boned lamb loin (12 ounces), tenderloin included (3 ounces)
2 large handfuls of very young lettuces (rocket and rocket flowers, frisée, bronze leaf, ruby red leaf, Romaine, Verona chicory, dandelion greens, garden cress)
2 large eggs

4 salt-packed anchovies (8 filets)
6 tablespoons clarified butter
8 ounces golden chanterelles, thickly sliced
Salt and pepper
Extra virgin olive oil
2 Russet potatoes (1 pound)
Nasturtium petals

Remove and discard all fat, skin, and sinew from the boned lamb loin. Wash and spin-dry the lettuces and refrigerate. Put the eggs in a pan and cover them with water. Bring the water to a boil, turn off the heat, and let the eggs sit in the hot water for 8 minutes. Drain off the water, cool the eggs under cold water, then peel them.

Filet the anchovies and soak them in several changes of cold water for 20 minutes. Meanwhile, melt 1 tablespoon of the clarified butter in a sauté pan, add the chanterelles, and salt and pepper them lightly. Cook until all of the water they release evaporates and the mushrooms are slightly crisp and mahogany colored. Transfer to a small bowl. Drain the water and pat the anchovies dry with a paper towel. Cut them into ⅛-inch-thick strips and toss in about a teaspoon of extra virgin olive oil.

Peel the potatoes and cut them on a mandoline, or by hand, into fine julienne strips. Put the cut potatoes in a large bowl and cover them with several changes of cold water until the water is clear and no longer milky. Let them soak for 1 hour.

For the garlic sauce:
⅙ cup neutral-flavored oil (peanut or vegetable)
1 egg yolk
1 clove garlic, peeled
½ teaspoon Champagne vinegar
1/16 teaspoon salt
1/16 teaspoon pepper
½ teaspoon water

Prepare the garlic sauce: In a small bowl, whisk the oil into the egg yolk drop by drop at first and then as it thickens, in a more steady, thin stream until all of it has been added. Pound the garlic clove in a mortar, add it to the egg and oil, and whisk in the seasonings and water. You should have a smooth, pourable sauce.

For the vinaigrette:
2 shallots (2 ounces), finely diced
1 tablespoon plus 2 teaspoons sherry vinegar
½ teaspoon finely chopped fresh oregano
½ teaspoon finely chopped fresh thyme
Salt and pepper
3 tablespoons extra virgin olive oil

Prepare the vinaigrette: Combine the shallots, vinegar, herbs, a little salt and pepper and mix well to dissolve the salt. Stir in the olive oil.

Drain the potatoes and spin them dry in the lettuce spinner. Melt 4 tablespoons of the clarified butter in a well-seasoned 8-inch steel sauté pan or nonstick pan. Warm the butter until it sizzles when you touch a potato to it. Add one half of the straw potatoes to cover the bottom of the pan, salt and pepper the layer, then add the other half and salt and pepper it. Compress the potatoes lightly with the lid of a pan or a spatula. Cook the potatoes for about 5 to 8 minutes. Keep the heat high enough so that you hear a gentle sizzle. (If the heat is not high enough the potatoes will not brown and crisp.) Several times during the cooking move the pan back and forth. The potatoes are ready to be flipped when you see browned compacted edges and the aroma changes from steamy to nutty. To flip the cake, place a flat lid over the pan and invert the pan. Carefully slide the cake back into the pan. Continue to cook the cake another 8 minutes or so, until it is thoroughly browned and crisp on the second side. When it is done, transfer it to a plate and place it in a warm oven.

After boning, the lamb loin and tenderloin are each sautéed in one piece so that they retain their juices during cooking. The tenderloin is a much more tender muscle and cooks in less time. Salt and pepper the loin and tenderloin on both sides and sauté them over high heat in the remaining 1 tablespoon clarified butter to medium-rare. This should take about 8 minutes for the loin and 5 minutes for the tenderloin. Turn the pieces often so that the lamb browns but does not toughen on the surface. Let the meat rest in a warm spot for 5 minutes. Reserve the juices.

Assembling the salad: Have six large plates ready. Combine the lettuces and nasturtium petals with the mushrooms and dress with the vinaigrette. Add any juices from the lamb to the salad as well. Construct each salad in a similar way: Lay down the lettuces and mushrooms to cover the bottom of the plate. Slice the lamb thin and arrange it among the lettuces. Lay strips of anchovy on the lamb slices and drizzle a little garlic sauce over the meat. Break up the potato cake in 6 rough pieces and add a piece to each plate (the potatoes have a nice look if broken up by hand). Chop the eggs coarse and sprinkle all over the top of the salad. Grind a little black pepper over each plate and serve.

Lamb Shank Soup with Tomatoes and Shell Beans

For 8

This soup is very substantial and can serve as a meal in itself. It is really a braise modeled after *pot au feu*. The soup broth derives from the slow simmering of the lamb in water with tomatoes and vegetables. The shanks are later boned and added back to the soup. Since the primary liquid is water, it is essential that the vegetables be fresh and flavorful or else the broth will taste flat.

The garnish for this soup consists of chopped garlic, lemon zest, and Italian parsley, a mixture the Milanese call *gremolata*. Sprinkled on top of the soup (not stirred in!) at the moment of serving, it provides a fresh accent. Make the *gremolata* just before you serve the soup so that its flavor will be lively. The addition of a little virgin olive oil to each bowl is welcome.

2½ tablespoons olive oil
Salt and pepper
2 lamb shanks (2 pounds, 5 ounces), trimmed of all fat
1½ carrots (6 ounces), diced
1½ red onions (13 ounces), diced
1 large stalk of celery (4 ounces), diced
12 cloves garlic (½ cup), peeled
4 bay leaves
3 sprigs parsley
2 sprigs fresh thyme
4 large, very ripe tomatoes (2 pounds, 8 ounces), peeled, seeded, cut into ½-inch dice, juice strained and reserved
1 tablespoon balsamic vinegar
9 cups water
1 cup mixed fresh shell beans (cranberry, flageolet, black-eyed peas)

For the gremolata:
4 tablespoons chopped fresh Italian parsley
1 clove garlic, very finely chopped
Grated zest of ½ lemon

Warm 1 tablespoon of the olive oil in a soup pot. Salt and pepper the shanks, add them to the pot, and cook over low heat for 30 minutes, turning them to brown all sides thoroughly. Remove the shanks from the pot. Discard the rendered fat, add the remaining 1½ tablespoons olive oil and the carrots, onions, and celery. Raise the heat and brown the vegetables for 15 minutes, stirring often to keep them from burning.

Wrap the garlic cloves, bay leaves, parsley, and thyme in cheesecloth and add it to the pot. Stir in the tomatoes, tomato juice, and balsamic vinegar. Set the lamb shanks on the bed of vegetables and cover with the water. Bring to a gentle boil and immediately reduce the heat to a bare simmer. Cook the shanks for 2 hours, undisturbed and uncovered. When done, remove them from the pot and transfer to a plate to cool. Remove the cheesecloth-wrapped seasonings from the pot and discard.

While the shanks are cooking, simmer the beans in 1 quart water with 1 teaspoon salt. When they are tender, remove from heat and set aside.

Raise the heat and let the pot bubble gently for 15 minutes. During this time skim all fat and orangeish foam that rises to the surface. (Another purpose for this additional cooking is to reduce the amount of broth and intensify the flavor of the soup.) When the shanks are cool enough to handle, remove the meat from the bones, pull it apart into bite-sized pieces, and add it back to the soup. Drain the shell beans, add them to the pot, and bring the soup to a simmer. Mix together the parsley, garlic, and lemon zest to make the *gremolata*. Correct the soup for salt, generously pepper it, and serve in warm bowls. Sprinkle *gremolata* over each bowl.

Put a flask of your best olive oil on the table and plenty of warm bread to dip into the soup.

Braised Lamb Shanks with Gratin of Flageolet Beans

For 4

Lamb shanks are rich in gelatin and exude the characteristic flavor of the animal. Braising is the logical method for cooking them; several hours in a pot render lamb shanks sumptuously tender. A minimum of liquid is added to the braising pot and the flavorful juices the shanks release combine with vegetables, herbs, and garlic to form a richly scented sauce. I prefer to use water to cook the shanks as the sauce ends up tasting more direct; however, good red wine is another possible option.

Presenting the shank whole, with the bone on, on a large plate surrounded only by its sauce is dramatic, but in consideration of your guests, who may find it intimidating to take what appears to be a cumbersome quantity of meat, you may bone it after it cooks (the meat will fall off easily) and serve it in more manageable pieces.

Lamb and beans go together famously. There are two cooking processes in making the gratin: first, the beans are cooked until tender in lamb broth (substitute beef broth or even water if you don't have time to make lamb broth) with tomatoes, aromatic vegetables, herbs, and a prosciutto hock. Next, the cooking liquid is reduced, the beans are poured out into a baking dish, topped with bread crumbs, and put into the oven to form a golden crust.

The shanks are freshened at the last minute with a *gremolata* of chopped parsley, garlic, and lemon zest. It is a good idea to chop and combine the ingredients for the *gremolata* just before you serve the shanks so that their freshness doesn't fade.

4 lamb shanks (5 pounds)
Salt and pepper
3 tablespoons carrot (1 ounce), finely diced
2 shallots (2 ounces), finely diced
9 cloves garlic, unpeeled
1½ cups water
3 leafy sprigs thyme
1 tablespoon chopped celery leaves

For the gremolata:
4 tablespoons chopped fresh parsley
1 clove garlic, very finely chopped
Grated zest of ½ lemon

Have your butcher saw off 2 inches of the bone at the foot end of the shank (foreleg); otherwise, the shanks are unwieldy. Trim the fat off the shanks, leaving only a thin layer. You will need a large pan with a lid that fits tightly for cooking the shanks. A heavy 12-inch sauteuse, 3½ inches deep, is ideal. The shanks should rest side by side without crowding one another. Preheat the pan over low heat. Meanwhile lightly salt and pepper the shanks. Place them in the pan and brown them on all sides over low heat allowing about 15 minutes per side. The shanks should sizzle gently in the pan. This will take about 1 hour. When the shanks are brown, remove them from the pan. Add the carrot, shallots, and garlic to the pan and cook for 5 minutes to release their flavor, stirring occasionally.

Deglaze the pan with ½ cup water, scraping up all the brown bits adhering to the bottom. Add 1 more cup water, the thyme sprigs, and celery leaves, and set the shanks on top. Adjust the heat to the barest simmer and cover tightly so no steam escapes. Braise the shanks for 2 hours, undisturbed.

Remove the shanks from the pan and keep them in a warm place while you finish the sauce. Pass the cooking juices, aromatic vegetables, and garlic through the fine blade of a food mill into a clean pan. Warm the sauce over low heat, pepper it generously, and thin it if necessary with a little water so that it remains slightly viscous but still pours in an even stream.

Mix together the *gremolata*. Serve the shanks on individual plates, pour the sauce over and around each, and sprinkle liberally with the gremolata.

Gratin of Flageolet Beans

1¼ cups flageolet beans, washed, picked over, soaked in cold water overnight

2 tablespoons pure olive oil
1 small carrot (2 ounces), finely diced
½ large stalk of celery (2 ounces), finely diced
1 small yellow onion (5 ounces), finely diced
6 cloves garlic, peeled
2 leafy sprigs thyme
4 tomatoes (14 ounces), peeled, seeded, diced
Piece of prosciutto hock with rind attached (5 ounces)
5 cups beef broth (see page 427) or water
1 teaspoon salt
4½ tablespoons chopped fresh parsley
1½ cups bread crumbs
3 tablespoons extra virgin olive oil
2 tablespoons grated fresh Parmesan

Warm the olive oil in a 6-quart noncorroding pot. Add the carrot, celery, onion, and garlic and cook over medium heat for 5 minutes, until the vegetables soften slightly and release their perfume. Add the thyme, tomatoes, prosciutto hock, and beans. Cover with the broth and stir in the salt. Bring the beans to a simmer, cover, and cook for 1½ hours. Remove the cover after 1 hour, raise the heat slightly so that the liquid bubbles all over its surface, and allow the liquid to reduce during the last 30 minutes so that it is at the same level as the beans. When stirred, the beans should appear saucy.

Preheat the oven to 350°F. Remove the prosciutto hock and the thyme sprigs. Cut the meat and rind from the prosciutto, chop it into coarse bits, and add it to the beans. Stir in 2½ tablespoons of the parsley.

Pour the beans into a baking dish (10 by 8 by 2 inches). Mix the crumbs with the remaining 2 tablespoons parsley, extra virgin oil, and Parmesan and spread them over the beans in an even layer. Bake the beans in the oven for 40 minutes, or until the edges bubble and the crumbs are evenly browned.

Lamb Tartare

The same process for making beef tartare can apply to very tender cuts of lamb or veal. It is essential that the meat you use be absolutely fresh. Furthermore, it is advisable that you choose meat from a source that is known to you to be assured that the animal was raised in a clean, healthy environment and that it preferably was fed on an organic diet and without chemicals or medications (see page 351 on naturally grown meat).

Lamb tartare is different from beef tartare both in flavor and texture—it has a buttery smoothness, particularly if you use the loin muscle. Keep the meat cold before you chop it and then afterward work quickly over a bowl of ice. I prefer to keep the seasoning simple because the flavor and texture of lamb are quite fine. However, optional additions may include small capers, or chopped cornichons, a little mustard, or in keeping with the classic recipe, raw egg. You may mix the tartare an hour or two ahead of time. If so, keep it cold and add the vinegar just before you serve it, otherwise the color of the meat will fade.

8 ounces very lean fresh lamb, preferably from the loin, trimmed of all fat, skin, or
  sinew
1 tablespoon extra virgin olive oil
1 large shallot (1 ounce), finely diced
4 salt-packed anchovy filets, soaked for 15 minutes in several changes of cold water,
  squeezed out, finely chopped
1 tablespoon chopped fresh Italian parsley
¼ teaspoon salt
¼ teaspoon freshly ground black pepper
½ teaspoon balsamic vinegar

Using a very sharp knife, slice the lamb as thin as possible, cut it into thin strips, then dice it fine. Combine the lamb in a bowl with the olive oil, shallot, anchovies, parsley, salt, and pepper. Season it with the vinegar and mix well. Divide the lamb tartare between chilled plates and serve it in a small mound surrounded by croutons or toast points that have been brushed with butter and baked crisp in the oven. Alternatively, serve the lamb tartare directly on the toasts as a passed hors d'oeuvre.

Lambs' Tongues with Herb Sauce

For 4

Lambs' tongues have a delicate flavor and texture. The combinations of boiled tongue and a tart vinaigrette thick with herbs and accented with chopped capers and anchovies are pleasing; the sauce adds interest and enlivens the meat, which tastes somewhat plain on its own. The same principle applies here as for any boiled meats and is exemplified by the Italian boiled dinner, *bollito misto*, a grand assembly of chicken, cotechino sausage, tongue, beef, and veal served with salsa verde, and on occasion, freshly grated horseradish doused with white vinegar.

If lambs' tongues are not available, substitute veal tongues, which are larger and will require more time in the pot. (Remove them when they yield easily to the tip of a knife.) This recipe is intended as a simple appetizer, but may be embellished as a full course with a few boiled new potatoes and turnips, Beets with Vinegar and Tarragon, and leeks vinaigrette or parboiled scallions and rosettes of lamb's lettuce.

2 quarts water
2 teaspoons salt
1 small stalk of celery (1 ounce)
1 medium carrot (3 ounces)
1 small onion stuck with 3 cloves
4 sprigs thyme
4 lambs' tongues (12 ounces)

Combine the water, salt, vegetables, and thyme and bring to the boil. Add the lambs' tongues, reduce to a simmer, cover, and cook for 2 hours, or until tender. The tongues should offer no resistance to the tip of a knife. Remove the tongues from the pot, allow the cooking liquid to cool to warm, then return the tongues to the liquid until you are ready to serve them.

For the herb sauce:
2 tablespoons chopped fresh Italian parsley
1 teaspoon chopped fresh tarragon
1 teaspoon chopped fresh oregano
1 teaspoon chopped fresh thyme
1 small clove garlic, finely chopped
1 small shallot (½ ounce), very finely diced

*4 salt-packed anchovy filets soaked in several changes of cold water for 15 minutes,
    squeezed, finely chopped*
1 tablespoon capers, rinsed in water, finely chopped
5 tablespoons extra virgin olive oil
1 teaspoon white wine vinegar
Pinch of salt and pepper
1 large hard-cooked egg, finely chopped

Stir together all the ingredients except the egg. Correct the sauce with a few drops more of vinegar, if necessary, so that it is slightly tart.

To serve: Remove any fat clinging to the underside of the thickest part of the tongues and cut them lengthwise into thin slices. Arrange the tongue on plates. Spoon the sauce over each slice, covering it, then sprinkle with the chopped egg.

Roast Loin of Cured Pork

For 8

Brining is the best method I know of tenderizing and enhancing the flavor of various cuts of pork. Brining is like marinating, although the effect is more radical: The pork is entirely submerged for 2 to 5 days and the flavors of the brine reach to the very center of the meat, imparting characteristics of a mildly cured ham. The brine in this recipe is a solution of salt and sugar ($2\frac{1}{2}$ percent by weight) in water with aromatic vegetables, herbs, and spices. It is effective in penetrating cuts of pork that are not too thick. The loin of pork—whole, boned, or cut into chops—and the shoulder butt roast, ribs, and belly flaps are all suitable to be brined. The leg, with bone in, tends to be too thick and dense to permit the penetration of this mild cure. The length of the cure will vary according to the thickness of the cut. Loin or shoulder (3 to 4 inches thick) takes 5 days; ribs and chops ($\frac{1}{2}$ inch to 2 inches thick) will cure in 2 to 3 days.

The choicest cut to brine comes from the loin because it is lean and without much muscle separation or connective tissue. In the restaurant we prefer the shoulder blade end of the loin that has been cut from just behind the shoulder and nine ribs down. The meat at this end of the loin is dark, moist, and very flavorful. The blade and loin can be cured on or off the bone. To prepare this cut for the spit roast or the oven, cut the meat away from the ribs but leave it attached to the chine and feather bones. This allows for an easy penetration of the brine. Later the roast is trimmed of excess fat and a portion of the blade bone it contains, fresh herbs are placed between the ribs and the meat, and it is tied securely between each bone, resembling a rack of lamb. Roasting with the bones on protects the meat from the drying effect of direct heat and also helps conduct heat to the center of the roast. Alternatively, the loin can be removed from the bone for brining, tied, and cooked slowly on the charcoal grill. The roast is superb this way, sliced and served with grain mustard and rocket salad.

Curing the roast with the bone attached requires a larger container and more space in the refrigerator. But the boneless roast fits well, cut in half, in a container with a capacity slightly larger than a gallon. Make certain that the meat is entirely submerged in the brine and that the container is tightly covered to prevent contamination from the outside. Store the meat in the refrigerator at a temperature not higher than 40°F.

For the brine:
¾ cup additive-free kosher salt (3 ounces)
Scant ⅔ cup granulated sugar (3 ounces)
1 gallon ice water
20 whole juniper berries
20 whole allspice berries
1 teaspoon whole black peppercorns
1 leafy stalk of celery (4 ounces), thinly sliced
1 medium carrot (3 ounces), thinly sliced
¼ yellow onion (2 ounces), thinly sliced
3 sprigs thyme
3 sprigs parsley
3 bay leaves

1 bone-in, blade-end loin of pork (8 pounds, 2 ounces), cut in half
Freshly ground pepper
6 sprigs rosemary

Prepare the brine: In a large bowl dissolve the salt and sugar in the water. Crack the juniper, allspice, and pepper in a mortar. Add the vegetables, herbs, and spices to the water.

Cut the meat away from the ribs but leave it attached where it rests on the chine and feather bones at the base of the ribs. Position the meat so that it is resting on the tips of the rib bones and chine, and make a cut along the length of the meat just behind the eye of the roast. Remove this strip of meat and fat and cut out the fatty pieces of meat between each rib. Remove the blade bone by sliding the knife directly under it. Trim the roast to even it out into a cylindrical form resting on the bones and remove any excess fat, leaving a layer about ¼ inch thick.

Wash and scald a plastic bucket, stainless-steel pot, or ceramic crock large enough to contain the meat and brine, with minimal headroom. Place the meat in the container and pour the brine over it. The meat should be completely submerged. Store in the refrigerator at 40°F for 5 days.

Preheat the oven to 350°F.

Remove the meat from the container and discard the brine. Dry the meat with a towel. Pepper the meat all over, including the portion cut away from the ribs. Place the rosemary sprigs between the meat and ribs and tie the roast from bone to bone. Allow the meat to come to room temperature. Roast the pork in the oven for 1 hour and 20 minutes, or to an internal temperature of 140°F. Allow the meat to rest in a warm place for 5 minutes. To facilitate carving, first cut the meat away from the bone, then slice it thin, transferring each piece as you slice it to a warm platter. Garnish the meat with the rosemary sprigs that have perfumed it.

Braised Pork Shoulder with Tomatoes, Fennel, and Olives

For 8

The forequarter of pork is divided into two prime cuts: the picnic shoulder, which is the foreleg (sold rind on, with hock included); and the shoulder butt roast, also called Boston shoulder, which rests behind the head on either side of the animal. The shoulder butt roast is an excellent cut to braise. Although it contains some small muscles, fat, and connective tissues, the proportion of dark, succulent meat is high.

The goal of braising is to simmer the meat in a moist medium until meltingly tender. Unlike poaching, where the food to be cooked is entirely submerged in the hot liquid, braising is accomplished with less liquid and the pot is covered tight to retain steam as it cooks. While the meat cooks, it releases its juices, which blend with the cooking liquid, aromatic vegetables, and herbs. The cooking liquid is later reduced and skimmed of any fat to form a sauce wherein the essential flavors of the braise are concentrated. The pork may also be braised in water, in which case the resulting sauce will be light and direct; a liquid such as stock will produce a richer sauce with more body.

The pot you use for braising should be heavy, preferably of ceramic, enameled steel, or any of the laminated steel pots with a stainless-steel interior. The pot should also have a tight-fitting lid. If you lack the proper pot, a deep baking dish tightly covered with aluminum foil will suffice.

Serve the braised pork with browned new potatoes.

Salt and pepper
1 boneless pork shoulder butt roast (3 pounds, 12 ounces), fat trimmed to ⅛ inch, tied to form a rough rectangular shape
3 tablespoons vegetable oil
1 large carrot (4 ounces), finely diced
1 medium stalk of celery (2½ ounces), finely diced
2 small yellow onions (12 ounces), finely diced
1½ teaspoons fennel seeds, crushed in a mortar
4 leafy sprigs thyme
3 large ripe tomatoes (2 pounds, 14 ounces), peeled, seeded, diced, juice strained and reserved
3 tablespoons vegetable oil
30 slices of garlic (4 large cloves)
2½ cups water or meat broth (see page 427)
½ cup pitted Niçoise olives (if the olives taste strongly of salt, rinse them in several changes of water before adding to the sauce)
1 heaping tablespoon chopped fresh Italian parsley

Salt and pepper the roast and place it, fat side down, in a cast-iron pan preheated over low heat. Raise the heat to medium and brown the roast for 12 minutes on the fatted side, pouring off fat as it renders, and about 5 minutes on the remaining three sides. Transfer the roast to a plate and set it aside.

Preheat the oven to 325°F. Clean out the cast-iron pan, warm the vegetable oil, add the carrot, celery, and onions, and cook the vegetables over moderate heat for 12 minutes. Raise the heat in the final 4 to 5 minutes, add the fennel seeds, and allow the vegetables to color lightly.

Place the cooked vegetables and the thyme sprigs in the bottom of a 6-quart braising pot. Add the tomatoes and their juice, sprinkle them with 1 teaspoon salt, and grind a little pepper over them. Stud the roast with the garlic slices and set it on the bed of vegetables. Pour the water or meat broth into the braising pot and bring it to a simmer. Cover the pot tightly and place it in the oven for 2 hours.

Remove the roast from the pot and set it on a warm place. Remove 3 cups of sauce and vegetables from the pot and put them through the fine blade of a food mill back into the braising pot. Reduce the vegetables and liquid by half, or until the two are combined in a thick, saucy blend. Skim away any fat that rises to the surface during the reduction. Test the consistency of the sauce by placing a spoonful on a plate. If a thin liquid bleeds out, reduce it further. The sauce will appear quite thick. When the sauce has reduced sufficiently, stir in the olives and parsley.

Slice the roast, cutting away and discarding any internal pockets of fat. Arrange the meat on a large warm platter or individual plates and place a generous spoonful of sauce on each slice. Spread the sauce to cover the meat. Alternatively, you may slice the meat ahead of time and in a large earthenware or ceramic dish layer it with the sauce. This can be accomplished well ahead of serving; the braise can then be gently warmed in the oven just prior to serving.

Fresh Pork Sausages

About 2½ pounds of sausage, eight 5-inch links

If you have a hand meat-grinder or mixer with sausagemaking attachments, a batch of sausage can be made up quickly. It is essential, however, that the cutting blade be as sharp as possible to prevent the meat from being crushed, which destroys its juice-retaining structure and results in a drier, less succulent sausage. Furthermore, the meat and fat should be nearly frozen so that the machinery remains cool during the cutting process; cold meat and fat will leave the grinder more cleanly. If you have neither a hand grinder or sausage attachment for the mixer, the meat and fat may be chopped by hand, which actually produces the best results. Chopping with a heavy chef's knife or sharp, thin-bladed cleaver keeps the structure of the meat intact and allows for varying textures of chopped meat, which makes the sausage all the more interesting. Chopping by hand is less feasible, however, if you are preparing a large batch.

Stuffing the sausage may be accomplished in several ways. Funnels for stuffing come as attachments to grinders, or can be used manually. A stuffing funnel is a hollow, cylindrical tube, tapered slightly at the end. The casing is slipped over the end of the tube where it rests, ready to receive the sausage mixture that is forced through the other end. (See page 256 for a source for sausage-making equipment.)

To prevent air from entering the casing, it is best to first push some of the meat through the tube to create a vacuum, then to slip on the casing. Sausages should not be packed too tightly, or they will tear when twisted off in portions, or will burst when cooked. Casings come in a variety of sizes for different applications. For fresh pork sausage, I generally choose natural hog casings with a diameter of about 1½ inches. Sheep casings are another possibility, but are thinner and more fragile than hog casings. Casings are available in bulk from manufacturers of sausage-making equipment, or it may be possible to order them in smaller quantities from your butcher if you give him a few days. Casings are generally packed in dry salt and must be soaked ahead of time. Unused casings will last indefinitely if they are repacked in salt and refrigerated.

Another option for serving sausage is to wrap it in caul, the veil-like stomach membrane of lamb or pork, also available from butchers: Form the chopped meat into a patty and cut out a piece of caul about 2½ times as large as the patty. Wrap the caul around the patty (a bay leaf set on top adds flavor and is nice to look at), enclosing it entirely, and press the loose sides gently in place. Cook the patty first on the side where the ends overlap. The caul will adhere to itself.

Sausage should contain about 30 percent fat to be moist. Pork butts already contain a fair amount of fat, but need a little extra. Use the firm, tender, very white fat from the back of the animal rather than that from the belly, which tends to be tougher and flabbier.

This pork sausage can be grilled or fried and served on its own, or used as part of a mixed grill, or served with pasta or bean dishes. These sausages will keep in the refrigerator for 2 to 3 days.

2 pounds pork butt
6 ounces fresh pork back fat
1 large clove garlic
¼ teaspoon anise seed
¼ cup dry red wine
1½ teaspoons salt
1 teaspoon freshly ground black pepper
⅛ teaspoon ground cayenne

BY MACHINE: First cut the meat and fat by hand into small chunks and in a bowl chill it thoroughly. If you are using a meat grinder, attach the ¼-inch plate. Run the fat through once alone, then pass it through the second time with the meat. Pound the garlic to a paste in a mortar, add the anise seed, and crush it. Add the garlic and anise to the ground meat. Wash out the mortar with the red wine and add it to the meat with the salt, pepper, and cayenne. Mix thoroughly by hand until the fat is well distributed.

BY HAND: First cut the fat into thin slices, cut the slices into strips, then dice the strips fine. Do the same with the meat and if you wish to vary the texture, leave a portion of the meat in larger dice and set this portion aside. Combine the fat and meat together and chop them to a similar consistency. Add the seasonings as above and mix well. Stuff the sausage into casings or make patties and wrap them in caul, each with a bay leaf.

Grill the sausages over a low fire for about 5 minutes per side, or until they become slightly firm to the touch in the center.

Source for sausage-making equipment:
The Sausage Maker
177 Military Road
Buffalo, New York 14207
(716) 876-5521

Cotechino Sausage

2 large sausages, enough for 6

In the first week of December we celebrate the new vintage of Zinfandel made for us by the Phelps Vineyard. The menus for the week are in keeping with the fruity, high-spirited, rough qualities of this new wine, which we serve from the barrel. Roast chicken with garlic, cassoulet, spit-roasted suckling pig, confit of duck, onion panade, baked squid, and salt cod hash are representative of the style of dishes that are served. And we always include sausage, which I remember Alice encouraged several years ago with a memory of a dish she ate in Paris—*cervelas*, a large sausage studded with black truffles and served with boiled leeks and potato purée. Her more specific description reminded me of Italian cotechino, a coarsely chopped, highly spiced pork sausage containing the boiled rinds and skin of the pig, which give it a nearly creamy texture.

This sausage is essentially a cotechino with the addition of pistachio nuts, and, if possible, diced black truffle. The sausage will be no worse without the truffle, but including it will add an extra dimension of flavor and interest.

This recipe contains curing salt (half the quantity that federal regulations permit) as an ingredient. Curing salt is a mixture of salt and sodium nitrite or nitrate. Since the sausage is eaten fresh, this salt has no effect on flavor. It contributes the characteristic flavor of cured meats and sausages only when used in more extended cures. Here it is used to stabilize and prevent any fading of the color of the sausage mixture. Without curing salt, the sausage will have an unappetizing gray-brown color. Its use, however, is entirely optional. Curing salt containing nitrites should be used with care; before proceeding with this recipe read the information on page 432.

The simplest method of forming the sausage is to roll it up in a double sheet of plastic wrap and tie off each end tightly with kitchen string. In this way, no stuffing is necessary, the sausage poaches well, and it is easy to remove for slicing. If you prefer to stuff the sausage, the beef "middle" casing, derived from the large intestine, is the right size. You may have to special-order this casing from a sausage house, or perhaps your butcher will be able to get it for you. Refer to the source on page 256 for sausage-making equipment.

Serve these sausages with boiled leeks and carrots tossed in a little butter and a purée of potatoes. Homemade Sauerkraut, pulled from the crock before it develops its full sourness and tossed in a little Champagne, is a good contrast to the richness of the sausage. It is also delicious sliced and served with stewed lentils or cannellini beans that have been simmered in lightly salted water with sage leaves and garlic.

12 ounces fresh pork jowls (available in Chinese markets, or ask your butcher)
2 teaspoons salt
2½ quarts water
3 bay leaves
2 pounds pork from the shoulder
4 ounces fresh pork back fat
3 small cloves garlic, smashed to a paste in a mortar
½ cup pistachio nuts, parboiled 1 minute, peeled, coarsely chopped
1½ teaspoons salt
½ teaspoon freshly ground pepper
⅛ teaspoon ground cloves
¼ teaspoon ground cinnamon
¼ teaspoon freshly grated nutmeg
Optional: 1 black truffle (1½ ounces), diced
½ teaspoon curing salt containing 6¼ percent sodium nitrite by weight (see page 432)
    dissolved in 1 tablespoon water

Combine the pork jowls, salt, water, and bay leaves in a pot. Bring to the boil, skim off the white froth that comes to the surface, reduce to a simmer, cover, and cook for 2 hours and 15 minutes, or until the pork is very tender. While the pork jowls are cooking, cut the pork shoulder into thin slices, then thin strips, and dice it. Do the same with the back fat but keep it separate from the meat for the time being. Set aside about one third (10 ounces) of the diced meat. Chop it very finely until it resembles a coarse paste. Combine the fat with the remaining diced pork and chop it fine with a heavy sharp knife, turning the mass of meat over upon itself with the blade as you proceed, moving the meat on the bottom to the top. Chopping the meat by hand produces a more distinct texture than a meat grinder and preserves its juice-retaining structure. Chop until the fat and meat are reduced to ⅛-inch bits and well mixed together. Combine all of the meat in a bowl.

Remove the pork jowls from the water and test their tenderness. The thickest portion should yield easily to the blade of a knife. Drain in a colander, let the jowls cool thoroughly, then turn them out onto the cutting board. Chop the jowls into very fine bits. Add them to the bowls with the meat. Add the garlic paste, pistachio nuts, salt, pepper, spices, and truffle, if you have one. Mix briefly with your hands, then sprinkle the curing salt over the meat, and mix very thoroughly.

Forming the sausages: Divide the mixture in two. Cut a piece of plastic wrap 14 inches long. Place half the sausage mixture in the center of the wrap, spreading it out to form a log about 10 inches long and 3 inches wide. Compact the meat with your hand to prevent air pockets. Fold one half of the wrap tightly over the meat, then the other. Roll the meat gently to form a rough cylinder. Cut another piece of wrap and place the wrapped sausage as before, but closer to the edge, and roll it up. Roll the sausage in yet another piece of plastic wrap. Twist the ends of the wrap in opposite directions so that the sausage tightens, its length reduces to 8 inches, diameter to 2 ½ inches, and a neat cylinder forms. Be careful not to tighten the sausage so much that it bursts in the poaching pot. Tie off the ends tightly with string as close as possible to the sausage (an extra hand to hold the twisted end is a help here.) Do the same with the remaining sausage mixture. Let the sausage sit for at least 1 hour (the mix can be made up to 1 day ahead, if necessary) before cooking so that the curing salt will take effect.

Cooking: Plunge the sausages into a large pot of boiling water and reduce the heat to a bare simmer. Keep the sausages submerged (they will float to the top) under an undersized lid or ceramic plate for 1 hour. Remove the sausages carefully with a slotted spatula. Working over a deep platter, puncture the casing in several spots to expel the fat the meat has released, then remove the plastic. Slice the sausages with a sharp, thin-bladed knife into thick pieces and serve.

Terrine of Pork

16 slices

A terrine is a seasoned, baked forcemeat, so named after the deep, oval, or rectangular mold in which it cooks. For lack of a better translation it is often inadequately described as a meat loaf. The method of making a terrine is similar. However, the result is worlds apart. A terrine is a much richer, more highly seasoned preparation akin to cured meats and sausages. Terrines can be made of meat, poultry, game, fish, and even vegetables, and their composition can be a simple or complex variety of ingredients bound with different forcemeats. This recipe is an uncomplicated version with the number of ingredients kept to a minimum.

You will need no fancy tools or mechanical gadgets to make this terrine. In fact, I urge that you resist the temptation to use a meat grinder or a food processor. The forcemeat is best when chopped by hand—the texture of the finished terrine is noticeably more distinct in appearance and flavor and it has a pleasantly irregular consistency. Putting the meat through a grinder or the blade of a rotary cutting processor is damaging to the juice-retaining structure of meat and the terrine will taste greasy. A mechanically chopped forcemeat loses considerably more juice and fat while cooking than one that is hand-chopped. If you must use a meat grinder or food processor for time's sake, make certain that the blades are very sharp and the meat and fat to be cut are cold (just above freezing is ideal).

I have found the most efficient tool for chopping to be a thin-bladed, medium-weight Chinese cleaver. If the cleaver is very sharp and you handle it vigorously, the job of chopping can be accomplished in minutes. Furthermore, the wide blade of a cleaver makes it easy to turn the mass of meat over upon itself during chopping. (The most finely chopped bits are always on the bottom.)

Traditionally, meat terrines are enclosed in thin sheets of back fat or caul fat to assure that the forcemeat remains moist while cooking. Although it is important to protect the surfaces of the terrine from the dry heat of the oven, the fat enclosure is unnecessary (it would have to be removed anyway before serving). Instead, parboiled chard leaves are used in this recipe to line the mold and protect the open surface. The spice proportions make this a highly seasoned terrine, and you may wish to cut back or include your own mixture. At home I make this terrine for special occasions and usually when a large group is expected; because of its richness, it is better shared among many than held for leftovers.

Serve the terrine at room temperature with homemade pickles, good crusty bread, and condiments such as whole-grain mustard or horseradish.

8 ounces fresh pork back fat
2½ pounds shoulder of pork
7 ounces fresh pork liver, trimmed of all veins
1 tablespoon pure olive oil
4 shallots (4 ounces), finely diced
1 cup (2 ounces) white bread crumbs
½ cup dry white wine
4 cloves garlic (1 ounce), pounded into a paste in a mortar
2 tablespoons chopped fresh parsley
⅓ cup pistachio nuts, parboiled for 1 minute, skins removed
Spices, all finely ground:
  ½ teaspoon allspice
  ½ teaspoon bay leaf

½ teaspoon dried oregano
½ teaspoon dried thyme
1½ teaspoons black pepper
3 teaspoons salt
¼ teaspoon cayenne
8 to 10 large, intact, red or green chard leaves, parboiled 2 minutes until limp and
well drained

Slice the back fat into thin strips and dice into regularly sized pieces about ⅛ inch thick. Cut the pork into thin strips, dice it, distribute the fat on top of the pork, then divide the mixture in half on the cutting board. Chop the mixtures more and less so that you obtain a varied forcemeat of fine and coarse bits of pork, ranging from ⅛ to ⅜ inch in size. When chopping, go over the mixture with the cleaver or knife several times, turn the mixture over with the blade of the knife and continue in this manner until the consistency is right. Slice the liver, dice it, then chop it as fine as possible, to a near liquid consistency (it won't be absolutely smooth). Transfer the chopped meat, fat, and liver to a large mixing bowl.

Preheat the oven to 325°F. Warm the olive oil in a small sauté or saucepan, add the shallots, and cook them for 5 minutes, without browning, until softened. Meanwhile, in a separate bowl combine the bread crumbs and white wine and stir until the crumbs are soaked. Add the wine and bread crumbs, the shallots, garlic, parsley, pistachio nuts, and ground spices to the pork forcemeat and mix thoroughly by hand.

Line a 1½-quart terrine or loaf mold with the chard leaves: Arrange a large leaf to cover the bottom of the mold. Fit the other leaves, overlapping the bottom leaf and each other, around the sides of the mold allowing them to drape over the edge about 2 inches. You may have to trim them. Pack the forcemeat mixture into the mold (it will be slightly mounded) and fold the leaves over the top to enclose it. Rap the bottom of the mold against the table to settle the contents. Place the terrine in a baking dish with enough water to come two thirds of the way up the sides of the terrine. Bake in the oven for 1½ to 1¾ hours, or until a meat thermometer reads 130°F in the center of the terrine.

Remove the terrine from the oven and allow to cool for ½ hour. Then place a dish or flat board and about a 3-pound weight over the top of the terrine. Allow to cool at room temperature for several hours under the weight. When the terrine is cool and quite firm, remove the weight, wrap the terrine on the counter, and put it in the refrigerator to ripen for a day before eating.

Prosciutto with Warm Wilted Greens

For 6 as an appetizer

This is a quick and simple appetizer made by wilting a variety of greens in vinaigrette and then rolling them up in thin slices of prosciutto. Any green that is sturdy but not tough is suitable for wilting. Those that quickly go limp and heavy, such as spinach, should not be used. Young collards, bok choy, red mustard, escarole, curly endive, the large leaves of rocket, and some of the oriental brassicas, such as Mizuna and the flowering shoots of Hon Tsai Tai, Tendergreen, and Tat Tsoi, all work well. You will find it easiest to wilt the greens directly over the flame in a large stainless-steel bowl or wok. The size of the bowl will make it easy to turn the greens without spilling them and you will be able to better control the brief cooking—the wilted greens can be more easily moved from the hot base of the bowl to the cooler sides. A pair of V-shaped tongs is a great help tossing the greens.

Ideally, the greens should be rolled up in the prosciutto while they are still warm; the steam they release will cause the prosciutto to soften and the flavors to meld.

For the vinaigrette:
¼ teaspoon salt
2 tablespoons red wine vinegar
1 large shallot (1 ounce), finely diced
1 clove garlic, mashed in a mortar
Freshly ground pepper
4 tablespoons extra virgin olive oil

3 large handfuls greens (about 9 ounces; see above), washed and dried
12 very thin slices prosciutto

Prepare the vinaigrette: Dissolve the salt in the vinegar. Stir in the shallot and garlic, add pepper to taste, and stir in the olive oil. Put the vinaigrette in a stainless-steel bowl or wok large enough to hold the greens comfortably, and warm it over a direct flame.

Add the greens and toss them continually with a pair of tongs for about 1 minute, until they are slightly wilted but have not gone entirely limp. Remove the bowl or wok from the stove. Working directly from the bowl, place a small mixture of greens loosely on each prosciutto slice and roll up the slice. Serve while still warm.

Roast Chicken

For 4

More than a recipe, this is a tribute to roast chicken, which can hardly be improved upon by the additions of a sauce or fancy seasonings. A well-roasted chicken requires neither of these embellishments. By itself it is plenty juicy and its crisp skin heightens the flavor of the flesh much like a sauce.

To transport a roast chicken from the wonderful to the sublime, cook it on a spit in front of a live fire of burning oak or fruit wood. What has come to be viewed as an archaic method of cooking still surpasses, in its results, a gas or convection oven. For more information on spit roasting, see page 264. To make this recipe choose a fresh, plump roasting hen.

1 roasting hen, about 4 pounds, at room temperature
1 teaspoon fennel seed
¼ teaspoon cayenne pepper flakes
1½ teaspoons additive-free kosher salt
½ teaspoon ground black pepper
A small bunch of fresh thyme

Preheat the oven to 400°F.

Remove any excess fat inside the cavity of the chicken and in the neck flap. Crack the fennel seeds in a mortar with a pestle and mix them with the cayenne, salt, and pepper. Salt the cavity and stuff the bunch of thyme inside. Truss the legs loosely so that all areas, particularly the inner thighs, are exposed to the heat. Turn the wings behind the neck of the bird and fix them in place. Use the remaining mixture of seasonings to salt the bird all over, particularly the breast section that is milder in flavor than the darker parts of the bird. Set the bird in a roasting pan without a rack, and cook it for 1 hour. Remove it from the oven and allow it to relax for 5 minutes before carving it.

Spit Roasting

Among the many ways to cook, the most appealing is spit roasting over a live fire. Spit-roasted birds, lambs, and roasts of all kinds are served frequently on the nightly menus and for festive occasions at Chez Panisse. Apart from the immediate comfort and warmth of the hearth, roasting food over a crackling fire fills up the senses, and is both visually exciting and stimulating to the appetite. Less practical, more time-consuming, and perhaps less fuel efficient, spit roasting over a fire has for the most part disappeared. It is certainly an anomaly in restaurants. Nevertheless, the benefits of this method far exceed the extra trouble. There is no better way to cook whole animals, large roasts, and poultry. With a well-made fire and a spit that turns with a slow regular rhythm, heat penetrates gradually and consistently, producing self-basted meat that is moist, redolent of burning oak or fruit wood, and cooked evenly from the center to the exterior. Unlike cooking in the oven, spit roasting requires more active attention on the part of the cook. The whole process is immensely gratifying, however, and with a little practice an easy rhythm is established.

The key to successful spit roasting lies in maintaining the fire and gauging the space between the food and the flame. The fire should be started early enough so that in addition to burning logs there is a substantial bed of hot embers. This is most important for roasts that spend over an hour on the spit.

The fire should be neither too hot nor too cool and the food should be placed far enough from it so that it does not char or spin aimlessly. The alternatives in this case are to move either the food or the fire, depending upon the versatility of the spit mechanism and the dimensions of the hearth.

The most desirable firewood is seasoned oak. Being very dense, it burns slowly and produces a pleasing aromatic smoke. Fruitwoods such as apple, olive, cherry, or grape can be used, but softer woods, such as pine, should be avoided as they burn too quickly.

Care must also be taken in preparing the roasts and loading the spit. With the exception of very small birds, poultry and large animals should be trussed so that no parts hang free to burn or put the spit out of balance as it spins. As a general rule, truss a roast so that it is as close as possible to a compact, cylindrical form and arrange the roasts on the spit so that the weight is evenly distributed. In the case of poultry, turn the wing joints under and secure the legs inside the skewers. Legs of lamb work best with the H-bone removed and the whole roast tied at one-inch intervals beginning above the shank. Loins of pork retain more moisture and cook more quickly if they are roasted with the bone on. This does not always follow for beef, however, as roasts such as prime rib and cross rib are too cumbersome and heavy in this form. The filet of beef, being for the most part cylindrical, is ideally suited. The tail section, that is, where the filet tapers, is best trimmed off and used for some other purpose. Small birds, pheasant, partridge, and guinea fowl, should be barded—pancetta or smoked bacon sliced into large very thin sheets ("leaves") is tied securely around the breast. This follows for lean cuts of meat such as loin or leg of veal.

Cooking times vary according to the thickness of the roast and not the overall weight. Provided the heat is steady, spit roasting takes no more time, notwithstanding the preparation of the fire, than cooking in the oven, and the end result is without comparison.

Chicken Breast Stuffed with Wild Mushrooms

For 4

Chicken is greatly enhanced by marinades and stuffings; flavors easily penetrate the breast portion, particularly if the bones are removed. The stuffing for this recipe is made of wild mushrooms, Italian bacon, herbs, onions, and garlic. The filet of chicken (the thin, tapering muscle on the underside of the breast) contains a fair amount of natural gelatin and is also added to the stuffing to bind the other elements. Because there is no cavity in a chicken breast, any stuffing must be enclosed inside a protective coating. Caul fat, the membranous, lacelike lining of the pig's stomach (available in Chinese markets or by special order from some butchers) is used to contain the stuffing, which is spread onto the underside of the breast. When the breast is cooked, the caul melts away, leaving an attractively browned surface.

The horns of plenty (*Craterellus cornucopioides*) called for in this recipe can be replaced with a similar amount of any other available mushroom. In the spring we make this dish when the morels arrive from Oregon. If you use other mushrooms, make sure that you cook them until they have released all their moisture and are quite dry.

Although the stuffed chicken is sufficiently moist on its own, you may wish to include a sauce to unify the other elements you have chosen to accompany it. A reduction of chicken broth, mounted with a little butter, peppered, and sprinkled with some of the same herbs in the stuffing, is a simple option. Plain or parsleyed noodles are delicious, as is a purée of root vegetables such as potatoes, celeriac, parsnips, or green garlic. A gratin of soft-flavored vegetables such as artichokes, fennel, or endives is likewise harmonious. If you decide to make this chicken for lunch, serve it without a sauce and surround it with lettuces vinaigrette. When cooked, the stuffing adheres to the breast and can be cut into ¼-inch slices on the bias to make an attractive presentation.

4 boneless chicken breasts (1 pound, 8 ounces), skin removed
Salt and pepper
2 tablespoons unsalted butter
¼ cup leek (2 ounces), white parts only, diced
2 ounces pancetta, diced
5 ounces horns of plenty or other wild mushrooms
1 large clove garlic, finely chopped
1 tablespoon chopped fresh Italian parsley
½ teaspoon chopped fresh thyme
1 pound caul fat

From each chicken breast remove the filet, the small tapering muscle on the underside of the breast, and cut out the white sinew running through it. Set the filets aside. With a meat mallet or the back of a heavy knife or cleaver, flatten, without smashing, the thick end of the breast so that the whole breast is a uniform thickness, about ⅜ to ½ inch thick. Lightly salt and pepper both sides and set aside. Dice the filets and pound them to a coarse paste in a mortar.

Melt the butter in a 3-quart saucepan, add the leek, and cook slowly for 5 to 8 minutes, until thoroughly softened. Add the pancetta and mushrooms and cook another 10 minutes, or until all of the water that the mushrooms release has evaporated. Turn the mixture out onto a cutting board and chop coarse. Combine the mixture in a bowl with the pounded chicken filet, garlic, and herbs. Add ¼ teaspoon salt and a liberal grinding of pepper. When mixed together the stuffing should yield a heaping 1⅓ cups. Divide the mixture in four. Spread one fourth of the mixture on the underside of each breast to cover the entire surface in an even layer.

Rinse the caul fat in cold water. Hold the caul up and examine it for tears. Cut intact pieces from the sheet that are large enough to enclose the breast and stuffing with minimal overlapping. (You will have more caul than you need, but it is good to buy a little extra so that you can select choice pieces; the rest can be frozen.) Place each chicken breast in the middle of a piece of caul and fold the caul over the breast so that it is completely sealed. Set the stuffed breasts aside on a plate until you are ready to cook them.

Preheat a 12-inch cast-iron pan over low heat. Lay the chicken breasts in the pan side by side, seam side down (stuffing side down), raise the heat a little, and cook for 4 to 5 minutes per side, or until the caul fat has rendered and the chicken is well browned and firm throughout. Serve the chicken breasts immediately.

Chicken Sausages

10 sausages, roughly 4 ounces each

These sausages resemble bockwurst or *boudins blancs*. The fine-textured force-meat consists primarily of chicken, but can be made with other light meats or poultry—veal, rabbit, or pheasant. These sausages are suited to browning in a sauté pan rather than on the charcoal grill; the flavors are soft and satisfying in their own right without the additional smoky aroma.

To achieve a smooth texture, without graininess, and a juicy succulent quality, you will need to reduce the meat and fat to a very fine consistency. This can be accomplished in a number of ways: by passing it three times through a meat-grinder fitted with a 3/16-inch plate; by chopping it in a food processor; or by pounding the mixture in a mortar. The goal is a fine mousseline-like consistency. The natural gelatin in the meat mixes with the other elements of the mixture to create a seamless bonding of meat, fat, and seasonings.

Serve the sausages with sautéed onions and apples or Cabbage Braised with Riesling and Bacon and a smooth, not-too-hot mustard.

1 tablespoon unsalted butter
½ yellow onion (4 ounces), finely diced
¼ cup dry white wine
¼ cup fresh white bread crumbs
1 cup heavy cream
2 pounds chicken breasts, skin removed
10 ounces lightly smoked fatty bacon
1½ teaspoons salt
⅛ teaspoon freshly grated nutmeg
¼ teaspoon thyme
⅛ teaspoon ground bay leaf
¼ teaspoon ground white pepper
⅛ teaspoon ground cayenne

Warm the butter in a sauté pan. Add the onion and wine and soften the onion over medium heat for 7 to 8 minutes. Allow the wine to fully evaporate. Set aside to cool. Combine the bread crumbs in a bowl with ½ cup of the cream and let them soak a few minutes. Cut the chicken and bacon into cubes and pass them once through a meat grinder fitted with a 3/16-inch plate. (If you use the mortar or food processor work the chicken, bacon, cooked onions, bread crumbs, and ½ of the cream to a very smooth mousselinelike consistency.)

Mix the ground meat-bacon mixture with the onions, cream, and bread crumbs. Work the mixture together with a spoon to bring it together, then pass it two more times through the meat grinder. Transfer to a bowl, add the seasonings, and work in the remaining ½ cup cream with a wooden spoon until the mixture has a stiff but slightly fluffy consistency. Stuff into hog casings about 1½ inches in diameter and form links by twisting the length of sausage at 4- to 5-inch intervals, each new twist made in the *opposite* direction relative to the previous. Otherwise, the individual sausages will quickly unwind. The other option for forming links is to tie them off with thin kitchen string.

To cook the sausages: First bring a large pot of water to the boil. Without cutting the sausages into individual links, plunge them into the boiling water, turn off the heat, and let them stand for 8 minutes. Remove the sausages and let them cool, and cut into links. Once parboiled, the sausages will keep for several days. Before serving, brown the sausages in a cast-iron pan in a light film of clarified butter over low heat, for 4 to 5 minutes per side.

Steamed and Roasted Duck

For 2 as a main course

Perhaps the greatest challenge in cooking Peking or Long Island duck is coping with the abundance of fat under the skin, which does not break down easily when simply roasted, grilled, or braised. Two cooking processes are necessary: the first to soften and render most of the fat, the second to brown and crisp the skin. Although it is possible to accomplish the first step by deep-frying the duck (a common practice in Chinese restaurants), it is a messy business at home and does not produce the best results in preparing the duck for finishing in the oven. Steaming the duck is an effective method for breaking down the tough fat, and causes it to render readily. Because it cooks in a hot, steamy medium the flesh of the duck retains moisture and is sumptuously tender.

I have had best results using White Peking duck (available fresh in Chinese markets). The first steaming process takes an hour and may be done far ahead of time, if necessary. Roasting the duck to brown and crisp the skin requires about 45 minutes.

If you do not have a large Chinese basket strainer, one may be improvised: A large, oval, enameled, deep roasting pan, in which most people cook their Thanksgiving turkey, is ideal for steaming, provided it is somewhat larger than the duck. Place a square rack on the bottom of the roasting pan about 1½ inches above the bottom by setting it on top of several ramekins (or even two clean rocks of similar dimension) at either end of the rack. It is important that as little steam escape as possible. Cover the pan first with cooking parchment, then with heavy-duty foil, squeezing the foil tightly at the edges of the pan. The foil covering should be tight enough that it puffs up with the pressure of the rising steam. If the foil is not wide enough to cover the pan in one piece, fold two or more pieces together as tightly as possible.

Rather than carving the meat off the bones, I prefer to serve it as the Chinese do, divided into small chunks. Leaving the bones attached preserves the succulence of the meat, particularly if you leave your fork and knife on the table and dig in with your hands. A sharp, thin-bladed cleaver is ideal for cutting up the duck, but a pair of poultry shears will work as well.

Accompaniments might include braised mustard or collard greens, bok choy, blanched curly endive dressed fresh with a vinaigrette, and steamed vegetables such as carrots, turnips, rutabagas, or parsnips tossed in butter.

1 fresh White Peking duck, head and feet included (5 pounds)
1½ tablespoons additive-free kosher salt
½ teaspoon freshly ground black pepper
The leafy top of a stalk of celery
1 small carrot (1 ounce), cut into chunks
½ small onion (3 ounces), cut up rough
3 cloves garlic, peeled
1 small bunch of fresh thyme
½ cup dry white wine
1 tablespoon balsamic vinegar
1 heaping tablespoon honey
1½ teaspoons chopped fresh thyme

Cut the neck, head, and feet off of the duck. Sever the wing at the first joint, leaving the small arm or drumette. Remove the fatty deposit just inside the cavity of the duck. Reserve the neck (skin removed), feet, and wings for your next poultry broth and render the fat (cook it over low heat in a saucepan) from the neck and cavity for use in warm salads, or as a tasty cooking fat for potatoes.

Prick the duck all over with the tines of a fork, particularly underneath the wing joints along the breast and wherever you notice deposits of fat. Combine the salt and pepper. Sprinkle the cavity of the bird and rub it evenly all over the surface with the salt mixture. Put the celery, carrot, onion, garlic, and bunch of thyme inside the cavity. Place the bird breast side up in the steamer. Pour about an inch of water in the bottom of the pan, cover it tightly as described above, and steam the duck over medium heat (or high enough so that the foil covering puffs up and trails of steam are released) for 1 hour. The skin of the duck should feel very tender after this amount of time.

Preheat the oven to 425°F. Combine the wine, balsamic vinegar, honey, and thyme in a small saucepot. Warm the mixture gently to dissolve the honey. Place the duck on a rack set on a flat baking pan and roast it for 30 minutes. Reduce the heat to 375°F and begin brushing the bird all over with the warm wine and honey mixture. Brush the bird repeatedly during the course of the next 15 minutes until it is a dark mahogany brown. You should be left with a little more than half the basting liquid.

When the duck is sufficiently browned, remove it from the oven and let it rest in a warm spot for about 5 minutes. Then cut it up and arrange the pieces on a warm platter. Bring the remaining basting liquid to a boil, pour it over the duck, and serve.

Duck Legs Braised with Onions and Cabbage

For 4

An alternative to roasting a duck whole is to remove the breasts and legs and cook them separately. The leg meat of a duck is dark and tends toward toughness. As such, it is suitable for braising, which tenderizes the meat and keeps it moist throughout. If you remove the legs yourself, make certain that you leave enough skin, which shrinks during cooking, to slightly overlap the meat (the legs are not entirely submerged in the braising liquid and the skin helps keep the meat moist). Set the duck in front of you, breast side up (feet removed) and make a cut through the skin connecting the thigh to the carcass. Turn the duck slightly on its side and make a neat circular cut around the thigh catching the "oyster," the small, plump piece of meat resting in the shallow cavity under the thigh against the backbone of the bird. Bend the whole leg away from the carcass until the ball of the thighbone frees itself from the hip socket. Cut between the ball and socket and remove the leg. Repeat with the other leg. Cut the breast meat free and reserve for sautéing or grilling. Set aside the carcass for broth.

This dish is a good choice in the fall when you can use the last tomatoes of the season and serve it with sautéed apples. A crisp Straw Potato Cake is another option that provides contrast to this dish of soft textures.

4 duck legs (2 pounds)
1 tablespoon additive-free kosher salt
¾ teaspoon freshly ground black pepper
1 teaspoon thyme
3 large red onions (2 pounds), halved, cut into thick slices
¼ of a savoy or Dutch white cabbage (12 ounces), roughly cut up
Heaping ½ teaspoon salt
3 tablespoons balsamic vinegar
2 cups full-bodied poultry (see page 426) or beef broth (see page 427)
3 tomatoes (12 ounces), cored, peeled, quartered

Trim the fat in the pockets against the skin around the flesh of the duck legs. Hold the flat end of the knife blade to the fat and scrape it to the side or cut it free. Trim the excess skin so that it extends slightly beyond the flesh of the leg.

Mix together the kosher salt, freshly ground pepper, and ½ teaspoon of the thyme, and sprinkle both sides of the legs with the mixture. Set the legs on a plate at room temperature for 1½ hours to absorb the salt.

Preheat the oven to 350°F. Warm a 12-inch cast-iron pan. Place the duck legs in skin side down (it isn't necessary to add any fat to the pan) and cook them slowly for 20 minutes, or until they achieve an even mahogany color. As the ducks cook, pour off the fat that collects in the pan and reserve it. The legs should not fry in their fat. When the legs are browned thoroughly on the skin side, remove them from the pan.

Wash out the cast-iron pan and return it to the stove. Measure out ¼ cup of the rendered duck fat and warm it in the pan. Add the onions and soften them over medium heat, stirring often, for 7 to 8 minutes. Add the cabbage, regular salt, and the remaining ¼ teaspoon pepper, balsamic vinegar, and the remaining ½ teaspoon thyme, and cook the mixture for 5 minutes, until the cabbage is wilted. Transfer the cabbage and onions to a ceramic or enamel baking dish and lay the duck legs on top of them. Pour the broth over the legs and set the tomatoes (lightly salted and peppered) around them. Cover the pan tightly and place it in the oven for 1½ hours. When done, the legs should be tender throughout and should yield easily to a toothpick.

Remove the duck legs from the baking dish and pour the braising liquid through a sieve into a wide sauté pan. Arrange the braised vegetables on a serving platter, place the legs on top, and hold the platter in a warm oven while you finish the sauce. Set the pan with the strained braising liquid slightly off the burner and turn the heat as high as it will go. Reduce the liquid until it is slightly thick and about 1 cup remains.

Serve the duck on warmed plates with a healthy portion of the onions, cabbage, and tomatoes. Spoon some of the sauce over each.

Duck Liver Croutons

2 cups, enough for about 24 croutons

Liver croutons are a common appetizer in the restaurants of Florence and the Tuscan countryside and are distinctive there by the addition of veal spleen, which adds a richness and depth to the liver mixture. Unfortunately, veal spleen is not sold in our markets. Nevertheless, these flavors are not radically diminished, particularly if you use the fine-tasting livers of ducks or pigeons (chicken livers have a stronger, less-refined flavor).

The livers are sautéed gently so that they are still pink in the center, chopped coarse, and combined with cooked Italian bacon, shallots, anchovies, and capers. Traditionally, the mixture forms a coarse spread for country bread that has been doused in poultry broth. It is more manageable, particularly as a passed hors d'oeuvre, if served on bread slices that have first been fried in olive oil or crisped on the charcoal grill. The flavors of liver croutons are most fully present if served slightly warm and are complemented with a glass of chilled, dry Marsala.

3 ounces pancetta, cut into small bits
2 shallots (2 ounces), finely diced
2 tablespoons dry Marsala
1 tablespoon pure olive oil
12 ounces duck livers, veins and fat removed, lightly salted and peppered on both sides
1 clove garlic, mashed to a paste in a mortar
2 tablespoons extra virgin olive oil
¼ teaspoon salt
6 salt-packed anchovy filets, soaked in several changes of water to remove excess salt, drained, squeezed out, chopped
1 tablespoon capers, soaked in several changes of cold water for 20 minutes, and drained
Freshly ground pepper
Sourdough bread

Put the pancetta into a 10-inch sauté pan over medium heat. After about 1 minute, the pancetta will begin to render some of its fat. Add the shallots, lower the heat, and cook for 5 minutes, until the shallots have softened. Add the Marsala and scrape up any bits adhering to the bottom of the pan. Let the Marsala evaporate, transfer the mixture to a plate, and set aside.

In the pan warm the olive oil. Lay the livers in side by side and cook them over low heat for 3 to 4 minutes, turning them over every minute so as not to brown them. Keep a plate nearby and remove those that are just firm throughout. The livers should remain pink in the center. Let the livers cool. Meanwhile, mince the shallots and pancetta. Chop the livers coarse and combine them in a bowl with the shallots and pancetta and any juices from the plate they rested on. Add the garlic, extra virgin olive oil, salt, anchovies, and capers, grind black pepper over the ingredients, and mix well.

Grill or fry small squares of sourdough bread until golden and rub them with raw garlic. Spread the liver mixture on top of the warm croutons and serve while still warm.

Pigeon

Because of its flavor and versatility, we serve pigeon more frequently in the restaurant than any other poultry. Like pheasant, partridge, and other so-called game birds that are commercially available, pigeon is domesticated and raised in cages on simplified grain diets. Surprisingly, it retains more of the flavor of the wild than other birds. Its flesh, although not as firm as pigeon that has flown free, is similarly dark with a slight but distinctive liver flavor. Its heart, giblets, and liver are excellent added to sauces or used as the bases for salad vinaigrettes in which pigeon is the main ingredient; the richly flavored livers are delicious in pastes and in chopped forcemeats.

Pigeon is ideally suited to the grill; the smoke of an oak or charcoal fire particularly enhances it. Care should be taken to prepare a medium-hot fire and to leave plenty of room between the pigeons as the fat is very flammable. Most of the cooking should occur on the skin side of the bird if the backbone is removed and the bird flattened. The fat will render, the skin slightly crisp, and the bird will baste itself as it cooks. Although it is a dense meat, heat penetrates quickly when it is turned and it is soon done. Pigeon should be cooked to medium-rare. Beyond this point, it quickly loses its juice, toughens, and turns an unpleasant color. It is also advisable to rest the birds in a warm place for 5 minutes after they come off the grill to allow the meat to relax. Pigeon can be deboned, that is, legs and breasts removed and the carcass reserved for sauce, if the intention is to eat without effort, but it is much more savory grilled on the bone. In this form as with other small birds it should be eaten with the hands.

Because of its rich, dark flesh, pigeon has an affinity for fruits such as currants, raspberries, blackberries, cherries, and figs. It benefits by being dressed while still warm from the grill, and fruit vinegars, or Italian balsamic vinegar, are good additions.

The carcass of pigeon makes exceptional broth and should not be discarded when the bird is boned. It can either be browned in the oven or, if a smoky taste is desirable, on the grill. The carcass should then be well crushed up. In the restaurant we use a large mixer fitted with a paddle, at home a heavy cleaver will do. Add the crushed bones to light beef broth or poultry broth, or a combination of both, and simmer for a full hour. The resulting broth is a rich essence and can serve as a consommé, or in reduced form as the basis for sauces and vinaigrettes. For the latter, strain the liquid through a heavy conical sieve or a food mill and work as much of the meat and bone marrow through as possible to add body to the essence.

Roast Pigeon Salad

Pigeon is superb in composed salads where its rich, slightly gamey flavor is dominant. Throughout the seasons we make various pigeon salads at the restaurant. A mixture of garden lettuces (heavy in the varieties that are assertively flavored or slightly bitter such as rocket, curly endive, dandelion, the passionately colored leaves of Verona, or variegated Castelfranco radicchio) dressed with the juices of the roasted birds is indispensable to all of these salads. The combination is one of the most savory I know. The rich dark flesh of pigeon goes naturally with such fruits as figs, raspberries, fresh currants, and even prickly pears, the fruit of the cactus plant.

The unifying ingredient of this salad is the dressing, which is derived from the pigeon in one of two ways. In the restaurant we often remove the legs and breasts of the birds (later to be sautéed or grilled to a juicy pinkness) and roast the carcasses. We then chop and crack the carcasses and simmer them in previously made poultry broth. This broth simmers for two hours after which it is strained; the bones are pounded in a heavyweight conical sieve to extract as much flavor as possible and the resulting liquid is reduced. This reduction is then used as the basis of the dressing; it is sharpened with balsamic or fruit vinegar, and shallots, olive oil, and pepper are stirred in. The key to using fruits in pigeon salads so that they do not appear gratuitous is to combine a mashed portion of them in the finished reduction, mingling their flavors with the pigeon.

The second method of introducing the pigeon flavor into the salad is simpler and is the one used in this recipe. First, roast the pigeon and after it comes out of the oven, pour off the fat and juices into a small bowl. Pour a little of the fat over the lettuces and other ingredients and skim the rest away. Drizzle what remains in the bowl, the dark flavorful juice of the bird, over the salad just before serving.

Composed salads such as these fall into a different slot in a menu than do simpler salads, which provide relief or contrast. I think of them more as a main event around which other simpler courses are planned.

2 pigeons, about 2 pounds, livers reserved
6 sprigs thyme
Salt and pepper
1 head garlic (about 20 cloves), unpeeled
3 tablespoons plus 1 teaspoon extra virgin olive oil

16 croutons (small ¼-inch-thick slices of baguette)
1 shallot, finely minced
½ tablespoon balsamic vinegar
8 thin slices bacon (2½ ounces)
2 large handfuls mixed lettuces (blanched curly endive, rocket, rocket flowers, red or
   bronze leaf, dandelion, escarole), washed and spun dry

Preheat the oven to 450°F.

Turn the wings under the pigeons, place 3 thyme sprigs in each of their cavities, and salt and pepper them well. Place the pigeons in a small baking dish. Toss the garlic cloves in 1 teaspoon of the olive oil and strew them around the birds. Roast the birds for about 35 to 40 minutes, until browned and the breast meat is slightly firm to the touch, basting them every now and then with their own juices. In the meantime, set the croutons out onto a baking pan and brush them with 2 tablespoons of the olive oil; put them in the oven 15 minutes before the pigeon is scheduled to come out. Make a vinaigrette; combine the shallot and vinegar and a little salt. Stir in the remaining 1 tablespoon olive oil and set aside.

When the croutons are golden brown and crisp, remove them from the oven. Pour off the juices and fat in the baking pan into a small, deep bowl. Tip the cavity of the pigeons over the bowl so that the juices run out. The fat will rise to the surface leaving the dark flavorful juices on the bottom. Let the pigeons cool for 5 minutes. Fry the bacon until crisp and transfer it to a paper towel-lined plate to drain. Discard the bacon fat, salt and pepper the pigeon livers, and while the pan is still hot, in it cook the livers over low heat for about 1½ minutes per side, until just firm but still pink in the center.

Put the lettuces in a mixing bowl; add the vinaigrette and 2 tablespoons of the rendered pigeon fat from the roasted birds. From the bowl, skim off and discard the remaining pigeon fat until you reach the dark juices and set aside. Chop the livers and bacon coarse and add them to the lettuces. Remove the legs and breasts from the pigeons and slice the breasts into thin pieces. Toss the lettuces well with the liver and bacon. Correct for salt to your taste and add a few more drops of vinegar, if necessary. Arrange the salad on a platter and distribute the breast meat and legs of the pigeons on top. Surround the salad with the croutons and place a roasted garlic clove on each. Instruct your guests to squeeze the softened garlic out of its skin onto the croutons. Spoon the reserved pigeon juices over the meat and lettuces and serve.

Roast Pigeon and Green Garlic Soup

This recipe uses the entire pigeon. The flesh of the roasted bird is removed and pounded to a fine paste in a mortar, and then added to a purée of green garlic and new potatoes that has been moistened with broth in which the bones of the pigeon have simmered. The mixture is put through a sieve to make a fine texture, enriched with a little cream, seasoned, and peppered generously.

Another dimension may be added to this soup by cooking the pigeons on the grill over a wood or charcoal fire. Brown the pigeons slowly, making certain the fire is low.

The soup is satisfying in its own right and needs nothing in the way of garnish. However, rather than wasting the liver, heart, and gizzards of the birds, you may wish to sauté them in butter (cut the gizzards away from the tough connective membrane and slice them thin along with the heart), with a little chopped garlic and thyme, pound them in a mortar, combine the mixture with melted butter and brush it onto grilled or baked croutons to serve with the soup.

2 fresh pigeons (about 2 pounds), heads and feet attached
3 tablespoons unsalted butter
3/4 cup water
12 green garlic plants, 1/2 inch in diameter at the base, white part only (6 ounces), thinly sliced
1 pound new red potatoes, peeled, cut into a small dice
4 cups chicken broth (see page 426)
1/4 cup heavy cream
1/2 teaspoon white wine vinegar
Salt
Freshly ground black pepper

Preheat the oven to 450°F.

Salt and pepper the birds all over and cook them in a small roasting pan in the oven for 30 to 35 minutes, until the breast meat still retains a pink juiciness. Let the pigeons cool on a plate and transfer any juices they have released, and any from the baking pan, to a bowl and reserve it. In the meantime, melt the butter in a 3-quart saucepan, add the water, the garlic plants, and potatoes, and bring to the simmer. Cover the pot tightly and stew the mixture for 15 minutes, or until the potatoes and garlic are very soft. Check the pot after 10 minutes to make sure that it is cooking gently and that the water has not evaporated. If it has, add a little more and continue cooking the vegetables.

Working over a plate so as to catch as much of the juice as possible, cut away the breast meat and legs from the cooled pigeons. Remove the skin and separate as much of the meat as possible from the legs and carcasses. Break up the carcasses and leg bones with a cleaver and combine them in a saucepot with the chicken stock. Bring to a boil, reduce immediately to a low simmer, cover, and allow it to bubble gently for ½ hour. Strain the hot broth into the garlic and potatoes. Pass the mixture through the finest blade of a food mill or purée it in batches in a blender for 1 minute. Pour into a clean saucepan.

Pound the pigeon meat little by little in a mortar, moistening it as you proceed with the reserved, fat-skimmed juices of the roasted birds. Reduce the pigeon meat to a very fine, smooth paste, then whisk it into the garlic and potato purée. Pass the soup through a fine sieve into a clean pan, pressing through as much of the pigeon meat as possible with the back of a spoon.

Stir in the heavy cream and vinegar and season the soup with about ¾ teaspoon salt and a generous grinding of pepper. Taste the soup and correct it if necessary with a few more drops of vinegar or salt.

Rewarm the soup gently (do not boil it) and serve with warm bread.

Pigeon Marinated in Muscat Wine

For 2

The sweetness and fragrance of Muscat easily penetrates the rich flesh of pigeon, particularly if you remove the breasts and legs from the carcass. The sweet wine turns the skin a deep caramel color when cooked.

Grilling the pigeons will greatly enhance their flavor, while sautéing or roasting the whole, unboned bird will express the flavor of the wine more clearly. Whichever method you choose, do not overcook the pigeon. It is at its most juicy and flavorful if cooked to medium-rare pink.

If you bone the bird as I describe below, you will have a ready source of a delicious sauce in the remaining carcasses—an essence made by browning the carcasses, chopping them into bits, and combining them with poultry or beef broth; later the pigeon broth is strained, added to the vegetables from the marinade, and then reduced to concentrate the consistency and flavor. A little black truffle in the marinade is more than welcome.

Pigeon is a versatile partner to vegetable accompaniments. In winter, consider braised cabbage or Brussels sprouts, a gratin of potatoes with a layer of celery root in the center, baked acorn or butternut squash, or wild mushrooms. Yet, I can't think of a more satisfying companion to grilled pigeon and its sauce than a salad bed of mixed young lettuces. Let peppery rocket leaves dominate, dressed with olive oil and a little vinegar. The exciting combination weds the lightness and tingle of an appetizer with the full savor of a saucy main course.

For the marinade:
1 tablespoon pure olive oil
1½ tablespoons finely diced carrot (½ ounce)
1½ tablespoons finely diced celery (½ ounce)
2 tablespoons finely diced yellow onion (½ ounce)
3 cloves garlic, sliced
3 sprigs thyme
½ cup Beaumes des Venise or other sweet Muscat wine

2 fresh pigeons, about 2 pounds
cups poultry broth (see page 426) or beef broth (see page 427)
1 tablespoon unsalted butter

Prepare the marinade: Warm the olive oil in a sauté pan, add the carrot, celery, onion, garlic, and thyme, and soften the vegetables over medium heat for 5 minutes to release their flavor. Turn off the heat and combine the vegetables and herbs in a bowl with the Muscat wine.

Remove the breasts and legs from the pigeons, being careful to keep the skin intact so that it covers the legs and breasts well. Reserve the necks, heads, feet, and carcass for the sauce. Combine the breasts and legs with the marinade and let stand for at least 3 hours at room temperature or refrigerated overnight.

To make the sauce: Preheat the oven to 400°F. Put the carcasses, neck (remove skin first), head, and feet on a baking pan and roast them in the oven for 35 to 40 minutes, or until they are thoroughly browned. Transfer any juices from the pan to a small bowl and set aside. With a cleaver, chop the pigeon into very small bits. Combine the chopped carcasses in a saucepan and cover with the chicken or beef broth. Bring to a boil, immediately reduce to a low simmer, skim, and let cook for 40 minutes. Strain the broth through a fine sieve, pressing firmly to extract as much liquid as possible. About 1¾ cups should remain.

Remove the pigeons from the marinade, strain the vegetables, and discard the wine. Melt the butter in a sauté pan and lightly brown the vegetables over medium heat. Pour the pigeon broth over the vegetables. Adjust the heat to high and set the pan slightly off the burner. Skim away any fat or scum that collects at the side of the pan. Reduce the sauce until it thickens slightly and about ½ cup remains. Pour the sauce into a small bowl and set it aside until you are ready to use it.

To cook the pigeon: Prepare a medium-hot charcoal fire. Salt and pepper the breasts and legs on both sides. The pigeon legs will take a little longer to cook than the breasts so place them on the grill first, skin side down, and add the breasts to the grill when the legs have begun to brown after about 3 minutes. Turn the legs over when they have taken on a mahogany-brown color. Grill the breasts skin side down for 4 to 5 minutes, or until they are similarly colored. Turn the pigeon breasts and continue to cook them, about 3 to 4 minutes, until the undersides brown lightly and they are just firm to the touch. The legs by this time should be nicely browned on the underside. Don't overcook the birds—they will dry out quickly and lose their succulence. Let the pigeon rest for about 5 minutes in a warm place. In the meantime, heat the sauce, but don't reduce it any more. Arrange the pigeon on warm plates and pour the sauce over and around it.

Stuffed Quail

For 4

It is best to purchase quails that have been semi-boned (rib cage removed, skin left intact) for this recipe; they are much easier to eat this way. The stuffing fills the cavity and plumps it nicely when cooked. If only bone-in quails are available, you can remove the rib cage yourself: Position the quail with its legs facing away from you. Open the skin flap at the neck and make a small incision in the breast meat on either side of the collar bone. Using your forefinger, carefully press through the breast meat along either side of the breast bones and along the ribs. Gently pull the wing joints free, taking great care not to rip the skin of the bird. Working from the neck, carefully turn the released flesh inside out, freeing it from the rib cage as you go. Resist the temptation to use a knife as the likelihood of tearing the skin is greater. Also, do not pull the flesh free; using your fingertips, probe through the flesh, pushing it off the bone. When you reach the legs and the quail is nearly fully inside out, locate the thigh joint and carefully pull it free. Work the meat away from the thigh bone with your fingers and sever it from the drumstick bone; at this point the entire rib cage should come free. Then turn the quail, which is now entirely inside out, back into its original position with the skin on the outside. The skin should be fully intact. If there are a few rips, it is not critical; the quail will later be sealed inside a coating of egg and bread crumbs.

There are two steps involved in cooking the quails—first they are sautéed in pure olive oil or neutral-flavored vegetable oil to brown and crisp the breading, then baked in the oven to cook fully. For a wonderful lunch or dinner course, nestle the quails in a mixture of lettuces vinaigrette.

4 quails (12 ounces)

For the stuffing:
1 large clove garlic, finely chopped
2 shallots (2 ounces), finely diced
2 tablespoons olive oil
1 tablespoon white wine vinegar
Pinch of salt and pepper
4 ounces escarole leaves, washed, spun dry, roughly cut up
¼ cup ricotta cheese
1 ounce prosciutto, finely chopped
2 tablespoons freshly grated Parmesan
1 teaspoon chopped fresh thyme

1 large egg, beaten
1 cup fresh bread crumbs
1½ cups pure olive oil or vegetable oil

Prepare the stuffing: Combine the garlic, shallots, olive oil, vinegar, salt and pepper and add it to a sauté pan over low heat. When the mixture begins to sizzle, add the escarole, turning the leaves over and over for about 1 minute, until they are wilted but not entirely limp. Turn the leaves immediately out onto a cutting board and chop them fine. Transfer the escarole to a bowl and combine it with the ricotta, prosciutto, Parmesan, and thyme. The stuffing should not require any more seasoning. Nevertheless, taste it and add a little more salt and pepper if it does not suit you.

Open the cavity of each quail and fill it by hand with the stuffing. Or use a pastry bag fitted with a large plain tip to pack the birds loosely and evenly with the stuffing. If they are too full, they will break open when cooked.

Preheat the oven to 400°F. Dip the quails first in the egg, then lay them in the crumbs. Surround the quails with the crumbs and pat them on firmly, so that they adhere. Set the quails aside on a plate until you are ready to fry them.

Heat the oil in a 12-inch cast-iron pan until it sizzles when a crumb is dropped in. Set the quails in gently and fry them for about 2 minutes per side. Adjust the heat higher if the quails appear not to be browning, turning them with a pair of V-shaped tongs.

Place the quails on a baking sheet or oven platter and set them in the oven for 10 to 12 minutes more, until the breast feels a little firm to the touch.

Rabbit Salad with Browned Shallots

For 4

This salad made from the whole rabbit, liver and kidneys included, makes a full course, but a light lunch. A richly flavored reduction is made from the carcass and forelegs of the rabbit, which bear only a scanty amount of usable meat. No vegetables or herbs are added to this reduction as the delicate flavor of rabbit is easily interfered with. The reduction is used as a sauce, rather than being mixed into the vinaigrette for the salad, so that the flavor of rabbit is foremost.

When sautéed or grilled, rabbit has a tendency to toughen, to lose its juices and go dry. Besides cooking rabbit in a moist braise (the legs are best suited to this), frying is the best method for sealing in the juices and the flavor. Browning the shallots, used as the basis for the vinaigrette, gives the dressing an entirely different character—the caramelized flavor makes the salad much more savory than if the shallots were added raw.

To satisfy larger appetites, additional garnishes to this salad might include steamed carrots and little turnips tossed with butter and chervil, sautéed wild mushrooms, pan-fried potatoes, or Straw Potato Cake served on the side.

1 fresh-killed rabbit (2¾ pounds)
7 tablespoons pure olive oil
6 cups water
1 large egg, beaten
2 cups fresh sourdough bread crumbs
¼ teaspoon balsamic vinegar

Salad and garnishes:
4 handfuls curly endive, tender pale centers only
1 large handful of rocket leaves
2 ounces pancetta, sliced thinly, then diced
2 hard-boiled eggs, coarsely chopped
¼ cup rocket flowers

For the vinaigrette:
2 shallots (2 ounces), finely diced
¼ teaspoon finely chopped fresh garlic
½ teaspoon Dijon mustard
¼ teaspoon chopped tarragon leaves
⅛ teaspoon freshly ground black pepper
1 tablespoon Champagne vinegar
3½ tablespoons extra virgin olive oil

First cut up the rabbit. The back legs, saddle, tenderloin, liver, and kidney will be served in the salad; all other parts will be used to make a reduction. Set the rabbit on a large cutting board. Remove the back legs, the forelegs, and the saddles (the long, cylindrical muscles on either side of the backbone starting below the front legs and extending just above the back legs). Set them aside. Turn the rabbit over, remove the liver and kidneys, trim the livers and kidneys of any veins and fat, and set them aside. Cut out the tenderloins—the thin strips of flesh inside the cavity of the rabbit and underneath the saddles. With a heavy cleaver, chop the forelegs and the rest of the carcass into small pieces.

Warm 2 tablespoons of olive oil in a pot large enough to contain the rabbit pieces side by side and brown them (all but the back legs, tenderloin pieces, kidneys, and liver) well over medium-high heat. This process takes up to 20 minutes, in which time the rabbit should be turned often to expose all sides to the heat. Keep the heat high enough so that the rabbit doesn't steam. At the end, the rabbit should have taken on a mahogany-brown color and the bottom of the pot should be encrusted with brown bits. Raise the heat and add 1 cup of the water, a little at a time. Use a wooden spoon with a flat edge to scrape up the bits that are clinging to the bottom of the pot. When all are free add the remaining 5 cups water just to cover the rabbit. Bring to the boil, reduce to a simmer, cover, and cook for 30 minutes.

In the meantime, debone the back legs entirely; beginning at the top of the thigh, make a cut along the bone. Follow the bone through the thigh joint and down the shank. Cut around the bone to remove the meat. Add the leg bones to the simmering rabbit sauce. Divide each of the boned legs into 2 large chunks and cut them into ½-inch-thick slices, the size of small medallions. Proceed in the same manner with the boned saddles and tenderloins, making slantwise cuts to obtain similar sized slices as those of the leg. Salt and pepper the slices lightly on both sides. Dip them first in the beaten egg, then in the soft bread crumbs. Lay the pieces out on a plate.

After 30 minutes, remove the cover of the pot containing the rabbit and simmer for another 30 minutes.

In the meantime, wash the curly endive and the rocket, transfer it to a large bowl, and chill. Make the vinaigrette. In small sauté pan, warm 1 tablespoon of the olive oil. Add the diced shallots and brown them lightly. Transfer the shallots to a bowl. While the sauté pan is still hot, salt and pepper the reserved kidneys and liver and cook them briefly on both sides so that both are pink inside. Set aside to cool. Combine the shallots in a bowl with the garlic, mustard, tarragon, pepper, and vinegar. Stir in the olive oil. Whisk well. Correct with salt if necessary.

Strain the rabbit stock, discard the bones, and return the liquid to the saucepot. Reduce to ½ cup, sharpen it with the vinegar, and keep it in a warm place on the back of the stove.

Assembling the salad: Have ready four dinner plates. In a small sauté pan, soften the pancetta over medium heat, without rendering its fat, for 1 minute. Turn off the heat and let the pancetta remain in the pan. Chop the rabbit liver and kidneys into small bits and add them along with the pancetta to a bowl containing the endive and rocket.

In a 12-inch cast-iron pan, heat the remaining 4 tablespoons olive oil until a bread crumb sizzles when dropped in. In it fry the breaded rabbit pieces for a little over 1 minute on each side, until well browned on both sides. Transfer the pieces to a plate lined with paper towels. Quickly dress the salad, tossing it well with the vinaigrette, and distribute greens on the plates. Surround the greens on each plate with the fried rabbit, drizzle 2 tablespoons of the rabbit sauce over the rabbit in each salad, scatter chopped egg and rocket blossoms on top, and serve immediately.

Desserts

Marsala Cream Pots

Fruit Compote

Compote of Strawberries, Nectarines, and Peaches

Seckel Pears Poached in Red Wine with Burnt Caramel

Old-Fashioned Vanilla Ice Cream

Muscat Grape Sherbet

Chestnut Honey Ice Cream

Blood Orange Sherbet

Fig Jam Tart with Thyme

Preserved Fruit Cake

Persimmon Cake with Apple and Quince Sauce

Ricotta Cheesecake

Meyer Lemon Cake

Panettone

Panettone Bread Pudding

Bitter Almond Bavarian with Apricot Sauce

Strawberry Semifreddo

Walnut Biscotti

Puff Pastry

Puff Pastry Tart Shell

Strawberries in Puff Pastry

Yeasted Puff Pastry (Croissant Pastry)

Yeasted Puff Pastry Pear Tart

Marsala Cream Pots

For 4

This is a very simple dessert to make. It is a flavored cream bound with egg yolks, which results in a velvety texture. Serve these custards warm. When they are cool the marsala is not as volatile, and the difference is much like drinking brandy from a chilled, versus slightly warmed, snifter.

If marsala is not to your liking, substitute other fortified wines or spirits such as port, Calvados, or marc brandy. An unusual alternative is *nocino*, the green walnut infusion produced in France and Italy and drunk there as a digestif.

Duck eggs, if you can find them, produce a subtle but unmistakable refinement in this recipe—an ever-more luscious and silken consistency that will make you want to eat more than is prudent.

1 ½ cups heavy cream
½ cup sugar
4 large egg yolks (or 3 duck egg yolks)
2 tablespoons dry marsala

Preheat the oven to 350°F.

Heat the cream and sugar in a saucepan until the sugar dissolves and the cream is scalded. Put the yolks in a bowl and whisk them together without allowing them to foam. Pour the hot cream into the yolks little by little, stirring constantly. Strain the mixture through a fine sieve into a bowl, add the marsala, and divide the custard among 4 ramekins. Put the ramekins in a baking pan. Pour hot water into the pan to two thirds the level of the ramekins, tightly cover with foil, and bake in the oven for 15 to 20 minutes, or until the custards are just set. They should be no longer wet but jiggle slightly in the center. Remove from the oven and cool the custards on a rack. The custards are ready to serve when the ramekins are still warm to your bare hand.

Fruit Compote

Fruit compote ends a meal on a light note. It is one of the simplest desserts to prepare and is always refreshing. Fruit compotes are made of ripe fruit cooked or served fresh in a syrup and the options are innumerable for both elements. For fresh fruits that are ripe and flavorful, a simple sugar syrup is best. Simple syrups can also be infused with herbs and spices or made with wine instead of water. For those fruits that require cooking, such as Bosc pears and quinces, the syrup is derived from the poaching liquid. In any case the liquid medium should be harmonious with the fruit and should be chosen to enhance rather than overpower.

In composing fruit compotes in the restaurant we use the season as our guide. Summer fruits offer numerous irresistible possibilities: berries, melons, plums, peaches, nectarines, and tropical fruits in combination with each other or by themselves. The interim between late summer and fall might suggest a combination of the last summer raspberries and *fraises des bois* with the first fall figs and pomegranates, all in a Muscat-flavored syrup. Later on in fall, citrus is at its peak and the compote will include grapefruit, blood oranges, tangerines, and Meyer lemons in Champagne syrup. Winter is a time for dried fruit compotes that are laced with spices such as vanilla, cinnamon, and clove.

In any season choose ripe but not overly soft fruit. Fruit that is ideal for jam is not the best for making compotes as it breaks down too much in the syrup and the result is a kind of fruit soup. This too can be delicious, although the flavors become melded and indistinct if more than one fruit is involved.

Compote of Strawberries, Nectarines, and Peaches

The following is a favorite basic recipe for summer fruit. Depending on the sweetness and fragrance of the fruit or your own taste, the amount of sugar in the syrup may have to be increased or decreased. We include a red wine syrup as an alternative.

For simple syrup:
3½ cups water
1 cup sugar

For red wine syrup:
1 cup Zinfandel wine
2½ cups water
1 cup sugar

3 nectarines, washed (Suncrest or Fairlane)
3 peaches (Babcock, Elberta, or O'Henry), peeled
1 pint strawberries, hulled

Prepare the syrup: Combine the water and the sugar, or in the case of the red wine syrup, the wine, water, and sugar in a small saucepan. Bring to the boil, remove from the heat, and chill over a bowl of ice or in the refrigerator until very cold. Transfer the syrup to a bowl large enough to contain it and the fruits.

Leave the skins on, and slice the nectarines in ¼-inch pieces directly into the syrup. Slice the peeled peaches similarly. Slice the berries and add. Let the fruit sit, refrigerated and covered, for 12 to 24 hours. Serve it with its syrup in chilled bowls.

Seckel Pears Poached in Red Wine with Burnt Caramel

For 8

Seckel pears are small, have reddish-brown skin, and appear in the market in the early fall. Like Bosc pears, they are meaty fleshed and quite firm when fully ripe. Seckel pears are ideal for poaching because they resist turning to mush when cooked and their skins do not crack or wrinkle. Although the pears can be peeled for this dish, they seem nude this way and it is best to present them with their skins on.

Caramelization of sugar occurs at temperatures from 310°F to 350°F and is evidenced by a change in color and aroma. As the temperature increases, white sugar transforms to various shades of gold to brown, and the aroma from buttery to nutty. The best indication of the finished stage of the caramel for this recipe is the dark, red-amber color the caramel takes on seconds after it begins to caramelize. The addition of wine at this point will stop the cooking. It is a good idea to have your lower arm and hand covered with a long oven mitt when adding the wine—caramel burns terribly if it lands on you.

This is not a refined dessert; because the skins are left on the pears and because of the bittersweet sauce, its effect is more rustic. When Seckel pears are cooked, their pale yellow color is transformed to a faded tawny brown; glistening under the wine glaze they are strongly evocative of autumn. These pears are light and fresh tasting and fit well after a rich main course such as Duck Legs Braised with Onions and Cabbage.

⅔ cup granulated sugar
1 cup water
4 drops lemon juice
2 cups dry red wine (preferably Zinfandel)
8 Seckel pears
¾ teaspoon balsamic vinegar
1 tablespoon dark molasses

Put the sugar and water into a deep 3-quart saucepot. Put the pot on the stove over medium-high heat and stir the mixture until the sugar is completely dissolved. With a brush dipped in hot water, wash down the sides of the pan where any undissolved sugar crystals may have attached during stirring—undissolved sugar clinging to the pan can later fall back into the syrup and cause crystallization. Bring to a low boil. Add the lemon juice. At this point, and until the sugar caramelizes, do not stir or move the pot at all. As water evaporates, the solution becomes more sugar saturated, unstable, and prone to recrystallization. When the water has evaporated, after about 10 minutes, the sugar temperature rises rapidly until it reaches 310°F and begins to take on color. The advanced stage of caramelization, which gives this dessert a desirable bittersweetness, is evidenced by a light smoke rising from the pan, a dark red-amber color, and the aroma of toasted marshmallows. Stand back to add the wine; the pan will sputter violently. The wine will harden some of the caramel. Whisk the mixture until all the caramel is dissolved. Place the whole pears in the pot. Reduce to a simmer and cover. Poach the pears gently for 20 minutes.

Remove the pears and transfer them to a platter. Reduce the wine syrup to a scant cup. Add the vinegar and molasses and stir well. Taste the syrup. If you have taken the caramel too far and it is too bitter, correct it by dissolving more sugar in the hot wine syrup to your taste. Pour the syrup over the pears. The pears should be served at room temperature. As the pears cool, repeatedly spoon the syrup over them. As the syrup cools, it will thicken and form a glaze over and around the pears.

Old-Fashioned Vanilla Ice Cream

1 gallon

Richness is currently the prevailing style in ice cream, both the popular commercial brands and the homemade offerings of restaurants. Unfortunately, ice cream has become glamorized and the richness of its blended ingredients, I suppose, justifies its claims. The old dimestore triple scoop has been supplanted by boutiques with Italianate names that dish up miserly portions in plastic cups at fabulous prices. One leaves with the feeling of having eaten too little or paid too much, or both. Never mind—to feel guilty about eating ice cream is also fashionable.

I like ice cream that makes my head hurt from the cold and I like a generous bowl of it. Ice creams made from extra rich creams, or egg yolks, or both, are very smooth but never as cold-tasting as those made without.

I imagine that the original ice cream was little more than sweetened, frozen milk with various flavorings or fresh fruits added for variation. Cream and egg yolks were probably later refinements. Rich ice cream doesn't freeze as hard as that made with a less rich base and has a more malleable consistency for scooping. This may have something to do with the addition of cream to "improve" or extend the life of ice cream in the freezer.

The recipe below illustrates the "simple is better" axiom. But for the freezing, this ice cream takes minutes to prepare. The reader may dismiss the suggestion to use a hand-cranked machine as asking too much. A motorized machine will, of course, do the job as well with far less strain.

3 quarts cold half-and-half
1 cup granulated sugar
2½ teaspoons vanilla extract
Rock salt

Pour the half-and-half directly into the ice cream maker's metal canister. Add the sugar and vanilla extract and whisk it thoroughly until all of the sugar is dissolved. (I freeze this ice cream in a wooden ice cream maker with a gallon capacity.)

For proper freezing, the bucket must be packed correctly with layers of crushed, not cubed, ice and coarse rock salt. Salt lowers the freezing point of water. Crushing ice greatly multiplies its surface area and in combination with salt brings more coldness into contact with the canister. Coarse rock salt is less likely to escape through the ice and rest on the bottom of the machine, and it dissolves more slowly so that the temperature of the surrounding ice lowers gradually. If the ice is too cold, a coarse, dense ice cream is the result. Gradually cooling ice produces smoother, more voluminous ice cream as many more and smaller crystals form simultaneously.

Set the canister into its bucket, paddle in place. Surround the canister with a 2-inch layer of crushed ice and sprinkle about 3 tablespoons rock salt all around and on top of the ice. Continue in this manner until you have reached the top of the canister. Then start cranking by hand or turn on the ice cream maker. Add more ice and salt as the level drops below the top of the canister. Crank the machine for 25 to 35 minutes. When the crank offers strong resistance and you can see that the ice cream has thickened and nearly fills the container, stop.

Remove the canister from the bucket and pull out the paddle. Spoon the excess back into the canister or give the paddle to a pleading child to lick clean. At this point the ice cream is at its ethereal best, but it will benefit from repacking to firm up its texture. Stir the ice cream with a long-handled spoon to distribute its coldness (slightly more so at the edges of the canister). Cover the ice cream with two layers of plastic wrap. Press the film against the ice cream and draw the excess out and around the canister. This will prevent salt or salty water from entering. Return the canister lid and cover the lid tightly with foil. Put the canister back into the bucket and repack it with ice and salt as before. When you reach the top, mound the lid with ice and salt as well. Put in a cool place or wrap up the entire bucket in a picnic blanket and let stand for 3 hours before serving.

This ice cream is best eaten the day it is made. Its texture will become much harder in the refrigerator freezer. If possible, serve it in chilled bowls.

Muscat Grape Sherbet

1 quart

Refreshing sherbet may be made of any wine grape. During harvest season in the fall, friends of the restaurant bring boxes of their vineyard grapes, which we make up into a sampler plate of sherbets, each expressing a varietal character.

The Muscat grape is a large, meaty grape equally adaptable to winemaking, table, or raisin use, and has a strong, easily distinguishable quality that is delicious all by itself.

3½ pounds Muscat grapes
3 tablespoons sugar
1⅓ tablespoons corn syrup
2 teaspoons Muscat wine, such as Beaumes des Venise

Wash the grapes and remove their stems. Put the grapes in a saucepan, cover, and cook for 15 to 20 minutes, stirring occasionally, until they are soft and juicy. Purée the grapes through a food mill (a blender or food processor will also work) into a bowl. Strain through a fine-mesh sieve. Measure 4 cups of the juice. While still hot, stir in the sugar, corn syrup, and wine. Mix until the sugar is dissolved. Chill. Freeze in an ice cream maker. It is best to make this sherbet the same day it will be served.

Chestnut Honey Ice Cream

We were introduced to the unique flavor of chestnut honey by our friends who produce it at the Badia a Coltibuono in Chianti. The honey is made from the nectar of chestnut blossoms, is a deep amber color, and sweet, slightly bitter in taste, with a wild aroma suggesting spring acacia, yeast, and toasted nuts. Like *chartreuse* or authentic balsamic vinegar, its flavor reaches far back in time, as though something ancient were embodied. In cooking, the honey is very potent and should be used in small quantity or mixed with other more neutral-tasting honey to moderate its strength. Besides this recipe for ice cream, chestnut honey is incomparable drizzled over warm walnut crêpes.

6 tablespoons chestnut honey (see Note)
2 tablespoons clover honey
1 cup half-and-half
¼ cup sugar
2 cups heavy cream
6 large egg yolks

Warm the chestnut and clover honeys in a small saucepan. In another saucepan, heat the half-and-half, sugar, and 1 cup of the cream; stir until the sugar is dissolved. Whisk the egg yolks in a bowl. Add the hot half-and-half mixture to the yolks, whisking constantly together. Return the mixture to the saucepan and cook over low heat, stirring constantly, until the custard is thick and coats the spoon. Strain through a fine sieve into the remaining 1 cup cream. Stir in the warmed honeys. Chill and freeze in an ice cream maker. Serve slightly soft in chilled bowls.

Note: De Medici Imports, currently located at 1775 Broadway, New York, New York 10019, imports and distributes the products of Badia a Coltibuono, including their olive oil, vinegars, and unusual chestnut honey. De Medici Imports does not itself offer mail-order service. Paul Farber, who owns the firm, would be happy to suggest where you might find this honey in your area, however. The telephone number is: (212) 974–8101.

Blood Orange Sherbet

Blood oranges are generally tarter than most of the plain-colored varieties. When left on the tree to ripen, they also turn sweet, which balances their acidic quality. At their peak, blood oranges are deeply tinted, juicy, and suggest ripe raspberries. They are available in California in the winter months, beginning in mid-January through March. Wait until the season is in full swing—early blood oranges can be harsh and sour and lack color. Blushes of red on the skin, however, usually mean the pulp itself will be suffused with color. Select small fruits with taut skins that feel heavy for their size (Moro and Tarocco are predictably fine varieties).

Serve blood orange sherbet as a refreshing dessert with slices of the fruit, peel and pith cut away, and Walnut Biscotti.

12 to 16 blood oranges, to yield 1 quart juice
Grated peel of 2 of the oranges
1 cup sugar

Grate the peel of 2 of the oranges and set it aside. Juice the oranges and strain through a fine-mesh sieve. Place the juice in a pan or bowl and add the sugar and the peel. Stir the mixture thoroughly until the sugar is entirely dissolved. Test to see if the sugar is dissolved by dipping your finger in and rubbing your fingers together. You should feel no grains. Chill the mixture over ice or in the refrigerator, then freeze in an ice cream maker. Serve on the day it is made.

Fig Jam Tart with Thyme

For 8

With its latticework top and jam-filled center, this tart resembles the classic Linzertorte. This recipe calls for no sugar except for that in the crust, so use only the ripest figs (those that have matured fully on the tree would be ideal). Choose figs that are soft with skins that have not been broken—this is the best indication of ripeness. When cut open the figs should be moist and jamlike. If only firmer figs are available, give them a chance to ripen a day or two at room temperature. This tart can also be seasoned with fresh mint (substitute 2 teaspoons), which is more pronounced in flavor than thyme but complementary.

First, make the short crust pastry. This may be made several days in advance, wrapped tightly, and kept in the refrigerator. It can also be frozen (wrapped in foil as well as plastic) for up to a month.

For the short crust:
2 cups all-purpose flour
2 tablespoons sugar
½ teaspoon salt
½ teaspoon grated lemon peel
16 tablespoons unsalted butter, chilled but not hard-cold
2 tablespoons water
1 teaspoon vanilla extract

Prepare the short crust: In a bowl, mix the flour, sugar, salt, and lemon peel. Cut the butter into ½-inch slices and work it into the flour mixture with your hands, until it is mostly incorporated in cornmeal-size pieces and the mixture just begins to hold together. Avoid overworking the mixture. Combine the water and vanilla and work it into the flour and butter mixture until the pastry is just blended and will hold together if you press it. Gather into a ball, divide it in half, wrap it in plastic, and allow it to rest for 30 minutes. Half the pastry will be used to line the tart pan, the other half to form the latticework top.

Press half the pastry into a 9-inch tart pan, making sure that it is of an even thickness over the bottom and sides. (If the thickness is uneven, some parts will bake too much before other parts are cooked.) Prick the bottom of the tart with a fork. Before baking the tart shell, set it in the freezer, wrapped in foil, for 30 minutes or overnight. Bake, unwrapped, in a preheated 375°F oven for 25 minutes, or until the shell is a light golden brown and baked all the way through. Cool on a rack.

For the fig jam: makes 2 cups
20 very ripe black Mission figs (1 pound, 9 ounces)
½ teaspoon fresh thyme leaves

Prepare the fig jam: Trim the tips off the figs, cut the figs into small pieces, and put them in a saucepan. Add the thyme. Cook over medium heat until the figs are hot and begin to boil. Reduce the heat to low and cook for approximately 45 minutes, stirring occasionally, to prevent the figs from burning. As they cook, the figs will first appear watery, and then, as they reduce, the mixture will begin to thicken. The jam is finished when it is a dark purple color and very thick. Set aside to cool.

Assembling the tart:
Fig jam
1 egg yolk
1 tablespoon heavy cream

Assemble the tart: Roll the remaining short crust dough into a circle approximately 10 inches in diameter and ⅛ inch thick. Put it on a baking tray and let it rest in the refrigerator for 10 minutes. Fill the prebaked tart shell with the fig jam, spreading it evenly. Remove the rolled dough from the refrigerator and let warm slightly, for a minute or so. Using a knife (or a zigzag pastry cutter), cut the dough into ¼-inch-wide strips for the lattice top. Arrange the strips on top of the jam in the following way: Place one strip vertically on the tart shell about 1 inch from the left side. Then place one strip diagonally across the tart at a 45-degree angle to the vertical strip, starting at the top left corner. Repeat this process, alternating vertical and diagonal strips, maintaining 1-inch spaces between. It should take 12 strips in all. Be sure the strips are evenly spaced. Trim the ends of the strips so they touch the edge of the tart shell. Where the strips touch the shell, brush with a dab of water and press each strip gently onto the edge of the shell.

Preheat the oven to 375°F.

Beat the egg yolk with the cream. Brush the egg wash carefully onto the lattice strips. Bake the tart at 375°F for approximately 45 minutes, until the pastry is cooked. Cool on a rack. Serve by itself, or with unsweetened mascarpone (see page 313).

Preserved Fruit Cake

I remember vividly the taste of two cakes my mother made frequently for our family. One was a light lemon cake with a sweet-tart glaze made from our backyard lemon tree (see page 306). The other was a boiled cake containing a mixture of dried fruits and nuts, which appeared on our table most often in the fall.

The recipe here has been altered (Sauternes and water substituted for the strong coffee my mother used) so that it could accompany Sauternes for a special luncheon in the restaurant. If you enjoy the flavor of coffee, it can be used instead and will make the cake much darker. The large proportion of fruit in the recipe makes the cake quite moist, and it will become more balanced in flavor if allowed to sit, well covered, a day or so after being made.

½ cup golden raisins
¼ cup dark raisins
¼ cup dried currants
¾ cup dried apricots
½ cup dried pears
¼ cup dried figs
1 cup water
1 cup Sauternes wine
1 cup sugar
8 tablespoons unsalted butter
½ teaspoon salt
1 teaspoon ground cinnamon
¼ teaspoon ground cloves
¾ cup walnuts
¼ cup pinenuts
2 teaspoons baking soda
2 cups cake flour

Preheat the oven to 350°F.

Put the raisins, currants, and other dried fruits in a 2-quart saucepan. Cover with water and bring to a boil. Reduce heat and simmer for 5 minutes. Remove from heat and let stand for 5 minutes, or until all the fruit is softened. Drain well, cool, and chop coarsely. In a separate pan, combine the water, wine, sugar, butter, salt, cinnamon, and cloves. Bring to a boil, reduce the heat, and simmer for 5 minutes. Pour the liquid into a mixing bowl and cool to room temperature.

Lightly toast the walnuts in the oven for 5 minutes. Chop medium fine and set aside. Lightly toast the pinenuts for 2 minutes. Combine with the walnuts. Reduce the oven to 325°F.

When the liquid mixture has cooled, stir in the baking soda and mix well. Stir in the flour. When combined well, stir in the nuts and dried fruits. Pour into a buttered and floured 9-inch cake pan or Bundt pan and bake for about 45 to 55 minutes, until the cake feels firm and set all the way through. Let cool, and store the cake, covered, at room temperature. Serve with a glass of Sauternes.

Persimmon Cake with Apple and Quince Sauce

One 9-inch cake, for 8 servings

There are few things as striking as a persimmon tree in autumn—fruit clinging like Christmas ornaments to the dark arms of the bare tree in the quickening air. Melancholy, fruition, and the close of the circle of the seasons are summed up in this image of withering branches and ripening fruit.

The most distinguishing feature of a ripe persimmon is its texture. It is like a slippery jelly that lingers in the mouth, which may account for its unpopularity. There are few foods in Western cooking with which to compare the sensation of eating a persimmon. Raw oysters on the half shell come close. Some varieties of persimmons can be eaten while still firm, the Fuyu, for instance. For this recipe I use the larger varieties, such as Hachiya, that require full ripening. Unripe persimmons are very astringent, so allow them to ripen on a plate at room temperature until very soft. The ripening period is variable and can take from three to four days to several weeks, particularly if they are bought while still hard. Cutting a ripe persimmon open should reveal a very soft, almost translucent pulp all the way to the center of the fruit.

Persimmons are valued primarily as a moisture retainer in baked breads, cakes, and puddings and for the gingerbread-brown color they contribute to batters and doughs. This cake, as well as the sauce made from apples and quince, should be served warm, and it is well matched with a glass of Armagnac.

3 very ripe persimmons (1½ pounds), to yield 1½ cups pulp
1 cup coarsely chopped walnuts
2¼ cups all-purpose flour
1½ teaspoons ground cinnamon
Pinch salt
3 whole eggs
1⅛ cups sugar
¾ cup pure olive oil
1½ teaspoons baking soda
¾ cup dark raisins

Preheat the oven to 350°F.

Scrape the pulp from the peel of the persimmons. Break up the pulp with a fork to a purée, with no chunks of fruit. Lightly toast the walnuts in the oven for 5 minutes, then reduce the oven temperature to 325°F. In a bowl, sift together the flour, cinnamon, and salt. In another bowl, mix together the eggs, sugar, and olive oil.

In a third bowl, whisk the persimmon purée with the baking soda. When well mixed, add this to the egg mixture and combine well. Fold the dry ingredients into the persimmon mixture until well combined and no floury streaks appear. Fold in the walnuts and raisins. Pour the batter into a buttered and floured 9-inch cake pan and bake for approximately 1 hour and 15 minutes, or until a toothpick comes out clean. Cool on a rack. Serve warm with apples and quince sauce. Store, covered, at room temperature; persimmon cake will keep for several days.

Apple and Quince Sauce

Makes about 4 cups

4⅓ cups water
1⅓ cups sugar
2 quinces (1 pound)
7 Jonathan or Pippin apples (3 pounds)

Combine 4 cups of the water and the sugar in a saucepan and bring to a boil to dissolve the sugar. Peel and core the quinces and cut them into ⅓-inch-thick slices. Add them to the hot sugar syrup, reduce the heat, and simmer, partially covered, for approximately 2 hours. The quinces should cook very slowly. When they are finished, they will appear pink to salmon in color and feel very soft.

While the quinces are cooking, peel, core, and chop the apples coarse. Place in a separate saucepan with the remaining ⅓ cup water. Cover and cook over medium heat for 15 to 20 minutes, stirring occasionally, until soft. When cooked, remove the lid, and cook 5 minutes longer. Set aside.

When the quinces are cooked, drain the slices, reserving the poaching liquid. Mash the quinces with a fork and combine with the applesauce. The mixture will be somewhat chunky. Add 3 tablespoons of the reserved quince liquid, and if it does not seem sweet enough, correct the mixture with more liquid. Reserve the remaining quince poaching liquid for use as a glaze or as a sweetener for another dessert. Serve warm with persimmon cake.

Ricotta Cheesecake

1 cake for 10 to 12 servings

A favorite memory I have is that of eating freshly made sheep's milk ricotta in the Florentine countryside. There, a Sardinian family kept a small herd of sheep and daily produced ricotta and a firmer, aged pecorino in a massive, vaulted stone cellar. The ricotta was unusually good when it was bought while still warm, rushed home, and seasoned with new green oil, salt, and pepper. This we ate with the traditional saltless Tuscan loaf, slices of prosciutto, and a salad of wild greens collected in the fields. We washed it down with spritzy young Chianti. To this day I don't believe I have enjoyed a meal more.

Ricotta is an altogether distinctive fresh cheese, wonderfully light and wholesome. It is traditionally made from whey as a by-product of the cheesemaking process or a combination of whey and whole milk. Since a culture of bacteria is not used to coagulate or flavor ricotta, it is clean and fresh tasting with no sourness whatsoever. Ricotta is essentially a lean, unpressed cheese; the small curds are clearly discernible and leave their characteristic soft, dry sensation in the mouth. Ricotta is moist and nearly soufflé-like in consistency when very fresh.

Make certain you drain the ricotta well before beginning this recipe. Pour it out into a colander lined with a double thickness of cheesecloth. The cheese should be as firm as possible so that excessive moisture does not interfere with the binding action of the eggs. If it is still very moist, tie off the cheesecloth and suspend the ricotta for several hours over the sink or a container to catch the drips.

Since ricotta is mild and so agreeable in texture it is a very effective carrier of flavor. This cheesecake is seasoned with both almond and vanilla extracts, dry Marsala, cinnamon, golden raisins, and pinenuts. In the final time spent in the oven, it rises and resembles a soufflé, but it soon retreats into its crumb crust when cooled. It nevertheless maintains a lightness, and is sublime when served while still warm from the oven with a glass of sparkling Muscat.

For the cheesecake crust:
12 tablespoons unsalted butter
¾ cup sugar
1 large egg
¼ teaspoon vanilla extract
1½ cups all-purpose flour
¾ teaspoon baking soda
Pinch salt

Prepare the cheesecake crust: Cream 8 tablespoons of the butter and the sugar until light and fluffy. Mix in the egg and the vanilla. Beat until smooth. Sift together the flour, baking soda, and salt. Stir the dry ingredients into the butter mixture. Stir only until combined. Wrap the dough in plastic wrap and chill it at least 2 hours.

Preheat the oven to 350°F.

Cut the dough into two pieces. Roll each piece into a rectangle, about ⅛ inch thick. On a baking tray bake the dough for about 10 to 15 minutes, until golden brown. Cool. Place the dough on a flat surface and smash it with a rolling pin to make fine crumbs. Melt the remaining 4 tablespoons butter and stir it into the crumbs. Butter an 8½-inch-round springform pan. Place the cookie crumb mixture in the pan. Using your hand, press the crumb crust against the sides of the pan to form an even crust.

For the cheesecake filling:
¼ cup plus 1 tablespoon Marsala
½ cup golden raisins
½ cup pinenuts
4 cups whole-milk ricotta
¾ cup heavy cream
4 large eggs
9 tablespoons sugar
Large pinch cinnamon
½ teaspoon vanilla extract
¼ teaspoon almond extract
5 tablespoons all-purpose flour

Preheat the oven to 375°F.

Prepare the cheesecake filling: Heat the Marsala and pour it over the golden raisins. Let stand for 20 minutes. Toast the pinenuts in the oven for 2 to 3 minutes and set aside. Place the ricotta, cream, eggs, sugar, cinnamon, vanilla, and almond extract in a bowl. Sift the flour over the top. With a heavy whisk, mix the ingredients for about 4 minutes, until very well combined. The mixture will never be absolutely smooth because ricotta has a very finely coagulated curd. Add the raisins and Marsala and the pinenuts and stir them in with a large spoon. Taste the mixture and adjust the sweetness if necessary (different types of ricotta may need more sugar than others).

Spoon the cheesecake filling into the prepared pan. Place the pan on a baking sheet and bake for approximately 1¼ to 1⅓ hours. The top will turn deep brown and will puff up. Cool the cake for 20 minutes on a rack. Run a metal spatula or thin knife around the edge of the cake and remove the springform pan. Serve the cake while still warm from the oven. The texture is best if it is not refrigerated before serving.

Meyer Lemon Cake

The Meyer lemon is different from the common commercial lemon. It has a much rounder form, smooth, unpitted skin, and when mature, takes on a deep yellow to orange color. Meyer lemons have a wonderful tangy aroma and are sweeter and less acidic than the standard lemon. The juice of Meyer lemons is a fine substitute for vinegar in salad dressings. Here it is added to the cake batter and later combined with confectioner's sugar to form a syrupy glaze. The glaze is spooned over the cake while it is still warm. The Meyer lemon makes this cake distinctive, but if you can't find them, substitute standard lemons. For this recipe you will need eight lemons.

8 tablespoons unsalted butter
4 large eggs, separated
1¼ cups sugar
⅔ cup buttermilk
⅓ cup Meyer lemon juice
1 tablespoon Meyer lemon zest
2 cups cake flour
1¼ teaspoons baking powder
¼ teaspoon salt

For the glaze:
⅓ cup Meyer lemon juice
1⅔ cups confectioner's sugar

Preheat the oven to 325°F.

Melt the butter in a saucepan. Cool and set aside. In a mixing bowl, beat together the egg yolks with 1 cup of the sugar until thick and light in color, about

2 to 3 minutes. Beat in the buttermilk, Meyer lemon juice, and zest. Sift together the cake flour, baking powder, and the salt. Beat the egg whites until they hold soft peaks. Then add the remaining ¼ cup of sugar and continue beating until stiff peaks form. Alternately, fold one half of the flour mixture into the egg yolk mixture, followed by one half of the egg whites. Fold carefully so as not to deflate the batter. Repeat with the remaining flour and egg whites. Take about 1 cup of the batter and stir it into the melted butter. Gently fold the butter into the cake batter. Pour into a buttered and floured 9-inch cake pan or Bundt pan and bake for about 50 to 60 minutes.

While the cake is baking, make the glaze: Combine the ⅓ cup Meyer lemon juice and the confectioner's sugar in a saucepan. Heat until the sugar is dissolved. Set aside until the cake is done.

When the cake is finished, cool for 5 minutes in the pan. Turn the cake out of the pan and invert on to a cooling rack. With a long toothpick or skewer, poke the top of the cake to make many small holes. Slowly spoon the warm glaze over the cake. Allow the glaze to sink into the cake before adding more. Poke more holes if necessary. Use all of the glaze. Cool the cake completely and serve with crème Chantilly, if desired.

Panettone

1 loaf

Panettone is the traditional Christmas bread of Lombardy and is particularly associated with the city of Milan. It combines the qualities of cake and bread and is similar to French brioche, also yeasted, and enriched with egg yolks and butter. This enrichment of the dough and the addition of sultana raisins and candied citrus peel account for the celebratory status of panettone.

A slice of panettone is perfect with afternoon coffee, tea, or a glass of vin santo. Toasted and buttered, it is splendid for breakfast.

A variation of bread pudding can be made with the leftover loaf. Slices of panettone are lightly toasted, brushed with butter, and set in a baking dish. Vanilla custard is poured over the bread and the pudding is baked in the oven until just set in the center. The bread slices rise to the surface to form a golden brown gratin, with a soft custard layer beneath.

⅓ cup lukewarm water
¾ ounce (3 packages) active dry yeast
¼ cup sugar
6 large egg yolks
1 teaspoon vanilla extract
¼ teaspoon grated lemon peel
½ teaspoon salt
2¼ to 2½ cups all-purpose flour
8 tablespoons unsalted butter, softened
⅓ cup chopped candied orange peel
⅓ cup chopped candied lemon peel
½ cup dark raisins
½ cup golden sultana raisins
1 tablespoon unsalted butter, melted

Place the lukewarm (80°F) water in a small bowl. Sprinkle the yeast and 1 tablespoon of the sugar over it. Stir to dissolve the yeast and sugar, then let stand for 15 minutes, until the yeast is bubbly. Put the egg yolks, vanilla, lemon peel, salt, and the rest of the sugar in a large mixing bowl. Add the yeast and mix well. Gradually add 1½ cups of the flour. Stir until combined. Add the butter and mix until the dough becomes a sticky ball. Gradually mix in ½ cup more flour. Turn the dough out onto a floured board. Knead the dough with ¼ to ½ cup more flour until it is no longer sticky to the touch. Then knead it for 10 minutes more, until it is smooth and elastic.

Shape the dough into a ball and place in a large bowl. Cover and put in a warm (80°F to 90°F) spot for 1 hour, or until doubled in volume. While the dough is rising, finely chop the candied orange and lemon peels. Mix with the dark and golden raisins and set aside. Preheat the oven to 400°F.

Punch the dough down and knead in the candied peels and raisins. Shape the dough into a ball and place it on a buttered baking sheet. Cut a cross on top of the ball. Cut a collar out of parchment or heavy brown paper about 5 inches wide and 22 inches long. Butter one side and wrap it loosely around the dough (to allow for some expansion). Fasten the ends of the collar with a paper clip and set the loaf in a warm place for a second rise. Allow the bread to expand for 30 to 45 minutes, or until again doubled in volume.

Brush the top with some of the melted butter and bake the bread at 400°F for 10 minutes. Reduce the oven temperature to 350°F. Brush the top again with melted butter and bake for 30 to 35 minutes more. The panettone is done when it is brown on the outside and sounds hollow when the bottom is tapped.

Panettone Bread Pudding

4 cups milk
11 tablespoons sugar
5 whole eggs
5 egg yolks
1 teaspoon vanilla extract
⅓ loaf Panettone (recipe precedes)
2 tablespoons unsalted butter

Heat the milk with the sugar until it is just hot and the sugar has dissolved. Place the eggs and egg yolks in a bowl. Whisk in the hot milk until well combined. Stir in the vanilla extract and strain the custard through a fine-mesh sieve into a bowl.

Preheat the oven to 350°F.

Slice the panettone into pieces ¼ inch thick and cut each slice in half. Place on a baking sheet and bake for 6 to 8 minutes, or until crisp and lightly toasted. Melt the butter and brush one side of the panettone slices with it. Arrange the slices evenly in a baking dish (8 by 8 inches), pour the custard over the slices, and let stand for 15 minutes. Place the dish of bread pudding in a larger baking dish containing enough hot water to come halfway up the sides of the bread pudding. Bake for about 35 to 40 minutes. When the custard puffs around the sides of the baking dish and is only just set in the center, the pudding is done. Remove from the water bath and cool slightly. Serve while still warm.

Bitter Almond Bavarian with Apricot Sauce

A Bavarian cream is an exquisite texture, rivaled only by barely set custards that melt away in the mouth, a texture that dissolves into flavor. Whipped cream is folded into a flavored custard to which a small amount of gelatin has been added. A surprisingly soft, smooth, tremulous consistency takes hold when chilled and unmolded.

This particular dessert was developed to accompany Sauternes, which goes well with bitter almonds. Ladyfingers are used to completely encase the Bavarian. Dried apricots, rehydrated in boiling water, are puréed and sweetened for the sauce. If time does not permit, you may wish to make the almond Bavarian without lining the mold with ladyfingers. In this case, follow the directions for making the Bavarian cream using only 1 tablespoon gelatin. Scoop it out onto chilled dessert plates and serve it with or without the sauce but with a glass of Sauternes.

Bitter almonds might be difficult to find. If you live near a Chinese marketplace, seek out an herbalist; they usually sell them in bulk with the skins removed. Otherwise, substitute the kernels inside the pits of stone fruits such as apricots, cherries, and peaches. Without them the Bavarian is not nearly as interesting. Bitter almonds and stone fruit kernels are strong and must be used in combination with regular almonds and almond extract to balance the flavors. If you use stone fruit pits, break them up with a nut cracker or hammer, extract the kernels and crush them in a mortar. Add the crushed kernels and the regular almonds (also crushed) to the milk and bring it to just under the boil. Remove from the heat and let steep for 30 minutes before sieving.

For the ladyfingers (for one 9- by 5-inch loaf pan):
⅔ cup cake flour
Pinch salt
4 large eggs
½ cup sugar
½ teaspoon almond extract

Preheat the oven to 325°F.

Prepare the ladyfingers: Line a baking sheet with parchment paper. Using a rectangular loaf pan (9 by 5 by 3 inches), draw the dimensions of the bottom, top, and the longest sides of the pan onto the parchment paper. The drawings will be used as a guide for piping the ladyfingers.

Sift together the cake flour and the salt. Separate the eggs. Beat the egg yolks with ¼ cup of the sugar until thick and pale yellow and they form a ribbon. Mix in the almond extract.

In a separate bowl, beat the egg whites until they hold soft peaks. Gradually add the remaining ¼ cup sugar and continue beating until the whites hold stiff, glossy peaks. Sift one third of the cake flour into the egg yolks. Fold in the flour as lightly as possible. Fold in one half of the egg whites. Sift in and fold the remaining flour into the batter. Gently fold in the remaining egg whites without deflating the batter.

Put some of the batter into a pastry bag fitted with a plain tip ½ inch in diameter. Turn the parchment paper over so that the pencil outlines are on the underside. Pipe the ladyfinger batter onto the baking sheet in strips about ³⁄₁₆ of an inch apart, straight up and down, using the drawings as a guide. When baked the ladyfingers will be in one piece. Refill the pastry bag as needed. Bake for 15 to 18 minutes. The ladyfingers will be lightly golden on top, firm on the outside, and slightly soft on the inside. Cool and remove the ladyfingers from the paper. Line the loaf pan with plastic wrap. Reserve the remaining ladyfingers for the top then place the ladyfingers on the bottom and long sides of the pan. Trim the ladyfingers even with the rim of the pan.

For the Bavarian cream:
1½ cups whole almonds (skin on)
¼ cup bitter almonds, skinned, or stone fruit kernels
3 cups milk
4 tablespoons water
1 tablespoon plus ½ teaspoon gelatin
6 egg yolks
6 tablespoons sugar
¼ teaspoon almond extract
1 cup heavy cream

Preheat the oven to 375°F.

Lay the regular almonds out on a baking sheet and toast them for 7 to 10 minutes, until they lose some of their moisture and become crunchy. Add the skinned bitter almonds to the tray during the last 3 minutes (if you use the kernels of stone fruits, you need not toast them). Put all the almonds in a mortar and crush them fine. Combine the milk and the almonds in a saucepan and heat to just below a simmer. Remove from the heat and let steep for 30 minutes. Strain the almond milk through a fine-mesh sieve in a bowl, pressing as much of the milk through as possible. Discard the almonds. Set aside 2 cups of the almond milk.

Put the water in a small saucepan. Sprinkle the gelatin over the water and allow the gelatin to soften for 3 minutes. Warm the gelatin over very low heat until dissolved. Do not overwarm it or it will lose its binding ability. Set aside.

Put the egg yolks in a bowl. Heat the 2 cups almond milk with the sugar in a saucepan until hot. Whisk together the egg yolks, then whisk a small amount of the almond milk mixture into them. Add the yolk mixture to the hot milk, continuing to whisk, and cook over medium-low heat, stirring constantly with a spoon, until the mixture thickens slightly and coats the back of the spoon. Strain the custard into a bowl and set the bowl on a bowl of ice. Stir in the almond extract. When the mixture is tepid, whisk in the dissolved gelatin.

In the meantime, beat the heavy cream to soft peaks. Stir the almond mixture over the ice until it begins to thicken and is nearly the same consistency as the whipped cream. If the almond mixture sets prematurely, warm it slightly and try again. Fold in the whipped cream and pour the mixture immediately into the ladyfinger-lined loaf pan. Tap the pan gently on the table. Set the reserved ladyfingers in place on top and trim any edges so that the ladyfinger top fits evenly. Cover with plastic film and refrigerate overnight.

To serve, center a platter over the Bavarian and invert it. Peel away the plastic wrap and slice the Bavarian with a thin-bladed knife into pieces about 3/4 inch thick. Dip the knife in hot water between each slice. Pour several tablespoons of the apricot sauce around each slice and serve.

For the apricot sauce: makes 2 cups
1 cup dried apricots
3½ cups water
1 tablespoon sugar
3 tablespoons Sauternes

Place the dried apricots and the water in a saucepan and simmer over low heat for 20 minutes. The apricots should be completely softened and the water will have reduced by about one third. Pour the water and the apricots in a blender or food processor and purée until smooth. Strain the sauce through a fine-mesh sieve. Add the sugar and Sauternes and stir until the sugar has dissolved. The sauce should be slightly viscous but pourable. Thin with a little water if too thick.

Strawberry Semifreddo

For lack of a better term, this dessert has been called a semifreddo; strictly speaking, it is not. A true semifreddo contains a frozen element, usually ice cream, between layers of sponge cake or biscuits such as savoyardes, and whipped cream or cooked meringue. The cake or cream element accounts for the half-cold effect of a semifreddo and the derivation of its name.

This dessert is a cross between a trifle and a semifreddo. Several layers of sponge cake are brushed with a kirsch-flavored syrup, spread with sweetened mascarpone (a thickened cream), and scattered with chopped strawberries. The combination is refrigerated for at least 8 hours. In the meantime, the cake and mascarpone drink up some of the juices of the strawberries, resulting in a voluptuous puddinglike texture.

To make this recipe you will need to begin 4 days ahead to allow time for the mascarpone to thicken.

For the mascarpone: makes 1 heaping cup
2 cups heavy cream
⅛ teaspoon tartaric acid (available in pharmacies)
3 tablespoons sugar
2 large eggs

Four days before assembling the semifreddo, prepare the mascarpone: Place the cream in a stainless-steel bowl over a hot water bath on the stove. Heat the cream to 180°F. Stir in the tartaric acid and stir continuously for 30 seconds. Remove the bowl of cream from the water bath and continue to stir for 2 minutes. Place a fine-mesh sieve inside a deep bowl so that it doesn't touch the bottom. Line the sieve with a double layer of cloth, such as a cotton dish towel. Pour the hot mascarpone slowly into the lined sieve. The cream should not seep through the cloth. Place in the refrigerator. When cool, cover with plastic wrap. If a small amount of cream has seeped through after the mascarpone has cooled, pour it back into the strainer.

Let the mascarpone stand in the refrigerator for 3 to 4 days. A small amount of clear liquid will drain as it stands. After 3 to 4 days, the mascarpone will be firm and ready to use; it is at this point that the sugar and eggs are beaten into the cream.

For the sponge cake:
4 eggs
½ cup sugar
⅛ teaspoon vanilla extract
½ cup all-purpose flour
⅙ cup cake flour
Small pinch salt

Preheat the oven to 325°F. Butter, flour, and line one 17- by 11-inch jelly-roll pan with parchment paper.

Place the eggs and the sugar in a mixing bowl. Whisk the eggs and sugar over hot water or above a flame until slightly warm. Remove from the heat, add the vanilla, and beat until the mixture is thick, pale in color, tripled in volume, and falls in a ribbon. Sift together the flours and salt. Slowly sift the flours over the egg mixture. Fold very gently with a rubber spatula so as not to deflate the eggs. Continue folding until all the flour is incorporated. Pour the batter into the prepared jelly-roll pan. Using a spatula, carefully spread the batter evenly into the pans. Bake for about 15 minutes or until the cake is golden brown. Set on a rack to cool. Peel the cake away from the parchment paper and set aside.

For the kirsch syrup:
¼ cup water
1 tablespoon sugar
⅛ teaspoon kirsch

Place the water and sugar in a saucepan. Heat until the sugar is dissolved. Cool and stir in the kirsch.

Strawberries:
2 pints strawberries
2 tablespoons sugar
Few drops lemon juice
Kirsch

Rinse the strawberries with water and let them drain in a colander. Remove the stems, chop the berries coarse, and place them in a bowl. Stir in the sugar, lemon juice, and kirsch to taste. Let stand for 5 minutes and stir again until the sugar is dissolved and the berries have begun to release juice.

Assembling the semifreddo: Put the mascarpone in a mixing bowl. Using a large whisk, beat in the 3 tablespoons sugar. Then beat in the eggs, 1 at a time. The mascarpone should remain thick, although immediately after the whisking in of each egg it will begin to lighten. After all the eggs have been added, continue to beat the mascarpone until it reaches the consistency of whipped cream.

Spoon one quarter of the whipped mascarpone into an 8- by 8-inch Pyrex dish and spread it evenly into a thin layer. Cut the sponge cake into pieces roughly 4 inches square. Make a layer of sponge cake on top of the mascarpone. Using a pastry brush, lightly moisten the cake with some of the kirsch syrup. Spoon another quarter of the mascarpone over the cake and spread it evenly to form another layer. Spoon half the chopped strawberry mixture over the mascarpone until it is evenly distributed. Place the second layer of sponge cake over the strawberries. Brush on some more kirsch syrup until lightly moistened. Cover with another quarter of mascarpone and the remaining strawberries. Form the final the layer with the rest of the cake, brush with kirsch syrup, and cover with the last of the mascarpone. Cover with plastic wrap and refrigerate at least 8 hours, or overnight, before serving. Spoon the semifreddo into chilled bowls.

Walnut Biscotti

There are myriad types of Italian cookies known as *biscotti*, but few as appealing as those baked in a long sausagelike form, cut on the diagonal, and then baked a second time to dry. These cookies have a rough charm, both crunchy and nutty, and are designed to be dipped into coffee (the Italians eat them for breakfast) or a glass of wine. With time these biscuits will dry out even further and become bone-hard, but the flavors still balance very nicely. The recipe can be varied depending on what you wish to serve them with. Substitute almonds or other nuts for the walnuts or sprinkle the dough with anise seeds.

Walnut biscotti are lovely with Chestnut Honey Ice Cream or simply a glass of vin santo.

¾ cup walnuts
8 tablespoons unsalted butter, softened
¾ cup sugar
2 eggs
1 teaspoon vanilla extract
1 tablespoon Cognac or brandy
2 cups plus 2 tablespoons all-purpose flour
1½ teaspoons baking powder
¼ teaspoon salt

Preheat the oven to 350°F.

Toast the walnuts in a baking pan for 5 minutes. Let cool and chop them coarse. Reduce the oven to 325°F.

Cream the butter with the sugar in a large bowl. Beat in the eggs and mix well. Add the vanilla and Cognac. In another bowl, stir together the flour, baking powder, and salt. Add to the butter mixture with the chopped nuts. Stir just until combined. On a lightly floured surface, roll the dough into cylinders about 1½ inches wide and 12 inches long. Place on a baking sheet about 2½ inches apart and bake for about 25 minutes, until lightly browned on top. Remove from the oven and let cool for 5 minutes.

Carefully remove the cylinders to a cutting board. Slice the cookies about ½ inch wide on the diagonal. Return them to the baking sheet, the cut surfaces down. Bake for 5 to 10 minutes, until the tops are lightly brown. Let cool and store in an airtight container.

Puff Pastry

Puff pastry is as satisfying to make as it is to eat. Unfortunately, it has the reputation of being an intimidating, time-consuming task, requiring special skills. It is unforgiving—it either works or it doesn't. Unlike the braising pot, left alone for hours to work its own magic, the success or failure of puff pastry is directly connected at every stage to the cook's work and attention. The challenge lies in developing a feel and a more-than-casual understanding of the principle of this pastry and the variables that favorably or adversely affect it.

Making puff pastry from start to finish takes time, although the amount spent actively working with the pastry is minimal. The brief process of rolling and turning the pastry takes minutes and is followed by longer periods in which the pastry is put away to rest. Making a batch of puff pastry can easily be incorporated into a day devoted to other chores around the house.

Puff pastry is composed of thin layers of dough separated by fine films of butter. Gluten, an insoluble wheat protein containing about twice its weight in water, is largely responsible for the rise of the pastry. The generation of steam during baking and the pressure of water vapor within the gluten structure cause the dough layers to expand. Meanwhile, the melting butter insulates one layer from the next. As the temperature increases, the gluten becomes rigid, the layers cook and absorb the butter, and the greatly expanded structure becomes fixed.

The process is begun by forming a dough with flour, butter, and water. The flour used for making puff pastry should be strong (contain a high gluten content) with a gluten that is resilient enough to stand up to the manipulation involved in rolling the pastry and that will also assist in giving lift to the pastry during baking. Bread flour, a high gluten white flour, is generally used in significant proportion in the following recipes.

The dough is rolled out to a rectangle. Cold butter, which has been smoothed and softened through kneading, is wrapped in this rectangle of dough. The proportion of butter to flour can be equal by weight, or the butter may be reduced to half or quarter the weight of the flour, which will make a leaner pastry. There are different ways to fold the dough around the butter. It can be spread onto half of the sheet to form an envelope, resulting in two layers of dough and one of butter. Or, if two thirds of the sheet is covered with butter and the dough is folded in three, two layers of butter to three layers of dough result. The difference may seem insignificant at the outset, but actually accounts for a difference of hundreds of layers in the finished pastry. Later the dough is rolled out and repeatedly folded upon itself to create a succession of layers in a rapidly multiplying geometric progression. The final number of layers is directly related to the initial ratio of dough and butter layers, how the dough is folded, and the number of times it is folded.

After the butter has first been enclosed in the dough, it is turned 90 degrees, rolled to form a rectangle, and then folded upon itself in three, or in bookfold—each end is brought to the center and the whole is folded in the center like a book. This is known as a half-turn and describes the change of position after folding, which ensures that the pastry is always rolled against the open ends. It is easier to roll against the open ends than a folded edge. A full turn is two half-turns, one immediately following the other without resting the dough. Maintaining a rectangle with square corners and straight edges throughout the folding and turning is essential, or many layers could be lost, which results in uneven lifting of the pastry and shells that are distorted in shape.

Between rolling and folding, the dough is allowed to rest to reduce elasticity. The time will vary from 20 minutes to 1 hour depending upon the temperature and condition of the dough. An insufficient resting time, both initially and after subsequent turns, results in a dough that must be worked excessively with the rolling pin, which may damage the layers.

Puff pastry is given a minimum of three half-turns and a maximum of three full turns. Too many turns will cause excessive layering and a lack of volume, as the gluten and butter are only so extendable. If the dough is not turned enough, the layers of butter will be too thick and will not be absorbed by the dough layers during baking. The butter runs out, and heavy, greasy pastry is the result.

During the rolling and folding of the dough, it is important to remember to flour the dough and table only as necessary, and to brush away any dusting flour from the surface of the dough before each fold. The pastry should never be allowed to become warm. If the butter becomes too soft it has a tendency to squeeze out during rolling and the layers are ruined. This should not be a problem, even in the warmest weather, provided the pastry is handled efficiently, and immediately put into the refrigerator after the turns. The dough should rest on a flour-dusted pan covered with plastic wrap or closed in a large plastic storage bag, pan and all. This will keep the dough from drying out and forming a skin.

Don't abuse the dough while rolling, or the laminated structure that is being built will tear down. The rolling pin should never be dropped on the dough, nor should it be used to pound and flatten it before rolling. If the butter is too cold and unyielding, allow the dough to rest on the table until it is the right temperature to roll. If the gluten in the dough is relaxed and the butter is plastic the job of rolling should not require much force at all. I prefer to use a pin with a roller that turns free at the handles. If the dough springs back and fights the pin it is a sure sign that the dough has not rested enough. If it is stiff and uncooperative, it is likely that it is too cold.

After the final turn and a final resting time, the dough is ready to be rolled and cut. The thickness of the dough, as well as the number of layers, will determine how well it rises. Here it is worthwhile to mention that the method of initially enclosing the butter and the number of times the dough is folded should be suited to the preparation. If the plan is to make a rustic tart, for instance, where a dramatic lift is not called for, make an envelope of dough and butter and give it the minimum number of half-turns. On the other hand, if the goal is a crisp and airy dessert celebrating the pastry itself, enclose the butter within the dough folded in thirds and give it full-turns, which will guarantee more layers.

When you are ready to shape the pastry, cut it with a very sharp, thin-bladed knife: A dull blade will only smash or compress layers at the edges of the pastry and cause them to lift unevenly. Puff pastry is generally cooked at high heat (375°F to 400°F) at the start of baking to encourage a vigorous release of steam, and then midway through baking the temperature is lowered to ensure even and thorough cooking. If oven temperatures are too low or erratic at the start, the gluten will expand poorly and volume will be lost. Often the pastry will need some drying out even after being fully cooked. For a crisp bottom and top and dry layers, turn the oven off and let the pastry sit 10 minutes or so.

Do not be discouraged if your first attempts do not succeed. Making light, distinctly layered, well-lifted puff pastry requires a practiced feel for the consistency of the butter and dough that form layers in the raw pastry, skill with the rolling pin, and good judgment. There are many aspects of the technique to remember, yet they can all, in a sense, be forgotten when you gain a tactile understanding, and control and confidence in correcting for the variables at each stage of the process. Once achieved, you will take pleasure in your handiwork and the sophisticated charm of this risen dough.

Puff Pastry Tart Shell

This recipe for puff pastry calls for flour and butter in equal proportion by weight with a minimum of three half turns. It is suitable for light, crisp, tart shells, which can be filled with either sweet or savory fillings. It is possible to create pastry with more layers by giving the same dough as many as three full-turns. This is for desserts or savory dishes where the pastry itself is the main attraction.

¾ cup bread flour (high gluten white flour)
1¼ cups all-purpose flour
16 tablespoons cold, unsalted butter
¼ teaspoon salt
10 tablespoons ice water

First make the dough: Sift the two flours together in a bowl. Cut 2 tablespoons of the butter into small bits. With a knife and fork, cut the butter into the flour until it is distributed throughout. Dissolve the salt in the ice water, make a well in the center of the flour, and pour in the water. Using a fork, gradually bring the flour into the center until it has absorbed the water and the mass resembles torn rags. Working quickly, without kneading the dough, squeeze the dough together, gathering up all the bits of flour to form a rough rectangular shape. It need not be homogeneous; it will become so later on as it is rolled. Wrap the dough in plastic wrap and chill for 1 hour.

The next step is to soften the cold butter. This is a critical step in the process. To roll and form the pastry successfully, both the dough and the butter must be soft and cool and of a similar texture so that they will move the same way under the rolling pin. The goal is to smooth and soften the butter and yet keep it cool so that it will spread in a thin film without much force from the rolling pin.

After the dough has chilled 1 hour, remove the butter from the refrigerator. On a cool surface, cut the butter into small pieces and knead with a metal scraper, or bat it with a rolling pin, or work it in a mixer fitted with a paddle until it is soft. (Working the butter manually will help you develop a feel for the texture and progress of the butter as it softens. But do not use your hands as they transfer too much heat.) The butter should yield easily when poked with a finger and should feel dry, not greasy. If the butter is too cold or hard bits remain in the mass, it will not roll easily. If the butter is too warm or soft, return it to the refrigerator for 15 minutes.

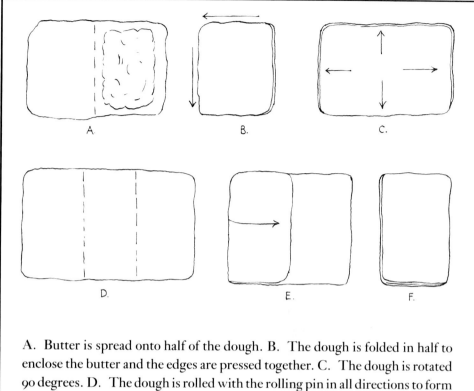

A. Butter is spread onto half of the dough. B. The dough is folded in half to enclose the butter and the edges are pressed together. C. The dough is rotated 90 degrees. D. The dough is rolled with the rolling pin in all directions to form a large rectangle and divided in three by eye. E and F. The dough is folded in three and put in the refrigerator to rest. This is called a half turn. After recovery the dough is positioned on the table as in F and is ready to be similarly rolled, folded, and turned.

When the butter is cool and soft, remove the dough from the refrigerator, dust the work surface and the dough with flour, and roll it out into a rectangle that is about 10 by 8 inches and ¼ inch thick. Locate a center line and distribute the butter on one side of the dough. Press the butter out with a fork so that it rests on the dough in a layer ¾ inch from the edges and the center line. Fold the dough over the butter so that the edges meet evenly and press them together lightly so that the butter is sealed in. Turn the dough 90 degrees and roll the dough from the center out in alternating directions to produce a rectangle about 18 by 12 inches and a little less than ¼ inch thick with corners as square as possible. Work quickly with efficient strokes of the rolling pin and with only as much pressure as is required to extend the sheet. (Overworking the pastry will make it elastic and difficult to roll and will result in pastry that is tough and does not hold its shape while baking.) Brush any excess flour off the surface of the sheet. Fold the pastry onto itself in even thirds, again making sure to brush dusting flour away. Do not worry if the dough itself still looks a little rough— rolling and folding a second and third time will make it smoother and the shape of the rectangle will become well defined. Transfer immediately to a lightly floured baking sheet and cover with plastic wrap, or put the pan in a plastic storage bag, and refrigerate for 30 minutes. Take it out of the refrigerator. Repeat this process of rolling the pastry and folding it in thirds two more times, allowing 30 minutes rest between each turn.

Forming the shell: When the dough is sufficiently rested, at least 1 hour, remove it from the refrigerator and cut it in half with a thin-bladed sharp knife. If you are not planning to make more than one shell, wrap the remaining pastry tightly and freeze it. Lightly flour the table and roll the dough into a rough 12-inch square about ⅛ inch thick. Cut the corners off the pastry so that you are left with a rough circular form. Make little folds around the circumference of the pastry—grasp the edge of the pastry between your index finger and thumb. Place your other index finger on the dough's edge in an opposing position. Fold over about an inch of it toward the center, bringing the pastry around the tip of your other index finger. Press lightly where the folded edge meets the bottom of the shell to make a little half-circle rim. In a similar manner make another fold that slightly overlaps the first, and continue in this way all around the edge. Slide your hands under the shell and move it to a baking sheet, cover it with plastic wrap, refrigerate, and let it rest for 1 hour before baking.

While the shell is chilling, preheat the oven to 400°F.

Bake the shell for 35 minutes. If your oven is outfitted with baking stones, line them with foil and bake the shell directly on the stones. Otherwise, bake the shell on the baking sheet. After 35 minutes, when the tart is well browned and puffed, turn off the oven and let the shell dry out for 8 to 10 minutes. Remove from the oven and cool the tart on a rack with air circulating underneath it.

Strawberries in Puff Pastry

For 4

There are some desserts that never fail to please and strawberries in puff pastry is a shining example. The pastry is rolled out in a thin sheet and baked with a cooling rack or another pan on top, which prevents the pastry from rising and creates a crisp, crackerlike texture. Rectangles are then cut from the pastry and layered with lightened vanilla pastry cream and sugared strawberries, resulting in a roughly shaped napoleon. Stacked high, this dessert has a dramatic appearance and is very festive, well suited to Champagne or sparkling Muscat.

½ recipe puff pastry (from Puff Pastry Tart Shell, see page 322)
2¼ cups sliced ripest strawberries
1 tablespoon sugar

For the pastry cream:
¾ cup milk
2 tablespoons all-purpose flour
2 tablespoons sugar
2 egg yolks
⅛ teaspoon vanilla extract

⅓ cup heavy cream
1 tablespoon confectioner's sugar

Roll out the pastry into a thin, rectangular sheet, about 16 by 8 inches and about ¹⁄₁₆ inch thick. Transfer the pastry to a baking sheet and let it rest in the refrigerator for 45 minutes. Toss the strawberries with the sugar in a bowl, cover, and refrigerate them.

Preheat the oven to 400°F.

When the puff pastry has rested sufficiently, place in the oven with another baking sheet or a cooling rack covering and resting on the dough. Bake for a total of 25 minutes, or until lightly browned and crisp. Remove the baking sheet or cooling rack after the first 12 to 15 minutes. Cool on a rack.

While the pastry is baking, make the pastry cream: Scald the milk. Put the flour and sugar into a small, heavy saucepan. Whisk the hot milk slowly into the flour mixture, making sure to catch the edges of the pot. Bring the mixture to a gentle boil over medium heat and cook for 2 minutes. Put the yolks into a bowl and whisk them together thoroughly. Whisk a small amount of the hot milk

DESSERTS   325

mixture into the yolks, then pour them into the pan containing the milk mixture, stirring constantly. Bring the mixture to just under the boil and strain it immediately back into the bowl. Stir in the vanilla. Whisk the pastry cream occasionally while it is cooling. Cover and chill.

When the pastry has cooled to room temperature, cut it into 16 rectangular pieces, about 4 by 2 inches each. Whisk the heavy cream to soft peaks and fold it into the chilled pastry cream.

Assembling: Have four 8-inch dessert plates ready. Lay down a piece of puff pastry, spread it with about 1 tablespoon of the pastry cream, and spoon about 1 tablespoon of the strawberries over it. Dot the berries all over with pastry cream. The layering need not be neat—the dessert looks best if the strawberries are spilling out. Repeat this layer two more times. Each pastry will then have three layers of strawberries, six layers of pastry cream, and four layers of pastry (the last being the top). Finish the last layer of pastry cream with a piece of puff pastry and sift powdered sugar over the top. Make three more pastries in the same manner and serve immediately.

Yeasted Puff Pastry (Croissant Pastry)

Dough for two 9-inch tarts

The flavor of the yeast is perhaps the greatest difference between yeasted and non-yeasted puff pastry. Yeasted puff pastry is light and tender with a crisp, blistered surface. Inside, the wild aroma of fermentation is pervasive. This pastry is not as delicate as that made without yeast. When baked it is less flaky, more elastic, and breadlike. It is an excellent pastry for enclosing meat, poultry, or fish, and makes a fine crust for fruits such as apricots and pears.

Making yeasted puff pastry requires an additional step besides rolling, turning, and resting the dough. It must be allowed to rise, as for bread, in a warm place (85°F to 95°F) before baking. Because the dough is yeasted, I prefer to work with it cold so that it remains inactive until moved to a warmer temperature to rise. Cake yeast is called for in this recipe because it can be dissolved in cold water without a loss of fermenting power. Dry yeast must be rehydrated in warm water to be fully active.

1 tablespoon plus 1 teaspoon cake yeast
3/4 cup ice water
1/2 teaspoon salt
2 tablespoons sugar
2 cups bread flour
2 tablespoons plus 2 teaspoons cake flour
12 tablespoons unsalted butter

In a bowl, mix the yeast and the ice water until the yeast is dissolved. Add the salt and sugar and stir until dissolved. In another bowl, mix together the bread and cake flours. Add the flours to the water and mix only until combined. The dough will appear crumbly. It need not be homogeneous. Use your hands to form a rough rectangular shape. Cover with plastic wrap and refrigerate for 20 minutes.

Follow the instructions on page 322 for Puff Pastry Tart Shell on kneading the 12 tablespoons butter called for in this recipe and on forming, filling, rolling, and turning this dough. Give the pastry three half turns with 20 minutes of recovery time between turns.

Yeasted puff pastry can be made one day and used the next if it is well wrapped and kept refrigerated. Otherwise, freeze the pastry, which can be done successfully. It will keep very well for 4 to 6 weeks. Move the pastry from the freezer to the refrigerator one day before you intend to use it.

Yeasted Puff Pastry Pear Tart

More than a simple vehicle for the pear, yeasted puff pastry provides a crisp, flaky enclosure, which not only supports the fruit but adds a rich dimension of texture and yeasty flavor.

½ recipe Yeasted Puff Pastry (recipe precedes)
3 large French Butter or Bosc pears
3 tablespoons sugar
1 egg
2 tablespoons warm glaze (quince, pear, or apricot)

Roll the pastry on a lightly floured board into a round 12 inches in diameter and about ¼ inch thick. Chill the pastry on a baking sheet, covered, in the refrigerator for 30 minutes. Peel and slice the pears into ⅓-inch-thick slices. Trim the edges of the pastry to form a circle. Arrange the pear slices in the center of the pastry in a circular pattern, slightly overlapping each other, leaving a 3-inch border of pastry around the edge. Sprinkle the pears with the sugar. Pull the pastry border up over the pears to partially cover them. The pastry will slightly overlap itself.

Beat the egg with a fork until mixed and brush the tart with the egg wash. Be careful not to let the egg wash drip over the sides onto the baking sheet. Enclose the tart, pan and all, in a large plastic storage bag (preferably clear so that you can watch the tart's progress) for proofing. Inflate the bag so that the tart is not touching it and tie off the opening with kitchen twine. Place the bag in a warm part of your kitchen—85°F to 95°F. Allow the pastry to rise until it doubles in volume (about 1½ hours). If your kitchen is cold, turn on your oven and place the tart near it. You may place the baking sheet on top of the oven, but be careful not to let it get too warm. If the tart proofs too warm, the butter will begin to ooze from the pastry.

While the tart is proofing, preheat the oven to 425°F.

Bake the tart for 15 minutes, reduce the oven temperature to 400°F, and bake the tart for approximately 25 minutes more, until the bottom is brown and crisp. If, while baking, the top of the tart is browning too quickly, gently cover the edges with aluminum foil. When baked, cool the tart for 5 minutes, then brush the pear slices with the warm glaze. Serve warm. (If necessary, the tart may be reheated in a 400°F oven for 5 minutes.)

Pickles
and
Preserves

Pickles

I must confess to a continual craving for pickles, pickled anything really—cucumbers obviously, but capers, anchovies, onions, beans, chili peppers too . . . , and when I am hungry, a pickle overloads my senses and I become ravenously hungry. I am sure I am not alone. Vinegary and slightly salty foods stimulate the appetite; it is for this reason that dishes with these sharp accents are often planned as appetizers at the restaurant, though why vinegar and salt should so appeal I am not quite sure. Perhaps it is their startling effect on sleepy taste buds.

In an informal meal the tartness of pickles cuts through richness (I think of pâté and pickles, steak or ham and pickles, or lamb and chutney pickle). At the risk of sounding heretical (I'll say it anyway), I don't find wine entirely antithetical to food and pickles since when one is in the mood to eat with gusto conventions evaporate. Nevertheless, don't serve a really fine wine along with pickles—it will quickly fall from grace in such coarse company.

To make pickles, choose only the freshest and best produce and move it quickly from market shelf or kitchen garden to the pickling jars. Once picked, vegetables, in particular, rapidly lose moisture, flavor and texture.

Use only additive-free, plain, pure salt. This is different from common table salt, which is iodized and causes pickles to darken, or contains anti-caking agents, which make pickling liquids cloudy. Use a high-quality pasteurized vinegar (your homemade vinegar won't do here) of minimum 4 to 6 percent acidity (40 to 60 grain). I prefer a good white wine, red wine, or cider vinegar. Distilled vinegar is raw-tasting and lacks the depth of vinegars subjected to less purgative treatment. Since acidity is the barrier to spoilage, it is critical that you use vinegar with known acidity, often not always displayed on the bottle. If you like the flavor of a particular vinegar and its acidity is not listed, consult the manufacturer or dealer before you begin pickling.

Pickled Artichokes

Artichokes are essentially thistles, and in my repertoire of pickles they are pre-eminent. Alone, artichokes leave slightly bitter, sweet traces in the mouth. Add to this the tart and salty accents of a pickling solution and you have the entire spectrum of appreciable taste sensations.

Serve pickled artichokes alongside rich, cold meats, fresh or cured, or as part of a platter of appetizers that might include marinated beans, olives, poached fish, or salted anchovies. For this recipe, you will need the smallest artichokes, called "loose" artichokes, which have a tender heart and undeveloped choke.

4 pounds small artichokes
3 cups white wine vinegar
1 cup water
½ teaspoon cayenne pepper flakes
½ teaspoon whole coriander seeds
3 bay leaves
3 whole cloves
2 teaspoons salt
9 cloves garlic (1½ ounces), coarsely chopped
2 tablespoons fresh thyme leaves
Pure olive oil

Remove the outer leaves of the artichokes until you reach the pale green to yellow hearts. Cut the artichoke where the leaves begin to taper to a point, about two thirds of the way up from the base to the top of the bud. Cut off the stem of the artichoke, trim the leaves around the base, and cut each in quarters.

Pour the vinegar and water into a stainless-steel pot. Add the cayenne, coriander, bay leaves, cloves, and salt and bring to a boil. Add the artichokes to the boiling mixture, reduce to a simmer, and cook them for 10 full minutes.

Sterilize two 1-pint canning jars and their lids and seals by washing them thoroughly. Then put them in a large pot, pour water over them, and bring slowly to a boil. Remove the artichokes from the pickling liquid with a flat strainer and pack the jars with them, spices too, in layers. As you fill the jars, sprinkle the chopped garlic and thyme leaves on each layer. Top the artichokes with olive oil, leaving ½ inch of headroom, place the seals and lids on the jars, and process the jars in a boiling-water bath (see page 343) for 10 minutes.

The artichokes will be ready to eat after 1 day and will keep for several months in a cool spot. Strain the pickling liquid in which the artichokes are cooked and use it in vinaigrettes.

Pickled Yellow Wax Beans

3 pints

I owe the idea for this recipe to our friends at the Chino Ranch, who occasionally send along jars of their preserves with our weekly produce. These beans retain their crisp, snappy texture because they are packed in the jars raw. They are hot-processed for 10 minutes in a boiling-water bath—the brief processing period is adequate for beans because of the high acidity of the vinegar used in combination with a low-acid food.

Serve the beans cold from the refrigerator to enjoy them fully.

1 pound very fresh yellow wax beans
3 sprigs fresh dill
3 cloves garlic, sliced
3 small dried red chiles
2 cups water
2 cups white wine vinegar
1 tablespoon plus 1 teaspoon additive-free kosher salt

Sterilize three 1-pint canning jars and their lids and seals by washing them thoroughly. Then put them in a large pot, pour water over them, and bring slowly to the boil. In the meantime, cut the stems and tips off the beans and wash them. Remove the jars from the hot water and place a sprig of dill, a third of the garlic, and a red pepper in each jar. Pack the beans upright in the jars, leaving about 1 inch of headroom (you may have to trim some of the beans to fit). Bring the water, vinegar, and salt to a boil and pour it over the beans, filling each jar to ½ inch from the top. Place the seals and lids on the jars and process the jars in a boiling-water bath (see page 343) for 10 minutes. Remove and let cool. Check to see that the seals are complete (see page 343), then store in a cool place.

The beans will be ready to eat after 1 day, but will be much better if you wait 2 weeks.

Pickled Eggplants

Pickled eggplants are first cooked in vinegar, then hot-packed in oil with fresh basil leaves and sliced garlic. If you can find very young Japanese eggplants (the elongated, curving variety) no longer than 3 inches, they are ideal; otherwise, cut larger eggplants into chunks about 1 inch thick. It is not necessary to peel the eggplants; the skins will soften considerably when cooked. Sliced pickled eggplants are delicious in lamb sandwiches or as an accompaniment to cured meats.

2 pounds, 6 ounces small Japanese eggplants, about 3 inches long and 3/4 inch thick
4 cups red wine vinegar
4 cups water
1/4 onion (2 ounces), finely diced
1/2 teaspoon cayenne pepper flakes
2 teaspoons salt
10 cloves garlic, sliced
Fresh basil leaves
Pure olive oil

Wash the eggplants. Pour the vinegar and the water into a 6-quart stainless-steel pot, add the onion, cayenne, and salt, and bring to the boil. Plunge the eggplants in. Set a clean ceramic plate on top of the eggplants to keep them submerged. Adjust the heat so that the pot simmers, and cook the eggplants for 10 minutes, or until they are soft all the way through.

Sterilize four 1-pint canning jars (preferably short, wide ones). Pack the jars while they are still hot. Set the eggplants in on their sides, bending them gently to fit the contours of the jar, and sprinkle the garlic and basil leaves between the layers. Leave 1/2 inch headroom and top the eggplants to the same level with the olive oil. Place the seals and the lids on the jars and process the jars in a boiling-water bath (see page 343) for 15 minutes. Strain the pickling liquid for use in vinaigrettes.

Let the pickled eggplants sit for 1 day before serving.

Pickled Shallots

Red onions may be substituted for the shallots in this recipe with similar effect. Besides their pleasing shades, red onions strike a clear tone in composed salads and when served with rich meats.

1 pound firm, unsprouted shallots
2 tablespoons plus 2 teaspoons sugar
1 tablespoon additive-free kosher salt
¾ cup water
¾ cup red wine vinegar
⅛ teaspoon ground cayenne

Peel the shallots and slice them ⅛ inch thick. Combine the sugar, salt, water, vinegar, and cayenne in a saucepan and bring to the boil. Sterilize three ½-pint canning jars and their lids and seals by washing them thoroughly. Then put them in a large pot, pour water over them, and bring slowly to a boil. Pack the jars with shallots and pour over the boiling vinegar mixture. Seal the jars and loosely fit the lids. Process in a boiling-water bath (see page 343) for 10 minutes. Let the jars cool, check the seals, and store in the refrigerator, cupboard, or cellar.

The shallots will be ready to eat in 5 days.

Sweet and Sour Turnip Pickles

6 pints

Our friends at the Chino Ranch send us a remarkable variety of turnips, each with its own pastel color and distinct flavor. These turnips make crunchy pickles with a slightly peppery aftertaste.

Use small, firm turnips about 1½ inches in diameter. Larger turnips can be watery. You may wish to add other vegetables as well, such as carrots, cauliflower, small onions, or butternut squash.

1 quart water
1 quart white wine vinegar
1 cup light red wine vinegar
1 cup sugar
1 tablespoon salt
¼ teaspoon ground cayenne
6 cloves garlic, sliced
1 ounce unpeeled fresh ginger, thinly sliced
3 fresh thyme branches
¼ cup fresh mint leaves
4 pounds young turnips, topped (leaving ½ inch of the stems attached), peeled, sliced
  into ¼-inch pieces

Sterilize six 1-pint canning jars and their lids and seals by washing them thoroughly. Put them in a large pot, pour water over them and slowly bring to a boil. Combine all the ingredients except the turnips, and bring to the boil in a stainless-steel pot. While the jars are still hot, pack them with turnips. Pour about 1 cup of the pickling liquid into each jar and leave ½ inch headroom. Place the seals and lids on the jars and process the jars in a boiling-water bath (see page 343) for 15 minutes.

The pickles will be ready to eat after 3 days.

Homemade Sauerkraut

All that is required to makes sauerkraut at home is a large crock, cabbage, a little salt, and time. Homemade sauerkraut has a mild acidity, a pleasing crunchy texture, and a fresh cidery quality that is altogether different from the commercial canned variety. Cooking or canning sauerkraut makes its sour quality more pronounced and causes the fresh cabbage flavors to fade. For this reason I prefer to eat it directly from the crock, like a condiment or pickly salad, alongside sausages and rich meats and poultry, such as pork and duck.

To make sauerkraut, choose very fresh, large cabbages (mature cabbages are higher in sugar) with firm, tight leaves. The common Dutch winter white cabbage works very well. Leafy savory cabbages produce sauerkraut with a less crisp texture. To prepare the cabbage for the crock, slice it as thin as possible. This encourages the flow of juice, the formation of brine, and the eventual onset of fermentation.

The ratio of salt to sliced cabbage as expressed by weight is very important. The correct amount of salt, and the juices that the cabbage releases, provide a medium in which desirable microorganisms flourish, converting sugar to lactic acid, which accounts for the tartness of sauerkraut. Too much salt inhibits fermentation, while too little can cause spoilage. If you decide to make a larger batch, adjust the amount of salt so that its weight is 2½ percent of the weight of the cabbage (4 ounces or 6 level tablespoons salt for each 10 pounds of cabbage). Measure carefully and use only food grade pickling salt or additive-free kosher salt.

Throughout the period of fermentation a consistent temperature must be maintained. Room temperature 70°F is ideal and will cause the sauerkraut to be ready in 8 to 14 days. The temperature at which the sauerkraut is stored should not exceed 75°F. Beyond this point you court spoilage. At lower temperatures (60°F to 65°F) the sauerkraut will still be active but fermentation will proceed at a slower rate. It is wise to purchase a thermometer, preferably one that registers maximum and minimum temperatures, to monitor the temperature throughout the process (these are available in home-brewing and winemaking shops).

While it is fermenting, store the sauerkraut in a large (3- to 5-gallon capacity), heavy, glazed ceramic crock. Most hardware stores stock these crocks in varying sizes. Before packing the crock, wash and rinse it thoroughly, then scald it with boiling water. Once it has been packed in the crock, the cabbage needs to be covered with plastic wrap and weighted to keep it submerged in the brine that forms. The goal is to keep the cabbage out of contact with the air so that yeasts and molds do not contaminate the batch. A clean, heavyweight plastic bag, partially filled with water and tied off, works well as it fits snugly against the sides of the crock and does not permit air to enter.

5 pounds freshest whole cabbage
3 level tablespoons additive-free kosher salt

Cut the cabbage in half and cut out the hard core. With a sharp knife, divide the cabbage into manageable pieces and slice it as thin as possible. Wash out a 3-gallon crock in hot, sudsy water, rinse it, then scald it with boiling water. Dry the crock with a clean towel.

Put the sliced cabbage in a large bowl, sprinkle the salt over it, and mix it thoroughly with clean hands until the cabbage feels wet. Pack the cabbage in the crock in 2-inch layers, compacting each layer with the palm of your hand before adding the next. If you are working with a large batch for which you have no bowl large enough to contain it, pack the sauerkraut directly in the crock in 1-inch layers and sprinkle salt lightly and evenly over each layer, making certain to use up all the salt, and to distribute it equally among the layers. Tamp each layer with your palm and repeat the process with the rest of the cabbage.

Cover the top layer of cabbage with plastic wrap. Open up a large, clean, heavy-gauge plastic bag and place it *in* the crock on top of the cabbage. Add about 1 gallon of water to the bag so that it weights the cabbage and adjust it so that the water flows to the sides of the crock to form an airtight seal. Tie the bag with string and store the crock at 70°F.

After 24 hours, lift the bag from the crock and set it temporarily in a large clean bowl. Remove the plastic wrap and examine the cabbage. If you notice a film on top, scald a stainless-steel spoon and remove it. If the cabbage has not released enough liquid to just cover the cabbage by about ½ inch, prepare additional brine (1 quart boiling water and 1½ tablespoons salt) cooled to room temperature and use it to top the cabbage. Replace the covering with new plastic wrap and the water-filled bag.

After 8 days sample the cabbage. You may wish to use it at this point when it is mildly tart. Otherwise, allow it to continue to sour 6 days or more. Move the covered crock to a very cool cellar (38°F). Or transfer the sauerkraut to scalded jars, top with ¾ inch brine and scalded lids, and store in the refrigerator. The sauerkraut will keep well for at least a week, but it is advisable to can it if you intend to store it for a longer period.

Tomato Sauce

Tomato sauce is a good pantry staple, useful in soups, sauces, pasta dishes, and braises. The summer is of course the best time to make a supply of it, particularly if you grow tomatoes in your own garden (there is always an excess), or if you have access to a country farm or greengrocer who sells vine-ripened tomatoes in bulk. This recipe is a very basic tomato sauce with few additions. Ripe tomatoes are quartered, stewed in olive oil with a handful of basil leaves, and seasoned with salt and pepper. The mixture is passed through the fine blades of a food mill to catch the skins and seeds, then reduced to allow the sauce to thicken. Italian plum tomatoes with their meaty and comparatively drier flesh are perhaps most naturally suited, but any sweet ripe tomato will do.

My own cache of tomato sauce has saved me on more than one occasion when the cupboard was bare. Although by now the formula is well worn, tomato sauce, buttered or perfumed with good olive oil (or basil oil, see page 339), on freshly made pasta is a divinely simple pleasure. Care must be taken in the method of preserving tomato sauce for storing. Use only firm, ripe, unblemished tomatoes with unbroken skins. Discard any that have soft or rotten spots. Wash the tomatoes well and cut them up on a clean surface with a clean, stainless-steel knife. For processing in a boiling-water bath the U.S.D.A. recommends the addition of a small amount of crystalline citric acid to prevent the possible growth of bacteria. Citric acid is available in most drugstores and imparts no flavor to the tomatoes. Distilled white vinegar can also be used for the same purpose. Proportions are given below for both.

5 pounds tomatoes
3 tablespoons pure olive oil
Large handful fresh basil leaves
1 teaspoon salt
¼ teaspoon ground black pepper

Wash the tomatoes and quarter them. Warm the olive oil in a large stainless-steel pot (7- to 8-quart), add the tomatoes, basil, salt, and pepper. Cook over medium heat for 30 minutes, stirring every so often, until the tomatoes are well softened. Pass the tomatoes through the fine blade of a food mill. Return the purée to the pot and reduce the sauce to a consistency halfway between juice and paste. About 2 pints should remain.

Sterilize two 1-pint canning jars by washing them thoroughly. Then place them in a large pot, pour water over them, and bring slowly to a boil. Pour the hot sauce into the hot jars, leaving ½ inch headroom. Add ¼ teaspoon pure crystalline citric acid (or 3 teaspoons distilled white vinegar) to each jar, adjust the seals, and fit the screw lids snugly but not tightly on top. Process the jars in a boiling-water bath (see page 343) for 30 minutes. Cool, check for tight seals, and store in a cool, dark, dry place.

Basil Oil

1 pint

This is a scented oil—a cold infusion of basil leaves in olive oil. It is to be used sparingly as a condiment; drizzled on pasta, rice dishes, grilled fish, or on ripe tomatoes from the garden, it lends its delicate perfume. Use fresh, preferably just-picked, glossy basil leaves and a fruity extra virgin olive oil.

This simple combination applies to other herbs as well, particularly rosemary, sage, and oregano and is a wonderful way of capturing the scent of the black truffle (slice it thin into the oil). It does not work to similar effect with the white truffle, however.

1 cup very fresh basil leaves
2 cups extra virgin olive oil

Sterilize a 1-pint canning jar. Wash the basil leaves and dry them in a towel. While the jar is still hot, pack it with the leaves. Pour in the olive oil, secure the lid tightly, and store in a cool, dark place.

The oil will be ready to use in 10 days.

Green Tomato, Raisin, and Mint Chutney

2 quarts

The green tomato with its firm meaty texture and lemon-sour flavor is a good candidate for chutney preserve. Green tomato chutney is slightly sweet, sour, and piquant, and is a natural complement to pork, turkey, and particularly lamb.

4 pounds green tomatoes, cut into ½-inch dice
2½ cups light brown sugar
1 cup cider vinegar
3 cups diced onions (12 ounces)
1 cup golden raisins
1 cup black raisins
¾ cup sliced fresh ginger (2½ ounces)
1 teaspoon cayenne flakes
½ teaspoon salt
½ cup fresh small mint leaves, coarsely chopped

Combine all the ingredients, except the mint, in a 6-quart stainless-steel pot. Bring to a simmer and cook, uncovered, for 1 hour and 15 minutes. Thoroughly wash four 1-pint jars, lids, and seals. Then put in a large pot, pour water over them, and slowly bring to a boil. Add the mint to the simmering mixture and pack loosely in the hot jars. Screw the tops on and place in a large pot, cover with water by 1 inch, bring to the boil, and process the jars for 15 minutes. Store in a cool, dark place. The chutney will keep indefinitely.

Bitter Apricot Preserves

Eleven ½ pints

These preserves are slightly bitter because of the kernels inside the apricot pits, which are added to the fruit as it cooks. The kernels have the flavor of bitter almonds and make wonderful ice creams and Bavarian creams (see page 310), so think twice before you discard the apricot pits. As well as a topping for morning toast, a spoonful of bitter apricot preserves reinforces a bowl of vanilla ice cream. The preserves may also be used in place of fresh figs in the recipe for Fig Jam Tart with Thyme, if it is further reduced to a thick, spreadable consistency.

8 pounds apricots, split, pitted, pits reserved
1 cup sugar

Set aside half of the pits and, using a hammer, gently crack their outer shells (don't smash them). Extract the kernels inside. You will need ⅓ cup.

Put the apricots in a large, wide stainless-steel pot (6- to 7-quart capacity), stir in the sugar, and set over medium-high heat. Stir the pot often to prevent sticking and reduce the heat, if necessary, so that the apricots bubble gently. Cook the apricots for 45 minutes, or until the liquid surrounding the fruit has thickened and there is about as much of it as chunks of apricot.

Sterilize eleven ½-pint canning jars by washing them thoroughly, then put them in a large pot, cover with water, and bring slowly to a boil. While they are still hot, pack them with the hot preserves. Place the seals and lids on the jars and process the jars in a boiling-water bath for 10 minutes (see page 343). Store the preserves in a cool place.

Conserve of Cèpes

This recipe is a response to a bumper crop of cèpes, which was more than we could use. It is an excellent way to preserve the mushrooms if drying them is not a possibility.

Slightly pickled and mixed with the flavors of rosemary and garlic, these mushrooms are delicious in salads, on grilled bread, or when served with veal chops or roast fowl.

12 ounces fresh cèpes (Boletus edulis), *cut into ¼-inch slices*
2½ teaspoons very good white wine vinegar
¼ teaspoon salt
⅛ teaspoon freshly ground pepper
½ cup olive oil
Six 2-inch sprigs fresh rosemary
3 cloves garlic, thinly sliced

In a stainless-steel pot, with a perforated insert or fold-up steamer basket, steam the cèpes in two batches over ½ inch boiling water for 6 minutes. Remove the cèpes and while they are still hot, toss them with the vinegar, salt, and pepper. Reduce the water in the steamer, now flavored by the cèpes, to 2 tablespoons and mix it with the mushrooms as well. Gently warm the olive oil in a saucepan. Add the rosemary and garlic and let it sizzle in the oil for 2 minutes. Remove from the heat and let cool.

Sterilize a 1-pint jar by thoroughly washing it, its lid and seal. Place in a pot, cover with boiling water, and slowly bring to a boil. Pack the cèpes in the hot jar adding the flavored oil, rosemary leaves, and garlic slices to each layer of mushrooms. Seal the jar and keep it refrigerated.

The conserve will keep well in the refrigerator for 1 month. It is ready to eat immediately and is best served at room temperature.

Boiling-Water Bath

Most of the recipes in this chapter call for a boiling-water bath, which is used in the canning of strong acid foods—vinegared items, tomato sauce, pickles, sweet jams, and some conserves. The boiling-water bath eliminates any airborne microorganisms present in raw or partly cooked foods, or in the pickling jar while it is being filled and sealed, and forces air out of the food and canning liquid, creating a vacuum and perfect seal that prevents spoilage. Processing in a boiling-water bath is not optional and should be done with care.

Boiling-water bath canners are sold commercially, but it is also easy to adapt a deep kitchen broth pot to the purpose. The pot must be deep enough to accommodate the jars that rest on a rack 1 inch above the bottom of the pot and enough water to cover the tops of the jars by 2 inches, with sufficient room between the water and the top of the pot to provide that briskly boiling water does not spill out. Additional boiling water may be required to maintain 2 inches of water above jars. The holding rack can be made easily of hardware cloth, or other sturdy screen cut to fit the diameter of the pot bottom, tacked or stapled to unpainted or untreated strips of wood. The purpose of the rack is to allow boiling water to freely circulate around the jars.

To use the boiling-water bath, place the rack in the bottom. Pack the food in cleaned, sterilized jars according to the individual recipe. If the jars and pickling solution are very hot, they can be placed directly into boiling water. Cool jars plunged into boiling water are likely to crack. Set cool jars in the pot, then pour cool water over them, and bring to the boil.

Lower and lift jars into and out of the pot with a pair of tongs, grabbing the jars beneath the flange of the lids. Stores that sell canning equipment have tongs specifically designed for this purpose.

The most commonly used containers for storing pickles are closures—a flat lid with a band of rubber outlining the circumference, and a screw cap. Never tighten the screw cap before or after processing or the air in jars won't escape. Tightening the lid excessively after cooling may break the seal. Remember, it is not you that is making the seal but the jar itself as it expels air, creates a vacuum, and sucks the lid down firmly onto the rim of the jar. Screw the lids snugly, but not tightly, after cooling. Use lids only once (they are sold separately) to ensure a good seal.

Check the seals after one day. The lids should appear slightly concave. If not, press them. If they click and spring back, the seals are not complete and the contents should be eaten right away; or the entire process should be repeated from the beginning.

Fresh and Pure Ingredients

Everyone agrees that fresh, pure food is better than the alternative. The problem begins when one tries to set specific standards for freshness and purity: One man's meat turns out to be another man's health code violation. An apple can be fresh from the supermarket or fresh from the tree or its juice can be freshly made from concentrate. Freshness is an elusive quality.

The plain fact is that most food not locally produced and sold is now either processed to preserve it on its long journey to the supermarket, or shipped by air at great cost. Unlike patrons of the open-air food markets found in most European cities, the American consumer has little access to the farmer. If you do buy produce at a farmer's market, or at your local fruit and vegetable stand, the people there should be able to tell you how the food was grown and handled. Above all, realize that you do have choices in your diet. The most pleasing alternative for yourself and your family is to plant a garden. If this is not possible, you can become aware of seasonal foods and buy the food that is naturally ripe or ready at that time of year, and seek out local farmers' markets. As a last resort, badger your local supermarket into carrying foods you want to eat. You are not alone in your search; government agencies and private organizations can help you locate and identify whole and pure foods in your area. The following section describes the legal and political status of organic food.

Organic Foods: Standards and Definitions

Despite a diversity of legal definitions, practitioners of organic farming share a common philosophy, rooted in the belief that a healthy soil, high in organic matter, is the basis of any viable agriculture. In this view, the health of the soil, including the natural processes of decay of vegetative and animal matter and the flow of nutrients resulting therefrom, is to be nurtured as much as the crops grown in the soil. Heavy applications of synthetic chemical fertilizers and pesticides interrupt these processes.

Organic farming, therefore, involves the care and feeding of the soil as well as the cultivation of the plants it bears, through practices such as mulching, cover cropping, crop rotation, companion planting, and the use of naturally occurring products of mineral, plant, or animal origin to maintain soil and plant health.

Chemical-based agriculture, on the other hand, driven by the economic competition for volume production in the mass market, relies on the forced feeding

346   FRESH AND PURE INGREDIENTS

of crops with highly soluble, artificially synthesized nutrients; under such regimes the soil becomes little more than a sponge to sop up the additives. This intensive, usually monocrop, form of cultivation is so alien to the natural history of the various plant species—and by extension of the argument, animal species as well—and to the established checks and balances of nature that the resulting crops are more susceptible to the depredations of their natural enemies. So in addition they must be artificially protected with large quantities of laboratory devised insecticides, herbicides, and fungicides.

In contrast to this, organic farmers attempt to use the land in a way that respects the long and intricate process that fosters the relationships between the earth and the living organisms it sustains. As stated in a California Certified Organic Farmer's brochure, "Organic food has been grown with care for the whole ecosystem that supports us. Healthy soil supports healthy plants feeding healthy people and animals."

Implicit in this approach to agriculture is the basic principle of ecology: that all creatures and living things are mutually interdependent and they in turn depend on the proper use of the material bases of existence. The claim it makes is that only farming practices that are compatible with this principle result in an agriculture that is sustainable over the long haul. This is not only because it does not depend on an accelerating input of exhaustible resources, but because it is consistent with a civilized view of the relationship between humankind and the finite world we live in. It is a principle consistent with the biblical injunction to "replenish the earth," rather than to lay it waste.

Organic farming is not merely a return to the old, pretechnological methods of farming, although it embraces the wisdom of traditional practices: ". . . organic farming is *not* the farming our ancestors did. The same 'science and technology' that gave us chemicals also gave us insect ecology, microclimatology, soil analysis, permaculture, conservation techniques, and a host of other new knowledge that our farming ancestors never dreamed of. Organic farming is the *new* farming of today and the future, a blend of the best of the new sciences and of the old wisdom" (*Organic Directory and Yearbook* [Davis: California Agrarian Action Project, 1987]).

There is one more claim made by the organic approach to agriculture: that it will produce not only healthier, but also tastier food, food that is pleasing to the senses because it partakes of the essence of the earth. At its finest, such food is not only sensually pleasing, but also appealing to the aesthetic sense: It partakes of beauty. And this is so because beauty, or gracefulness, is something that cannot be forced, but rather is the expression of a set of appropriate and fitting relationships.

National standards for definitions for organic foods have not been established yet, though several of the organizations listed below are working toward national and international standards. We may soon be able to rely on the exact wording of the claim on a piece of fruit, for instance. States, however, do regulate the commercial use of words like "natural," "organic," and "fresh." Your state will doubtless differ from others, but you can ask for information about its regulations. States that have passed such laws controlling the use of the word "organic" include Washington, Oregon, Maine, California, New Hampshire, Montana, Minnesota, Nebraska, and Massachussetts. Iowa's law is pending, and others are being added to this list all the time.

In California, the terms "naturally grown," "ecologically grown," "wild," and "organically grown" are legally defined. The California code requires that food with any of these labels must be "produced, harvested, distributed, stored, processed, and packaged without the application of synthetically compounded fertilizers, pesticides, or growth regulators." The laws may include labeling requirements, which affect both the grower and retailer. In California, any food sold as "organically grown" must also bear the label "grown in accordance with California Health and Safety Code Sec. 26569.11."

Unfortunately, the mere existence of a law controlling the label "organic" does not guarantee that the law is working. Few states provide for enforcement, nor do they fund what can be expensive efforts to verify that organic growing practices are actually being used. In California, for instance, enforcement is the province of the Health Services Department, Food and Drug Branch; this branch handles many problems much more urgently life-threatening than one farm's fertilizer practices. As a consequence, their policy is to check claims about "organic" foods only when a consumer has filed a specific complaint.

In several states, groups of farmers have reacted to this neglect of enforcement by state governments by forming independent organizations to verify each other's claims by auditing farm records, inspecting farms, and performing laboratory analyses of food, soil, and feeds. These groups certify member farms annually and they encourage the use of a highly visible logo to help the consumer recognize a reputable purveyor of organic products. The standards for certification by these growers' organizations tend to be stricter than the legal requirements for the use of the "organic" designation. They also are usually more comprehensive, specifying not only what must *not* be used in the production of crops, but also stipulating that certain practices must be followed to insure the maintenance of the balance of fertility of the soil. The following is a partial list of certifying organizations:

Ozark Organic Growers Association,
HCR 72 Box 34,
Parthenon, Arkansas 72666

California Certified Organic Farmers,
P.O. Box 8136
Santa Cruz, California 95061-8136

Maine Organic Farmers and Gardeners Association
P.O. Box 2176
Augusta, Maine 04330

Organic Growers of Michigan
3031 White Creek Road
Kingston, Michigan 48741

Organic Growers and Buyers Association
P.O. Box 9747
Minneapolis, Minnesota 55440

Natural Organic Farmers Association
White Farm
150 Clinton Street
Concord, New Hampshire 03301
     NOFA has chapters in Connecticut, Illinois, Massachusetts, New York, and
Vermont, and members at large throughout the United States and Canada.

New York State Natural Food Associates, Inc.
One Cobey Terrace
Poughkeepsie, New York 12601

Oregon Tilth
P.O. Box 218
Tualitin, Oregon 97062

Organic Crop Improvement Association
Route 1, Box 729A
New Holland, Pennsylvania 17557

OCIA has chapters in several states, including Pennsylvania, Vermont, and Ontario, Canada, and affiliated organizations and members at large in the United States, Canada, and Central America.

Tilth Producers Cooperative
1219 Sauk Road
Concrete, Washington 98234

Wisconsin Natural Food Association, Inc.
6616 CTH I
Waunakee, Wisconsin 53597

Aside from your state's Department of Agriculture or its Department of Consumer Affairs, you may also contact the organizations listed below to learn more about organically grown foods:

Organic Food Producers Association of North America
P.O. Box 31
Belchertown, Massachusetts 01007
OFPANA is a trade association formed by organic farm organizations, processors, distributors, and supporters.

Americans for Safe Food
1501 16th Street N.W.
Washington D.C. 20036
ASF promotes the sale of organic food and publishes a list of organic food mail-order suppliers. Send a stamped self-addressed envelope to receive the list.
ASF has also published a booklet entitled *Guess What's Coming to Dinner: Contaminants in our Food*, which is very informative and is available upon request.

Potomac Valley Press
Suite 105, 1424 16th Street N.W.
Washington D.C. 20036
Healthy Harvest, an annual directory of organizations involved in sustainable agriculture, $10.95, including tax and shipping.

California Agrarian Action Project
P.O. Box 464
Davis, California 95617

CAAP publishes perhaps the most complete list of organic farms, businesses, certifying organizations, and other information about sustainable agriculture in its annual directory and yearbook. $22, including tax and shipping.

Some groups work to persuade larger stores to stock organic foods. Natural foods are reaching the mainstream distribution channels as more demand for them is created. In 1982, the U.S. Department of Agriculture released a Report and Recommendations on Organic Farming that was very encouraging. In the 69 organic farms studied, ranging in size from a few acres to nearly 1,500, it found that organic farms are successfully competing with farms that use chemical pesticides and fertilizers.

All states require that food packagers comply with certain labeling requirements. By learning the legal definitions that apply in your state, you can greatly improve your control over your diet.

Specific Points About Meats and Poultry

Standards for "organic" meats and poultry are not well defined, and those that do exist differ from state to state. The safest course is to find butchers who you can trust and ask them to describe the meat-raising practices of the farms that supply them. If you cannot find a butcher concerned about such things, you can turn to the action groups listed in the section above. Americans for Safe Food is organizing a national campaign to let grocery stores know that consumers want food free of potentially dangerous pesticides, fumigants, growth promotants, antibiotics, hormones, and additives. Without loud noises from consumers, the food industry has no incentive to provide safe food. You can help by participating in their campaign. Write to ASF (listed above) for more information.

Traditionally, attention has focused on the way meat was treated after the animal was slaughtered. We have been warned to beware of beef dyed to look fresher, and to treat raw chickens carefully to avoid salmonellosis. But these warnings ignore the fact that the live animal may have been subjected to practices that affect the wholesomeness of the meat.

Recent concerns about the safety and quality of fresh meats are aired in three different questions: How was the animal treated, how was the animal fed, and how was the meat treated after the animal was slaughtered. The slaughtering of most animals and the processing of meat after slaughter is regulated by the U.S. Department of Agriculture, and you can certainly do your part to make sure your meat is handled carefully by buying it from a reputable butcher. The questions regarding the treatment and feeding of the animal are, unfortunately, less easy to answer.

The treatment of the food animal is a point of real controversy. Most livestock-raising practices turn a blind eye to the comfort of the animal, as long as the creature is putting on flesh quickly enough. Poultry is particularly subject to cruel practices, such as confinement to small or extremely crowded cages to discourage movement and the removal of beaks or the placement of permanent, tinted lenses on the eyes of the birds to discourage fighting. Consumers who care about such things find that the economics of the meat-raising industry have made it difficult to find companies who follow even minimally humane practices in raising meat animals. The meat industry, on the other hand, points back to the consumer, saying that demand for "milk-fed" veal, for instance, has created and perpetuated the practice of isolating calves in pens, denying them exercise, and feeding them whey-based formula feeds that are low in iron so the meat will be as white as possible. Veal is raised humanely at some farms where calves have access to pasturage, but such places are very much the exception.

One type of naturally raised flesh that is increasingly popular is the free-range chicken. In farmers' markets in the English countryside, the belief that the well-being of the animal affects the flavor of the food has popularized even the eggs of free-range chickens. Organic eggs are available in the United States as well. The term "free-range" refers to the open space and natural pasturage available to the animal, but the use of the word is not regulated, so the amount of space actually available to the chicken should be investigated in each case before such a label is taken literally. An interesting irony of free-range chickens in this country is that the most common breed raised for meat—the Hubbard—is not particularly interested in roaming around. In fact, the chicken will not leave its coop as long as it has a trough full of feed in front of it. Some free-range farms take the trouble to shoo the birds out for a stroll by setting their food outside, for instance, while other farmers simply leave the door open so the chickens can go out if they are so inclined.

One aspect of humane treatment is not controversial, however. It is generally agreed that meat animals yield better meat if they are not subject to panic immediately before slaughter. Evidently the rush of panic-induced adrenaline affects the flavor of the meat. For this reason, organic farms take considerable trouble to find humane abattoirs, and ranchers may escort the animals there to ensure their humane slaughter.

Although the cruel treatment of meat animals is the most sensational failure of those regulating the modern meat industry, it is by no means the only one.

The dependence of modern agriculture upon synthetic chemicals has led to three classes of chemical residues making their way into the meat from animals raised according to the conventional practice of animal husbandry. These are antibiotics, hormones, and pesticides. Antibiotics are usually added to the feed in sub-therapeutic amounts—amounts less than would be used for the treatment of illness—not only to prevent disease, but also because this practice has been found to increase the growth rate of the animals. The effect of the antibiotics in preventing disease has also made it possible to crowd more animals into a given space without spreading certain diseases among the herd or flock. The addition of hormones to the feed, or their injection in slow-release form, also speeds up the growth of animals. Pesticide residues make their way into the flesh of animals because they have been used on grain and hay crops that make up the bulk of animal feeds.

There is a tendency to minimize the issue of pesticides when discussing meats because the animal is one step removed from any toxic residues in the plants it eats. In fact it has been found that for some of these compounds the animal acts not as a filter but as a concentrator. This became evident when the effects of DDT contamination were studied. The complex organic chemicals used in some pesticides tend to concentrate in the fatty tissues and liver of the animals that eat the treated plants.

In May 1987, a committee of the prestigious National Research Council of the National Academy of Sciences published a report, *Regulating Pesticides in Foods*, which concluded that the nation's food supply is inadequately protected from residues of cancer-inducing pesticides. This study found beef to contain the second highest levels of pesticide residues (tomatoes were first), with pork and chicken among the fifteen most contaminated foods. It complained that a "crazy-quilt" of laws and regulations is permitting high levels of some of these chemicals to reach the consumer. Earlier studies by the General Accounting Office of the U.S. Congress ascertained that probably less that 1 percent of foods appearing on the market are tested for pesticide residues by the USDA and the U.S. Food and Drug Administration. The same 1 percent figure appears in a 1983 National Research Council study as the estimate of the percentage of slaughtered animal carcasses tested for antibiotic residues by the USDA. The incidence of illegal levels of antibiotics in those carcasses tested was 1½ percent overall, but in certain animals, particularly calves and swine, contamination has run several percentage points higher in some regions of the country.

The danger to human health of the routine use of antibiotics in animal feed is not limited to the possible toxic or allergic consequences of residual contamination of meat. There is a growing conviction among health officials and consumer advocates that this practice is compromising the treatment of human disease because of the spread of antibiotic-resistant bacteria from animals to humans.

The problem stems from the fact that the continual presence of antibiotics in the gastrointestinal tract of an animal results in the development of antibiotic-resistant strains of pathogenic bacteria, particularly salmonella, which cause bacillary dysentery, a serious form of diarrhea in human beings. There is a significant death rate from such infections, many times higher than that from infections with salmonella strains that are susceptible to antibiotics. The paradox of this situation is that the use of antibiotics for animals has negated the ability of physicians to save human patients with these same antibiotics in a growing number of cases. In March 1987, a report of outbreaks of antibiotic-resistant salmonellosis traced to hamburger from dairy farms in the Los Angeles area brought national attention to this problem. The report published in the *New England Journal of Medicine* stated in summation: "We conclude that food animals are a major source of antimicrobial-resistant *salmonella* infections in humans and that these infections are associated with antimicrobial use on farms."

The unwanted consequences of the use of hormones as growth-promoting agents have affected children, perhaps numbering in the thousands in Puerto Rico, according to another report published in the *New England Journal of Medicine* in June 1984. Traces of a synthetic female hormone used to promote growth in animals was found in the blood of some of these patients. This drug, called zearalenone, has been found to be potentially cancer-inducing in laboratory animals, as excessive doses of other female hormones have proven to be in humans.

A good deal of public attention has been focused on these various problems in the past few years. (See *Modern Meat* by Orville Schell [New York: Random House, 1984] for a very graphic description of some of the objectionable practices of the modern meat industry.) The rising level of concern about these practices has recently induced the USDA to step up its monitoring of meat for residues of additives. A nationwide system of spot checks of carcasses, known as the National Residue Program, has emphasized the selective monitoring of antibiotic and pesticide residues where problems of contamination are suspected. Now a more intensive monitoring system, the Verified Production Control Program, is underway. Carcasses are inspected at the slaughterhouse, but there is also surveillance of the animals at the participating ranches and feedlots to ensure that they are free of additive residues well before slaughter. Inclusion of a ranch in such a program does not signify that the animals are raised without the use of antibiotics and hormones. But some ranchers use the program to verify that they do not use these additives at all.

The use of the program has, incidentally, compounded confusion in the public mind regarding the meaning of terms used in the labeling of meats. When the USDA permits the term "natural" to be used in the labeling of meat, it signifies, at the present time, only "that the product is a natural food because it contains no artificial ingredients and is only minimally processed"; in other words, that no chemicals or other additives have been applied to the meat after the animal is slaughtered. It indicates nothing about the way the animal was raised. Some growers whose animals are raised without medications use the term "natural beef," for example, as part of the labeling and advertising scheme. The USDA is planning to modify the terminology, which hopefully will lessen the existing confusion.

The use of the term "organic" is another bewildering matter. There is no Federal definition of the term and its legal import, in regard to meat, varies from state to state. In California, the term "organically produced" and its several variations are defined by law as follows: "Meat, poultry, or fish produced without the use of any chemical or drug to stimulate or regulate growth or tenderness and without any drugs or antibiotics administered or introduced to such animal by injection or ingestion, except for treatment of a specific disease or malady and in no event administered or introduced within 90 days of the slaughter of such animal; at least the final 60 percent of the sale weight of each animal, bird, or fish shall have been raised on feed without medication which complies with subdivision (a)." "Feed without medication" of subdivision (a) refers to raw agricultural commodities which "are produced, harvested, distributed, stored, processed, and packaged with application of synthetically compounded fertilizers, pesticides, or growth regulators."

The reason why organically raised feed is required only for the final 60 percent of the weight gain of the animal is that it enables ranchers to buy young animals at market or auction to supplement the offspring of their breeding stock, or to obviate the necessity of having breeding stock. The Oregon and Washington laws are ambiguous about whether they require the animal to have been raised entirely on organically grown feed, but the organic growers' organizations, including California Certified Organic Farmers and Oregon Tilth, are moving in the direction of requiring that slaughter animals be fed organically grown feed throughout their lifetime.

The distinctions among conventionally raised animals, animals that are raised without medications, and animals not only raised without medications but also fed organically raised feed account for the differences in the cost of raising livestock. Most organic farms are small, and the per unit cost of producing animals is greater when it is done in small numbers than in large. Animals raised without antibiotics, chemical parasiticides, and worming medicine cannot be crowded into small spaces, nor are the practitioners of organic farming inclined to do so—the evolving standards of organic certifying organizations specify that humane practices be followed in the production of livestock. Animals raised without antibiotics and hormones gain weight more slowly, so the number of animals raised in a given space and the turnover rate over time are both reduced. More important, the amount of animal weight gained per quantity of feed consumed is significantly reduced; this is usually where the greatest expense is. It takes more time and more feed to raise a healthy animal.

The cost of organically raised feed is high, particularly grains such as corn, barley, and soybeans. There are now a few farms raising grains and hay organically, including some volume growers of wheat and corn for the organic flour market, but in most areas such sources of supply are few and transportation and storage costs high, so that the cost of organically raised feed will usually in itself raise the cost of producing an animal some 20 to 50 percent. Lambs and goats, which can be nourished entirely or primarily on a farmer's own pasture, are generally the least expensive to raise according to organic principles. Chickens and rabbits, which require high proportions of grain and other feed supplements, are the most expensive. Although pigs usually are fed a diet based on grain, the organic feeding problem can be at least partially solved by feeding them organic by-products, such as the whey from goat's milk used for making cheese and other otherwise unmarketable produce from organic farms. Beef cattle can be pasture raised, particularly on large ranges in the West, although supplemental feeding of hay and grain, or the combination as silage, is usually required at some times of the year. The American taste in beef also demands a finishing period of several months in a feed lot with a high intake, grain-enriched diet, although this is changing somewhat with the increased emphasis on the production of lean meat.

To no longer produce what is on our table, as our forefathers did by the sweat of their brows, is, I suppose, a mark of progress. Such progress has relieved the burden of necessity, and the accompanying sense of responsibility for the quality of food. Yet, to realize the larger meaning of progress, understood as an advance toward a more fulfilling life for ourselves and for all who inhabit the earth, a sense of responsibility is critical, both on the part of those who supply our food and those who demand it. This sense of responsibility is rooted in the simple fact that food is eaten by people; it is our life's sustenance. To care for food is to care for ourselves.

Lately, in light of encouraging, cooperative efforts on the part of farmers, ranchers, food brokers, retailers, government agencies, and restaurants, there is cause to wonder whether the distance between ourselves and our forefathers, who by necessity knew their food intimately, is really that great. For it has become quite clear that it is still possible to enjoy the food that springs innocently from the earth.

Making a Menu

Seasonal Menus
Menus for Friends
Celebration Menus
Wine Menus

Making a Menu

Nearly every Friday morning for the past six years I have written the following week's nightly changing menu for Chez Panisse. The basis for the menus has not altered since the restaurant's inception; more than an arena for wild experimentation, the menus are an opportunity to swing with the seasons and make the most of their bountiful variety.

The best kind of cooking is improvisation that develops from a receptive attitude on the part of the cook, and from the enjoyment he or she takes in the whole process. An ever-changing menu permits a freedom that encourages this attitude and approach. The vigor of seasonal, fresh, raw foods in their prime is a powerful incentive to a cook whose imagination is not limited by the strictures of a fixed, repeated menu. Logically, many restaurants operate on the premise that the same people will not be back the next night. This fact, along with added control and predictability, is the *raison d'être* of a fixed menu. The potential pitfall, of course, is the tendency for a fixed menu to resemble a broken record, less so perhaps to the clients of a restaurant than those who prepare its dishes. A menu that does not excite those who cook it will not excite those who eat it; this is as true at home as it is in a restaurant. I say these things with some reservations: I know the problems of restaurants and of households in which busy schedules often reduce cooking and the pleasures of the table to the simple act of being fed. Nevertheless, a menu that reflects a cook's joy and whimsy makes the table an abiding source of pleasure.

Another benefit of menus that chart their way through the seasons is that ideas for dishes are generated from the work itself. A flavorful bouillabaisse inspires a variation for another night, perhaps a sieved thick broth for a fish and bread soup. Grilled onions and pigeon, served in separate courses, suggest another pairing of those flavors in a risotto. The seasonal coincidence of squid and shrimp results in a baked dish of whole squid stuffed with chopped shrimp, basil, and bread crumbs. Our runs of local salmon beget salmon in court bouillon beget salmon salad beget baked salmon with bacon and onions, and so forth.

A successful menu is a harmony of parts and a succession of individual dishes, each of which declares a mood, weight, and style. There are at least as many ways of filling and articulating the form of a menu as there are ways to plant a garden. And it is not any simpler to make a good menu of three courses than one of seven. Although the meal of seven may require more detail, the challenge remains the same, to unify and make whole the various statements.

A good menu has a style that reflects the season, weather, time of day, and the tastes of those who partake of it. Often it is the occasion itself that suggests the style of menu. This is particularly true of celebrations, New Year's Eve, for instance, the first day of fall, Valentine's Day, or Thanksgiving. A menu often elaborates a food or wine theme or celebrates a particular person by associating its dishes with the tastes or character of the honored. These initial considerations supply a menu with a point of origin. The next step is to choose individual dishes that suit the style and complement one another. A common pitfall is to preconceive ideas of food in making a menu. Ground yourself in the season, for this is the best frame of reference. It would be ideal if you could make your menu based on what looks vibrant in the marketplace.

With an idea of the style of menu in mind, begin by choosing one particular food that captures your eye and imagination. In spring, for instance, you might expect to encounter artichokes, asparagus, peas, salmon, and strawberries; in the fall, wild mushrooms, apples, and shellfish; in summer, tomatoes, peppers, peaches, and rockfish. Among these choices at least one will stand out. Before coming to any conclusions about its place in the menu and deciding its destiny in a particular dish, first evaluate what captures your interest. If you are unsure of what you are dealing with, ask questions of your fishmonger, greengrocer, butcher, or cheese merchant. The spring salmon you choose, delicate and not at all fatty, may best be poached rather than exposed to the smoky charcoal grill. The apples you select with a pie in mind may be better eaten raw or even quickly sautéed. Often the fate of a particular food will be obvious, such as braising a particular cut of meat; or a perfectly ripe tomato, which would be a sacrilege to eat any other way but raw.

Once one dish is decided upon, a menu begins to take shape. But before going any further, I should digress to say that I don't usually begin a menu with thoughts about dessert. I think of dessert as the final stroke, the most diplomatic course in a menu. When well planned, dessert can crown a meal with grace and good feeling, or soothe or smooth out prior difficulties. It is a good idea to decide upon your dessert course after the other dishes are planned. This is particularly true if you have taken some risks in your menu or decided to present dishes you suspect might appear controversial. In the restaurant, for instance, it is often the case than on the heels of dishes that are composed of variety meats, which the public is, in general, predisposed to shun, we plan desserts that are sure to please. Who, with suspicions or displeasure aroused at the prospect of a bowl of braised tripe, brains in brown butter, or grilled sweetbreads, would not later be lulled into sweet contentment by the offering of an individual warm chocolate cake in a thin pool of crème anglaise (one of our most obvious ploys), or a puff pastry with mixed berries and peaches with a glass of chilled Sauternes? Calculated as it is, out of sympathy or salutation, dessert merits special consideration.

The other end of a menu is also significant. If hors d'oeuvres are not offered, a first course, since it initiates the meal, should be a genuine appetizer. A first course should be a provocation to eat that is designed to appeal to sluggish appetites or the high pitch of hunger; never should it dampen or make dull, in its character or quantity of proportion, the anticipation or surprise of what is to follow. First courses are most often effective when they contain an element of mild shock—bright colors, tart, vinegary, or salty accents, piquancy or astringency, and when they have a quality of ease and spryness about them.

Discovering what precedes, follows, or frames a dish, whatever its placement in a menu, involves making associations and balancing the whole. Consider first the dish you have chosen as your starting point. What would best harmonize with it? Is it rich or lean? What food category does it belong to? What is its color and texture? What is its weight? (By weight I do not mean how much you provide in portion, but the overall character of the dish, which is related to the manner in which it is cooked or otherwise prepared. Dishes that have considerable weight usually have deep, lingering, or complex flavors accompanied by an intensity or richness. Those that are less so state their flavors simply, and are fresh and bright with a certain leanness.)

Continued interest in a meal is sustained by providing contrast and relief. A tart first course served cold with sharp, clean flavors might be followed by a warm soup, saucy sauté, pasta, or risotto. A pasta dish that contains a saucy stewed meat might be followed by a grilled filet of fish with a wedge of lemon. A plate of mixed lettuces after a braised course, or a roast, is a way of refreshing the appetite prior to dessert. In a menu of more than three courses, it is often necessary to work at the planning of several courses at once, revising, discarding, shifting, or substituting one element of one course to another place in the menu to achieve balance and good pairings. Often this kind of juggling can get hypothetical. Return to the food itself if you find your decisions are becoming heady or difficult. Tasting and working with it will reveal its appropriate placement and an inner logic in the menu.

Avoid repetition. The recurrence of an ingredient, if not significantly masked, will appear as a regression, will thwart the element of surprise, and block the forward momentum of a menu. Variety sustains interest. When you have placed your dishes in the form of a menu, step back and look at it. It is at this point that you may consider how balanced the menu is and may make some mental notes about the size of portions you plan to give relative to one another. Think too about the color of the food and avoid serving meals that are chromatically monotonous—this is one subtle way of introducing contrast.

Unless the menu is specifically designed to complement wine, it is also time to think about how you will include it. Wine punctuates a menu, is a way of announcing a new course, and provides logical breaks. Often in extended menus the presentation of wines maintains a slightly separate agenda. The usual progression of wines in a menu is from simple to complex, from young to old. But there are really no rules regarding this practice; age isn't necessarily a reliable indicator of a wine's character. Generally speaking, wine should mirror the food in its style and tone.

Making a menu is a discovery process that beckons you to follow your nose and your hunches down a circuitous route led by the lure of the season's produce. You will find that the best ideas for a menu and its dishes come about not as a result of abstract formulations, but from the food itself.

Seasonal Menus

A good seasonal menu has a catch-of-the-day appeal, expresses an awareness of time and place, and the urgency of the moment. There are few things worse than being served pallid tomatoes in dead winter, or frozen, out-of-season salmon. Besides their disappointing appearance and flavor, forced as they are by the miracle of artificial ripening and the deep freeze, they strike a discordant tone, all the more jarring if you have become used to enjoying them in the prime of their season. The following are examples of seasonal menus derived from recipes throughout the book, and they illustrate, along with the other menus that follow, the principles of menu making set forward in the introduction. In general, a seasonal menu reflects the season of its locality. Still, there are some exceptions to this, such as when the food of a season of a different place comes available. Here in California we enjoy Italian white truffles in November and Chesapeake Bay soft-shell crabs in late spring.

The seasonal menus presented here may seem overwhelmingly localized in their focus. You may be able to use them or not depending on where you live. At any rate, more than providing a recipe for a menu, they are intended to encourage you to look around your locality for inspirations in your menu making.

Spring Menus

Pan-Fried Soft-Shell Crabs with Yellow Pepper Sauce

Spinach Soup

Butterflied Filet of Beef with Herbs

Morels Baked with Bread Crumbs, Garlic, and Parsley

Garden Lettuces

Meyer Lemon Cake

––––––––––

Lambs' Tongues with Herb Sauce

Tortellini of Veal, Ricotta, Spinach, and Parmesan

Grilled Sea Bass with Sliced Artichokes Stewed in Olive Oil

Garden Lettuces Vinaigrette

Marsala Cream Pots

––––––––––

Spring Salmon Salad

Green Garlic Soup

Veal Meatballs with Artichokes, Tomatoes, Green Olives, and Sage

Strawberry Semifreddo

Summer Menus

Eggplant Croutons

Lamb Salad with Garden Lettuces, Straw Potatoes, and Garlic Sauce

Fig Jam Tart with Thyme, Chestnut Honey Ice Cream

———

Ratatouille

Corn Soup with Garlic Butter

Fried Flounder and Poached Flounder with Tomato Sauce and Basil

Garden Salad

Fresh Fruit

———

Menu for a Hot Summer Day

Champagne

Chilled Red and Yellow Tomato Soups with Peppers, Cucumbers,
Onions, and Basil

Garlic-Baked Squid

Salad of String Beans and Shell Beans

Compote of Strawberries, Nectarines, and Peaches

Fall Menus

Duck Liver Croutons

Grilled Late-Season Tomato Soup with Bacon, Garlic, and Croutons

Steamed and Roasted Duck with Garden Lettuces

Muscat Grape Sherbet

———————

Cèpes Baked in Parchment

Pasta with Giblet Sauce

Roast Pork with Gratin of Florence Fennel

Garden Salad

Seckel Pears Poached in Red Wine with Burnt Caramel

———————

Sea Bass Grilled in Fig Leaves with Red Wine Sauce

Ravioli of Chicken with Pancetta and Browned Garlic and Rosemary Oil

Roast Loin of Cured Pork with Wild Mushrooms

Radicchio Salad

Persimmon Cake with Apples and Quince Sauce

Winter Menus

Poached Cod with Pickled Vegetable Relish

Bread and Onion Soup with Red Wine

Roast Chicken with Wild Mushrooms

Garden Salad

Chestnut Honey Ice Cream

Leeks Vinaigrette with Anchovies and Eggs

Braised Lamb Shanks with Gratin of Flageolet Beans

Citrus Fruit Salad

Yeasted Puff Pastry Pear Tart

Crab Cakes

Black Truffle Soup

Pigeon Marinated in Muscat Wine

Garden Lettuces Vinaigrette

Blood Orange Sherbet

Menus for Friends

The occasion for this menu was a celebration of a dear friend, Angelo Pellegrini, who, through his writings and gracious presence, has become something of a spiritual benefactor and inspiration to us at the restaurant. Angelo's recently reprinted book *The Unprejudiced Palate* (first published in 1948; a must for any serious cook) suggested this menu. Little birds cooked on the spit was the central event, and was derived from the amusing story he tells of a botched courtship. Invited to the family ranch of his *innamorata*, he cannot resist the temptation to indulge his appetite for "anything that flies." He goes off hunting. To his host's horror he returns with his catch, and decides to cook them for supper. "But for some succulent meadowlarks fattened in the wheat fields of the west I might have married a farmer's daughter and inherited a wheat ranch. . . . During dinner I ate the larks, head, bones and all, with more than permissible relish." Although we couldn't locate meadowlarks for that day, we loaded the spits with quails, ortolans, and pigeons, and turned them slowly in front of an oak wood fire.

In reference to our guest's regard for the garden as the source of the good life and the best kind of cooking, we made a colorful salad of an assortment of fresh shelling beans, string beans, and yellow and red tomatoes dressed with a sweet red onion vinaigrette and garnished with anchovy filets and chopped Italian parsley. A fish soup followed and included some of the odder varieties of our Coast's rockfish, which I knew our friend would appreciate. After the birds, we had a chunk of Gorgonzola to swallow with the remaining red wine in the pitcher, and then a refreshing salad of bitter greens to wipe the slate clean. Knowing the Italian disinclination for fancy desserts, we served ripe, black figs poached in Muscat wine, and then passed plates of anise *biscotti*.

A Sunday Lunch from the Garden
in Honor of Angelo Pellegrini

Salad of String Beans, Shell Beans, and Tomatoes

Fisherman's Soup

Little Birds Roasted on the Spit
Rosemary Noodles

Gorgonzola Dolce and Garden Lettuces

Poached Fresh Figs and Italian Cookies

15 June 1986

For Richard Olney, friend and mentor of the restaurant, I wanted to create a menu that would illustrate the idea that in the best of cooking, the cooking itself does not show. This notion, which I believe is the essential doctrine of his book *Simple French Food*, is based on "noble products and simple preparations." Planning a menu of this kind is a little precarious since any shortcomings of the ingredients or the cooking compromise the larger intent. The challenge in such a menu is to cook without intruding upon the food, to tailor the preparation to maintain the primitive or pristine character of the ingredients, to present things as they are.

The first course was composed of nearly translucent shavings of fennel, young, rock-hard bolete mushrooms from our Mendocino Coast, Italian white truffles, and Parmesan cheese, all anointed with a buttery, extra virgin olive oil, a squeeze of lemon juice, and salt and pepper. Next came large sea scallops from the coast of Maine that arrived live in their shells. These we shucked quickly, browned in clarified butter, sprinkled with chopped parsley and grated lemon peel, and rushed to the table with baskets of grilled sourdough bread rubbed with garlic. Two weightier courses followed: a plate of golden risotto moistened with turkey broth and flavored with saffron, and spit-roasted loin of veal with straw potatoes and baked chanterelles. After salad and cheese (we chose the milder varieties that wouldn't overpower the wine), a glass of chilled Sauternes alone made dessert. To complete the meal we served persimmon cookies with coffee. A particularly agreeable match was made by serving the Chablis with the sea scallops. The wine was on an equal plane with the scallops and offset their richness with a crisp acidity.

November Lunch for Richard Olney

Fennel, Mushroom, Parmesan Cheese, and White Truffle Salad

Vintage Tunina, Jermann

Sautéed Maine Sea Scallops

Raveneau Chablis (Blanchots), 1984

Saffron Risotto

Rubesco riserva in magnum, Lungarotti, 1975

Spit-Roasted Veal and Straw Potatoes with Chanterelles

Château Margaux in jeroboam, 1966

Garden Salad

Cheese

Nuits Meurgers, Henri Jayer, 1978

Yquem, 1976

16 November 1986

A Magnum Dinner
to Celebrate Forty-third Birthdays:
Darrell's & Steve's

Boal Madeira 1941, C.D.G.C.

Oloroso PP, Duff Gordon

Salmon and Scallop Carpaccio

Dom Pérignon Rosé 1971

Comté Cheese Soufflé

Puligny Montrachet 1981, Clavoillon, Leflaive

Pear Rosemary Sherbet

Gratin of Veal Tripe, Penne, and Cabbage

Pichon Lalande 1953

Langoa Barton 1952

Spit-Roasted Shoulder of Cured Pork

Broccoli Roman-Style

Purée of Spring Favas

Assortment of Chino Ranch Vegetables

Clos des Lambrays 1949, Cosson

Musigny 1947, Vieilles Vignes, de Vogüé

Parmigiano Reggiano

Aceto balsamico 1730/1750, San Geminiano

Almond Charlotte Bavarian

Strawberry Napoleons

Yquem 1975

Coffee

Chartreuse Verte, pre-1935

Bénédictine, pre-1939

3 April 1985

A Bandol Dinner for François & Paule Peyraud

Warm Creamed Salt Cod with Garlic Toast

Marinated Mussels on the Half-Shell

Fish and Bread Soup

Grilled Summerfield Veal Chop with Wild Mushroom Gratin

Winter Garden Salad

California Goat Cheese

Yeasted Puff Pastry Pear Tart with Chestnut Honey Ice Cream

Wines from Domaine Tempier

22 January 1987

For Our Friends at Badia a Coltibuono

Squash Ravioli

Pacific Rockfish and Shellfish Soup

Lamb Shanks Braised in Chianti

Flageolet Beans

Fig, Rocket, and Prickly Pear Salad

Prune, Amaretto, Coffee, and Mascarpone Semifreddo with
Badia a Coltibuono Honey

13 October 1984

John Hollander's poem about the seasons and his visit to the restaurant inspired this autumn menu.

Beginnings

The shad and asparagus are over, the berries
And late bluefish still to come: and yet beyond these wait
The successive New Years at harvest, mid-darkness and
Arisen spring—three points each of which could be a pure
Spot of origin, or a clear moment of closure.
As it is, they whirl by as bits of what is being
Measured rather than as milestones, as parentheses
Which turn out to have been what was being put between
Brackets in the first place. Occasions usurp the false
Fronts of giddy centers on circumferences. How
The lazy susan of the seasons turns around! piled
Chock-a-block with delectables, eased about by Time,
Our most thoughtful and, ultimately, murderous host.

John Hollander

A Menu for John Hollander

Warm Salad of Fall Greens with Bacon and Wild Mushrooms

Butternut Squash Panade

Braised Duck Legs with Cabbage and Apples

Garden Salad

Comice Pear Bavarian with Crème Anglaise

15 November 1986

A Menu for Vikram Seth

The season's song, a summer ballad,

Tomatoes, basil, flowers, beans

In unison dance, LOBSTER SALAD.

Appetite wakened, dinner leans

To weightier course—a golden spice

Piatto di mezzo, SAFFRON RICE.

A brief hiatus, then to come

ROAST MARINATED QUAILS and some

BUTTERED TURNIPS. It clears the air:

YOUNG LEAVES, FRESH HERBS IN VINAIGRETTE

Primizia plucked *sans regret*.

To DESSERT and a final prayer—

May food and wine bring health and peace,

Welcome Mr. Seth to Chez Panisse.

10 June 1987

Celebration Menus

This menu was conceived as a "meal of little tastes," but what resulted was an extravagantly ample lunch. People are hungriest at the beginning of a meal and it was my intention to shift the weight of the menu away from any central main course. The first three courses were not only meant to satisfy the expectation of eating, but also of seeing food and I consciously made them very colorful and eye-appealing. We had five different kinds of marvelous shellfish including abalone and our large Monterey Bay prawns with the roe attached. All were charcoal-grilled, scattered with black truffles, and painted with the olive oil in which the truffles had been left to infuse for several weeks. What followed were two dishes with salt and vinegar components: capers, olives, anchovies, and herb vinaigrette, all of which serve to stimulate appetites. On the table we placed crocks of pickled eggplants, artichokes, and beans. The wines to match the appetizers were clean, cold, and without complexity.

The problems in a menu of ten different courses are of balance, pacing, and judging the size of portions. This we achieved by sending the appetizers in quick succession followed by a rest. The arrival of the soup then felt like a new beginning. Following the appetizers, the portions were gradually scaled down. The wine service added punctuation as did the smell of burning fig branches, which we allowed to waft into the dining room, signaling the lamb course. Next came a succession of savory courses. Both the pigeon noodles and lamb chops with beans were foils for two wonderful and relatively soft Nebbiolo wines. I have always been attracted to the ruggedness of Piemontese wines, Nebbiolo in particular, and the task of matching them with food, which is not simple. The food must approach the intensity of the wine or absorb it, otherwise it is overwhelmed. The meal was also an opportunity to present an authentic Aceto Balsamico and an unusual green walnut liqueur, *nocino*, from the Emilia-Romagna. This we served in thimble glasses with strong espresso.

A Menu for Feasting

Prosecco di Conegliano-Valdobbiadene, Santa Margherita

Shellfish with Truffled Olive Oil
Soave Classico 1982, Pieropan

Braised Veal Loin and Calves' Brains with
Tuna Sauce, Capers, Olives, and Anchovies

Baby Veal Tongues with Herb Sauce and Shallots
Gavi 1982, Giorgio Carnevale

Fish Soup with Roasted Peppers

Risotto of Squid in Its Own Ink
Gavi dei Gavi 1981, La Scolca

Rosemary Noodles with Pigeon Essences
Gattinara 1961 Riserva Speciale, L. Caldi

Grilled Marinated Lamb Chop with Savory Beans
Spanna di Gattinara 1955, L. Caldi

Salad of Wild and Cultivated Greens, Herbs, and Flowers,
with 1951 Balsamic Vinegar from the Violi Acetaia

Blood Orange Sherbet, Italian Cookies

Prune, Amaretto, Espresso, and Mascarpone Semifreddo
Coffee, Nocino San Geminiano di Montericco

One of the highlights of the year is the arrival in late November of fresh white truffles from Italy. When we first began cooking with white truffles, our approach was to spread them thinly among the dishes—the idea of eating anything so dearly priced (several dollars a bite) continues to be inhibiting. We concluded, however, that the careful and miserly apportioning of the truffle appeared halfhearted and did not succeed in fulfilling the expectations of our guests. Nor did it adequately deliver the promise of its mysterious, wonderful aroma. So we abandoned the casual placement of the truffle in the menu throughout the season in favor of one or two nights of indulgence. The plan for the menu was to present three truffled dishes, each of which would reveal an aspect of its potential. The first, an escalope of veal pounded to a translucent thinness, was topped with shavings of Parmesan cheese, slices of raw fennel heart, and dressed with lemon juice and olive oil. The truffle, presented in its most basic form, was shaved over the top like a raw vegetable.

When the white truffle is sliced over something warm its full aroma is released. The second course, a risotto moistened with poultry broth, garnished with duck giblets, and generously buttered was its carrier. As each table received this course, the dining room was filled with the truffle's unmistakable scent.

The white truffle can also act as a powerful influence, passing its aroma to whatever it is placed in contact with. The third dish, a roast capon, was stuffed under the skin and inside the cavity with truffle slices, which resulted in a soft penetration of the truffle's aroma in the flesh and skin of the bird.

Italians generally favor Piemontese red wines with the white truffle. A harmonious wine that stands out in my mind, however, was a bottle of Château Ygrec, the dry wine made from half Sauvignon, half Semillon, that is produced by Yquem.

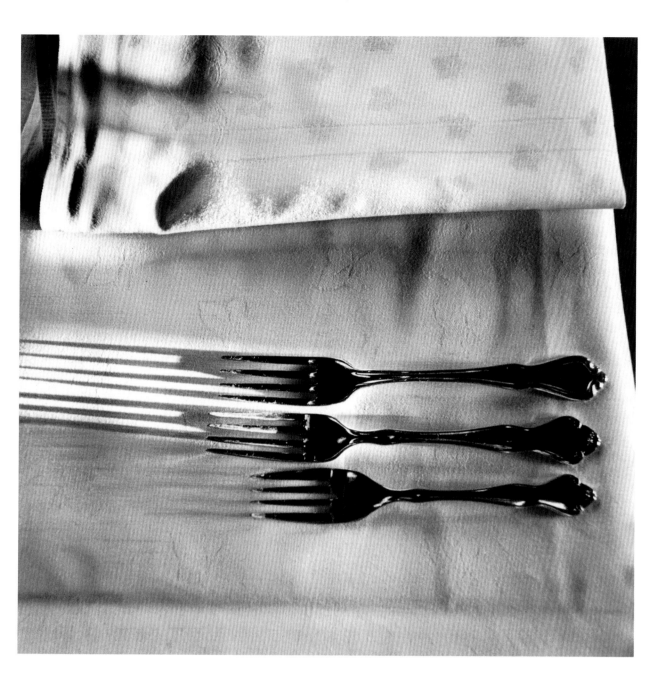

A White Truffle Dinner

Carpaccio of Veal with White Truffles

White Truffle Risotto

Roast Capon with Truffles Stuffed under the Skin

Salad of Radicchio and Garden Onions

Upside-Down Pear Tart with Vanilla Ice Cream

Chez Panisse 10th Annual Garlic Festival

Grilled Squid with Garlic Vinaigrette

New Potatoes with Pesto

Shell Bean Salad with Aioli

Spanish-Style Flatbread with Chino Ranch Peppers,
Rosemary, and Garlic

Coulee Ranch Lamb with Two Sauces:
Garlic Tomato and Garlic Parsley

Tricolor Bombe with Garlic Meringues

House Zinfandel & Sauvignon Blanc

Domaine Tempier Rosé 1984

Neyers Chardonnay 1983

Green & Red Zinfandel 1982

Van der Kamp Sonoma Sparkling Brut 1982

Bastille Day, 14 July 1986

This menu extended beyond the parameters of wine and food to include the larger context of a meal, its setting and surrounding influence. The occasion was the celebration of the fall season and the end of the harvest in Napa Valley. Joseph Phelps was kind enough to allow us to use the cellar room in his winery, which displayed a magnificent panoramic view of the expansive vineyard ablaze with autumn colors. It was a hot day and the high-ceilinged room had a church-like coolness that bore the musty scent of fermenting grapes.

The menu itself was an example of the way in which weight might be distributed differently, and was conceived in two acts. The classic format of a menu is to proceed from the light to the more weighty, from young wines to old. After a light appetizer, two courses, braised veal tripe and tortelli of pigeon, declared a more immediate gravity. The wines to match (two riserva chiantis) were the oldest wines to be presented. Following intermission—a stroll in the vineyard—the guests were called back to the table. The placement of a fresh, crisp wine (1982 vintage Tunina) in contrast to those that had preceded it, punctuated a new beginning. The courses that followed, an array of grilled seafood and vegetables, were served on platters so that each guest could take as much or as little as he or she desired. As the light began to fade, the meal progressed to three sweet dishes—a salad of sweet cactus fruit dressed with balsamic vinegar, Gorgonzola cheese with honey and walnuts, and a warm puff pastry tart of prunes and figs poached in black tea. The *coup de grâce* was an unusual digestive, a marc brandy made from Gewürztraminer grapes. The service of a digestive, often a potent alcoholic distillation, is more common in Europe than it is here. My Italian friends maintain that its reputation as an aid to the digestion is euphemistic; they think of it, more realistically, as a very good excuse to remain at the table.

Fall Menu in the Napa Valley

Marsala Vergine Soleras, Carlo Pellegrino

Cured Filet of Beef with Virgin Olive Oil and Lemon
Freisa 1982, Aldo Conterno

Braised Veal Tripe

Villa Antinori Riserva 1967, Marchesi Antinori

Pigeon Tortelli with Giblet Sauce

Villa Antinori Riserva 1964, Marchesi Antinori

Assortment of Fish and Shellfish
Grilled Vegetables
Vintage Tunina 1982, Jermann

Prickly Pear Salad

Pears, Gorgonzola, Honey, and Walnut Bread
Barolo 1970, Giuseppe Mascarello

Warm Fig and Prune Tart with Mascarpone
Scheurebe 1983 Late Harvest, Joseph Phelps

Coffee, Marc Brandy of Gewürztraminer, St. George Spirits

30 September 1984

New Year's Eve invites a certain extravagance at the table—foods with special qualities and elegance, dishes that suggest generosity and perhaps something novel for the new year. When I overheard our friend Phillip Paine, who raises our pigeons, complain of some annoying problems he was having with the noisy peacocks on his property, I lit on an idea and offhandedly (but with serious intent) suggested a solution. I had read of Roman banquets in which peacocks were served stuffed and readorned with their feathers. With the prospect of only four hens, we abandoned the idea of a grand entrance and decided instead to braise the birds and make ravioli out of the meat and a flavorful broth out of the carcasses, which we garnished with black truffles. The meal began with a Champagne and bitter orange aperitif. An array of appetizers preceded the raviolis—little salads of local Dungeness crabs with lemon mayonnaise, cucumbers and caviar, oysters on the half shell with mignonette sauce, and lobster vinaigrette with sliced Chinese radishes. We offered suckling pig for the main course, which was chosen for its auspicious associations, and vegetable accompaniments strongly suggestive of the winter season—braised cabbage, apples, chestnuts, and turnips. After salad and cheese, each table received its own baked Alaska, a fanciful amalgam of sponge cake, citrus fruit sherbets (blood orange and tangerine), ice cream, adorned with a filigree of browned meringue. Upon leaving, each guest was given a gilded box of New Year's Eve candies.

New Year's Eve 1986

Aperitif

New Year's Appetizers . . .

Ravioli of Braised Peacock with Black Truffles in Consommé

Spit-Roasted Legs of Suckling Pig
Sautéed Apples, Braised Cabbage, and Turnips

Garden Salad and Cheese

Baked Alaska

This menu was designed to celebrate Chez Panisse's thirteenth birthday with dishes that clearly represent the style of cooking at the restaurant, its roots in the cuisines of northern Italy and the south of France, and the emphasis on local, seasonal ingredients: grilled rockfish from our coastal waters, artichokes from Pescadero, pigeon and summer lamb from Sonoma County, and fruits and vegetables from nearby farms and gardens.

Chez Panisse's Thirteenth Birthday

Anchoiade

Grilled Fish and Artichoke Stewed with Rosemary

Pigeon and Rocket Tortelli

Rack of Lamb and Fresh Flageolets

Garden Salad

Salal Berry Crêpes

28 August 1984

Saint Valentine's Day

Oysters on the Half Shell

Maine Lobster Cooked in Court Bouillon with Garlic Mayonnaise

Fried Potatoes

Garden Salad

Strawberry Tart Hearts

14 February 1986

A Mouton-Rothschild Dinner

Warm Lobster and Bean Salad

1982 Château Haut-Brion Blanc

Chanterelle and Pigeon Lasagna

1982, 1975, 1970, & 1966 Château Mouton-Rothschild

Spit-Roasted Sonoma Lamb with Potatoes and Turnips

1962, 1961, 1959, & 1945 Château Mouton-Rothschild

Garden Salad

Adriatic Fig Salad

1929 Château Caillou "Crème de Tête"

14 September 1985

Lunch for Robert Chevillon and Michel Juillot

A Richard Olney Menu

Cervelles de veau froides à la crème

Tranches de saumon au court bouillon

Jarret d'agneau à l'essence de vin rouge aux aulx

Salade et fromage

Tarte aux poires et figues

1982 Mercurey blanc en magnum, Michel Juillot

1976 Mercurey blanc en magnum, Michel Juillot

1979 Nuits St. Georges "les Vaucrains," Robert Chevillon

1971 Nuits St. Georges "les Cailles," Robert Chevillon

19 August 1984

Stephen's Luncheon for Grand Bottles

Composed Seafood Salad

1964 Taittinger Comtes de Champagnes, en magnum

Pasta with Pigeon

1961 Château Margaux, en magnum

1959 Château Lafite-Rothschild, en magnum

Double Veal Chop with Roasted Potatoes

1953 Château Pavie, en jeroboam

. . . More Potatoes

1953 Château Pétrus, en magnum

Cheese

1947 Château Mouton-Rothschild, en magnum

Cake with Preserved Fruit

1921 Château d'Yquem

1 June 1986

Wine

Eating and drinking go together. It is in the context of a meal with friends or family that wine is best expressed and appreciated. Naturally, there are times when just a glass of wine is fitting—offered in anticipation of a meal it gives edge to the appetite, it is a gracious way of summoning and focusing social attention, and it is an invitation to set aside one's worries and relax. Some wines are best without food to interfere. I think of the dessert I once made to accompany an old bottle of Château d'Yquem. There was only one bottle to be shared among twenty guests. Had I tasted this amber-colored, liquorous nectar prior to preparing the menu, I would have realized that it was a wine of great dimension and needed nothing to complete it.

Most everyone who enjoys wine, or eats out, or purchases it for regular consumption must choose or decide on an appropriate bottle to accompany a meal. The sheer breadth of the subject, and the quantity and varieties available, make this a daunting task. There has been a good deal written about matching wine and food, yet these observations often appear to be dryly or abstractly conceived, failing to adequately convey the richer context of a meal in which a particular pairing was successful or disappointing. In practice, it is nearly impossible to predict the outcome of food and wine together unless both are well known ahead of time. Moreover, one of the delights in bringing food and wine together is the element of surprise; great marriages of wine and food are more often than not accidental.

I seldom think of matching a particular wine with a certain food. Rather, I think in more general terms about styles of wine. Selection of a wine begins with the food itself—what is its character and quality and how was it cooked? Is the food delicate, spicy, complex, or simple in flavor, rich or lean, was it grilled or sautéed, braised or roasted? With these questions answered, it then becomes possible to begin to choose a wine. The wine should neither overpower nor be a weak partner to the food; generally speaking, it should be of a similar pitch or tone value. It would be a miscalculation, for instance, to pair a weighty, highly perfumed, or coarse wine with foods that have delicate, refined flavors or fresh simple scents. The first runs of spring salmon are small, firm, bright-colored fish. They are the most delicate of the year and are not at all fatty; the fine texture and flavor is subtly stated and requires a wine on a similar plane. The same is true of roast young lamb, angel hair pasta with peas, cream, and ham, or a sauté of tender spring vegetables. However, later runs of salmon bring fish that are more strongly flavored and that can stand up to sturdier wines; and it follows that an older, fatter lamb with a more pronounced flavor would suggest a meatier wine.

Just as the strength of the wine should not compete with that of the food, neither should its complexity. If the food is aromatically complex, it is wise to choose a wine with a perfume that is simple or direct. Conversely, foods with aromas that are straightforward and limited are enhanced by wines with the opposite characteristic.

Like food, wine has mood and weight, which is reflected in the place, occasion, climate, and manner in which it is served. A hot summer day suggests a simple meal of the bright produce of the season, perhaps prepared outdoors on the grill. The wine should be light and uncomplicated, meant to be quaffed rather than quietly savored, and served chilled so that it is both quenching and refreshing. By contrast, in the slower pace of winter when you plan a more formal meal, you might consider a weightier, more ceremonious wine. The wine you choose should likewise suit your own state of mind. It is probably better to reserve your rarer or more complex bottles for times when you are most alert and best disposed to appreciate them. An evening after a particularly hard day at work is not the best time to savor your finest bottle.

Learning about wine is the practice of engaging the senses. The color of a wine gives a clue to its age and health, method of vinification, perhaps even the grape varietal and the climate in which the grapes were grown. Observing the color helps form an expectation of the wine, its weight and style. Often there is a direct relationship between the intensity of the color of wine and its aromas. Some wines have syrupy, viscous qualities, while others are thin; it usually follows that syrupy wines are accompanied by dark, warm tints and those that are thin by fairness or pallor. When gazing at a glass of wine, look beyond the general color category for finer shadings. Find a wine not only red but ruby, purplish, brick red, bluish-violet, rust red, vermilion, cherry red, blood red, salmon-colored, reddish brown. Allow these impressions to form slowly.

The perfumes in wine are less quantifiable, more elusive, more unbridled than wine's other characteristics. When tasting wine, four basic sensations are registered in the mouth and on the tongue—bitterness and sourness (called astringency and acidity when applied to wine), sweetness, and saltiness (not usually present in wine). While these sensations and their relation to one another tell of anatomy or structure, the aroma of a wine describes its spirit or soul.

It is difficult to identify or pinpoint the scents in wine. They escape before there is time to register them. But more often than not this is a problem of language. Scents are an order by themselves and do not require language to justify them. Knowing what kind of blossoming tree produces a pleasing scent does not, strictly speaking, qualify it, nor does it add to or diminish the pleasure we experience when we smell it. Language tends to limit our experience of scent. The standard jargon of wine (although necessary to help order our experience and to converse about wine) is often inadequate in describing scent perceptions and is invariably overly politic. Create your own language if you feel the need to, and base this on olfactory memory without forcing the issue. There are no names for many of the scents in wine. Resist the temptation to tailor your impressions to fit the standard language unless it is a genuine coincidence, for this will take you further from appreciating the aroma of wine on its own merits.

Tasting wine often gives meaning to its scent; although we also smell when we taste (aromas enter the nasal cavity via the mouth), often the more ethereal scents are lost the moment we tip the glass. Tasting wine reveals its framework and constitution. The first impressions received can be identified quite clearly. The sweetness of the wine is perhaps the simplest to detect. Bitterness or astringency is associated with tannin in the wine. It registers in the mouth as a drying, puckery sensation on the tongue, cheek tissues, and gums; it is similar to the effects of strong tea, unripe persimmon, or raw artichoke. Sourness, better described as acidity, stimulates somewhat the opposite of tannin, causing the saliva to flow and producing a tingling sensation. The alcohol in wine can also produce sensations when you taste it. Alcohol gives wine warmth and texture, which is appreciable often as a soft viscosity. It is helpful when evaluating a wine to be conscious of these varying sensations.

Generally speaking, wine mellows with time; color fades or softens, and the rough edges of its youthful structure become smoother and more harmonious. To say that a wine is young is to acknowledge that its structural components have not yet come into balance. Hard, steely, and raw are words used to describe young wines with high levels of tannin or acid. When a well-made wine matures, these qualities subside, the flavors of the grape come forward and when balanced with alcohol the wine is called supple, velvety, round. If you become seriously interested in pursuing wine, it is not at all a bad idea to taste young vintages next to older ones. In this way it is often easier to distinguish structural characteristics and to understand something of their progress in the process of maturing.

Generally speaking, if our food tastes lively, fresh, and is full of savor, it is safe to assume that it was grown or raised with care, gathered at the right time, handled with respect, and manipulated with skill and attention in the kitchen. Wine is the product of a similar process, a cooperation between man and nature. Neglect, carelessness, mishandling, or disinterest will naturally be reflected in the wine.

If your thirst for wine expands to include a desire to know more about it, study it by drinking it and do so with an open mind. There is also a great deal of information and opinion about wine, some of it by experts whose extraordinary olfactory awareness, palate reckoning, and cataloging of a wide range of wines, entitles them to speak out. They are the close observers of the trade, and information from these sources can be helpful for those in pursuit of an understanding of the standards by which wine is evaluated, the language used to describe it, and a sense of perspective. However, it is not particularly meaningful to those who have neither the experience nor the opportunity to verify it. It is not necessary to know about wine to appreciate it; what there is to know, beyond the glamour of vintage, producer, and varietal, is in the glass in front of your nose. By sampling an assortment of wines you will quickly form preferences and you will discover which wines please you and which don't. Once you have discriminated, there is no reason to be shy in stating your preference for a particular wine or style of wine; it is no more unseemly than saying you prefer salmon over sole, or veal instead of beef.

There are many conventions associated with wine that tend to fix it rigidly, define it, categorize it, assign it status and a place in a menu or in combination with food, in effect, to make it predictable. Wine is a living substance and resists these limitations of its potential. The average European, for whom wine is a daily necessity, is contentedly ignorant of such etiquette and the glamorous fascination that surrounds it. Rules concerning food and accompanying wine simply do not exist; the most common conventions are consistently confounded. While it is true that white wine can successfully complement a fish dish, it is absurd to conclude that it always does and that red wine would be inappropriate.

Often it is interesting to serve what would be considered an unlikely choice, even what you yourself consider to be a long shot, to confirm your own reservation or to be pleasantly surprised by an unpredicted harmony. Successful pairing of wine and food ultimately means that both the wine and the food taste better by virtue of their having been brought together. Although consumed as a beverage, wine is also like a sauce that accents and enhances flavor in food. Conversely, food will draw forth component flavors in the wine. When this happens, you will have discovered a rich source of pleasure in the wine and food on your table.

Basics

Clarified Butter

Whole butter consists of water, milk solids, and butterfat. The milk solids are soluble in water. When heated, water evaporates, the solids precipitate, and the butterfat remains. This is the basis for making clarified butter for use in high-temperature cooking (sautéing and pan-frying), where the milk solids in whole butter would otherwise scorch. Clarified butter is also used in place of other oils or fats for a milder, buttery flavor.

There are two ways to clarify butter: The first is a gentle process over low heat, which produces a delicately perfumed yellow oil; the second is quite different in that the milk solids are burnt, leaving a darker tea-colored oil. This brown butter is used in sautés, where a nutty flavor is preferable, or for saucing certain dishes, such as raviolis, where olive oil would be too lean a flavor. You can flavor the darker oil by adding herbs, such as rosemary or sage, to the butter as it boils. The resulting flavored oil adds an allusive perfume to sautéed cutlets of veal, quail, or spring lamb chops. When clarifying butter by either method, bear in mind that it loses about 25 percent of its original volume.

Yellow clarified butter

Unsalted butter, cut into small pieces

Melt the butter in a small, heavy saucepot over low heat. Remove the pot from the heat and let the butter stand for 5 minutes. Skim off the white froth from the surface. Carefully pour the yellow oil through a sieve lined with a double thickness of rinsed and wrung-out cheesecloth, leaving the milky solids in the pot. Use the solids to spread on toast. Transfer any unused clarified butter to a jar with a lid and store it in the freezer. Tightly covered, clarified butter will keep indefinitely.

Brown clarified butter

Unsalted butter, cut into small pieces

Melt the butter in a small, heavy saucepot over medium-high heat. Allow it to boil. As it boils, a thick froth will develop on top. Take care not to let the butter flow over. As the butter continues to boil, the foamy milk solids will collapse and when all the water has evaporated the sound of cooking will change from one of boiling to that of frying. When the froth on top begins to turn brown, skim it off to reveal a clear, golden-to-nutty-brown oil and dark sediment. The temperature rises quickly at this point, so remove the pot from the heat and strain the butter through a sieve lined with a double thickness of rinsed and wrung-out cheesecloth.

Oils and Their Uses

The recipes in this book call for many types of oils. These various oils, extracted from olives, seeds, and nuts, have specific uses in the kitchen, which are determined by their strength and flavor characteristics, their behavior when heated, and particularly in the case of olive oil, their grade and cost.

The traditional way to make olive oil, which is still the best, involves crushing sound, ripe or partially ripe olives under the weight of two opposing massive stone wheels. The paste is pressed and results in a cloudy liquid full of small particles of suspended fruit. The oil is then stored in a cool cellar in enormous terra-cotta urns in which the olive residue settles to the bottom before the oil is decanted. It is sometimes filtered, then bottled.

This first pressing, "cold" without heat and using only physical means, is called "virgin" oil, a delicate flavor-rich oil. There is also a quality designation applied to virgin oil, which is based upon the percentage of free oleic acid present. This percentage of acidity in oil indicates the extent to which fat has been broken down into its simplest components—free fatty acids, which lower the smoke point of oils when heated to high temperatures. "Extra virgin" oil must contain less than 1 percent acidity. The other grades are "superfine virgin" (less than 1.5 percent), "fine virgin" (less than 3 percent), and "virgin" (not more than 4 percent).

The other methods of extracting oil are through the application of heat, chemicals, and solvents. Further pressings contain substances that are harsh and undesirable, and refining the oil is necessary to remove them. Such oil, if it is not blended with other types, is called "pure" olive oil.

The production of cold-pressed virgin olive oil is a labor of love. In Italy the olives are still picked by hand, graded, and carted to the communal oil mill for pressing. Oil made in this way is fast becoming a rarity—the older generation of sharecroppers and peasants who tend the olive groves is not being replaced. Oil produced in the traditional way has dramatically decreased over the past thirty years as technology has supplanted artisanry.

Virgin olive oils vary greatly and, like wine, their flavor tells of the specific area of origin. There are producers in Tuscany who can distinguish oils made from olives of the particular hillsides of a small area. There is no best oil, only different oils, although the oils most prized for their delicacy and refinement come from cooler, temperate climates. Oils from the meridional climates of Spain, Italy, and Greece are characteristically heavier, often stronger in flavor (to the point of being overwhelming in cooking), than those coming from Tuscany or the French Riviera. When made from ripe fruit, the oil will have a buttery to nutty flavor. Oils produced from a blend of ripe and partially ripe olives, the kind preferred in Italy, is a deep green color with a distinctive sharpness, a feature that mellows with time.

Virgin oil is too delicate to cook with. It is simply a waste to expose extra virgin oil to the direct heat of a pan as its fruity character and color are soon lost. Furthermore, virgin oils scorch at relatively low temperatures. When sautéing or pan-frying it is better to use pure olive oil. Use first-pressed oils to season salads and appetizers, or as a final addition to grilled vegetables, meats, and poultry, as well as on soups and pasta. The exceptions are using virgin oils as flavoring in baked dishes or brushing bread for grilling.

Walnuts and hazelnuts are also pressed to extract oil. Dressings made from these potent oils must be blended with milder, blander oil to dilute their overpowering flavor. Nut oils are particularly delicious and have a balancing effect on salads containing bitter leaves such as dandelion, curly endive, and radicchio. They are also good for dressing salads containing fruit, such as pears with sorrel; or Belgian endive, apples, walnuts, and figs. Walnut oil can be substituted for olive oil in certain marinades, such as those for lamb or pheasant. Like extra virgin olive oil, walnut oil can also function as a condiment—a few drops on cooked meats, a veal chop, for instance, lend a unique flavor. The resounding presence of nut oils dictates that they be used discreetly. Like virgin olive oils, they are seasoning oils and should be used raw. Treat nut oils as you would an unusual perfume.

Refined peanut, corn, and safflower oils are the blandest of all the oils, and the least expensive. We use refined peanut oil frequently in the restaurant as the basis for mayonnaise. Once a quantity of mayonnaise has been built up, it can then be flavored with extra virgin olive oil. Mayonnaise made with virgin olive oil alone is too heavy. Refined oils are also best for frying. Their smoke points are very high relative to the other oils and because of their neutrality in flavor, they impart nothing to the food.

Flavored oils are used to season soups, salads, pastas, and meat and are made by the slow infusion of herbs and oil or by warming the herbs in the oil. Rosemary and garlic are two pungent flavors well represented in this way, and are delicious in bean and pasta soups and on grilled steak or sea bass. Basil oil, which is made by long infusion rather than heating, is used in seasoning salad or pasta with tomatoes.

Crème Fraîche

Crème fraîche, like yogurt, buttermilk, and sour cream, is a fermented dairy product thickened by the action of acid-producing bacteria. The discovery of yogurt and buttermilk was very likely due to fortuitous circumstances—fresh unpasteurized milk, if left untreated, is soon ripe with lactic acid bacteria that sour it. The same is true of buttermilk, the low-fat by-product of the butter-making process. If fermentation does not progress too far, the resulting flavor is pleasantly tangy. Crème fraîche, clotted cream, and sour cream differ from yogurt and buttermilk in that they derive from the high fat portion of milk.

Crème fraîche is simple to make. Fresh cream is mixed with a small amount of buttermilk, which contains an active culture of acid-producing bacteria (*Lactobacillus bulgaricus* is the strain listed on most buttermilk cartons). The bacteria are quite active at temperatures around 100°F, so the cream is first warmed before the buttermilk is stirred in. The cream is then stored in a warm spot (75°F) for about 24 hours, after which it will appear slightly thickened and have developed a tart flavor. At this point, the cream is put away in the refrigerator, where it will continue to ripen but at a much slower rate. If you want to make more, use the same proportion (listed below) of ripe crème fraîche instead of buttermilk to inoculate your new batch.

1 cup heavy cream
1 teaspoon buttermilk

Warm the cream to about 95°F in a noncorroding saucepan. Stir in the buttermilk, place the mixture in a very clean glass or plastic container, and cover tightly. Place the container in a warm spot in the house, between 70°F and 80°F for 24 hours. Thereafter, keep the crème fraîche in the refrigerator.

Crème fraîche will keep well, if refrigerated, for about 10 days.

Pesto

1 cup

Pesto is the past participle of the Italian verb *pestare*, which means "to pound." It is made in a mortar and was served as a condiment long before the invention of the blender or food processor. Although pesto can be made by machine, it is never as good as that made by hand. I am not against the use of machines in the kitchen (no professional cook can afford to be) yet, in the case of pesto, the use of a blender or food processor not only noisily curtails what would otherwise be an enjoyable and appetizing process, but alters the effect entirely. Handmade pesto has a pleasing coarseness and lack of uniformity; the blender makes a slick imitation of the original.

In a mortar, the earthy, compounded aroma of garlic, pinenuts, and basil wafts up as the pestle is worked, the basil changing hue from luscious green to a more somber shade. The addition of buttery olive oil and grated Parmesan unifies the flavors and smoothes the texture to a porridge-like consistency. The temptation to savor the whole bowl in fingerfuls is keen. These pleasures are lost under the closed lid of a blender, while one keeps company with the dull whir of the motor.

Beyond these aesthetic considerations is the noticeable taste difference in pesto made by the two methods. Basil that is puréed in oil to a fine consistency in the blender tastes bitter, perhaps because there is a wider dispersion of basil oils throughout the sauce. An increased amount of cheese, or oil, or both, is needed to correct the problem.

There are many varieties of basil to choose from, differing in size, shape, color, and pungency. Lemon basil and cinnamon basil are two basils with dominating flavors. They should be used discreetly and in the concentrated form of pesto these basils would likely be overpowering. They are, however, refreshing infused in sugar syrup and made into ices. Lemon basil is delicious in lobster salad and adds a fresh accent to fish and shellfish soup.

Ornamental opal basil, as its name suggests, is prettier to look at than to eat. It contains less of the aromatic quality than the other basils and more of the bitterness. Cut into a razor-thin chiffonade, it is a reliable garnish for salads, soups, pastas, and vegetables that need a tinge of passion. Do not make pesto out of it.

Lettuce-leaved basil has large pale green wrinkled leaves, like those of green leaf lettuce. It makes an acceptable if slightly mild pesto. Dwarf varieties are best avoided—their fragrance is specific, but the leaves themselves are insipid.

The two ideal basils for pesto are Genovese and Piccolo fino. The leaves of Piccolo fino are small and finely formed. Those of Genovese are large and slightly toothed. Both are smooth, soft, and cool to the touch. If bruised, they exhale the scent of mint and clove.

Mortars large enough to handle even a small batch of pesto can be difficult to find. The best solution is to seek a vendor of Japanese kitchenwares. Large Japanese mortars with a grooved inner surface are excellent and comparatively inexpensive. The inner surface provides grit and makes a simple job of reducing the leaves to paste. More than pounding, the Japanese mortar is designed for grinding. Working the basil to a paste is best accomplished by combining downward pressure with circular motion. Before you add basil to the mortar, chop the leaves fine with a sharp knife (using a dull knife will result in a loss of flavorful oils to the chopping block).

If pesto is to be used on pasta, substitute an equal amount of unsalted melted butter for half the olive oil. Butter coats pasta more effectively than olive oil and in this instance is a better carrier for the flavor of basil. It is preferable to use pesto immediately, but it will keep for several days if tightly covered and refrigerated.

¼ cup pinenuts, *lightly toasted in a sauté pan*
3 cloves garlic
2 cups basil leaves, *finely chopped with a sharp knife*
½ cup *extra virgin olive oil*
⅜ cup *Reggiano Parmigiano cheese*
⅛ teaspoon *salt*
⅛ teaspoon *freshly ground black pepper*

Put the pinenuts and garlic in the mortar and smash them to a paste. Add the basil leaves, a few tablespoons at a time, and work them to a coarse paste. As the basil becomes pasty and adheres to the pestle, add ¼ cup of the olive oil, a little at a time, continuing to grind the mixture to a paste. When the paste is smooth, switch to a rubber spatula, add the Parmesan cheese, salt, and pepper, and mix the remaining oil in well.

Essential Sauces

My taste in sauces may be thought of as simplistic, considering the complexity of the subject. Yet there is a single and impressive model of a sauce with which I am content. It is most like the pan gravy my grandmother derived from the bottom of the roasting pan in which our Thanksgiving turkey was prepared. Once done, the turkey was transferred to a warm place to rest, and the mingled fat and juices were poured into a bowl to settle and separate. Meanwhile, the encrusted bits of skin and flesh and the reduced juices that had stained the bottom of the hot pan were loosened and scraped free with a few ladlefuls of broth. To this she added the chopped gizzard, heart, and liver of the bird (cooked in the roasting pan along with the turkey) and the finely shredded, succulent meat from the neck. Finally, the previously poured-off fat was skimmed away, leaving only the essential juices of the bird, which were added to the pan scrapings and innards to further enrich them. The directness and full savor of this flavor is one to which I repeatedly refer.

This type of sauce, the integrity and the spirit of cooking it embodies, is also present in well-made braises. The principles by which such a sauce is made carries over into broth, soupmaking, and sautés, indeed any process in the kitchen that involves the capture of an essential flavor.

In my mind all sauces fall into two categories: those that are developed apart from, or are substantially unrelated to, the food they accompany, such as the butter- and egg-based sauces—hollandaise, béarnaise, beurre blanc, and flour-based sauces; and sauces that are derived directly from the food during the cooking process, the fat-skimmed juices a roast releases while it cooks, for example. My grandmother's turkey sauce is another, as is the liquid of a braise, or the residue left in a sauté pan, which can be made into a sauce by combining it with a liquid in the process of deglazing. Essences contain a high proportion of a substance's aroma in concentrated form. An essence can be a broth, or in more reduced form, a sauce. A simple broth may be made into an essence by further concentrating its flavor. A pigeon essence (see page 190) is made with a larger quantity of browned pigeon carcasses (or less liquid) than usual, and results in a broth highly infused with the flavor of the bird.

Capturing an essential flavor requires a reduced proportion of liquid to meat, carcasses, or trimmings, and shorter cooking time; this results in flavors that are fresh and pure. The method of making a sauce of this kind is the same for meat, poultry, fish, and shellfish. Scraps and trimmings, or meat from inexpensive flavorful cuts, necks and chopped carcasses in the case of poultry, are first browned well (fish bones and trimmings of course are not browned and need only be covered with liquid) in a saucepan until a crusty residue forms on the bottom of the pan. The pan is then deglazed with water or broth. It is not critical that the broth be derived from the same meat in the pan, since the flavor of the browned meat is predominant. In the restaurant we keep two broths on hand, beef and chicken, and use them by themselves or mixed together as a source of body for these essences. After deglazing, the browned pieces are covered with the liquid and simmered for one to two hours. The resulting essence is strained and quickly reduced to further concentrate its flavor. At this point the essence may be left alone, enriched with cream or butter, or other accents may be added—a little Madeira, chopped herbs, ground spices, or more solid additions such as chopped wild mushrooms, stewed mirepoix, or other vegetables.

You may wish to experiment along these lines. If you are making a roast, you may want your butcher to include some meaty trimmings for the sauce, or you can purchase cheap stewing meat from the shanks or shoulders of the animal. Poultry that has been boned or cut up for sautéing or grilling is a ready source of scraps and carcasses. The backs and breast bones, along with the necks and giblets, are a rich source of flavor.

Broths

The foundation of good soups and sauces is a well-made broth. The term broth, for all intents and purposes, means the same thing as stock. An older generation of cooks trained in times of scarcity advocate the use of bones only, stripped free of meat for their stocks or broths; others sacrifice whole chickens or fish and pounds of meat to the broth pot. Our own approach at the restaurant lies in between the two; while it is not possible to make good broth without some meaty components, neither is it necessary to go to great expense.

In the case of beef, for instance, the relatively inexpensive shank meat and bones can be utilized. The same is true of the foreshanks and necks of lambs. The meat and bones of these cuts is dark and flavorful, a good source for a rich broth. Before making chicken or other types of poultry broth, I remove the breast meat and thighs and reserve them for other purposes. The broth is made from the remaining carcass, drumsticks, wings, necks, heart, and gizzards. Fish stores that cut filets from flat fish or whole round fish are usually overwhelmed with an excess of the heads and carcasses. Provided you are prepared to remove the gills and clean the fish yourself (filets are removed without first eviscerating the fish), this broth can be made for next to nothing. The other possibility is that you learn to filet your own fish, and then clean and reserve the carcasses for brothmaking.

As much care should be taken in preparing broth as a well-made braise, a process which is roughly analogous. The meat, carcasses, and trimmings you select should be fresh and well trimmed of fat, and the proportion of meat and bones to aromatics should be properly gauged. There is a tendency to consider the broth pot a receptacle for kitchen debris—leftover fatty scraps, unusable peelings or trimmings, high or tainted meats—a better place for which would be the garbage can. A broth that is made with garbage will taste like garbage; one that is made without care will taste indifferent.

Although broths can be made without first browning the meat (this may be desirable for certain mild, light-colored soups or sauces), I prefer to do so. It is the appetizing aroma of browning meat that I try to capture in the broth. Apart from contributing a deep color, browning the meat encourages the release of its juices and adds a rich dimension of flavor to the finished broth. The easiest way to brown meat and bones is in a roasting pan in the oven. Aromatic vegetables are added halfway through the browning process so that their flavors are awakened and mingle with the bones and meat. In the case of fish, it is unnecessary to brown the bones or scraps; the release of the aroma of the fish and the rendering of their juices occurs in a matter of minutes when simply warmed in olive oil on top of the stove.

After the meat and bones are well browned, or the fish carcasses and trimmings are warmed, they are poured into a broth pot (stainless steel, an inert alloy, produces broth with the greatest clarity), covered with cold water, and brought slowly to the simmer. As the temperature rises, proteins in the meat and bones will rise to the surface as an albuminous froth. This should be skimmed away. After the surface clears, the herbs and spices are added to the pot. If added earlier, it would be difficult to avoid discarding them along with the rising scum.

A broth should never boil violently. Fats are invariably present, no matter how well the meat is trimmed, and they mix with the broth, making it cloudy and eventually less digestible. The heat should be adjusted to a peaceful simmer, the rising bubbles breaking the surface in an uneven rhythm. While the broth is cooking, it should give off an appetizing aroma of the meat, poultry, or fish it contains. Too much of one or all of the aromatics will be immediately

evident as an overriding vegetal odor (strong celery is often the culprit). If you are making beef broth, it should smell clearly of beef. The same applies to lamb, chicken, or fish. Err on the side of adding less than more aromatics; a finished broth that lacks these enhancements can always be corrected by adding more once the deficiency has been noted. On the other hand, it is impossible to remove them if a broth contains too much.

A well-made broth has a pleasing color and is bright and limpid. Depending on the type of broth, whether it is meat, poultry, or fish and the extent of the browning, the color of the broth will vary from a pale yellow to golden to deep amber. If for some reason your broth is cloudy, often the case with fish stock even when scrupulously attended (this is not necessarily a defect), strain it off and allow it to sit undisturbed. Fish broth, which is best used the same day it is made, will clear itself in a matter of hours; the suspended solids will sink to the bottom. The clear liquid can then be carefully ladled off the top. (Take care to disturb the broth as little as possible while you remove the clear liquid or the solids will rise up again.) Unclear meat or poultry broth should be left overnight. If the pot hasn't boiled too hard or too long, the fat that has clouded the broth may congeal at the surface in solid form and can then be removed easily with a spoon.

Cooking times vary according to the type of broth. Fish broth is the quickest, requiring 30 to 45 minutes from the point at which it begins to simmer. Poultry broth achieves its full flavor in 2 hours time. Meat broths take the longest and are generally allowed to simmer for 4 to 8 hours to encourage the release of gelatin, which gives body to a broth and a smooth glossiness and viscosity to sauces. If the broth is destined to moisten a pasta dish, simple risotto, or soup, it may be stopped after 3½ to 4 hours, since a flavorful liquid is all that is necessary. However, if the idea is to create a more full-bodied broth, cook the broth longer and the liquid will reduce and become more concentrated with gelatin. The bones and cartilaginous portions of young animals are a particularly rich source of gelatin, which is released faster than that from the heavy bones of older animals. If you are short on time, you may consider including these in the broth. The shin bones of veal, pork rinds or skins, and feet are good additions if you intend to make a full-bodied stock.

If you are making broth that will spend a long time on the stove, make it in a tall pot with a small surface to prevent evaporation. It is also wise to partially cover the pot for the same reason. Store broth covered in the refrigerator after it has cooled at room temperature. If you don't plan to use it up after several days either reboil it, cool and cover it, and return it to the refrigerator, or freeze it in plastic containers or empty milk cartons.

Chicken Broth

About 1 gallon

The following recipe for chicken broth may serve as a model for any poultry broth made of turkey, duck carcasses, pigeon, or a combination of the same. If you don't have the same quantity of carcasses listed here, reduce the other additions, keeping the proportions roughly the same.

6 pounds chicken carcasses, necks, wings, feet, and legs, fatty pockets inside cavity
* removed*
2 small carrots (5 ounces), sliced
½ large yellow onion (6 ounces), diced
½ large stalk of celery (2 ounces), sliced
6 quarts cold water
4 sprigs parsley
Small bunch of thyme
A few dry porcini mushrooms

Preheat the oven to 400°F.

Break up the bones and cut up the meaty sections of the chicken with a cleaver. Place the chicken in a roasting pan large enough to contain it without crowding and set it in the oven. After 20 minutes, stir the pieces around and strew the carrots, onion, and celery over the top. After 20 minutes, stir the chicken and vegetables so that the unbrowned portions are face up. Allow the chicken to roast for 1 hour, total time.

Transfer the bones, meat and vegetables to a deeper stainless-steel stockpot (10 to 12 inches in diameter). Add the water and set the pot to cook over medium heat. Skim the pot of the white to beige scum and any fat that rises to the surface as it begins to simmer. When the broth is clear on the surface (this may require repeated skimmings over a 30-minute period) add the parsley, thyme, and dry mushrooms. Maintain the broth at a gentle simmer for 2 hours with the lid half off.

When the broth is finished, strain it through a fine sieve, discard the carcasses, vegetables, and herbs, and allow the broth to cool at room temperature before pouring it into a warm, clean jar or bowl (with minimum headroom). Cover tightly. The broth will last 3 to 4 days in the refrigerator.

Beef Broth

8 pounds beef shank, sawed crosswise into pieces about 1 inch thick
2 tablespoons vegetable oil
2 small yellow onions (10 ounces), roughly diced
2 small carrots (6 ounces), cut up
1 small stalk of celery (2 ounces), sliced
1 whole head of garlic, cut in half
8 quarts cold water
1 pig's foot (about 8 ounces), split
Four 2-inch pieces dry porcini mushrooms
4 to 5 parsley sprigs
Small bunch of thyme
2 bay leaves

Preheat the oven to 400°F.

Cut away as much fat as possible from the outsides of the shank pieces. Dig the marrow out of the bones and reserve it for other purposes. (Wrap it tightly and freeze it; later it can be used as a cooking fat or to flavor risotti. Left in the bones, the marrow only melts in the broth, rising to the surface as fat, which is eventually skimmed away, and thus wasted.) Cut the meat away from the bones into 1-inch chunks. Toss the meat and bones in the vegetable oil and place them in a large roasting pan. Roast for 30 minutes, then stir the meat and bones around so that any unbrowned portions are face up. Mix in the onions, carrots, celery, and garlic. Roast the meat for 45 minutes to 1 hour more. If you take care to brown the meat well, your broth will develop a rich color.

Put the meat, bones, vegetables, and water into a stainless-steel stockpot, preferably with a small diameter (10 inches is ideal), to prevent too much evaporation. Pour off the fat in the roasting pan, then deglaze it with a little water, scraping free any crusty bits on the bottom, and add it to the pot as well. Bring the broth slowly to a simmer (this takes about 40 minutes) and skim off the froth and fat that rises to the surface. When the surface is relatively clear (after several skimmings), add the remaining ingredients, partially cover the pot, and continue to maintain a gentle bubbling simmer for 4 hours. Strain and store the broth as directed on page 426 for chicken broth.

Fish Broth

About 3 quarts

Central to any fish soup is the broth, and the success of the soup ultimately rests upon its quality. Oily-fleshed fish such as mackerel, herring, anchovies, tuna, bonita, and salmon should be avoided when making broth, except in special circumstances, such as a salmon stew or fish soups that are sieved. Fish belonging to the cod, sculpin, and bass family, flat fish such as halibut and sole, and Pacific rockfish of the low-fat, white-fleshed, or rose-colored variety will do. Flat fish are particularly rich in gelatin and give the broth structure. Mussels and certain varieties of clams (if their liquor is not too salty) add depth and flavor to the broth. The shells of crustaceans, shrimp, lobster, and crab contribute a spicy element, but these should be added in the last 15 minutes so that their flavors remain fresh.

After the fish has been fileted, the carcasses should be cleaned of all roe and viscera (the roe of our Pacific cabezone, a very common reef sculpin, is poisonous). Also remove the gills as their proximity to the digestive tract makes them suspect. Remove the blood running vertically down the backbone, noticeably present in Ling cod, and rinse the entire carcass thoroughly under cold water. The bones and bits of flesh clinging to the carcasses of fish render flavor very quickly. Thirty minutes, from the time at which the broth begins to simmer, is adequate time to extract the full flavor of the fish.

It is essential to a clean, fresh-tasting broth that the fish carcasses be of the freshest quality. Carcasses are very susceptible to rapid deterioration, even under refrigeration. It is wisest to buy whole fish if you can handle them, or find a cooperative fishmonger who is willing to filet and eviscerate the fish. Fish are less expensive purchased this way and quality and freshness are at once discernible. Soups can then be fashioned from the whole fish—the fileted portions are trimmed, cut into pieces, and poached in the broth made from the carcasses. There is a sense of economy in this approach, and pleasure comes from using all of the fish.

If you wish to make just broth, reserve the filets for another use. Fish broth, in the best of circumstances, should be used the day it is made. Even after one day under refrigeration the distinct perfume of fish in the broth will fade and the flavors and fragrance of the vegetables will become more pronounced. Extra fish broth keeps well if it is covered tightly and frozen as soon as it cools. Flavors will weaken in a broth that is held longer than about 12 hours. However, frozen broth can be used as a foundation for chowders and soups that require a flavor base but are not dependent upon the broth for their success. The broth for rockfish soup and consommé should be made fresh and used up each time.

Because fish broth cooks quickly, the aromatic vegetables are finely diced so as to release as much of their flavor as quickly as possible. Other herbs can be added such as lemon thyme, chervil, and the various basils. Strong herbs such as rosemary, oregano, and to a certain extent, tarragon, can unbalance the whole.

4 pounds assorted fish carcasses (Ling cod, Pacific rockfish, sea bass, halibut, or flounder), head included
1½ pounds mussels
3 tablespoons pure olive oil
1 cup dry white wine (such as Muscadet, Sauvignon Blanc, or Chablis)
½ stalk of celery (2 ounces), finely diced
1 carrot (3 ounces), finely diced
1 medium yellow onion (8 ounces), finely diced
2 tomatoes (10 ounces), diced
1 head of garlic, cut in half
A handful of fennel tops
4 sprigs Italian parsley
4 sprigs thyme
3 bay leaves
1 tablespoon Champagne vinegar
3 quarts water

Clean and rinse the fish carcasses. Scrub and de-beard the mussels. In a large pot (minimum 8-quart capacity) warm the olive oil. Add the fish carcasses and cook them, stirring continually to expose all surfaces to the heat for 5 to 8 minutes, until the color changes to white and the fragrance of the fish is released. Add the wine and scrape up any bits of fish adhering to the bottom of the pan. Add the mussels, vegetables, herbs, vinegar, and water and bring the liquid to a simmer. Skim off and discard the white froth as it rises to the surface. Maintain a gentle simmer for 30 minutes.

Remove the broth from the heat, strain it through a fine sieve, and discard all the remaining solids. Ideally, use this broth the same day it is made.

The Vinegar Barrel

If you regularly drink wine at home, it is likely that now and again you have unfinished bottles. There is no better use for these than the vinegar barrel, which will, in time, transform the wine into better vinegar than you can buy. Once established, the vinegar barrel requires no attendance on your part, and your salads and sauces will have a lively, down-home quality.

Vinegar means "sour wine" and is the result of the gradual fermentation of alcohol in wine. This is brought about by exposing wine to bacteria that gradually convert alcohol to acetic acid, which gives vinegar its characteristic pungency. It is possible to simply let your wine sour (I started my own barrel this way); vinegar bacteria are present in the air. The air, however, contains many other microorganisms that may not be beneficial to the vinegarmaking process and may compete with the bacteria that transform the wine into vinegar. To get predictable results, a pure culture is usually added to the barrel to inoculate it. This culture, known as the vinegar mother, works something like commercial yeast in breadmaking, and is available in most shops that sell winemaking supplies. The other way to introduce a culture is to add unpasteurized vinegar, which contain living bacteria, to the barrel along with the wine. Some specialty food shops or international groceries carry this in bulk.

To make vinegar, you will need a container that allows air to enter (oxygen is necessary to the fermentation process). The simplest container is a large glass jug that is covered at the top with a double thickness of cheesecloth. I prefer to use a wooden barrel, which imparts a pleasant woody quality to the vinegar. Vinegar produced in a glass jug will have a raw flavor and will lack a certain warmth that vinegar aged in wood contains. Barrels that are designed specifically for the purpose of making vinegar are sometimes available from dealers of winemaking equipment and supplies. Or you can adapt a small wine keg to fit the purpose. I have found that a three-gallon keg is an adequate size to keep me in vinegar throughout the year. To adapt a wine keg, you will need to purchase a small wooden spigot for drawing off the vinegar, and a funnel with a spout that extends nearly to the bottom of the barrel. If necessary, you can extend the spout of a short funnel with clear rubber hose from the wine supply shop. The funnel makes it easy to add wine to the barrel without spilling; the long neck allows the new wine you add to flow to the bottom without disturbing the vinegar culture, which collects on the top surface in a white film. Drill two holes, the first for the spigot, about 1 inch from the bottom of the barrel above the rim. Insert the spigot and tap it firmly into place. Drill another hole for ventilation, about 1 ½ inches in diameter above the spigot hole as close as possible to the top rim of the barrel. Cover the hole with fine door screen set in place with little tacks.

The top of the barrel contains an opening called the bunghole for which you will need a wide cork. The cork may also be drilled to accommodate the spout of the funnel, in which case the funnel can remain permanently in place. (If you decide to do this, keep the funnel covered to prevent dust or insects from entering the barrel.) Otherwise, the bunghole may be removed and the funnel gently inserted when you make new additions to the barrel.

Before adding wine to the barrel wash it out thoroughly to remove any dust. If you purchase a new wooden barrel, ask the dealer what he recommends for preparing it for use. New barrels contain bitter wood tannins and are generally treated with soda ash (sodium carbonate) and citric acid solutions before use.

To make vinegar, use only dry wine, white or red, of good quality. If you are using an unpasteurized vinegar to start the batch, add about a quart of vinegar to each gallon and a half of wine. Fill the barrel to just below the vent hole and store the barrel undisturbed at room temperature (around 75°F; the kitchen is a good spot). The vinegar should be ready to use in about three months. Taste it, however. If fermentation has not progressed far enough, its sourness will taste diluted, still more like wine than vinegar. Let it ferment further before drawing it off. When the vinegar has soured to your liking, draw off a quantity that will last four to five months and replace it with an equal amount of wine. The vinegar conversion process works best if it is left undisturbed. Rather than immediately adding leftover wine directly to the barrel, decant it into a bottle and seal it well until you are ready to draw off again. Vinegar should be stored in tightly corked bottles and kept in a cool, dark place. Once corked, the bacteria will cease to act in the absence of oxygen, but the flavors will develop and soften with age.

A Note on Charcoal

As grilling has come into vogue in the past years, there has been much written in cooking magazines and newspapers on the subject of fuel for the charcoal grill. Much of the media attention has focused on mesquite wood in particular, thought to be more desirable than commercially manufactured briquettes for the intense heat at which it burns and for its staying power. Furthermore, briquettes have become associated with petroleum by-products, which have discouraged many from using them. One of the major producers of briquettes indeed confirmed that in the past petroleum additives were used in the making of charcoal, but acknowledged that this is no longer the case. This is the reason for the disclaimer consumers might notice on bags of the major brands.

Briquettes, formed in a coking process from wood by-products, fibrous material, peach pits from the canning industry, and such things as walnut husks, are certainly an acceptable fuel for the charcoal grill. But it should be expected that briquettes burn faster and cooler than charcoal made from dense hardwoods such as mesquite. The woods that go into making briquettes are generally of the softer, cooler-burning, coniferous variety, such as Douglas fir, redwood, and pine.

Do not use lighter fluid that is sold as a companion product to briquettes. The kerosene odor it emits when burned is steadfast and will taint the food you cook.

On the Use of Nitrites in the Curing of Meats

This book contains a recipe for making sausages that specifies the use of chemical nitrite salts as curing agents. Because this is a book that emphasizes the importance of pure and fresh ingredients in the preparation of food, this paradox perhaps calls for an explanation.

Nitrites are indispensible for producing the traditional qualities of flavor and appearance of cured meat and for the prevention of spoilage and contamination, particularly for prevention of the growth of the bacteria that causes botulism. However, nitrites are a possible health risk because they can contribute to the formation of certain chemicals, called N-nitroso compounds, which have been found to cause organ destruction and to induce cancer in laboratory animals. Epidemiologic studies have produced suggestive evidence that stomach and esophageal cancers in humans may be associated with the traditional use of large amounts of nitrites and nitrates in the curing of foods in different regions of the world. (Nitrates, in the form of the naturally occurring saltpeters, were used in the past; it was subsequently discovered that nitrates act in curing because they are converted to nitrites.)

It has been possible to reduce, but not so far to eliminate, the amount of nitrite required for the curing of sausages and bacon by the use of other, nontoxic, chemical agents. Also, there is evidence that subsequent smoking of nitrite-cured meat destroys some of the residual nitrite in the meat without increasing the risk of botulism. Some makers of old-fashioned dry-cured bacon have been able to reduce the amount of nitrite they use to as little as one-third of that used in large-scale commercial pickling methods.

Cured meats are not the only source of exposure to nitrites, nitrates, and N-nitroso compounds. Bread, grains, and vegetables constitute a greater source of nitrite and nitrates in the typical American diet than the average of one ounce per day of cured meats. This has become especially true in recent years in some areas where residues from high nitrogen fertilizers and nitrogenous wastes accumulated from intensive animal husbandry have leached into the water table.

There are also occupations in which there are extremely high levels of exposure to N-nitroso compounds, including leather tanning and manufacturers of various rubber, plastic, and other refined products. In fact, the lifetime exposure of the average American to nitrosamines in the interiors of automobiles, as well as from the use of cosmetics, may each be equal to or greater than the estimated exposure from the ingestion of cured meat. And the amount of N-nitroso compounds inhaled in tobacco smoke by the one-pack-a-day cigarette smoker dwarfs the amount consumed in food. Also, oxides of nitrogen occurring in smoggy, polluted atmosphere may play a role in the generation of N-nitroso compounds.

An *ad hoc* Committee on Nitrite and Alternative Curing Agents in Food, appointed by the National Academy of Sciences/National Research Council in 1980, under contract with the U.S. Department of Agriculture and the Food and Drug Administration, concluded:

> From these calculations and speculations, it appears that a large reduction in exposure to nitrosamines in work environments, from cigarette smoke, and possibly from certain cosmetics and drugs would have a greater life-saving effect than the removal of nitrite from cured meats. The main reason

for this is that exposure to nitrosamines from nitrite in cured meats is small compared to the total exposure from all sources for all population groups, except for the high cured meat diet group. . . . Thus, it does not appear that the reduction of nitrite in cured meats will lead to a major decrease in risk to humans arising from total exposure to nitrosamines. However, if only dietary contributors to exposure to N-nitroso compounds are considered, the diminution in risk will be proportionately great if nitrites were removed from cured meats. . . .

(from *The Health Effects of Nitrate, Nitrite, and N-Nitroso Compounds*
Washington D.C.: National Academy Press, 1981)

A reasonable conclusion from this is that the moderate consumption of meats cured with nitrites in the amounts currently permitted in the United States is probably harmless, but the regular consumption of nitrite-cured meats as a staple of the diet may be risky, especially if it is adding to an already heavy load of these chemicals from smoking, occupational exposure, nitrate-rich water, etc. Also, people with certain chronic stomach troubles should be very sparing of nitrite-cured meats. Pregnant women should also be judicious about their consumption of nitrite-cured meats, and these products probably should not be fed to infants, because of the immaturity of their physiologic protective mechanisms. For this reason, neither nitrites nor nitrates are permitted in the United States in "baby, junior, or toddler foods."

The reader of this discussion is urged to decide whether the consideration of any possible risk of harm dims the pleasure of the prospect of concocting and savoring his or her own homemade sausage, even with the reduced amount of nitrite indicated in the recipe in this book. The safest guide, we suggest, is to follow the course one feels comfortable with, and if in doubt to play it safe, considering the fact that for most of us, unlike our ancestors, the curing of meat is something we do for the pleasure it gives us, and not because our survival depends upon preserving food in order to make it through the fallow seasons and the lean years.

Index

almond:
  biscotti, 316
  bitter, Bavarian with apricot sauce,
    310–12
anchovies:
  grilled tomato croutons with red on-
    ion vinaigrette, fresh basil and,
    140–41
  leeks vinaigrette with eggs and, 116–
    19
appetizers, 68–69, 362
  buckwheat crêpes with smoked
    salmon, crème fraîche, and capers,
    55–56
  crab cakes, 24–26
  creamed salt cod, 19–20
  duck liver croutons, 272–73
  eggplant croutons, 102
  grilled tuna and red onion salad, 68–
    69
  lambs' tongues with herb sauce, 249–
    50
  long-cooked broccoli, 88
  pickled artichokes, 331–32
  pickled eggplants, 333
  pickled shallots, 334
  pickled yellow wax beans, 332
  pickles, 330–37
  prosciutto with warm wilted greens,
    262
  salad of string beans, shell beans, and
    tomatoes, 81–82
  salmon carpaccio, 48
  straw potato cake, 136–38
  sweet and sour turnip pickles, 335

wild mushrooms, 123
apple(s):
  baked with orange and Riesling, 157
  and quince sauce, 301, 303
apricot:
  preserves, bitter, 341
  sauce, 310, 312
artichokes, 75–77, 107–8
  baked stuffed, 76–77
  "loose," 236, 331
  pickled, 331–32
  sliced and stewed in olive oil, grilled
    sea bass with, 57
  veal meatballs with tomatoes, green
    olives, sage and, 236–37
asparagus, grilled, with olive oil and
    Parmesan, 74

back fat, 260
bacon:
  Brussels sprouts leaves cooked with
    mirepoix and, 89
  cabbage braised with Riesling and, 90
  grilled late-season tomato soup with
    garlic, croutons and, 143–44
  potatoes cooked in the coals with,
    135–36
Badia a Coltibuono, 381
Bandol Dinner for François & Paule
    Peyraud Menu, 379
barrel, vinegar, 430–31
basil:
  pesto, 418–19
  types of, 418–19
basil oil, 338, 339, 417

bath, boiling-water, 343
Bavarian cream, bitter almond, with
    apricot sauce, 310–12
bean(s), 78–86
    fava, 107
    fava, with olive oil, garlic, and rose-
        mary, 85–86
    lobster salad with garden lettuces, to-
        matoes, basil, edible blossoms and,
        33–35
    pickled yellow wax, 332
    Romano, sautéed with oregano, 86
    Romano, squid, and tomato salad
        with garlic mayonnaise, 65–66
    soup, 78–89
    see also specific beans
béchamel sauce, 26–27, 28
beef:
    broth, 421, 427
    butterflied filet of, with herbs, 229–
        31
    spit-roasted, 265
    see also tripe
beets with vinegar and tarragon, 87
Belgian endive, 155
    gratin of, 106–7
biscotti, walnut, 316
bisques, 5
    shrimp, 60–62
blanching, 106
    radicchios, 155, 156
blossoms, edible, 150
    lobster salad with garden lettuces,
        beans, tomatoes, basil and, 33–35
    in salmon carpaccio, 48
boiling-water bath, 343
boletes, 107, 120, 121–22, 123, 175
bouillabaisse, 3, 5, 43–44
braising, 243, 250–51, 271
    broths and, 422
    peacocks, 396, 397
bread, 199–225
    after baking, 210–11
    basic ingredients of, 202–4
    country, 212–4
    fermentation in, 201–2

and fish soup, 7–8
levain, 218–25
making, 204–9
and onion soup with red wine, 128–
    29
panettone, 307–8
pudding, panettone, 307, 309
shaping dough for, 206–7
sponge method for, 205
spontaneously leavened sourdough,
    215–18
straight doughs, 205
yeast in, 200–202
bread crumbs:
    baked eggplants and tomatoes with
        basil and, 100–101
    in bisques, 5
    for fried shellfish, 58, 59
    in gratin of tripe, penne, and cab-
        bage, 233–34
    morels baked with garlic, parsley
        and, 127
    in veal meatballs with artichokes, to-
        matoes, green olives, and sage,
        236–37
brine for sauerkraut, 336–37
brining, 248–50
broad beans, 85
broccoli, long-cooked, 88
broth, 420–29
    beef, 421, 427
    chicken, 168, 175, 421, 426
    fish, 3, 4, 5, 10–11, 30, 43, 44, 168,
        169, 421–22, 425, 428–29
    green garlic, 111
    lamb, 421
    meat, 421–25
    poultry, 421–24
    for risotto, 165, 166
    turkey, 175
Brussels sprouts leaves cooked with ba-
    con and mirepoix, 89
buckwheat crêpes with smoked salmon,
    crème fraîche, and capers, 55–56
butter:
    clarified, 414–15

garlic, 99, 114
herb, 51, 52
in puff pastry, 317–18, 319
buttermilk, 417

cabbage, 90–91
braised with Riesling and bacon, 90
duck legs braised with onions and,
271–72
gratin of tripe, penne and, 233–34
homemade sauerkraut, 336–37
wilted flat black, 91
cakes:
Meyer lemon, 306–7
panettone, 307–8
persimmon, with apple and quince
sauce, 301–2
preserved fruit, 300–301
ricotta cheese, 304–6
sponge, 314, 315
straw potato, 136–38
cannellini beans:
grilled tuna, green onions, and radicchio with, 66–68
with pasta and rosemary, soup of,
78–79
capers, buckwheat crêpes with smoked
salmon, crème fraîche and, 55–56
caramelization of sugar, 292
carrot and red pepper soup, 93–94
casings, 257
sausage, 255
caul, 255
fat, 260, 265
caviar, white corn cakes with, 95–96
celebration menus, 363, 386–401
cèpes, 121
baked in parchment, 124–25
conserve of, 342
chanterelle, 120, 121, 122, 123
custard, 125–26
charcoal grilling, 234, 432
chard, smoked pigeon risotto with
grilled red onions and, 173–74
cheese:
and green garlic soufflés, 112–13

soufflés, 26–27
warm goat, and herb toast, fall fruit
salad with, 159–61
cheesecake, ricotta, 304–6
chestnut honey ice cream, 296
Chevillon, Robert, 403
Chez Panisse's Thirteenth Birthday
Menu, 398–99
Chez Panisse 10th Annual Garlic Festi-
val Menu, 393
chicken, 263–68, 353
breast stuffed with wild mushrooms,
265–67
broth, 168, 175, 421, 426
free-range, 352
ravioli of pancetta, browned garlic
and, with rosemary oil, 180–81
roast, 263–65
sausages, 267–68
stock, 168
chicoree frisée, 155
chicories, 149, 150, 155–56
chowders, 4, 5
lobster and white corn, 36–37
chutney, green tomato, raisin, and
mint, 340
citric acid, crystalline, 338
citrus fruit salad, 158–59
clam:
and sorrel soup with cream and mirepoix, 14–17
in soup, 3, 4–5
clarified butter, 414–15
clotted cream, 417
cod, poached, with pickled vegetable
relish, 17–18
cod, salt, 18–22
creamed, 19–20
hash, 21–22
poached, 19–20, 21–22
compote:
fruit, 290
of strawberries, nectarines, and
peaches, 291
condiments, x
basil oil, 339

old-fashioned vanilla ice cream, 293–
    95
panettone, 307–8
panettone bread pudding, 309
persimmon cake with apple and
    quince sauce, 301–2
preserved fruit cake, 300–301
puff pastry, 317–28
puff pastry tart shell, 320–22
ricotta cheesecake, 304–6
Seckel pears poached in red wine
    with burnt caramel, 292–93
strawberries in puff pastry, 325–26
strawberry semifreddo, 313–15
walnut biscotti, 316
yeasted puff pastry (croissant pastry),
    327
yeasted puff pastry pear tart, 328
double broths, 165
double soups, 92–94
dough:
    bread, 204–9, 213, 223
    bread, sour-, 217
    pasta, 177–80
    puff pastry, 317–28
    short crust pastry, 298, 299
duck, 268–73
    legs braised with onions and cabbage,
        271–72
    liver croutons, 272–73
    steamed and roasted, 268–70
duck eggs in marsala cream pots, 289

eggplant(s), 100–105
    baked, and tomatoes with bread
        crumbs and basil, 100–101
    croutons, 102
    grilled, with shallots and parsley, 103
    lasagna of tomato, basil and, 182–83
    pickled, 333
    tart, grilled, 104–5
eggs:
    chanterelle custard, 125–26
    leeks vinaigrette with anchovies and,
        116–19

in marsala cream pots, 289
    organic, 352
    soufflés, 26–28
endive, Belgian, 155
    gratin of, 106–7
escarole, 155
essences, 420, 421

Fall Menu in the Napa Valley, 394–95
fall menus, 369
fat, back or cawl, 260, 265
fava beans, 107
    with olive oil, garlic, and rosemary,
        85–86
Feasting, Menu for, 387–88
fennel, 107–10
    mushroom, Parmesan cheese, and
        white truffle salad, 107–8
fermentation, 205, 206, 207, 212, 216,
        218–21
    for sauerkraut, 336, 337
    of wine, 430
    of yeast, 201–2
fig jam tart with thyme, 298–99
fig leaves, grilled fish wrapped in, 12–
    13
filets, 229, 230
fine louviers, 155
fine maraîchère, 155
first courses, 364
    baked stuffed artichokes, 76–77
    fall fruit salad with warm goat cheese
        and herb toast, 159–61
    grilled eggplants with shallots and
        parsley, 103
    grilled eggplant tart, 104–5
    leeks vinaigrette with anchovies and
        eggs, 116–19
    risotto, 164–76
fish, 3–13, 17–22, 32–33, 43–57, 66–
    69
    broth, 3, 4, 5, 10–11, 30, 43, 44,
        168, 169, 421–22, 425, 428–29
    cakes, 25

November Lunch for Richard Olney,
374–75
nut oils, 415, 416

odors, x, xi, xv
oils, 415–17
  basil, 338, 339
  flavored, 417
  refined, 416–17
  rosemary, 180, 181
olive oil, 415–16
  basil, 338, 339
  herbs in, 339
olives:
  braised pork shoulder with tomatoes,
    fennel and, 250–52
  green, veal meatballs with artichokes,
    tomatoes, sage and, 236–37
onion(s):
  and bread soup with red wine, 128–
    29
  chilled red and yellow tomato soups
    with peppers, cucumbers, basil
    and, 145–46
  duck legs braised with cabbage and,
    271–72
  green, Dungeness crab soufflés with
    chervil and, 28–30
  green, grilled tuna with radicchio,
    cannellini beans and, 66–68
  grilled red, and smoked pigeon ri-
    sotto with chard and, 73–74
  and potatoes roasted with vinegar and
    thyme, 134
  red, and grilled tuna salad, 68–69
  red, pickled, 334
  red, vinaigrette, grilled tomato crou-
    tons with anchovies, fresh basil
    and, 140–41
  stewed in saffron, fish soup with, 10–
    12
orange(s):
  apples baked with Riesling and, 157
  blood, in citrus fruit salad, 158–59
  blood, sherbet, 297
organic foods:

certifying organizations of, 348–51,
  358
meats and poultry, 351–59
standards and definitions of, 346–51,
  357
ovens, stone or brick, 207–8
oyster soup, 4–5, 42–43

pain au levain, 218
pancetta:
  chicken breast stuffed with wild
    mushrooms and, 365–67
  ravioli of chicken, browned garlic
    and, with rosemary oil, 180–81
panettone, 307–8
  bread pudding, 307, 309
pan-frying, 58, 414, 416
pan gravy, 420–21
parchment, cèpes baked in, 124–25
Parmesan cheese:
  fennel, mushroom, and white truffle
    salad, 107–8
  grilled asparagus with olive oil and,
    74
  tortellini of veal, ricotta, spinach and,
    193–95
pasta, 177–98
  basic, 177–80
  dough, 177–80
  with giblet sauce, 183–87
  gratin of tripe, penne, and cabbage,
    233–34
  lasagna of eggplant, tomato, and
    basil, 182–83
  lobster raviolis, 187–89
  pumpkin tortelli with brown butter
    and sage, 192–93
  ravioli of chicken, pancetta, and
    browned garlic, with rosemary oil,
    180–81
  rosemary noodles with pigeon es-
    sences, 190–91
  saffron, and pan-fried bay scallops,
    with parsley and garlic, 195–96
  soup of cannellini beans with rose-
    mary and, 78–79

salads (*cont.*)

    fall fruit, with warm goat cheese and herb toast, 159–61

    fennel, mushroom, Parmesan cheese and white truffle, 107–8

    garden, 149–50

    grilled tuna and red onion, 68–69

    lamb, with garden lettuces, straw potatoes, and garlic sauce, 238–41

    lobster, winter, 37–39

    lobster, with garden lettuces, beans, tomatoes, basil, and edible blossoms, 33–35

    pickly sauerkraut, 336–37

    rabbit, with browned shallots, 282–84

    roast pigeon, 275–76

    spring salmon, 53–54

    squid, Romano bean, and tomato, with garlic mayonnaise, 65–66

    of string beans, shell beans, and tomatoes, 81–82

salmon, 45–56

    carpaccio, 48

    in court bouillon with herb butter, 51–52

    grilled, with tomatoes and basil vinaigrette, 52–53

    salad, spring, 53–54

    smoked, buckwheat crêpes with crème fraîche, capers and, 55–56

salt, 257, 432

    as breadmaking ingredient, 202, 203–4, 205

    for homemade sauerkraut, 336–37

    for pickling, 330

salting, of cod, 18–19

sauces, 420–21

    apple and quince, 301, 303

    apricot, 310, 312

    béchamel, 26–27, 28

    blue crab, 96, 98

    garlic, 238, 239

    giblet, 183, 184–87

    herb, 247–48

    lobster, 34, 38

    for lobster raviolis, 188–89

    pan, 420–21

    red pepper, 9

    red wine, 12–13

    sage, 192, 193

    tomato, 338–39

    tomato, and basil, 32, 33

    yellow pepper, 24

sauerkraut, homemade, 336–37

sausage:

    casings, 255

    chicken, 267–68

    cotechino, 257–59

    fresh pork, 252–56

sauté, mushroom, 125–26

sautéing, 414, 416

Sauternes in preserved fruit cake, 300–301

scallops, bay, pan-fried, and saffron pasta with parsley and garlic, 195–96

sea bass, griled, with sliced artichokes stewed in olive oil, 57

seafood, *see* fish; shellfish

seasonal menus, 362–63, 365, 366–71

Seckel pears poached in red wine with burnt caramel, 292–93

seed oils, 415

seeds, mail-order sources for, 156

semifreddo, strawberry, 313–15

Serrano chile, 9

Seth, Vikram, 385

shaggy parasols, 120, 122, 123

shallots:

    browned, rabbit salad with, 282–84

    grilled eggplants with parsley and, 103

    pickled, 334

shell beans:

    lamb shank soup with tomatoes and, 241–42

    minestrone of string beans, tomatoes, pesto and, 79–80

    salad of string beans, tomatoes and, 81–82

shellfish, 14–17, 22–31, 33–45, 58–65

soup, 148–49
truffle, white, 122
  dinner, menu for, 388–91
  fennel, mushroom, and Parmesan
    cheese salad, 107–8
  puddings, 146–47
tuna, grilled, 66–69
  and red onion salad, 68–69
  with green onions, radicchio and can-
    nellini beans, 66–68
turkey broth, 175
turnip pickles, sweet and sour, 335

vanilla ice cream, old-fashioned, 293–
  95
veal, 234–37
  controversy of, 234–35, 352
  marinated chops grilled over an oak
    fire, 234–36
  meatballs with artichokes, tomatoes,
    green olives, and sage, 236–37
  tortellini of ricotta, spinach, Parme-
    san and, 193–95
vegetable(s), xiv, 71–156
  in broth, 422
  garden salad, 149–50
  lamb salad with, 238–41
  lobster salad with, 33–35
  minestrone of shell beans, string
    beans, tomatoes, and pesto, 79–80
  pimiento soup with fried polenta,
    130–31
  ratatouille, 142–43
  relish, pickled, 17, 18
  for risotto, 165, 166
  soufflés, 26
  soup of cannellini beans with pasta
    and rosemary, 78–79
  soups, 3, 4, 5, 92–94
  in winter lobster salad, 37–39
  see also specific vegetables
vinaigrette, 39, 54, 81, 100, 101, 158,
  159, 240, 262, 283

for fruit, 160
garden salad, 150
herb, 247–48
leeks, with anchovies and eggs, 116–
  19
red onion, 140, 141
tomatoes and basil, 52, 53
vinegar, 430–31
  for pickling, 330
  for preserves, 338

walnut biscotti, 316
walnut oil, 416
wax beans, pickled yellow, 332
White Truffle Dinner Menu, 388–91
wine, 386, 407–11
  menus, 365, 395, 403–5
  into vinegar, 430
wine, red:
  bread and onion soup with, 128–29
  sauce, 12–13
  Seckel pears poached in, with burnt
    caramel, 292–93
  syrup, 291
winter lobster salad, 37–39
winter menus, 371
wood:
  for grilling, 234, 235, 274, 432
  for spit roasting, 264

yeast, 200–202, 204, 205, 207, 212,
  215–16, 218
  commercial vs. wild, 200–201, 203
  puff pastry (croissant pastry), 327
  puff pastry pear tart, 328
  starter for, 221
  types of, 327
yellow wax beans, pickled, 332
yogurt, 417

Zinfandel, New, mussels steamed with,
  41–42

About the Authors

PAUL BERTOLLI has been chef at Chez Panisse since 1982 and is responsible for the creation and execution of the restaurant's changing nightly menu. Prior to Chez Panisse, he worked in restaurants in Florence, Italy. He lives with his family in Kensington, California, and spends his spare time pursuing his interests in music and gardening.

ALICE WATERS started Chez Panisse in 1971, and Café Fanny in 1983. She has written the *Chez Panisse Menu Cookbook*, and co-authored the *Chez Panisse Pasta, Pizza & Calzone* cookbook. She has produced the *Chez Panisse Desserts* cookbook by Lindsey Shere, and *Chez Panisse Cooking* by Paul Bertolli. Alice is currently interested in writing a children's cookbook.

About the Photographer

GAIL SKOFF divides her time between Berkeley, California, and Provence. She photographs in black and white, prints the images (approximately 20 by 20 inches), then hand colors each image with oil paints. The prints are produced in limited editions of ten.

Design by Patricia Curtan
Type: Linotron Janson
Typesetting by Wilsted & Taylor
Color printing by Meriden-Stinehour Press
Two-color printing by Kingsport Press
Photography of color prints by M. Lee Fatherree